WORLD HISTORY IN JUVENILE BOOKS
A Geographical and Chronological Guide

WORLD HISTORY IN JUVENILE BOOKS

A GEOGRAPHICAL AND CHRONOLOGICAL GUIDE

By SEYMOUR METZNER

Director, Learning Resources Center
Northridge, California

NEW YORK
THE H. W. WILSON COMPANY
1973

Copyright © 1973
By Seymour Metzner
Printed in the United States of America

Library of Congress Cataloging in Publication Data

Metzner, Seymour.
    World history in juvenile books.

    1. Children's literature—Bibliography.
2. History—Juvenile literature—Bibliography.
I. Title.
Z1037.M324   028.52   72-11598
ISBN 0-8242-0441-7

ACKNOWLEDGMENTS

I wish to acknowledge with gratitude the help received from the staff and facilities of the Granada Hills branch of the Los Angeles Public Library and also the invaluable research assistance of Mr. Mark Wasserman, without whose endeavors this volume would still be unfinished.

CONTENTS

Acknowledgments	v
Introduction	xii
World History in Juvenile Books	1
I. Europe	1
General	1
Austria	11
Belgium	13
Bulgaria	14
Czechoslovakia	14
Denmark	15
Finland	16
France	17
Germany	27
Greece	35
Hungary	42
Iceland	43
Ireland	44
Italy	45
The Netherlands	54
Norway	56
Poland	58
Portugal	60
Rumania	62
Scandinavia	62
Spain	65
Sweden	69

Switzerland	70
Union of Soviet Socialist Republics (USSR)	71
United Kingdom (UK)	78
Vatican	114
Yugoslavia	116
II. Middle East	118
General	118
Biblical	118
Egypt	121
Iran	126
Iraq	126
Israel	128
Jordan	131
Lebanon	132
Saudi Arabia	132
Syria	133
Turkey	133
III. Asia	135
Afghanistan	135
Burma	135
Cambodia	135
Ceylon	136
China	136
Hong Kong	141
India	142
Japan	145
Korea	148
Malaysia	149

CONTENTS

	Nepal and the Himalayas	149
	Pakistan	150
	Southeast Asia	151
	Taiwan	151
	Thailand	151
	Vietnam	152
IV.	Africa	153
	General	153
	The Congo and Zaïre	159
	Ethiopia	159
	Ghana	160
	Kenya	160
	Liberia	161
	Nigeria	162
	North Africa (Algeria, Libya, Morocco, Tunisia)	162
	Rhodesia	164
	Tanzania	164
	Union of South Africa	164
V.	North America	166
	Canada	166
	Mexico	173
VI.	South America	179
	General	179
	Argentina	181
	Bolivia	181
	Brazil	182
	Chile	183

	Colombia	183
	Ecuador	184
	Guianas	184
	Paraguay	184
	Peru	185
	Uruguay	187
	Venezuela	187
VII.	Central America	189
VIII.	The Caribbean	191
	General	191
	Cuba	193
IX.	The Pacific Area	195
	General	195
	Australia	196
	Indonesia	198
	The Islands (Melanesia, Micronesia, Polynesia)	198
	New Zealand	199
	The Philippines	200
X.	The Polar Regions	202
	General	202
	Antarctic	202
	Arctic	205
XI.	History of Mankind: Political, Cultural, and Technological	208
	General	208
	Communication	213
	Exploration and Adventure	214

CONTENTS

  Geography and Maps 218
  International Organizations 219
  Prehistory 221
  Science and Technology 225
  Transportation 229
  Warfare 231
Directory of Publishers and Distributors 236
Author Index 241
Biographical Subject Index 295
Title Index 301

INTRODUCTION

The past three decades have seen the United States increasingly involved in the affairs of countries in all parts of the globe. Americans have become familiar with places which, as schoolchildren, they never even knew existed. The end of American isolation has resulted in a spate of juvenile literature admirably suited to encourage children to know and understand the larger world in which they live. Teachers and librarians must, of necessity, be leaders in this endeavor. It is hoped this book will make their task easier.

PURPOSE

This guide is a companion volume to the author's earlier bibliography, *American History in Juvenile Books* (1966). Its purpose is to provide a comprehensive listing of currently available trade books relating to world history which are meant for the elementary and junior high school age groups. The listing includes more than 2,700 titles of fiction and nonfiction. The arrangement of the titles is meant to be of maximum usefulness to the following groups:

1. School librarians and public librarians
2. Teachers conducting individualized reading programs
3. Teachers wishing information regarding supplementary reading material pertinent to the study of world history
4. Remedial reading specialists, particularly at the junior high school and high school levels

INTRODUCTION

5. Cultural and ethnic organizations interested in promoting the study and understanding of their ancestral heritage
6. Peace groups seeking to encourage international understanding
7. Parents interested in building up their children's sense of cultural identity
8. Authors and publishers wishing a ready reference to literature in specific areas of world history

CRITERIA FOR SELECTION

The books listed were selected from publishers' catalogs, review journals, *Books in Print*, and the *Publishers' Trade List Annual*. They were chosen on the basis of the following criteria:

1. Virtually all were available as of spring 1970.
2. They are primarily hard-cover trade books, available through regular bookstores and not basically intended for the school text market.
3. All books selected have reasonable relevance to world history. "World history" in this context is considered to include not only political events but also important moments and movements in the arts and letters, science and technology, and the general development of world civilization.

INFORMATION INCLUDED

The listing for each book includes author, title, suggested grade level, publisher, and publication date, and, insofar as possible, the number of pages and presence of textual illustrations and maps. This guide mainly concerns itself with cloth- and composition-bound books which are listed in *Books in Print*. Prices have been omitted since these are subject to frequent change. The most recent prices may be found in the publishers' catalogs or the latest issue of *Books in Print*.

A directory of publishers and distributors, an author index, a biographical subject index, and a title index are included in this volume.

Arrangement

Each of the first ten chapters covers a large geographical area, such as Africa. A general section on the area as a whole usually precedes the listing (by subheading) of smaller regions (North Africa) or individual countries (Tanzania) within the area.

The books given under each heading are categorized as "Fiction," "Nonfiction," or "Biography." The Fiction and Nonfiction sections are arranged in the following manner: Where the list is short, all books are simply listed in alphabetical order by last name of author; where the list is relatively long, as in the case of France or the United Kingdom, chronological subheadings are introduced. Works which cover several historical periods are listed first, followed by those which pertain only to a particular time.

Biographies for each country are arranged alphabetically by name of subject. Those dealing with multiple subjects are listed before those dealing with only one person. As a rule, a subject appears under the country in which his most important work was accomplished, rather than under the country of his birth. Thus, biographies of Pizarro are listed under "Peru," not "Spain." Readers should consult the Biographical Subject Index on pages 294-9 to determine the exact location of an entry.

INTRODUCTION

The suggested reading level of each book is contained within parentheses after each title. A plus (+) sign means that only the lower portion of the reading level continuum is given. These reading levels are obtained from the publishers' catalogs, book reviews, and *Books in Print*. As they are assigned in many different and often unspecified ways, they can be considered only as generally indicative of a book's suitability for any particular child and should not be viewed as definitive, inflexible guides. Indeed, the same book may be given widely varying grade level designations in different sources. Until publishers agree on a definite formula to be used by all, reading level designations will always be unsatisfactory; nevertheless, they are better than absolutely no information at all. In any case, most reading authorities would agree that a child's motivation and experiential background are major factors in determining the degree of success he will have in reading a book, and even the best readability formulas cannot take these into account.

Books are briefly annotated when their titles do not adequately indicate their relevance to world history or when they appear under a very broad topical heading.

The last chapter deals with subjects which are international in nature and therefore not amenable to area designations.

Recommended Procedure

It is recommended that after a reader has found a book under the appropriate topic and subheadings, he consult an authoritative review or booklist source for information concerning plot details and literary evaluation. Among the available sources are the following: The H. W. Wilson Company's *Children's Catalog* and *Junior High School Library Catalog*; Mary K. Eakin's *Good Books for Children*; Patricia Allen's *Best Books for Children*; The Association for Childhood Education International's *A Bibliography of Books for Children*; and *Adventuring With Books: A Reading List for Elementary Grades*, compiled by the Elementary Reading List Committee of the National Council of Teachers of English. Reviews of recently published books may be found in *Booklist, The Horn Book Magazine,* and *School Library Journal.*

I. EUROPE
General

FICTION

MOTT, MICHAEL. The Blind Cross: A Novel of the Children's Crusade. (3-7) Delacorte, 1970. 160p.

UNTERMEYER, BRYNA AND UNTERMEYER, LOUIS, eds. Adventure Stories. (3-6) Western, 1968. 256p. illus.
> Diverse historical settings in such stories as "The Three Musketeers" (France) and "Robin Hood" (England).

WHITE, A. T. The Golden Treasury of Myths and Legends. (6-10) Western, 1959. 164p. illus.
> Myths and legends from Classic and Norse sources.

NONFICTION

EPSTEIN, SAMUEL AND WILLIAMS, BERYL. European Folk Festivals. (2-5) Garrard, 1968. 64p. illus.

HILLYER, V. M. AND HUEY, E. G. Europe. (5+) Childrens, 1966. 126p. illus.

MERCER, CHARLES. Let's Go to Europe. (3-7) Putnam, 1968. 48p. illus.

VON MALTITZ, F. W. The Rhone: River of Contrasts. (4-7) Garrard, 1965. 96p. illus.

WOHLRABE, R. A. AND KRUSCH, WERNER. Picture Map Geography of Western Europe. (4-6) Lippincott, 1967. 160p. maps

Prehistory – A.D. 1300

ANSLEY, DELIGHT. The Good Ways. (7+) Crowell, 1959. 214p. illus.
> Exploration of monastic life.

APPEL, BENJAMIN. Illustrated Book of Knights – New Revised Edition. (5+) Grosset, 1970. illus.

ASIMOV, ISAAC. Dark Ages. (7+) Houghton, 1968. 288p. maps

EUROPE

BAILEY, ANNE AND REIT, SEYMOUR. The West in the Middle Ages. (7+) Western, 1966. 100p. illus. charts
> European history from 481 to 1485.

BELL, GERARD. The Crusaders. (7+) St. Martin's, 1967. 64p. illus. maps

BLACK, I. S. Castle, Abbey and Town: How People Lived in the Middle Ages. (4-6) Holiday, 1963. 101p. illus.

BOARDMAN, F. W. Castles. (7-9) Walck, 1957. 112p. illus.

BUEHR, WALTER. Chivalry and the Mailed Knight. (3+) Putnam, 1963. 96p. illus.

BUEHR, WALTER. The Crusaders. (4-6) Putnam, 1959. 96p. illus.

BUEHR, WALTER. Knights and Castles and Feudal Life. (4-6) Putnam, 1957. 72p. illus.

DUGGAN, A. L. The Castle Book. (4-7) Pantheon, 1961. 96p. illus.

FOSTER, HAROLD. The Medieval Castle. (4-6) Hastings [1957]. 126p. illus.
> Two boys train for knighthood in a medieval castle.

FREMANTLE, A. J. Age of Faith. (7+) Time-Life [c 1965]. 192p. illus. maps
> Life in the Middle Ages.

GLUBOK, SHIRLEY. Knights in Armor. (3-7) Harper, 1969. 48p. illus.

HAMILTON, FRANKLIN. The Crusades. (7+) Dial, 1965. 256p. illus. maps

HARTMAN, GERTRUDE. Medieval Days and Ways. (6+) Macmillan, 1937. 332p. illus.

HARTMAN, GERTRUDE AND SAUNDERS, L. S. Builders of the Old World. (4-6) Little, 1963. 468p. illus. maps
> History as people lived it, from earliest times to Columbus.

LEWELLEN, J. B. True Book of Knights. (K-4) Childrens, 1956. 48p. illus.

GENERAL

McLanathan, R. B. K. The Pageant of Medieval Art and Life. (7+) Westminster, 1966. 127p. illus.

Manz, Peter. Life in the Age of Charlemagne. (7+) Putnam, 1969. 208p. illus.

Oakeshott, R. E. A Knight and His Armor. (5-9) Dufour, 1963. 95p. illus.

Oakeshott, R. E. A Knight and His Horse. (5-9) Dufour, 1963. 95p. illus.

Oakeshott, R. E. A Knight and His Weapons. (5-9) Dufour, 1963. 95p. illus.

Sellman, R. R. The Crusades. (7+) Roy, 1955. 73p. illus.

Sobol, D. J. The First Book of Medieval Man. (4-6) Watts, 1959. 72p. illus.

Tappan, E. M. When Knights Were Bold. (7+) Houghton, 1911. 366p. illus.

Toussaint-Samat, M. Stories of the Crusades. (5+) World, 1970. 192p. illus.

Treece, Henry. Know About the Crusades. (6-9) Dufour, 1967. 62p. illus.

Tucker, E. E. The Story of Knights and Armor. (4-6) Lothrop, 1961. 214p. illus.

Uden, Grant. A Dictionary of Chivalry. (7+) Crowell, 1969. 352p. illus.

Uden, Grant. Hero Tales from the Age of Chivalry: Retold from the Froissart Chronicles. (7+) World, 1969. 159p. illus.

Vlahos, Olivia. The Battle-Ax People: Beginnings of Western Culture. (7+) Viking, 1968. 146p. illus.

Warwick, A. R. Let's Look at Castles. (4-7) Whitman, 1965. 64p. illus.

West, Anthony. The Crusades. (5-6) Random House, 1954. 192p. illus.

WILLIAMS, JAY. Knights of the Crusades; in consultation with Margaret B. Freeman. (6+) Harper, 1962. 153p. illus.

WILLIAMS, JAY. Life in the Middle Ages. (6-10) Random House, 1966. 160p. illus.

WILLIAMS, JAY. Tournament of the Lions. (7-9) Walck, 1960. 115p. illus.
Education for knighthood in 1448.

WILLIAMS, PAUL, il. The Warrior Knights; in pictures; writer: George Constable. (4-7) Time-Life, 1969. 52p. illus.

1300 – 1700

BIXBY, WILLIAM. The Universe of Galileo and Newton; by the editors of Horizon magazine; consultant: Giorgio De Santillana. (6+) Harper, 1964. 153p. illus.

BOWMAN, JOHN. The Age of Enlightenment. (7+) Western, 1966. 100p. illus. charts
Europe from 1543 to 1789.

BULL, G. A. The Renaissance. (6-9) Day, 1968. 112p. illus. maps

FOSTER, GENEVIEVE. The World of Columbus and Sons. (7+) Scribner, 1965. 406p. illus.
World events during the lifetime of Columbus and his sons.

FOSTER, GENEVIEVE. Year of Columbus, 1492. (4+) Scribner, 1969. 64p. illus.
The world scene during the time of the great voyage.

GAIL, MARZIEH. Life in the Renaissance. (7+) Random House, 1968. 160p. illus.

GRANT, NEIL. The Renaissance. (7+) Watts, 1971. 96p. illus.

JOHNSTON, JOHANNA AND STEFFENSEN, J. L. Reformation and Exploration. (7+) Western, 1966. 100p. illus. charts
Major Old World and New World events from 1415 to 1634.

GENERAL

MARX, R. F. The Battle of Lepanto 1571. (4-9) World, 1966. 128p. illus. maps
> Historic naval battle stops the westward expansion of the Ottoman empire.

MILLS, DOROTHY. Renaissance and Reformation Times. (7-9) Putnam, 1939. 345p. illus.

SHAPIRO, IRWIN. The Golden Book of the Renaissance. (7+) Western, 1962. 168p. illus.
> Europe from the thirteenth to the sixteenth century.

STEFFENSEN, J. L. The Renaissance. (7+) Western, 1966. 100p. illus. charts
> Great developments from 1277 to 1603.

1700 – 1920

COLBY, C. B. Aircraft of World War I: Fighters, Scouts, Bombers, and Observation Planes. (5-7) Coward, 1962. 48p. illus.

COOKE, D. C. The Planes They Flew in World War I. (4-6) Dodd, 1969. 64p. illus.

COWLEY, ROBERT. 1918: Gamble For Victory – The Greatest Attack of World War I. (6+) Macmillan, 1963. 96p. photos; maps; chronology

DUPUY, T. N. Naval and Overseas War, 1914-1915. (7+) Watts, 1967. 96p. illus. maps

DUPUY, T. N. The Naval War in the West: The Raiders. (7+) Watts, 1963. 96p. illus. maps

DUPUY, T. N. The Naval War in the West: The Wolf Packs. (7+) Watts, 1963. 96p. illus. maps

DUPUY, T. N. 1914: The Battles in the East. (7+) Watts, 1967. 96p. illus. maps

EUROPE

Dupuy, T. N. 1914: The Battles in the West. (7+) Watts, 1967. 96p. illus. maps

Dupuy, T. N. Stalemate in the Trenches. (7+) Watts, 1967. 96p. illus. maps

Dupuy, T. N. Summation: Strategic and Combat Leadership. (7+) Watts, 1967. 96p.

Dupuy, T. N. Triumphs and Tragedies in the East. (7+) Watts, 1967. 96p. illus. maps
> World War I.

Dupuy, T. N. The War in the Air. (7+) Watts, 1967. 96p. illus. maps
> World War I.

Dupuy, T. N. and Crick, Julia. 1918: Decision in the West. (7+) Watts, 1967. 96p. illus. maps

Dupuy, T. N. and Crick, Julia. 1918: The German Offensives. (7+) Watts, 1967. 96p. illus. maps

Dupuy, T. N. and Hayes, G. P. Naval and Overseas War, 1916-1918. (7+) Watts, 1967. 96p. illus. maps

Gurney, Gene. Flying Aces of World War I. (5-9) Random House, 1965. 192p. illus.

Jantzen, Steven. Hooray for peace, hurrah for war; the United States During World War I. (6+) Knopf, 1971. 327p. illus.

Lawson, Don, ed. Great Air Battles: World Wars I and II. (7+) Lothrop, 1968. 223p. illus.

Leckie, Robert. The Story of World War I. (5-9) Random House, 1965. 189p. illus.

Lindquist, Willis. The Age of Revolution. (7+) Western, 1966. 100p. illus. charts
> European and American revolutions and turbulence from 1765 to 1875.

Lindquist, Willis. Industrial Revolution and Nationalism. (7+) Western, 1966. 100p. illus. charts
> Major movements from 1702 to 1906.

GENERAL

PHELAN, J. A. Heroes and Aeroplanes of the Great War 1914-1918. (7+) Grosset, 1970. illus.

REEDER, RED (RUSSELL POTTER REEDER). The Story of the First World War. (6-12) Duell, 243p. 1962. illus. maps

RIBBONS, IAN. Tuesday 4 August 1914: The First Day of World War I. (5+) White, 1970. 80p. illus. maps

SELLMAN, R. R. The First World War. (7+) rev. & enl. ed. Criterion, 1962. 160p. illus. maps; tables

SNYDER, L. L. The First Book of World War I. (7+) Watts, 1958. 96p. illus. maps

TERRAINE, JOHN. The Great War, 1914-1918: A Pictorial History. (7+) Macmillan, 1965. 400p. photos

WERSTEIN, IRVING. The Many Faces of World War I. (7+) Messner, 1963. 192p. illus. maps

WHITEHOUSE, ARCH AND LANCELOT, MILTON. Fighting Wings: The Story of Aerial Combat in World War I. (5-8) Meredith, 1966. 96p. illus.

1920 – Present

BLIVEN, BRUCE. Story of D-Day: June 6, 1944. (6-8) Random House, 1956. 192p. illus.

COOKE, D. C. The Planes the Allies Flew in World War II. (4-6) Dodd, 1969. 64p. illus.

COWAN, LORE. Children of the Resistance. (6+) Meredith, 1969. 192p.

DUPUY, T. N. The Air War in the West; September 1939-May 1941. (7+) Watts, 1963. 96p. illus. maps

DUPUY, T. N. The Air War in the West: June 1941-April 1945. (7+) Watts, 1963. 96p. illus. maps

EUROPE

Dupuy, T. N. Asian and Axis Resistance Movements. (7+) Watts, 1965. 96p. illus.

Dupuy, T. N. Chronological Military History of World War II. (7+) Watts, 1967. 96p. maps

Dupuy, T. N. European Land Battles, 1939-1943. (7+) Watts, 1962. 96p. illus. maps

Dupuy, T. N. European Land Battles, 1944-1945. (7+) Watts, 1962. 96p. illus. maps

Dupuy, T. N. European Resistance Movements. (7+) Watts, 1965. 96p. illus.

Dupuy, T. N. Land Battles: North Africa, Sicily, and Italy. (7+) Watts, 1962. 96p. illus. maps

Dupuy, T. N. Strategic Direction of World War II. (7+) Watts, 1965. 96p. illus.

Dupuy, T. N. and Mayo, M. R. Campaigns in Southern Europe. (7+) Watts, 1967. 96p. illus. maps

Ellis, H. B. The Common Market. (7-10) World, 1965. 208p. illus.

Hine, Al. D-Day: The Invasion of Europe (consultant: S. L. A. Marshall). (5+) Harper, 1962. 153p. illus.

Howarth, D. A. D-Day, the Sixth of June, 1944. (7+) McGraw, 1959. 251p. illus.

Irving, Clifford. Spy: The Story of Modern Espionage. (7+) Macmillan, 1969. 208p. photos; glossaries

Leckie, Robert. Story of World War II. (5-9) Random House, 1964. 192p. illus.

Mason, H. M. Duel for the Sky: Fighter Planes and Fighting Pilots of World War II. (7+) Grosset, 1970. 160p. photos

Reeder, Red (Russell Potter Reeder). The Story of the Second World War: [v 1] The Axis Strikes (1939-1942). (5+) Meredith, 1969. 267p. illus. maps

GENERAL

REEDER, RED (RUSSELL POTTER REEDER). The Story of the Second World War: [v 2] The Allies Conquer (1942-1945). Hawthorn, 1970. 301p. illus. maps

RITCHIE, EDNA. Totalitarianism and the Great Depression. (7+) Western, 1966. 100p. illus. charts
Western history from 1890 to 1938.

RITCHIE, EDNA. World War II and the Modern Age. (7+) Western, 1966. 100p. illus. charts
World problems and events from 1934 to 1965.

SAVAGE, KATHARINE. Story of the Second World War. (7+) Walck, 1958. 272p. photos; maps

SELLMAN, R. R. The Second World War. (7+) Roy, 1966. 111p. illus.

SHAPIRO, W. E. ed. D-Day. (7+) Watts, 1968. 66p. illus.

SNYDER, L. L. The First Book of the Long Armistice. (7+) Watts, 1964. 96p. illus.
Issues and events between World War I and World War II.

SNYDER, L. L. The First Book of World War II. (7+) Watts, 1958. 96p. illus. maps

STRAUSS, RICHARD. Coal, Steel, Atoms, and Trade: Challenge of Uniting Europe. (6-8) Coward, 1962. 121p. illus.

SUTTON, FELIX. The How and Why Wonder Book of World War II. (3-6) Grosset, 1962. 48p. illus.

WERSTEIN, IRVING. Betrayal: The Munich Pact of 1938. (7+) Doubleday, 1969. 188p. illus.

WEYR, THOMAS. World War II. (7+) Messner, 1969. 224p. illus. maps

BIOGRAPHY

ARMY TIMES, EDITORS OF THE. Famous Fighters of World War I. (7-9) Dodd, 1964. 156p. illus.
Sketches of generals and soldiers.

BROOKS, P. S. AND WALWORTH, N. Z. The World Awakes: The Renaissance in Western Europe. (7-9) Lippincott, 1962. 224p. illus. maps
  Biographical sketches of Renaissance leaders.

BROOKS, P. S. AND WALWORTH, N. Z. The World of Walls: The Middle Ages in Western Europe. (7-9) Lippincott, 1966. 256p. illus.
  Biographical sketches of leaders in the Middle Ages.

BURCH, GLADYS. Modern Composers for Young People. (7+) Dodd, 1941. 207p. illlus.

BURCH, GLADYS AND WOLCOTT, JOHN. Famous Composers for Young People. (7+) Dodd, 1939. 184p. illus.

COWIE, L. W. The Reformation. (6-9) Day, 1967. 112p. illus. maps

DUPUY, T. N. Combat Leaders of World War II. (7+) Watts, 1965. 128p. illus.

FIROOZI, EDITH AND KLEIN, I. N. The Age of Great Kings. (7+) Western, 1966. 100p. illus. charts
  European history from 1469 to 1762.

FOSTER, GENEVIEVE. World of Captain John Smith. (5-11) Scribner, 1959. 416p. illus.
  World history during Captain John Smith's lifetime.

GOUGH, CATHERINE. Boyhoods of Great Composers, Book I. (4-6) Walck, 1960. 64p. illus.

GOUGH, CATHERINE. Boyhoods of Great Composers, Book II. (4-6) Walck, 1965. 64p. illus.

McKINNEY, R. J. Famous Old Masters of Painting. (7+) Dodd, 1951. 135p. illus.

NETTEL, REGINALD. Great Moments in Music. (7+) Roy, 1958. 128p. illus.

NICKEL, HELMUT. Warriors and Worthies; Arms and Armor Through the Ages. (7+) Atheneum, 1969. 122p. photos

AUSTRIA

O'NEILL, MARY. Saints: Adventures in Courage. (4-7) Doubleday, 1963. 187p. illus.

TREASE, GEOFFREY. Seven Sovereign Queens. (7+) Vanguard, 1969. 181p. illus.

UNSTEAD, R. J. Royal Adventurers. (5+) Follett, 1967. 144p. illus.
Short biographies of ten famous rulers.

UNSTEAD, R. J. Some Kings and Queens. (4-6) Follett, 1967. 128p. illus.

Austria

FICTION

KULLMAN, HARRY. Under Secret Orders. (7-9) Harcourt, 1968. 191p.
Intrigue in Austria during Napoleon's era.

NONFICTION

ESTERHÁZY, CHRISTA. Young Traveler in Austria. (7-10) Branford, 1956. 152p.

GRAHAM, FRANK. Austria. (7+) Macmillan, 1964. 128p. photos; map

TRAPP, M. A. The Story of the Trapp Family Singers. (7-9) Lippincott, 1949. 310p. illus.
Adventures of a singing Austrian family who flee from Nazism.

WOHLRABE, R. A. AND KRUSCH, WERNER. The Key to Vienna. (4-6) Lippincott, 1961. 128p. illus. maps

WOHLRABE, R. A. AND KRUSCH, WERNER. Land and People of Austria. (7-9) Lippincott, 1956. 120p. illus. maps

BIOGRAPHY

Freud

KLAGSBRUN, FRANCINE. Sigmund Freud. (7+) Watts, 1967. 150p.

STOUTENBURG, ADRIEN AND BAKER, L. N. Explorer of the Unconscious: Sigmund Freud. (7-11) Scribner, 1965. 192p. illus.

Haydn

KAUFMANN, H. L. The Story of Haydn. (4-6) Grosset [c 1962]. 179p. illus.

MIRSKY, R. P. Haydn. (5+) Follett, 1963. 160p. illus.

WHEELER, OPAL AND DEUCHER, SYBIL. Joseph Haydn: The Merry Little Peasant. (4-7) Dutton [c 1936]. 118p. illus.

YOUNG, P. M. Haydn. (7+) White, 1970. 78p. illus.

Mendel

GREENE, CARLA. Gregor Mendel. (4-7) Dial, 1970. 80p. illus.
   Austrian monk discovers laws of genetics.

SOOTIN, HARRY. Gregor Mendel: Father of the Science of Genetics. (7-10) Vanguard, 1958. 223p. illus.

WEBSTER, GARY (pseud. of WEBB BLACK GARRISON). The Man Who Found Out Why: The Story of Gregor Mendel. (6-9) Hawthorn [1963]. 188p. illus.

Metternich

ARCHER, JULES. Colossus of Europe: Metternich. (7+) Messner, 1970. 192p.

Mozart

BISHOP, C. H. Mozart: Music Magician. (4-7) Garrard, 1968. 144p. illus.

GASS, IRENE. Mozart: Child Wonder, Great Composer. (3-6) Lothrop, 1970. 64p. illus.

BELGIUM

JENKINS, ALAN. The Young Mozart. (6-10) Roy, 1961. 108p. illus.

KAUFMANN, H. L. Story of Mozart. (4-6) Grosset [c 1955]. 179p. illus.

KOMROFF, MANUEL. Mozart. (7-8) Knopf, 1956. 192p. illus.

MIRSKY, R. P. Mozart. (4-6) Follett, 1960. 144p. illus.

SEROFF, VICTOR. Wolfgang Amadeus Mozart. (7+) Macmillan, 1965. 128p. illus.

STEARNS, MONROE. Wolfgang Amadeus Mozart: Master of Pure Music. (7+) Watts, 1968. 256p. illus.

WHEELER, OPAL AND DEUCHER, SYBIL. Mozart, the Wonder Boy. (4-7) Dutton [1934]. 91p. illus.

WOODFORD, PEGGY. Mozart. (4-6) Walck, 1966. 104p. illus.

Schubert

WHEELER, OPAL AND DEUCHER, SYBIL. Franz Schubert and His Merry Friends. (4-7) Dutton [c 1939]. 124p. illus.

Belgium

FICTION

THOORENS, LEON. The Golden Compass. (7+) Roy, 1965. 142p. illus.

> In fifteenth century Antwerp, the Inquisition and Reformation clash.

WERSTEIN, IRVING. The Long Escape. (7+) Scribner, 1964. 192p.

> Belgian children and their nurse struggle to escape advancing Nazis.

NONFICTION

GERSON, N. B. Belgium. (7+) Macmillan [c 1964]. 118p. illus.

LODER, D. H. Land and People of Belgium. (7-9) Lippincott, 1966. 128p. illus.

EUROPE

STERLING PUBLISHING COMPANY, EDITORS OF. Belgium and Luxembourg in Pictures. (5-9) Sterling, 1966. 64p. illus.

WOLSELEY, R. E. Low Countries: Gateways to Europe. (6+) Nelson, 1969. 224p. illus.

BIOGRAPHY
Rubens

RIPLEY, ELIZABETH. Rubens. (7-9) Walck, 1957. 72p. illus.

WEDGWOOD, C. V. The World of Rubens, 1577-1640, by [the author] and the editors of Time-Life books. (5+) Time-Life, 1967. 192p. illus.

Vesalius

TARSHIS, JEROME. Andreas Vesalius: Father of Modern Anatomy. (7+) Dial, 1969. 144p.

Bulgaria

NONFICTION

BURT, OLIVE. Our World: Bulgaria. (4-6) Messner, 1970. 128p. photos

HALL, ELVAJEAN AND CRINER, C. L. Picture Map Geography of Eastern Europe. (4-6) Lippincott, 1968. 160p. maps

KOSTICH, D. D. The Land and People of the Balkans. (7-9) Lippincott, 1962. 160p. illus. maps

PERL, LILA. Yugoslavia, Romania, Bulgaria: New Era in the Balkans. (6-9) Nelson, 1970. 224p. illus. maps

Czechoslovakia

FICTION

BEATTY, J. L. AND BEATTY, PATRICIA. Witch Dog. (7-9) Morrow, 1968. 256p. map

ISH-KISHOR, SULAMITH. A Boy of Old Prague. (4+) Pantheon, 1963. 160p. illus.

DENMARK

McSwigan, Marie. All Aboard for Freedom! (5-9) Dutton, 1954. 249p. illus.
    Czechs escape communism by fleeing to West Germany.

NONFICTION

Hall, Elvajean. The Land and People of Czechoslovakia. (7-9) Lippincott, 1966. 160p. illus. maps

Hall, Elvajean and Criner, C. L. Picture Map Geography of Eastern Europe. (4-6) Lippincott, 1968. 160p. maps

Sterling Publishing Company, Editors of. Czechoslovakia in Pictures. (7+) Sterling, 1969. 64p. illus.

Denmark
See also Scandinavia

FICTION

Arnold, Elliott. A Kind of Secret Weapon. (6+) Scribner, 1969. 192p.
    Juvenile resistance to Nazis in occupied Denmark.

Garthwaite, M. H. The Locked Crowns. (5-7) Doubleday, 1963. 217p. illus.
    A novel of the days of Havelok the Dane.

Holm, A. S. North to Freedom. (7-9) Harcourt, 1965. 190p.
    Boy escapes from Nazi prison camp and seeks his home.

Levin, J. W. Star of Danger. (7-9) Harcourt, 1966. 160p.
    Two Jewish boys in Denmark evade the Nazis.

Werstein, Irving. That Denmark Might Live. (7+) Macrae Smith, 1967. 160p. photos
    Saga of Danish Resistance in World War II.

NONFICTION

Bailey, Bernadine. Denmark: Wonderland of Work and Play. (4-6) Dodd, 1966. 64p. illus.

LOBSENZ, N. M. First Book of Denmark. (4+) Watts, 1970. 96p. photos

O'NEILL, HESTER. The Picture Story of Denmark. (3-7) McKay, 1952. 56p. illus.

RUTLAND, JONATHAN. Looking at Denmark. (4-6) Lippincott, 1968. 64p. illus.

WOHLRABE, R. A. AND KRUSCH, WERNER. The Land and People of Denmark. (7-9) Lippincott, 1961. 128p. illus. maps

BIOGRAPHY

Andersen

COLLIN, HEDVIG. Young Hans Christian Andersen. (5-9) Viking, 1955. 216p. illus.

MANNING-SANDERS, RUTH. Story of Hans Andersen: Swan of Denmark. (7+) Dutton, 1966. 240p. illus.

MONTGOMERY, E. R. Hans Christian Andersen: Immortal Storyteller. (4-7) Garrard, 1968. 144p. illus.

SPINK, REGINALD. Young Hans Andersen. (6-10) Roy, 1962. 143p. illus.

WHEELER, OPAL. Hans Andersen, Son of Denmark. (3-6) Dutton, 1951. 183p. illus.

Havelok the Dane

CROSSLEY-HOLLAND, KEVIN. Havelok, The Dane. (5+) Dutton, 1965. 192p. illus.

SERRAILLIER, IAN. Havelok the Dane. (4-6) Walck, 1967. 72p. illus.

England
See United Kingdom (UK)

Finland
See also Scandinavia

FRANCE

FICTION

DEUTSCH, BABETTE. Heroes of the Kalevala. (6+) Messner, 1940. 340p. illus.
Stories of Finland's ancient heroes.

NONFICTION

BERRY, ERICK. The Land and People of Finland. (7-9) Lippincott, 1959. 128p. illus. maps

PALOHEIMO, LEONORA AND WATSON, J. W. Finland: Champion of Independence. (3-6) Garrard, 1969. 112p. illus.

France

FICTION

Prehistory – A.D. 1000

ALMEDINGEN, E. M. (MARTHA EDITH VON ALMEDINGEN). A Candle at Dusk. (7+) Farrar, 1969. 192p.
Struggles of a twelve-year-old in eighth century France.

ANDREWS, F. E. For Charlemagne. (7+) Harper, 1949. 207p.
Adventurers championing the cause of the emperor.

BOYCE, BURKE. The Emperor's Arrow. (4-7) Lippincott, 1967. 72p. illus.
Peasant boy helps Charlemagne.

CURREN, POLLY. Folk Tales of France. (4+) Bobbs, 1963. 126p. illus.

FINKEL, G. I. The Long Pilgrimage. (7+) Viking, 1969. 320p.
Story set in Charlemagne's time.

THE SONG OF ROLAND.
Available in several editions, some adapted for younger readers.

YONGE, C. M. Little Duke. (3-6) Dutton, 1963. 162p. illus.
Story of the childhood of Richard I, third Duke of Normandy, in the late 900s.

17

1000 – 1700

AGLE, N. H. Makon and the Dauphin. (3-4) Scribner, 1961. 126p. illus.
   Indian boy taken to sixteenth century France.

BUTLER, M. A. Ward of the Sun King. (7-11) Funk, 1970. 156p.
   Adventure and intrigue at the court of Louis XIV.

DUMAS, ALEXANDRE. The Three Musketeers. (6+)
   Available in several editions.

HEWES, A. D. A Boy of the Lost Crusade. (7+) Houghton, 1923. 288p. illus.
   French boy joins the Children's Crusade.

LOWNSBERY, ELOISE. The Boy Knight of Reims. (7+) Houghton, 1927. 336p. illus.
   Life in the fifteenth century.

SCOTT, SIR WALTER. Quentin Durward.
   Available in several editions.

WILLIAMS, PAUL, il. The Warrior Knights; in pictures; writer: George Constable. (4-7) Time-Life, 1969. 52p. illus.
   Follows boy from pagehood to knighthood in twelfth century France.

1700 – 1900

BOURLIAGUET, LÉONCE. The Guns of Valmy. (7+) Abelard, 1969. 159p.
   France fights to keep its Revolution alive.

DICKENS, CHARLES. A Tale of Two Cities. (7+)
   Available in several editions.

FOSTER, M. S. Red Carpet for Lafayette. (2-6) Bobbs, 1961. 159p. illus.

GARNETT, HENRY. The Red Bonnet. (7+) Doubleday, 1964. 192p. illus.
   Youthful adventures during the French Revolution.

KIMBALL, GWEN (pseud.). Puzzle of the Lost Dauphin. (5-8) Duell, 1964. 150p.
   Speculations regarding Louis XVII of France.

FRANCE

MAC ORLAN, PIERRE. The Anchor of Mercy. (7+) Pantheon, 1967. 224p. illus.
>Piracy and impending war on the French seacoast in 1777.

ORCZY, EMMUSKA, BARONESS. The Scarlet Pimpernel. (7+)
>Spy story of the French Revolution, written in 1905. Available in several editions.

RITCHIE, RITA. Night Coach to Paris. (5-9) Norton, 1970. 247p.
>Adventure during the Revolution.

ROBBINS, RUTH. The Emperor and the Drummer Boy. (2-6) Parnassus, 1962. illus.

TREASE, GEOFFREY. Victory at Valmy. (7-11) Vanguard, 1960. 255p.
>France defends her Revolution.

WALLOWER, LUCILLE. The Lost Prince: Louis XVII of France. (4-6) McKay, 1963. 128p. illus.
>Fictionalized biography of Charles Fontaine, who may have been the son of Louis XVI.

WILLIAMSON, J. S. Jacobin's Daughter. (5-6) Knopf, 1956. 224p. illus.
>Girl in Paris during the Revolution.

1900 – Present

BISHOP, C. H. Twenty and Ten. (4-6) Viking, 1952. 73p. illus.
>French children and a nun protect Jewish children from the Nazis.

KNIGHT, CLAYTON AND KNIGHT, K. S. We Were There With the Lafayette Escadrille. (4-6) Grosset [1961]. 182p. illus.

WHITEHOUSE, ARCH. The Laughing Falcon. (6-8) Putnam, 1969. 160p. illus.
>Americans fight for France in World War I.

WHITEHOUSE, ARCH. Spies With Wings: The Story of the Lafayette Escadrille. (6-9) Putnam, 1960. 160p. illus.
>Fictionalized account of Americans in France in World War I.

NONFICTION

BARRY, JOSEPH. France. (7+) Macmillan, 1965. 144p. photos; maps

EUROPE

BISHOP, C. H. French Roundabout. (6-10) Dodd, 1967. 384p. illus.

BISHOP, C. H. Here Is France. (7+) Farrar, 1969. 240p.

BRAGDON, L. J. The Land and People of France. (7-9) Lippincott, 1960. 128p. illus. maps

BROGAN, D. W. France. (4+) Time-Life, 1966. illus.

CHURCH, R. J. Looking at France. (4-6) Lippincott, 1970. 64p. illus.

CLEMENT, MARGUERITE. In France. (7+) Viking, 1956. 119p. illus.

DAVENPORT, WILLIAM. The Seine — from Its Source to the Sea. (5+) McGraw, 1968. 128p. illus.

DOUGLAS, M. S. The Key to Paris. (4-6) Lippincott, 1960. 128p. illus. maps

GEIS, DARLENE, ed. Let's Travel in France. (6+) Childrens, 1964. 88p. illus.

LONGLEY, JOHN (pseud. of JOHN DENTON). France: A First-Look-At-Geography Book. (2-6) Verry, 1966, 32p. illus.

NEWMAN, BERNARD AND CALDWELL, J. C. Let's Visit France. (4-6) Day, 1966. 96p. illus. maps

SASEK, MIROSLAV. This Is Paris. (3+) Macmillan [c 1959]. 60p. illus.

SMITH, IRENE. Paris. (5+) Rand McNally, 1961. 128p. illus.

STERLING PUBLISHING COMPANY, EDITORS OF. France in Pictures. (3-6) Sterling, 1965. 64p. illus.

WALLACE, J. A. Getting to Know France. (3-5) Coward, 1962. 72p. illus.

WHELPTON, BARBARA. Paris Triumphant. (7+) Roy, 1963. 155p. illus.
  Parisian history told through its monuments.

FRANCE

WILSON, HAZEL. The Seine: River of Paris. (4-7) Garrard, 1962. 96p. illus.

Prehistory – A.D. 1800

ALDERMAN, C. L. Liberty, Equality, Fraternity: The Story of the French Revolution. (7+) Messner, 1965. 192p. illus. maps

DOWD, D. L. The French Revolution; by the editors of Horizon in consultation with David L. Dowd. (6+) Harper, 1965. 150p. illus.

EIMERL, SAREL. Revolution: France 1789-1794. (7+) Little, 1967. 223p. illus.

LEVRON, JACQUES. Daily Life at Versailles in the 17th and 18th Centuries. (7+) Macmillan, 1968. 256p.

PRATT, STEPHEN. The French Revolution. (7-9) Day, 1970. 112p. illus. maps

SPENCER, CORNELIA. The Song in the Streets. (6-9) Day, 1960. 192p. illus.
  A brief history of the French Revolution.

1800 – 1900

BLASSINGAME, WYATT. The French Foreign Legion. (7+) Random House, 1955. 192p. illus.

DUPUY, T. N. The Battle of Austerlitz: Napoleon's Greatest Victory. (6+) Macmillan, 1968. 96p. illus. maps; chronology

PRINGLE, PATRICK. Napoleon's Hundred Days. (6-11) Warne, 1969. 95p. illus.

WERSTEIN, IRVING. I Accuse: The Story of the Dreyfus Case. (7+) Messner, 1967. 192p. illus.

WINWAR, FRANCES. Napoleon and the Battle of Waterloo. (5-6) Random House, 1953. 192p. illus.

1900 – Present

Bowen, R. S. They Flew to Glory. (4-6) Lothrop, 1965. 192p. illus.
> American pilots join the Lafayette Flying Corps to fight for France in World War I.

Jablonski, Edward. Warriors With Wings. (6+) Bobbs, 1966. 206p. illus.
> Story of the Lafayette Escadrille.

Nordhoff, C. B. and Hall, J. N. Falcons of France. (7+) Little, 1929. 332p.
> Americans fight in the sky for France in World War I.

Wilhelm, Maria. For the Glory of France: The Story of the French Resistance. (7+) Messner, 1968. 192p. photos; map

BIOGRAPHY

Anne of Brittany

Butler, M. A. Twice Queen of France: Anne of Brittany. (7-11) Funk, 1967. 190p.
> Biography of the wife of Charles VIII (1491-1498) and Louis XII (1499-1514).

Beaumarchais

Ruskin, Ariane. Spy for Liberty: The Adventurous Life of Beaumarchais. (7+) Pantheon, 1965. 192p. illus.

Bernadette of Lourdes

Stafford, Ann. Young Bernadette. (6-10) Roy, 1966. 125p. illus.

Catherine de Medicis

Vance, Marguerite. Dark Eminence: Catherine De Medici and Her Children. (7+) Dutton, 1961. 159p. illus.

Cézanne

Murphy, R. W. World of Cézanne. (5+) Time-Life, 1968. 192p. illus.

FRANCE

Charlemagne

KOMROFF, MANUEL. Charlemagne. (7+) Messner, 1964. 192p.

STEARNS, MONROE. Charlemagne. (7+) Watts, 1971. 192p. illus.

WINSTON, RICHARD. Charlemagne; by the editors of Horizon magazine; consultant: Harry Bober. (6+) Harper, 1968. 153p. illus.

Curie Family

McKOWN, ROBIN. Marie Curie. (7-10) Putnam, 1959. 128p.

McKOWN, ROBIN. She Lived for Science: Irène Joliot-Curie. (7+) Messner, 1961. 192p.

RUBIN, ELIZABETH. The Curies and Radium. (7+) Watts, 1961. 120p. illus.

THORNE, ALICE. Story of Madame Curie. (4-6) Grosset, 1959. 176p. illus.

De Gaulle

LESTER, JOHN. De Gaulle: King Without a Crown. (7+) Hawthorn, 1968. 192p. illus.

Descartes

HOYT, E. P. He Freed the Minds of Men: René Descartes. (7+) Messner, 1969. 192p.

Henry IV

WILKINSON, BURKE. The Helmet of Navarre. (7+) Macmillan, 1965. 176p. illus. chronology

Joan of Arc

CHURCHILL, SIR WINSTON. Joan of Arc. (7+) Dodd, 1969. 46p. illus.

FISHER, AILEEN. Jeanne d'Arc. (4-6) Crowell, 1970. 52p. illus.

MASEFIELD, JUDITH. Shepherdess of France: Remembrances of Jeanne d'Arc. (5+) Coward, 1969. 192p. illus.

NOLAN, J. C. Story of Joan of Arc. (4-6) Grosset, 1953. 178p. illus.

PAINE, A. B. The Girl in White Armor. (7+) Macmillan, 1967. 256p. illus. map; chronology

ROSS, N. W. Joan of Arc. (5-6) Random House, 1953. 192p. illus.

STRUCHEN, JEANETTE. Joan of Arc: Maid of Orleans. (7+) Watts, 1967. 96p. map

WILLIAMS, JAY. Joan of Arc; consultant: Charles Wayland Lightbody. (6+) Harper, 1963. 153p. illus.

Josephine

VANCE, MARGUERITE. The Empress Josephine from Martinique to Malmaison. (7+) Dutton, 1956. 160p. illus.

Lafayette

BISHOP, C. H. Lafayette: French-American Hero. (2-5) Garrard, 1960. 80p. illus.

CARTER, HODDING. The Marquis de Lafayette. (7+) Random House, 1958. 192p. illus.

GOTTSCHALK, FRUMA. The Youngest General: A Story of Lafayette. (5-6) Knopf, 1949. 169p. illus.

GRAHAM, A. P. Lafayette: Friend of America. (4+) Abingdon, 1952. 128p. illus.

MAUROIS, ANDRÉ. Lafayette in America. (7-11) Houghton, 1960. 192p. illus.

WILSON, HAZEL. Little Marquise: Madame de Lafayette. (7-11) Knopf, 1957. 256p. illus.
   The story of Lafayette's wife.

WILSON, HAZEL. Story of Lafayette. (4-6) Grosset, 1952. 182p. illus.

FRANCE

Lavoisier

MARCUS, R. B. Antoine Lavoisier and the Revolution in Chemistry. (7+) Watts, 1964. 190p.

RIEDMAN, S. R. Antoine Lavoisier — Scientist and Citizen. (7+) Abelard, 1967. 224p. illus.
  Scientific genius was also a statesman and social reformer.

Louis XIV

APSLER, ALFRED. The Sun King: Louis XIV of France. (7+) Messner, 1965. 192p.

STEARNS, MONROE. Louis XIV of France: Pattern of Majesty. (7+) Watts, 1971. 160p. illus.

WILKINSON, BURKE. Young Louis XIV: The Early Years of the Sun King. (7+) Macmillan, 1970. 160p.

Louis XVII

WALLOWER, LUCILLE. The Lost Prince: Louis XVII of France. (4-6) McKay, 1963. 128p. illus.
  Fictionalized biography of Charles Fontaine, who may have been the son of Louis XVI.

Marie Antoinette

KIELTY, BERNARDINE. Marie Antoinette. (7+) Random House, 1955. 192p. illus.

KOMROFF, MANUEL AND KOMROFF, ODETTE. Marie Antoinette. (7+) Messner [c 1967]. 192p.

VANCE, MARGUERITE. Marie Antoinette: Daughter of an Empress. (7+) Dutton, 1950. 159p. illus.

Napoleon

CAMMIADE, AUDREY. Napoleon. (7+) Roy [1963]. 112p. illus.

COOPER, LEONARD. Young Napoleon. (6-10) Roy, 1963. 134p. illus.

CORLEY, ANTHONY. True Story of Napoleon. (5+) Childrens, 1964. 143p. illus.

DUPUY, T. N. The Military Life of Napoleon, Emperor of the French. (7+) Watts, 1970. 221p. maps

GIMPEL, H. J. Napoleon, Man of Destiny. (7+) Watts, 1968. 320p. maps

HEROLD, J. C. Age of Napoleon. (5-9) Harper, 1963. 453p. illus.

KOMROFF, MANUEL. Napoleon. (7+) Messner, 1954. 192p.

Ney

FOSTER, J. T. Napoleon's Marshal: The Life of Michel Ney. (7-9) Morrow, 1968. 256p. maps

Pasteur

BURTON, M. J. Louis Pasteur: Founder of Microbiology. (7+) Watts, 1963. 208p. illus.

DOORLY, ELEANOR. Microbe Man. (6-8) Dufour, 1965. 164p. illus.
   Researches of Louis Pasteur.

LAUBER, PATRICIA. The Quest of Louis Pasteur. (7+) Doubleday, 1960. 55p. illus.

MALKUS, A. S. Story of Louis Pasteur. (4-6) Grosset [1952]. 178p. illus.

MANN, J. H. Louis Pasteur, the Germ Killer. (4-6) Macmillan, 1967. 48p. illus.

RICHARDSON, JOANNA. Young Louis Pasteur. (6-10) Roy, 1965. 128p. illus.

WOOD, L. N. Louis Pasteur. (7+) Messner, 1948. 224p.

GERMANY

Richelieu

WILKINSON, BURKE. Cardinal in Armor: The Story of Richelieu and His Times. (7+) Macmillan, 1966. 192p. illus. map; chronology

Rousseau

WEBB, R. N. Jean Jacques Rousseau: The Father of Romanticism. (7+) Watts, 1970. 128p. photos; map

Talleyrand

KOMROFF, MANUEL. Talleyrand. (7+) Messner, 1965. 192p.

St. Teresa of Lisieux

HAUGHTON, ROSEMARY. Therese Martin. (7+) Macmillan, 1967. 224p. photos

Verne

BECKER, BERIL. Jules Verne. (7-10) Putnam, 1966. 224p. illus.

BORN, FRANZ. Jules Verne: The Man Who Invented the Future. (5+) Prentice-Hall, 1964. 102p. illus.

PEARE, C. O. Jules Verne: His Life. (5-7) Holt, 1956. 122p. illus.

Germany

FICTION

Prehistory – A.D. 1800

ALMEDINGEN, E. M. (MARTHA EDITH VON ALMEDINGEN). The Treasure of Siegfried. (7-9) Lippincott, 1965. 160p. illus.

BALDWIN, JAMES. The Story of Siegfried. (7+) Scribner, 1931. 294p. illus.

DE VIVANCO, MARIA. Siegfried, the Mighty Warrior. (5-8) Western, 1969. 144p. illus.
> Twelfth century tale of legendary Germanic warrior of ancient Europe.

HOLBROOK, SABRA. Sir Tristan of All Time. (7+) Farrar, 1970. 192p. illus.
> An examination of the Tristan legend with much information about the Middle Ages.

HOLLAND, CECELIA. The King's Road. (4-6) Atheneum, 1970. 160p. illus.
> Novel about childhood of Frederick II, German emperor and crusader (1211-1250).

PYLE, HOWARD. Otto of the Silver Hand. (7+)
> Robber barons feud in medieval Germany. Available in several editions.

1800 – Present

BENARY-ISBERT, MARGOT. The Ark. (7-9) Harcourt, 1953. 246p.
> Postwar problems faced by a German family in a bombed-out city during World War II.

BENARY-ISBERT, MARGOT. A Time to Love. (7-9) Harcourt, 1962. 256p.
> Social conflict in Nazi Germany.

ECKE, WOLFGANG. Flight Toward Home. (5+) Macmillan, 1970. 128p.
> Ten-year-old East German boy attempts to flee to freedom in the West.

FORMAN, JAMES. Horses of Anger. (7+) Farrar, 1967. 224p.
> Growth of a German teen-ager in Nazi and postwar Germany.

FORMAN, JAMES. The Traitors. (7+) Farrar, 1968. 256p.
> Pastor fights Nazism in Bavarian town.

GOLDTHWAIT, PRISCILLA. Night of the Wall. (5-7) Putnam, 1964. 160p. illus.
> A story of the Berlin Wall.

HOLBROOK, SABRA. Bruno and Karen of Berlin. (4-6) Watts, 1967. 71p. illus.
> Fourteen-year-old girl escapes from East Berlin.

LEVITIN, SONIA. Journey to America. (4-6) Atheneum, 1970. 150p. illus.
> Struggle of a refugee family from Hitler's Germany.

GERMANY

ORBAAN, ALBERT. Duel in the Shadows. (7+) Doubleday, 1965. 240p.
>Underground resistance to the Nazis in World War II.

PILKINGTON, ROGER. The Eisenbart Mystery. (4-6) St. Martin's, 1963. 192p. illus.
>German boy escapes through the Iron Curtain.

STILES, MARTHA BENNETT. Darkness Over the Land. (7+) Dial, 1966. 284p. map
>A nine-year-old boy undergoes privations in Germany of World War II and the postwar years.

NONFICTION

DYRA, FRANCES, ed. Let's Travel in West Germany. (6+) Childrens, 1968. 88p. illus.

GOLDSTON, R. C. The Life and Death of Nazi Germany. (7+) Bobbs, 1967. 224p. illus. photos

HEAPS, W. A. The Wall of Shame. (5+) Meredith, 1964. 175p.
>Story of the Berlin Wall.

HOLBROOK, SABRA. Capital Without a Country. (6-8) Coward, 1961. 121p. illus.
>Story of modern Berlin.

HOLBROOK, SABRA. Germany: East and West. (7+) Meredith [c 1968]. 241p. illus. maps

HOLBROOK, SABRA. Getting to Know the Two Germanys. (3-5) Coward, 1966. 72p. illus.

HOMZE, ALMA AND HOMZE, E. L. Germany: The Divided Nation. (6-9) Nelson, 1970. 223p. illus.

HOYT, E. P. Swan of the East: The Life and Death of the German Cruiser Emden in World War I. (6+) Macmillan, 1968. 224p. maps

KNIGHT, D. C. The First Book of Berlin: Tale of a Divided City. (4-6) Watts, 1967. 96p. illus.

LOBSENZ, N. M. The First Book of West Germany. (4-6) Watts, 1959. 72p. illus.

MOORE, JAMES AND CALDWELL, J. C. Let's Visit Germany. (4-8) Day, 1970. 96p. illus. map

SAVAGE, KATHARINE. People and Power: The Story of Three Nations. (7-9) Walck, 1959. 250p. illus.
History of Germany, Russia, and Japan.

SHAPIRO, W. E. ed. Trial at Nuremberg. (7+) Watts, 1967. 66p. illus.

SHEPHERD, DAVID. We Were There at the Battle of the Bulge. (4-6) Grosset, 1970. illus.

STERLING PUBLISHING COMPANY, EDITORS OF. Berlin East and West in Pictures. (3-6) Sterling, 1962. 64p. illus.

STERLING PUBLISHING COMPANY, EDITORS OF. West Germany in Pictures. (6+) Sterling, 1967. 64p. illus.

WERSTEIN, IRVING. The Franco-Prussian War: Germany's Rise as a World Power. (7+) Messner, 1965. 192p. illus. maps

WOHLRABE, R. A. AND KRUSCH, WERNER. The Land and People of Germany. (7-9) Lippincott, 1964. 128p. illus. maps

BIOGRAPHY

Johann Sebastian Bach

ARKIN, DAVID. The Twenty Children of Johann Sebastian Bach. (3-7) Ritchie, 1968. illus.

HOLST, IMOGEN. Bach. (5+) Crowell, 1965. 80p. illus.

MANTON, JO. Portrait of Bach. (7+) Abelard, 1957. 176p. illus.

MIRSKY, R. P. Johann Sebastian Bach. (5+) Follett, 1965. 144p. illus.

REINGOLD, C. B. Johann Sebastian Bach: Revolutionary of Music. (7+) Watts, 1970. 128p. illus.

WESTCOTT, FREDERIC. Bach. (4-6) Walck, 1967. 96p. illus.

GERMANY

Beethoven

GIMPEL, H. J. Beethoven: Master Composer. (7+) Watts, 1970. 256p. illus.

GOSS, M. B. Beethoven: Master Musician. (7-9) Holt, 1946. 364p. illus.

HARRIS, PAULA. Introducing Beethoven. (6-10) Roy, 1965. 98p. illus.

KAUFMANN, H. L. Story of Beethoven. (4-6) Grosset, 1957. 192p. illus.

MIRSKY, R. P. Beethoven. (5+) Follett, 1957. 176p. illus.

SADIE, STANLEY. Beethoven. (5-8) Crowell, 1967. 76p. illus.

WHEELER, OPAL. Ludwig Beethoven and the Chiming Tower Bells. (3-7) Dutton [c 1942]. 144p. illus.

YOUNG, P. M. Beethoven. (7+) White, 1966. 69p.

Bismarck

APSLER, ALFRED. Iron Chancellor: Otto von Bismarck. (7+) Messner, 1968. 192p.

RICHTER, WERNER. Bismarck. (6+) Putnam, 1965. 416p.

SNYDER, L. L. Bismarck and German Unification. (7+) Watts, 1966. 168p. illus.

Brahms

DEUCHER, SYBIL. The Young Brahms. (3-7) Dutton, 1949. 152p. illus.

MIRSKY, R. P. Brahms. (4-6) Follett, 1966. 160p. illus.

Charles V

GRANT, NEIL. Charles V, Holy Roman Emperor. (7+) Watts, 1970. 224p.

Frederick the Great

DUPUY, T. N. The Military Life of Frederick the Great of Prussia. (7+) Watts, 1969. 160p. maps

SNYDER, L. L. AND BROWN, I. M. Frederick the Great: Prussian Warrior and Statesman. (7+) Watts, 1968. 192p. illus. maps

Gauss

SCHAAF, W. L. Carl Friedrich Gauss: Prince of Mathematicians. (7+) Watts, 1964. 168p.

Goethe

STEARNS, MONROE. Goethe: Pattern of Genius. (7+) Watts, 1967. 320p.

Handel

BERK, P. L. Duke's Command. (2-5) Lantern [c 1966]. illus.
The story of Handel.

SADIE, STANLEY. Handel. (5+) Crowell, 1969. 95p. illus.

WHEELER, OPAL. Handel at the Court of Kings. (3-7) Dutton, 1943. 135p. illus.

YOUNG, P. M. Handel. (7+) White, 1967. 70p. illus.

Hindenburg

DUPUY, T. N. The Military Lives of Hindenburg and Ludendorff of Imperial Germany. (7+) Watts, 1969. 160p. maps

Hitler

APPEL, BENJAMIN. Hitler: From Power to Ruin. (7-9) Grosset, 1964. 91p. illus.

BROWNE, HARRY. Hitler and the Rise of Nazism. (7+) Roy, 1969. 94p. illus.

DUPUY, T. N. The Military Life of Adolph Hitler, Führer of Germany. (7+) Watts, 1970. 179p. maps

GERMANY

KING-HALL, SIR STEPHEN. Three Dictators: Mussolini, Hitler, Stalin. (7+) Transatlantic, 1964. 132p.

SHIRER, W. L. Rise and Fall of Adolf Hitler. (7-11) Random House, 1961. 192p. illus.

SNYDER, L. L. Hitler and Nazism. (7+) Watts, 1961. 192p. illus.

Kepler

KNIGHT, D. C. Johannes Kepler and Planetary Motion. (7+) Watts, 1962. 190p.

LAND, BARBARA. The Quest of Johannes Kepler, Astronomer. (7+) Doubleday, 1963. 120p. illus.

ROSEN, SIDNEY. The Harmonious World of Johann Kepler. (7+) Little, 1962. 212p. illus.

Koch

KNIGHT, D. C. Robert Koch: Father of Bacteriology. (7+) Watts, 1961. 180p.

Ludendorff

DUPUY, T. N. The Military Lives of Hindenburg and Ludendorff of Imperial Germany. (7+) Watts, 1969. 160p. maps

Luther

ELDER, MICHAEL. The Young Martin Luther. (6-10) Roy, 1966. 126p. illus.

FOSDICK, H. E. Martin Luther. (7+) Random House, 1956. 192p. illus.

HUMMEL, R. S. Little Martin Luther. (K-1) Concordia, 1962. illus.

MCNEER, MAY AND WARD, LYND. Martin Luther. (4+) Abingdon, 1953. 96p.

PITTENGER, W. N. Martin Luther: The Great Reformer. (7+) Watts, 1969. 192p.

Marx

ALEXANDER, ALBERT. Karl Marx: The Father of Modern Socialism. (7+) Watts, 1969. 160p. map

APSLER, ALFRED. Prophet of Revolution: Karl Marx. (7+) Messner, 1967. 192p.

CARMICHAEL, JOEL. Karl Marx: The Passionate Logician. (7+) Scribner, 1967. 288p. photos

Richthofen

FISK, NICHOLAS. Richthofen, the Red Baron. (3-7) Coward, 1968. 40p. illus.

Röntgen

DIBNER, BERN. Wilhelm Conrad Röntgen and the Discovery of X-Rays. (7+) Watts, 1968. 160p. illus.

Schumann

KYLE, ELISABETH (pseud. of AGNES MARY ROBERTSON DUNLOP). Duet: The Story of Clara and Robert Schumann. (5-9) Holt, 1968. 192p. illus.

WHEELER, OPAL. Robert Schumann and Mascot Ziff. (3-7) Dutton, 1947. 167p. illus.

WHITE, HILDA. Song Without End: The Love Story of Clara and Robert Schumann. (7+) Dutton, 1959. 319p.

Wagner

STEARNS, MONROE. Richard Wagner: Titan of Music. (7+) Watts, 1969. 320p. illus.

WHEELER, OPAL. Adventures of Richard Wagner. (4-6) Dutton, 1960. 157p. illus.

Greece

FICTION

Prehistory – 400 B.C.

ALEXANDER, BEATRICE (pseud. of LOUISE RAYMOND). Famous Myths of the Golden Age. (5-6) Random House, 1947. 64p. illus.

AULAIRE, I. M. D' AND AULAIRE, E. P. D'. Ingri and Edgar Parin d'Aulaire's Book of Greek Myths. (7+) Doubleday, 1962. 192p. illus.

BARKER, SHIRLEY. The Trojan Horse. (5-6) Random House, 1959. 64p. illus.

COLUM, PADRAIC. The Golden Fleece and the Heroes Who Lived Before Achilles. (6+) Macmillan, 1962. 317p. illus.

COOLIDGE, OLIVIA. Greek Myths. (7+) Houghton, 1949. 256p. illus.

COOLIDGE, OLIVIA. Marathon Looks on the Sea. (7+) Houghton, 1967. 256p. illus.
  Son of a Greek general joins Darius and fights for the Persians.

COOLIDGE, OLIVIA. Trojan War. (7-12) Houghton, 1952. 256p. illus.

DARINGER, H. F. Yesterday's Daughter. (7-9) Harcourt, 1964. 156p. illus.
  Life on the Greek island of Delos in the fifth century B.C.

DOLCH, E. W. AND DOLCH, M. P. Greek Stories. (3+) Garrard, 1955. 176p. illus.

FADIMAN, CLIFTON. Adventures of Hercules. (5-7) Random House, 1960. 64p. illus.

FADIMAN, CLIFTON. The Voyages of Ulysses. (5-6) Random House, 1959. 64p. illus.

FORMAN, JAMES. Ring the Judas Bell. (7+) Farrar, 1965. 224p.
  Shepherd boy faces Communist problem in postwar Greece.

EUROPE

FORMAN, JAMES. The Skies of Crete. (7+) Farrar, 1963. 186p.
>A story of Nazi-occupied Greece.

GRAVES, ROBERT. Greek Gods and Heroes. (4-6) Doubleday [c 1960]. 160p. illus.

GRAVES, ROBERT. The Siege and Fall of Troy. (7+) Doubleday, 1963. 120p. illus. maps

GREEN, R. L. Heroes of Greece and Troy. (7+) Walck, 1961. 344p. illus.

HOMER. The Iliad.
>Available in several editions, some adapted for younger readers.

HOMER. The Odyssey.
>Available in several editions, some adapted for younger readers.

JOHNSON, D. M. Farewell to Troy. (4-6) Houghton, 1964. 224p. illus.
>Story of Priam and the fall of Troy.

KINGSLEY, CHARLES. Heroes.
>Tales of Greek mythology. Available in several editions.

LANG, ANDREW. Tales of Troy and Greece. (4-7) Roy, 1963. 299p. illus.

LOWREY, J. S. In the Morning of the World. (5-9) Harper, 1944. 168p. illus.
>Legends and myths of ancient Greece.

PALMER, M. T. At the Lion Gate. (7+) Houghton, 1962. 176p. illus.
>Crises in ancient Mycenae.

REEVES, JAMES. The Trojan Horse. (K-3) Watts, 1969. 32p. illus.
>Ten-year-old Trojan views history.

SERRAILLIER, IAN. The Clashing Rocks: The Story of Jason. (4-6) Walck, 1964. 104p. illus.

SERRAILLIER, IAN. A Fall from the Sky: The Story of Daedalus. (4-6) Walck, 1966. 64p. illus.

GREECE

SERRAILLIER, IAN. The Gorgon's Head: The Story of Perseus. (4-6) Walck, 1962. 80p. illus.

SERRAILLIER, IAN. The Way of Danger: The Story of Theseus. (4-6) Walck, 1963. 96p. illus.

SNEDEKER, C. D. Lysis Goes to the Play. (4-6) Lothrop [c 1962]. 63p. illus.
> Life in ancient Greece.

SNEDEKER, C. D. Theras and His Town. (4-6) Doubleday [c 1924]. 237p. illus.
> Tale of a sixth century Greek hero.

TREECE, HENRY. The Windswept City. (7+) Meredith [c 1967]. 110p. illus.
> Novel of the Trojan War.

VERGIL. The Aeneid.
> Available in several editions, some adapted for younger readers.

WITTING, ALISOUN. Treasury of Greek Mythology. (5-8) Harvey, 1966. 128p. illus.

400 B.C. – *Present*

ANDREWS, M. E. Hostage to Alexander. (6-9) McKay, 1961. 244p. map
> Alexander the Great and Darius III struggle for world power.

BAUMANN, HANS. Alexander's Great March. (7+) Walck, 1968. 144p.

COATSWORTH, ELIZABETH. The Hand of Apollo. (4-6) Viking, 1965. 79p. illus.
> Life in ancient Greece after the Roman destruction of Corinth.

POWERS, ALFRED. Alexander's Horses. (6+) McKay, 1959. 213p. illus.
> Young boys take care of Alexander the Great's horses.

SEEGER, M. L. The Day of the Earthquake. (4-6) Lothrop, 1967. 192p. illus.
> Adventure in the Antioch of early Christianity.

SNEDEKER, C. D. The Forgotten Daughter. (7+) Doubleday, 1933. 312p. illus.
Story of a Greek slave girl.

NONFICTION

BAUMANN, HANS. Lion Gate and Labyrinth. (7+) Pantheon, 1967. 184p. illus.
Archeologists reveal the secrets of Crete and Troy.

CONE, MOLLY. Green, Green Sea: A Story of Greece. (K-3) Crowell, 1968. 40p. illus.

COTTRELL, LEONARD. Crete: Island of Mystery. (5-9) Prentice-Hall, 1965. 71p. illus.

FENTON, S. H. Greece: A Book to Begin On. (1-4) Holt, 1969. illus.

GEIS, DARLENE, ed. Let's Travel in Greece. (6+) Childrens, 1964. 88p. illus.

GIANAKOULIS, THEODORE. The Land and People of Greece. (7-9) Lippincott, 1965. 160p. illus. maps

GOTTLIEB, GERALD. The First Book of the Mediterranean. (4-6) Watts, 1960. 68p. illus.

JOHNSON, D. M. Greece: Wonderland of the Past and Present. (4-6) Dodd, 1964. 64p. illus. map

MILLER, H. H. Greece. (7+) Scribner, 1965. photos; maps

NOEL-BAKER, F. E. Looking at Greece. (4-6) Lippincott, 1968. 64p. illus.

SASEK, MIROSLAV. This Is Greece. (3-5) Macmillan, 1966. 64p. illus.

TOR, REGINA. Getting to Know Greece. (3-5) Coward, 1959. 72p. illus.

WATSON, J. W. Greece: Land of Golden Light. (3-6) Garrard, 1967. 112p. illus.

GREECE

Prehistory – 700 B.C.

FIELD, G. L. The Minoans of Ancient Crete. (7+) Crowell, 1965. 100p. illus.

NEURATH, MARIE. They Lived Like This in Ancient Crete. (4-6) Watts, 1966. 32p. illus.

RAY, MARY. Standing Lions. (5-8) Meredith, 1969. 170p. illus.
Life and battle in preclassical Greece.

ROBINSON, C. A., JR. The First Book of Ancient Crete and Mycenae. (4-6) Watts, 1964. 76p. illus.

WILKENS, FRANCES. Ancient Crete. (6-9) Day, 1966. 112p. illus. maps

WILLETS, R. F. Everyday Life in Ancient Crete. (5-11) Putnam, 1969. 256p. illus.

700 B.C. – 400 B.C.

ASIMOV, ISAAC. Greeks: A Great Adventure. (7+) Houghton, 1965. 320p. illus.

BARBARY, JAMES. Ten Thousand Heroes. (7+) Roy, 1965. 150p. illus.
Greek soldiers battle through Persia in fifth century B.C.

BARKER, D. R. The Story of Ancient Athens. (7+) St. Martin's, 1960. 64p. illus. maps

BURLAND, C. A. Ancient Greece. (4-8) Dufour, 1961. 93p. illus.

CHUBB, M. A. An Alphabet of Ancient Greece; Book 1: Early Days. (4-6) Watts, 1968. 62p. illus.
Greece from 1500 to 480 B.C.

CHUBB, M. A. An Alphabet of Ancient Greece; Book 2: The Golden Years. (4-6) Watts, 1968. 64p. illus.
Greece after the defeat of the Persians in 480 B.C.

COOLIDGE, OLIVIA. The Golden Days of Greece. (4-6) Crowell, 1968. 211p. illus.

COOLIDGE, OLIVIA. Men of Athens. (7+) Houghton, 1962. 256p. illus.

EUROPE

DOWNEY, GLANVILLE. Stories from Herodotus. (5-9) Dutton, 1965. 160p. illus.

FOSTER, GENEVIEVE. Birthdays of Freedom, I. (7+) Scribner, 1952. 64p. illus.
> Growth of ideas of law and democracy in ancient Greece and Rome.

GREEN, R. L. Ancient Greece. (7-9) Day, 1970. 112p. illus. maps

JUPO, F. J. People and Things in Early Greece. (4-9) Grosset, 1971.

LEACROFT, HELEN AND LEACROFT, R. V. B. The Buildings of Ancient Greece. (7+) Scott, 1966. 40p. drawings

PRICE, CHRISTINE. Made in Ancient Greece. (7+) Dutton, 1967. 160p. illus.

QUENNELL, MARJORIE AND QUENNELL, C. H. Everyday Things in Ancient Greece. (7-9) Putnam, 1954. 272p. illus.

RENAULT, MARY, pseud. The Lion in the Gateway. (5+) Harper, 1964. 193p. illus.
> Battles of Greeks and Persians.

ROBINSON, C. A., JR. The First Book of Ancient Greece. (4-6) Watts, 1960. 68p. illus.

ROCKWELL, A. F. Temple on a Hill. (5-7) Atheneum, 1969. 108p. illus.
> Athens in its days of glory.

TAYLOR, DUNCAN. Ancient Greece. (7+) Roy, 1958. 76p. illus.

WEBSTER, T. B. Everyday Life in Classical Athens. (5-11) Putnam, 1969. 256p. illus.

WEISGARD, LEONARD. The Athenians in the Classical Period. (5-8) Coward, 1963. 64p. illus.

400 B.C. – Present

LEXAU, JOAN. Archimedes Takes a Bath. (2-5) Crowell, 1969. 56p. illus.

GREECE

WARREN, RUTH. The First Book of Modern Greece. (7+) Watts, 1966. 96p. illus.

BIOGRAPHY

PLUTARCH. Parallel Lives.
    Available in several editions, some adapted for younger readers.

Alexander the Great

DUPUY, T. N. The Military Life of Alexander the Great of Macedon. (7+) Watts, 1969. 176p. maps

GUNTHER, JOHN. Alexander the Great. (7+) Random House, 1953. 192p. illus.

MERCER, CHARLES. Alexander the Great; by the editors of Horizon magazine; consultant: Cornelius C. Vermeule III. (6+) American Heritage (distributed by Meredith) [c 1962]. 153p. illus.

MITCHISON, N. M. H. The Young Alexander the Great. (6-10) Roy [1961]. 118p. illus.

ROBINSON, C. A., JR. Alexander the Great: Conqueror and Creator of a New World. (7+) Watts, 1963. 172p.

SUGGS, R. C. Alexander the Great, Scientist-King. (3-6) Macmillan, 1964. 48p. illus.

Archimedes

BENDICK, JEANNE. Archimedes and the Door of Science. (7+) Watts, 1962. 140p. illus.

GARDNER, MARTIN. Archimedes: Mathematician and Inventor. (2-5) Macmillan, 1965. 48p. illus.

JONAS, ARTHUR. Archimedes and His Wonderful Discoveries. (3-6) Prentice-Hall, 1963. illus.

Aristotle

DOWNEY, GLANVILLE. Aristotle: Dean of Early Science. (7+) Watts, 1962. 160p.

Euclid

DE LACY, E. A. Euclid and Geometry. (7+) Watts, 1963. 120p. illus.

Hippocrates

GOLDBERG, H. S. Hippocrates: Father of Medicine. (7+) Watts, 1962. 124p.

Schliemann

BRAYMER, MARJORIE. Walls of Windy Troy: A Biography of Heinrich Schliemann. (7+) Harcourt, 1960. 189p. illus.

ELKIN, SAM. Search for a Lost City. (6-9) Putnam, 1967. 128p. maps
> Archeologist Heinrich Schliemann unearths ancient Troy.

SELDEN, GEORGE. Heinrich Schliemann: Discoverer of Buried Treasure. (1-5) Macmillan, 1964. 48p. illus.

Socrates

SILVERBERG, ROBERT. Socrates. (5+) Putnam, 1965. 192p.

TURLINGTON, BAYLY. Socrates: The Father of Western Philosophy. (7+) Watts, 1969. 256p.

Holland
See The Netherlands

Hungary

FICTION

DOMJAN, JOSEPH. Hungarian Heroes and Legends. (7+) Van Nostrand, 1963. 119p. illus.

HAMORI, LÁSZLÓ. Dangerous Journey. (4-6) Harcourt, 1962. 190p. illus.
> Two Hungarian boys flee from communism.

RITCHIE, RITA. Enemy at the Gate. (7+) Dutton, 1959. 250p. illus.
>Hungarian boy helps defend Vienna against Turks in 1529.

SEYMOUR, A. H. Toward Morning: A Story of the Hungarian Freedom Fighters. (5+) Follett, 1961. 144p.

NONFICTION

CSICSERY-RÓNAY, ISTVÁN. The First Book of Hungary. (7+) Watts, 1967. 96p. illus. maps

HALL, ELVAJEAN AND CRINER, C. L. Picture Map Geography of Eastern Europe. (4-6) Lippincott, 1968. 160p. maps

LENGYEL, EMIL. The Land and People of Hungary. (7-9) Lippincott, 1965. 160p. illus. maps

BIOGRAPHY

Kossuth

LENGYEL, EMIL. Lajos Kossuth: Hungary's Great Patriot. (7+) Watts, 1969. 160p. map

Iceland

See also Scandinavia

FICTION

BOUCHER, ALAN. The Land Seekers. (7+) Farrar, 1968. 144p.
>A novel of the Norwegian settlement of Iceland.

BOUCHER, ALAN. The Sword of the Raven. (7+) Scribner, 1969. 272p. illus.
>Seafarers in the days of the dragon ships.

TREECE, HENRY. The Burning of Njal. (6-10) Criterion, 1964. 191p. illus.
>Blood feud first recounted in the sagas.

TREECE, HENRY. Horned Helmet. (6-10) Criterion, 1963. 118p. illus.
>Vikings in Iceland.

EUROPE

NONFICTION

BERRY, ERICK. Land and People of Iceland. (7-9) Lippincott, 1959. 128p. illus. maps

CARY, STURGES. Volcanoes and Glaciers: Challenge of Iceland. (6-8) Coward [c 1959]. 94p. illus.

GOLDEN, G. B. Made in Iceland. (7+) Knopf, 1958. 192p. illus.

STERLING PUBLISHING COMPANY, EDITORS OF. Iceland in Pictures. (7+) Sterling, 1969. 64p. illus.

Ireland

See also United Kingdom (UK)

FICTION

CORDELL, ALEXANDER. The White Cockade. (7+) Viking, 1970. 160p.
> Bold deeds fighting the British in Ireland (1798).

DILLON, EILÌS. The Seals. (5+) Funk, 1969. 127p. illus.
> Young Irishmen struggle for freedom from England in 1920s.

PICARD, B. L. Celtic Tales. (6-10) Criterion, 1965. 159p. illus.
> Warrior tale of old Ireland.

POLLAND, M. A. Deirdre. (7+) Doubleday, 1967. 190p. illus.
> Legend of an Irish beauty who brings death and dishonor to heroes of Ulster.

REILLY, ROBERT. Red Hugh, Prince of Donegal. (4-6) Farrar, 1957. 160p.
> A story of the Irish rebellion against England in 1587.

VAUGHAN-JACKSON, GENEVIEVE. Carramore. (4-6) Hastings, 1968. 128p. illus.
> Young Irish girl faces Civil War in the 1920s.

NONFICTION

CALDWELL, J. C. AND OTHERS. Let's Visit Ireland. (4-6) Day, 1969. 96p. illus. maps

ITALY

ERDOES, RICHARD. Ireland: Bewitching Wonderland. (4-6) Dodd, 1968. 79p. illus.

JOY, C. R. Getting to Know England, Scotland, and Ireland. (3-5) Coward, 1966. 72p. illus.

NOWLAN, NORA. The Shannon: River of Loughs and Legends. (4-7) Garrard, 1965. 96p. illus.

O'BRIEN, ELINOR. The Land and People of Ireland. (7-9) Lippincott, 1953. 128p. illus. maps

QUIGLEY, L. F. Ireland. (7+) Macmillan, 1964. 128p. photos; maps

SASEK, MIROSLAV. This Is Ireland. (3+) Macmillan, 1965. 64p. illus.

STERLING PUBLISHING COMPANY, EDITORS OF. Ireland in Pictures. (6+) Sterling, 1962. 64p. illus.

BIOGRAPHY
de Valera

STEFFAN, JACK. The Long Fellow. (7+) Macmillan, 1966. 224p. photos
> Life of Eamon de Valera, fighter for Irish freedom.

St. Patrick

REYNOLDS, Q. J. The Life of Saint Patrick. (5-6) Random House, 1955. 192p. illus.

Italy

FICTION
Prehistory – A.D. 1000

ANDERSON, P. L. Pugnax, the Gladiator. (7-11) Biblo, 1939. 296p. illus.

ANDERSON, P. L. Slave of Catiline. (7-11) Biblo, 1930. 255p. illus.

EUROPE

ANDERSON, P. L. With the Eagles. (7-11) Biblo, 1929. 280p.
> Fighting with Roman legions.

BAUMANN, HANS. I Marched With Hannibal. (7+) Walck, 1962. 232p. illus.

BEHN, HARRY. Omen of the Birds. (7+) World, 1964. 160p. illus.
> Novel about Tarquin, the semilegendary Etruscan king of Rome.

CHURCH, A. J. Lucius: Adventures of a Roman Boy. (7-11) Biblo, 1960 (reprint). 341p.
> Originally published 1885.

DONAUER, FRIEDRICH. Swords Against Carthage; tr. from German by F. T. Cooper. (7-11) Biblo, 1932. 336p. illus.
> Action during the Punic Wars.

ESTES, ELEANOR. Miranda the Great. (4-6) Harcourt, 1967. 80p. illus.
> Cat saves kittens when barbarians sack ancient Rome.

GALE, ELIZABETH. Julia Valeria. (7-10) Putnam, 1951. 244p. illus.
> Novel of ancient Rome.

KENT, L. A. He Went With Hannibal. (7+) Houghton, 1964. 288p. illus.

MALVERN, GLADYS. Tamar. (6-9) McKay, 1952. 211p. decorations
> Novel of Rome in Jesus' day.

POWERS, ALFRED. Hannibal's Elephants. (6+) McKay, 1944. 272p. illus.
> Tale of Hannibal crossing the Alps.

SNEDEKER, C. D. A Triumph for Flavius. (4-6) Lothrop, 1955. 87p. illus.
> Life in ancient Rome.

TREASE, GEOFFREY. Word to Caesar. (7-9) St. Martin's, 1965. 270p. illus.

VERGIL. The Aeneid.
> Available in several editions, some adapted for younger readers.

ITALY

WALLACE, LEW. The Boys' Ben-Hur; a Tale of the Christ. (7+) abridged ed. Harper, 1928. 366p. illus.

WEBB, R. N. We Were There With Caesar's Legions; historical consultant: Courtney Whitney. (4-6) Grosset, 1960. 177p. illus.

WELLS, R. F. On Land and Sea With Caesar; or, Following the Eagles. (7-11) Biblo, 1926. 326p. illus.

WELLS, R. F. With Caesar's Legions. (7-11) Biblo, 1951. 336p. illus.

WHITEHEAD, A. C. Standard Bearer: A Story of Army Life in the Time of Caesar. (7-11) Biblo, 1943. 305p. illus.

WILLIAMSON, J. S. The Eagles Have Flown. (7+) Knopf, 1957. 224p.
  Life in the household of Brutus in ancient Rome.

WILLIAMSON, J. S. The Iron Charm. (5-6) Knopf, 1964. 204p.
  Roman patrician sold into slavery.

1000 – Present

CASSIDAY, BRUCE. Guerrilla Scout. (7+) Macmillan, 1965. 128p.
  American-born Italian boy helps fight the Nazis in World War II.

COOPER, L. U. The Twig of Cypress. (6-9) Washburn, 1966. 176p.
  Italian boy joins Garibaldi.

DALY, MAUREEN. The Small War of Sergeant Donkey. (4-6) Dodd, 1966. 85p. illus.
  World War II adventures of a twelve-year-old boy in southern Italy.

PATTON, WILLOUGHBY. The Florentine Giraffe: A Tale of the Italian Renaissance. (7+) McKay, 1967. 160p. illus.

NONFICTION

BARTLETT, VERNON AND CALDWELL, J. C. Let's Visit Italy. (4-6) Day, 1968. 96p. illus. maps

CRAZ, ALBERT. Getting to Know Italy. (3-5) Coward, 1961. 72p. illus.

EPSTEIN, SAM AND EPSTEIN, BERYL. The First Book of Italy. (4-6) Watts, 1959. 70p. illus.

GEIS, DARLENE, ed. Let's Travel in Italy. (6+) Childrens, 1964. 88p. illus.

GOTTLIEB, GERALD. The First Book of the Mediterranean. (4-6) Watts, 1960. 68p. illus.

MARTIN, RUPERT. Looking at Italy. (4-6) Lippincott, 1967. 64p. illus.

NOWLAN, NORA. The Tiber: The Roman River. (4-7) Garrard, 1967. 96p. illus.

ROBINSON, M. G. Rival Cities – Venice and Genoa. (5+) McGraw, 1970. 126p. illus.

SASEK, MIROSLAV. This Is Rome. (3-5) Macmillan, 1960. 64p. illus.

SASEK, MIROSLAV. This Is Venice. (3-5) Macmillan, 1961. 64p. illus.

STERLING PUBLISHING COMPANY, EDITORS OF. Italy in Pictures. (4-12) Sterling, 1966. 64p. illus.

WINWAR, FRANCES. The Land of the Italian People. (7-9) Lippincott, 1961. 128p. illus. maps

Prehistory – 100 B.C.

ASIMOV, ISAAC. Roman Republic. (7+) Houghton, 1966. 320p. illus.

BURLAND, C. A. Ancient Rome. (4-8) Dufour, 1961. 93p. illus.

COOLIDGE, OLIVIA. Roman People. (7+) Houghton, 1959. 244p. illus.

CORNEY, L. C. The Story of Rome. (7+) St. Martin's, 1964. 64p. illus.

ITALY

PIKE, E. R. Republican Rome. (6-9) Day [c 1966]. 112p. illus.

ROBINSON, C. A., JR. The First Book of Ancient Rome. (4-6) Watts, 1964. 72p. illus. maps

100 B.C. – A.D. 1000

ASIMOV, ISAAC. The Roman Empire. (7+) Houghton, 1967. 288p. illus.

COOLIDGE, OLIVIA. Caesar's Gallic War. (7+) Houghton, 1961. 256p. illus.

COWELL, F. R. Everyday Life in Ancient Rome. (7-9) Putnam, 1961. 200p. illus.

DUGGAN, A. L. The Romans. (6+) World, 1964. 128p. illus.

ERDOES, RICHARD. A Picture History of Ancient Rome. (4-6) Macmillan, 1967. 64p. illus. maps

FOSTER, GENEVIEVE. Augustus Caesar's World. (7+) Scribner, 1949. 352p. illus.

HADAS, MOSES. Imperial Rome. (7+) Time-Life, 1965. 200p. illus.

HAMILTON, EDITH. Roman Way. (7+) Norton, 1932. 281p.

KEATING, BERN. The Invaders of Rome. (6-9) Putnam, 1966. 192p.

KIRTLAND, G. B. One Day in Ancient Rome. (2-5) Harcourt, 1961. 40p. illus.

LAMPREY, LOUISE. Children of Ancient Rome. (7-11) Biblo, n.d. 262p. illus.

MELLERSH, H. E. Imperial Rome. (6-9) Day, 1964. 112p. illus. maps

MILLER, SHANE. The Romans in the Days of the Empire. (5-8) Coward, 1963. 64p. illus.

NEURATH, MARIE. They Lived Like This in Ancient Rome. (4-6) Watts, 1969. 32p. illus. maps

TAYLOR, DUNCAN. Ancient Rome. (7+) Roy [c 1960]. 80p. illus.

VON HAGEN, V. W. Roman Roads. (7+) World, 1966. 192p. illus.

WILKES, J. Roman Army. (4+) Cambridge, 1972. illus.

1000 – Present

CHUBB, T. C. The Venetians: Merchant Princes. (7+) Viking, 1968. 118p.

DOBRIN, ARNOLD. Italy: Modern Renaissance. (7+) Nelson, 1968. 224p. illus.

GAGE, JOHN. Life in Italy at the Time of the Medici. (6-8) Putnam, 1968. 207p. illus.

BIOGRAPHY

COOLIDGE, OLIVIA. Lives of Famous Romans. (7+) Houghton, 1965. 256p. illus.

COTTRELL, LEONARD. Great Leaders of Greece and Rome. (5-9) Prentice-Hall, 1966. 63p. illus.

PLUTARCH. Parallel Lives.
    Available in several editions, some adapted for younger readers.

Attila

WEBB, R. N. Attila: King of the Huns. (7+) Watts, 1965. 112p.

Caesar

DAVID, PETER. Julius Caesar. (7+) Macmillan, 1968. 128p. illus.

DUPUY, T. N. The Military Life of Julius Caesar, Imperator. (7+) Watts, 1969. 160p. maps

GUNTHER, JOHN. Julius Caesar. (7+) Random House, 1959. 192p. illus.

ITALY

ISENBERG, IRWIN. Caesar; by the editors of Horizon magazine; consultant: Richard M. Haywood. (6+) Harper, 1964. 151p. illus.

KOMROFF, MANUEL. Julius Caesar. (7+) Messner, 1955. 192p.

Cellini

CELLINI, BENVENUTO. Autobiography. (7+)
Available in several editions.

Cicero

BARBARY, JAMES. Young Cicero. (6-10) Roy, 1965. 139p. illus.

Copernicus

KNIGHT, D. C. Copernicus: Titan of Modern Astronomy. (7+) Watts, 1965. 232p. illus.

THOMAS, HENRY. Copernicus. (7+) Messner, 1960. 192p.

Dante

STEARNS, MONROE. Dante: Poet of Love. (7+) Watts, 1965. 248p. illus.

St. Francis of Assisi

LIVERSIDGE, DOUGLAS. Saint Francis of Assisi. (7+) Watts, 1968. 164p.

PELAGIE, DOANE. St. Francis. (4-6) Walck, 1960. 56p. illus.

Galileo

LEVINGER, ELMA. Galileo: First Observer of Marvelous Things. (7+) Messner, 1952. 192p.

MARCUS, R. B. Galileo and Experimental Science. (7+) Watts, 1961. 142p. illus.

ROSEN, SIDNEY. Galileo and the Magic Numbers. (7+) Little, 1958. 212p. illus.

Garibaldi

DAVENPORT, MARCIA. Garibaldi: Father of Modern Italy. (7+) Random House, 1957. 192p. illus.

SYME, RONALD. Garibaldi: The Man Who Made a Nation. (7-9) Morrow, 1967. 192p. illus.

Hannibal

DUPUY, T. N. The Military Life of Hannibal, Father of Strategy. (7+) Watts, 1969. 176p. maps

WEBB, R. N. Hannibal, Invader from Carthage. (7+) Watts, 1968. 144p.

Leonardo da Vinci

ALMEDINGEN, E. M. (MARTHA EDITH VON ALMEDINGEN). Young Leonardo da Vinci. (6-10) Roy, 1964. 143p. illus.

COOPER, MARGARET. Inventions of Leonardo da Vinci. (7+) Macmillan, 1968. 192p. illus.

GILLETTE, H. S. Leonardo da Vinci: Pathfinder of Science. (7+) Watts, 1962. 170p. illus.

HAHN, EMILY. Leonardo da Vinci. (7+) Random House, 1956. 192p. illus.

MCLANATHAN, R. B. K. Images of the Universe: Leonardo da Vinci, the Artist as Scientist. (7+) Doubleday, 1966. 240p. illus.

NEWCOMB, COVELLE. Leonardo da Vinci, Prince of Painters. (7+) Dodd, 1965. 265p. illus.

RIPLEY, ELIZABETH. Leonardo da Vinci. (7-9) Walck, 1952. 72p. illus.

SHIRLEY, JEAN. Leonardo da Vinci (adapted by the author from the original text). (4-6) Webster, 1967. unp. illus.

THOMAS, JOHN. Leonardo da Vinci. (6-10) Criterion, 1957. 191p. illus.

ITALY

WILLIAMS, JAY. Leonardo da Vinci; by the editors of Horizon magazine; consultant: Bates Lowry. (6+) Harper, 1965. 153p. illus.

Michelangelo

ALLEN, AGNES. The Story of Michelangelo. (7+) Roy, 1957. 198p. illus.

COUGHLAN, ROBERT. World of Michelangelo. (5+) Time-Life, 1966. 192p. illus.

RIPLEY, ELIZABETH. Michelangelo. (7-9) Walck, 1953. 72p. illus.

STEARNS, MONROE. Michelangelo. (7+) Watts, 1970. 256p. illus.

STONE, IRVING. The Great Adventure of Michelangelo. (7+) Doubleday, 1965. 288p. illus.

Montessori

SMARIDGE, NORAH. The Light Within: The Story of Maria Montessori. (5-9) Hawthorn [c 1965]. 172p. illus.
  Italy's first woman doctor pioneers educational innovations.

Mussolini

ABSOLEM, ROGER. Mussolini and the Rise of Italian Fascism. (7+) Roy, 1969. 96p. illus.

ARCHER, JULES. Twentieth Century Caesar: Benito Mussolini. (7+) Messner, 1964. 192p.

KING-HALL, SIR STEPHEN. Three Dictators: Mussolini, Hitler, Stalin. (7+) Transatlantic, 1964. 132p.

Raphael

GILLETTE, H. S. Raphael: Painter of the Renaissance. (7+) Watts, 1967. 160p. illus.

St. Thomas Aquinas

PITTENGER, W. N. Saint Thomas Aquinas, the Angelic Doctor. (7+) Watts, 1969. 160p.

    Catholic theologian dominates medieval thought.

Titian

RIPLEY, ELIZABETH. Titian: A Biography. (7-9) Lippincott, 1962. 72p. illus.

WILLIAMS, JAY. World of Titian. (4+) Time-Life, 1968. 192p. illus.

Verdi

KAUFMANN, H. L. Anvil Chorus: The Story of Giuseppe Verdi. (5-9) Hawthorn [c 1964]. 185p. illus.

Volta

DIBNER, BERN. Alessandro Volta and the Electric Battery. (7+) Watts, 1964. 144p. illus.

The Netherlands

FICTION

DE JONG, DOLA. The Level Land. (7+) Scribner, 1961. 176p. illus.

    Family faces danger in Holland in World War II.

JANSSEN, PIERRE. A Moment of Silence. (5+) Atheneum, 1970. 64p. illus.

    Story of a Dutch boy during the German occupation of Holland in World War II.

RHIJN, ALEID VAN. The Tide in the Attic. (6-10) Criterion, 1962. 126p. illus.

    A Dutch family fights the great flood of 1953.

SEYMOUR, A. H. When the Dikes Broke. (4-6) Follett, 1958. 144p. illus.

    Tale of the great flood of 1953.

THE NETHERLANDS

NONFICTION

BARNOUW, A. J. The Land and People of Holland. (7-9) Lippincott, 1961. 128p. illus. maps

CAREW, DOROTHY. The Netherlands. (5-7) Macmillan, 1965. 144p. photos; map

COHN, ANGELO. The First Book of the Netherlands. (4-6) Watts, 1962. 72p. illus.

IRWIN, THEODORE, ed. Let's Travel in Holland. (6+) Childrens, 1964. 88p. illus.

LAUBER, PATRICIA. Battle Against the Sea: How the Dutch Made Holland. (6-8) Coward, 1956. 121p. illus.

LOMAN, ANNA. Looking at Holland. (4-6) Lippincott, 1966. 64p. illus.

SPIER, PETER. Of Dikes and Windmills. (6-9) Doubleday, 1969. 187p. illus. maps

STERLING PUBLISHING COMPANY, EDITORS OF. Holland in Pictures. (6+) Sterling, 1962. 64p. illus.

WOLSELEY, R. E. Low Countries: Gateways to Europe. (6+) Nelson, 1969. 224p. illus.

BIOGRAPHY

Rembrandt

STEARNS, MONROE. Rembrandt and His World. (7+) Watts, 1967. 224p. illus.

Van Gogh

HONOUR, ALAN. Tormented Genius: The Struggles of Vincent Van Gogh. (7-9) Morrow, 1967. 192p. illus.

RIPLEY, ELIZABETH. Vincent Van Gogh. (7-9) Walck, 1954. 72p. illus.

WALLACE, ROBERT. The World of Van Gogh, 1853-1890, by [the author] and the editors of Time-Life books; consulting editor: H. W. Janson. (5+) Time-Life, 1969. 192p. illus.

Vermeer

KONINGSBERGER, HANS. The World of Vermeer, 1632-1675, by [the author] and the editors of Time-Life books. (5+) Time-Life, 1967. 192p. illus.

William the Silent

BAKER, N. B. William the Silent. (4-6) Vanguard, 1947. 271p.

HALL, G. L. William, Father of the Netherlands. (7+) Rand McNally, 1969. 240p. illus. maps

Norway
See also Scandinavia

FICTION

Prehistory – A.D. 1500

ASBJØRNSEN, PETER. Norwegian Folk Tales. (4-6) Viking, 1961. 69p. illus.

HAUGAARD, E. C. Hakon of Rogen's Saga. (7+) Houghton, 1963. 128p. illus.
   Saga of Norwegian Vikings.

UNDSET, SIGRID. Sigurd and His Brave Companions: A Tale of Medieval Norway. (7+) Knopf, 1943. 139p. illus.

NORWAY

WYATT, ISABEL. The Dream of King Alfdan. (4-6) Follett, 1961. 94p. illus.
>Viking Norway is united under one king.

1500 – Present

BALDERSON, MARGARET. When Jays Fly to Bárbmo. (7+) World, 1969. 240p. illus.
>Norwegian girl faces up to Nazi invasion.

BERNHARDSEN, CHRISTIAN. Fight in the Mountains. (7-9) Harcourt, 1968. 128p.
>Tale of Norwegian patriots fighting Nazis in World War II.

HOWARTH, D. A. We Die Alone. (7+) Macmillan, 1955. 248p.
>Young saboteur challenges Nazis in Norway.

MCSWIGAN, MARIE. Snow Treasure. (3-7) Dutton, 1942. 178p. illus.
>Norwegian children oppose the Germans during the occupation of Norway.

SOMMERFELT, AIMÉE. Miriam. (7+) Criterion, 1963. 160p.
>Norwegians suffer under German occupation in World War II.

NONFICTION

ASHBY, G. M. Looking at Norway. (4-6) Lippincott, 1967. 64p. illus.

HALL, ELVAJEAN. The Land and People of Norway. (7-9) Lippincott, 1963. 160p. illus. maps

HOPP, ZINKEN (SIGNE MARIE BROCHMANN HOPP). Great Day in Norway: the 17th of May. (1-4) Abelard, 1962. 32p. illus.
>Norway gets a constitution and a king on May 14, 1814.

MERRICK, H. H. The First Book of Norway. (7+) Watts, 1969. 96p. illus. maps

THORNE-THOMSEN, GUDRUN. In Norway. (5-9) Viking, 1948. 159p. illus.

BIOGRAPHY

Leif Ericson

AULAIRE, I. M. D' AND AULAIRE, E. P. D'. Leif the Lucky. (4-6) Doubleday, 1941. 64p. illus.

BERRY, ERICK. Leif the Lucky: Discoverer of America. (2-5) Garrard, 1961. 72p. illus.

SHIPPEN, K. B. Leif Eriksson: First Voyager to America. (7+) Harper, 1951. 150p.

STEELE, W. O. Story of Leif Ericson. (4-6) Grosset, 1954. 181p. illus.

WEIR, R. C. Leif Ericson, Explorer. (3+) Abingdon, 1951. 128p. illus.

Grieg

DEUCHER, SYBIL. Edvard Grieg, Boy of the Northland. (3-7) Dutton, 1946. 165p. illus.

KYLE, ELISABETH (pseud. of AGNES MARY ROBERTSON DUNLOP). Song of the Waterfall: The Story of Edvard and Nina Grieg. (5-9) Holt, 1970. 233p.

PURDY, C. L. Song of the North: The Story of Edvard Grieg. (7+) Messner, 1941. 256p. illus.

Poland

FICTION

BORSKI, LUCIA. Good Sense and Good Fortune, and Other Polish Folk Tales. (4-6) McKay, 1970. 96p. illus.

HAUTZIG, ESTHER. The Endless Steppe: Growing Up in Siberia. (7+) Crowell, 1968. 256p.
   A Polish deportee lives in Siberia during World War II.

KELLY, E. P. The Trumpeter of Krakow. (7+) Macmillan, 1966. 224p.
   Adventures in fifteenth century Poland.

POLAND

NONFICTION

CHARNOCK, J. T. The Land and People of Poland. (6+) Macmillan, 1968. 96p. photos; map

HALL, ELVAJEAN AND CRINER. C. L. Picture Map Geography of Eastern Europe. (4-6) Lippincott, 1968. 160p. maps

KELLY, E. P. AND KOSTICH, D. D. The Land and People of Poland. (7-9) rev. ed. Lippincott, 1964. 128p. illus. maps

STERLING PUBLISHING COMPANY, EDITORS OF. Poland in Pictures. (7+) Sterling, 1969. 64p. illus.

WALLACE, J. A. Getting to Know Poland. (3-5) Coward, 1960. 72p. illus.

BIOGRAPHY

Chopin

CHISSELL, JOAN. Chopin. (5+) Crowell, 1965. 94p. illus.

WHEELER, OPAL. Frederic Chopin, Son of Poland: Early Years. (3-7) Dutton, 1948. 156p. illus.

WHEELER, OPAL. Frederic Chopin, Son of Poland: Later Years. (3-7) Dutton, 1949. 155p. illus.

Kosciuszko

ABODAHER, D. J. Warrior on Two Continents: Thaddeus Kosciuszko. (6+) Messner, 1968. 192p.

Paderewski

HUME, PAUL AND HUME, RUTH. The Lion of Poland: The Story of Paderewski. (5-9) Hawthorn [c 1962]. 192p. illus.

LENGYEL, EMIL. Ignace Paderewski: Musician and Statesman. (7+) Watts, 1970. 128p. illus.

Pulaski

ABODAHER, D. J. Freedom Fighter: Casimir Pulaski. (7+) Messner, 1969. 192p.

Portugal

FICTION

BAUMANN, HANS. Barque of the Brothers. (7-9) Walck, 1958. 252p. illus.
   A tale of Prince Henry the Navigator.

FINGER, C. J. Courageous Companions. (6-9) Longmans [c 1929]. 304p. illus.
   English boy sails with Magellan around the world.

HEWES, A. D. Spice and the Devil's Cave. (5-6) Knopf, 1968. 352p. illus.
   Vasco da Gama seeks a route to India.

KENT, L. A. He Went With Magellan. (7-9) Houghton, 1943. 208p. illus.

KENT, L. A. He Went With Vasco da Gama. (7-9) Houghton, 1938. 272p. illus.

NONFICTION

BUEHR, WALTER. The Portuguese Explorers. (3-7) Putnam, 1966. 96p. illus.

CAREW, DOROTHY. Portugal. (7+) Macmillan, 1969. 144p. photos; map

MADDEN, D. M. Spain & Portugal: Iberian Portrait. (7+) Nelson, 1969. 224p. illus.

SANDERLIN, G. W. Eastward to India: Vasco da Gama's Voyage. (7+) Harper, 1965. 196p. illus. maps

SANDERLIN, G. W. ed. First Around the World: A Journal of Magellan's Voyage. (7+) Harper, 1964. illus. maps
   Antonio Pigafetta's account of his travels with Magellan.

STERLING PUBLISHING COMPANY, EDITORS OF. Portugal in Pictures. (4-12) Sterling, 1965. 64p. illus.

WOHLRABE, R. A. AND KRUSCH, WERNER. The Land and People of Portugal. (7-9) Lippincott, 1963. 128p. illus. maps

PORTUGAL

BIOGRAPHY

Buehr, Walter. The Portuguese Explorers. (3-7) Putnam, 1966. 96p. illus.

Da Gama

Syme, Ronald. Vasco da Gama, Sailor Toward the Sunrise. (4-6) Morrow, 1959. 96p. illus.

Henry the Navigator

Anderson, H. J. Henry the Navigator, Prince of Portugal. (7-12) Westminster, 1969. 124p.

Chubb, T. C. Prince Henry the Navigator and the Highways of the Sea. (7+) Viking, 1970. 192p.

Magellan

Finger, C. J. Courageous Companions. (6-9) Longmans [c 1929]. 304p. illus.
> The story of Ferdinand Magellan.

Granberg, W. J. Let's Go Exploring With Magellan. (3-5) Putnam, 1965. 48p. illus.

Groh, Lynn. A World Explorer: Ferdinand Magellan. (3-6) Garrard, 1963. 96p. illus.

Israel, C. E. Five Ships West — The Story of Magellan. (5-7) Macmillan, 1966. 160p. illus. map

Pond, S. G. Ferdinand Magellan: Master Mariner. (7+) Random House, 1957. 192p. illus.

Syme, Ronald. Magellan, First Around the World. (4-6) Morrow, 1953. 72p. illus.

Welch, Ronald (pseud. of Ronald Oliver Felton). Ferdinand Magellan. (6-10) Phillips, 1956. 178p. illus.

Wilkie, K. E. Ferdinand Magellan: Noble Captain. (4-6) Houghton, 1963. 192p. illus.

Rumania

NONFICTION

HALL, ELVAJEAN AND CRINER, C. L. Picture Map Geography of Eastern Europe. (4-6) Lippincott, 1968. 160p. maps

KOSTICH, D. D. The Land and People of the Balkans. (7-9) Lippincott, 1962. 160p. illus. maps

PERL, LILA. Yugoslavia, Romania, Bulgaria: New Era in the Balkans. (6-9) Nelson, 1970. 224p. illus. maps

Russia
See Union of Soviet Socialist Republics (USSR)

Scandinavia
See also Denmark, Finland, Iceland, Norway, Sweden

FICTION

AULAIRE, I. M. D' AND AULAIRE, E. P. D'. Norse Gods and Giants. (4-6) Doubleday, 1967. 160p. illus.

COLUM, PADRAIC. Children of Odin. (4-6) Macmillan, 1962. 280p. illus.

COOLIDGE, OLIVIA. Legends of the North. (7+) Houghton, 1951. 272p. illus.

CURREN, POLLY, ed. Folk Tales of Scandinavia. (4+) Bobbs, 1962. 125p. illus.

HAUGAARD, E. C. A Slave's Tale. (7+) Houghton, 1965. 132p. illus.
   Realistic novel of Norse life.

KEARY, ANNIE AND KEARY, ELIZA. Heroes of Asgard: Tales from Scandinavian Mythology. (4+) St. Martin's, 1930. 222p. illus.

SCANDINAVIA

KNIGHT, FRANK. Olaf's Sword. (2-4) Watts, 1970. 48p. illus.
> A twelve-year-old journeys to Vinland with the Vikings.

LEIGHTON, MARGARET. Voyage to Coromandel. (7+) Farrar, 1965. 224p.
> Norse hostage of Alfred the Great journeys to India.

NEWMAN, ROBERT. Grettir the Strong. (7+) Crowell, 1968. 190p. illus.
> Saga of the Norsemen.

SCHROEDER, MARY. The Hunted Prince. (6-8) Coward, 1969. 221p.
> Excitement in the Viking area.

SELLEW, C. F. Adventures With the Heroes. (1-3) Little, 1954. 145p. illus.
> Ancient stories of great Norse warriors.

TREECE, HENRY. The Last Viking. (5-6) Pantheon, 1966. 160p. illus.

TREECE, HENRY. Road to Miklagard. (6-10) Criterion, 1957. 254p. illus.
> Stirring Viking adventures.

TREECE, HENRY. Splintered Sword. (7+) Duell, 1966. 128p. illus.
> Tale of last days of Viking period.

TREECE, HENRY. Swords from the North. (5-6) Pantheon, 1967. 256p. illus.
> Adventures with the last of the Vikings from 1034 to 1044.

TREECE, HENRY. Viking's Dawn. (7-9) Criterion, 1956. 252p. illus.

UNDSET, SIGRID. True and Untrue. (5-6) Knopf, 1945. 264p. illus.

NONFICTION

BARKER, D. R. The Vikings at Home and Abroad. (7+) St. Martin's, 1967. 68p. illus. maps

EUROPE

BERRY, ERICK. Men, Moss, and Reindeer: Challenge of Lapland. (6-8) Coward, 1959. 121p. illus.

BURLAND, C. A. The Vikings. (4-8) Dufour, 1961. 92p. illus.

CHUBB, T. C. The Northmen. (6+) World, 1964. 128p. illus.

DONOVAN, F. R. The Vikings; by the editors of Horizon magazine; consultant: Sir Thomas D. Kendrick. (6+) Harper, 1964. 153p. illus.

EDWARDS, HARVEY. Scandinavia: The Challenge of Welfare. (7+) Nelson, 1968. 224p. illus.

INNES, HAMMOND (pseud. of RALPH HAMMOND-INNES). Scandinavia. (4+) Time-Life, 1963. 160p. illus.

JANEWAY, ELIZABETH. The Vikings. (5-6) Random House, 1951. 192p. illus.

NEURATH, MARIE. They Lived Like This: The Vikings. (4-6) Watts, 1971. 32p. illus.

PROCTOR, G. L. Ancient Scandinavia. (6-9) Day, 1965. 112p. illus.

RICH, L. D. The First Book of the Vikings. (4-6) Watts, 1962. 72p. illus.

SELLMAN, R. R. The Vikings. (7+) Roy, 1959. 68p. illus.

SIMPSON, JACQUELINE. Everyday Life in the Viking Age. (7-9) Putnam, 1968. 208p. illus.

WITKER, JIM. Getting to Know Scandinavia: Denmark, Norway, & Sweden. (3-5) Coward, 1963. 72p. illus.

BIOGRAPHY

BUEHR, WALTER. Viking Explorers. (3-7) Putnam, 1967. 96p. illus.

Scotland
See United Kingdom (UK)

Spain

FICTION

CERVANTES SAAVEDRA, MIGUEL DE. Don Quixote of La Mancha. (7+)
>Available in several editions, some adapted for younger readers.

KENT, L. A. He Went With Christopher Columbus. (7-9) Houghton, 1940. 317p. illus.

KIDWELL, CARL. Granada, Surrender! (7+) Viking, 1968. 288p. illus.
>Teenage boy fights the Moors in the fifteenth century.

LAWSON, ROBERT. I Discover Columbus. (4-6) Little, 1941. 110p. illus.

PAULI, H. E. America's First Christmas. (3-6) Washburn, 1962. illus.
>Story of Christmas with Columbus.

SPRAGUE, ROSEMARY. Fife and Fandango. (7-9) Walck, 1961. 256p.
>Fortunes of a loyalist family during the Napoleonic wars.

TREVIÑO, E. B. DE. Casilda of the Rising Moon. (7+) Farrar, 1967. 224p.
>Tale of a Moorish princess in medieval Spain.

NONFICTION

BRINTON, HENRY. Spain. (7-9) Dufour, 1962. 144p. illus.

BUCKLEY, PETER. Spanish Plateau: Challenge of a Dry Land. (6-8) Coward, 1959. 121p. illus.

DALY, MAUREEN. Spain: Wonderland of Contrasts. (4-6) Dodd, 1965. 64p. illus.

DAY, DEE. Getting to Know Spain. (3-5) Coward, 1957. 72p. illus.

GEIS, DARLENE, ed. Let's Travel in Spain. (6+) Childrens, 1964. 88p. illus.

GOLDSTON, R. C. Spain. (7+) Macmillan, 1967. 144p. photos; map

LODER, D. H. The Land and People of Spain. (7-9) Lippincott, 1963. 128p. illus. maps

MADDEN, D. M. Spain & Portugal: Iberian Portrait. (7+) Nelson, 1969. 224p. illus.

STERLING PUBLISHING COMPANY, EDITORS OF. Spain in Pictures. (3-6) Sterling, 1962. 64p. illus.

THOMAS, HUGH. Spain; by [the author] and the editors of Life. (4+) Time-Life, 1966. 160p. illus. maps

Prehistory – A.D. 1900

GOLDSTON, R. C. The Legend of the Cid. (5+) Bobbs, 1963. 159p. illus.

IRVING, WASHINGTON. Legends of the Alhambra. (7+)
Available in several editions.

LAURITZEN, JONREED. Blood, Banners and Wild Boars: Tales of Early Spain. (7+) Little, 1967. 151p. illus.
Struggles against tyranny and invasion.

SANDERLIN, G. W. ed. Across the Ocean Sea: A Journal of Columbus's Voyage. (7+) Harper, 1966. 275p. illus. maps
Selections from Columbus's Journal.

1900 – Present

GOLDSTON, R. C. The Civil War in Spain. (6+) Bobbs, 1966. 224p. illus.

WERSTEIN, IRVING. The Cruel Years: The Story of the Spanish Civil War. (7+) Messner, 1969. 192p. illus. map

BIOGRAPHY

Cervantes

BUSONI, RAFAELLO. The Man Who Was Don Quixote: The Story of Miguel Cervantes. (7-10) Prentice-Hall, 1958. 209p.

SPAIN

Columbus

AULAIRE, I. M. D' AND AULAIRE, E. P. D'. Columbus. (4-6) Doubleday, 1966. 192p. illus.

BAILEY, BERNADINE. Christopher Columbus: Sailor and Dreamer. (4-6) Houghton, 1960. 192p. illus. maps

BAKER, N. B. Story of Christopher Columbus. (3-4) Grosset, 1952. 179p. illus.

CARRISON, D. J. Christopher Columbus: Navigator to the New World. (7+) Watts, 1967. 256p. illus.

DALGLIESH, ALICE. The Columbus Story. (3-4) Scribner, 1955. illus.

DE KAY, ORMONDE, JR. Meet Christopher Columbus. (2+) Random House, 1968. 96p. illus.

DERLETH, AUGUST. Columbus and the New World. (4-7) Farrar, 1957. 190p. illus.

GRAHAM, A. P. Christopher Columbus, Discoverer. (3+) Abingdon, 1950. 128p. illus.

HODGES, C. W. Columbus Sails. (6-8) Coward, 1939. 224p. illus.

HOGEBOOM, AMY. Christopher Columbus and His Brothers. (4-6) Lothrop [c 1951]. 188p. illus.

JUDSON, C. I. Christopher Columbus. (3-6) Follett, 1959. 29p. illus.

KAUFMAN, M. D. Christopher Columbus. (3-6) Garrard, 1963. 96p. illus.

KNIGHT, FRANK. Young Columbus. (6-10) Roy, 1964. 144p. illus.

MCGOVERN, ANN. The Story of Christopher Columbus. (2-5) Random House, 1963. 53p. illus. maps

MEREDITH, R. K. AND SMITH, E. B. Quest of Columbus. (7+) Little, 1966. illus.

NORMAN, GERTRUDE. A Man Named Columbus. (K-3) Putnam, 1960. illus.

OLDS, H. D. Christopher Columbus. (1-2) Putnam, 1964. 64p. illus.

RUFFO, VINNIE. Let's Go to the New World With Christopher Columbus. (3-5) Putnam, 1969. 48p. illus.

SANDERLIN, G. W. ed. Across the Ocean Sea: A Journal of Columbus's Voyage. (7+) Harper, 1966. 275p. illus. maps
 Selections from Columbus's Journal.

SHOWERS, PAUL. Columbus Day. (K-3) Crowell, 1965. 40p. illus.

SPERRY, ARMSTRONG. The Voyages of Christopher Columbus. (7+) Random House, 1950. 192p. illus.

SYME, RONALD. Columbus, Finder of the New World. (4-6) Morrow, 1952. 96p. illus.

De Soto

MONTGOMERY, E. R. Hernando de Soto. (3-6) Garrard, 1964. 96p. illus.

SYME, RONALD. De Soto, Finder of the Mississippi. (4-6) Morrow, 1957. 96p. illus.

Ferdinand

MCKENDRICK, MELVEENA. Ferdinand and Isabella; by the editors of Horizon magazine [and the author]; consultant: J. H. Elliott. (6+) Harper, 1968. 151p. illus.

Franco

SNELLGROVE, L. E. Franco and the Spanish Civil War. (6-9) McGraw, 1968. 118p. illus.

Goya

RIPLEY, ELIZABETH. Goya. (7-9) Walck, 1956. 72p. illus.

SCHICKEL, RICHARD. World of Goya. (4+) Time-Life, 1968. 192p. illus.

STEARNS, MONROE. Goya and His Times. (7+) Watts, 1966. 288p. illus.

Saint Ignatius Loyola

LIVERSIDGE, DOUGLAS. Ignatius of Loyola: The Soldier Saint. (7+) Watts, 1970. 160p.

Isabella

CRISS, MILDRED. Isabella, Young Queen of Spain. (7+) Dodd, 1941. 219p. illus.

MCKENDRICK, MELVEENA. Ferdinand and Isabella; by the editors of Horizon magazine [and the author]; consultant: J. H. Elliott. (6+) Harper, 1968. 151p. illus.

NOBLE, IRIS. Spain's Golden Queen Isabella. (7+) Messner, 1969. 192p.

Picasso

STRUCHEN, JEANETTE. Pablo Picasso: Master of Modern Art. (7+) Watts, 1969. 128p. illus.

Velázquez

BROWN, DALE. World of Velázquez, 1599-1660, by [the author] and the editors of Time-Life books. (5+) Time-Life, 1969. 192p. illus.

RIPLEY, ELIZABETH. Velázquez. (7-9) Lippincott, 1965. 72p. illus.

Sweden
See also Scandinavia

NONFICTION

NANO, F. C. The Land and People of Sweden. (7-9) Lippincott, 1964. 128p. illus. maps

STERLING PUBLISHING COMPANY, EDITORS OF. Sweden in Pictures. (6+) Sterling, 1966. 64p. illus.

BIOGRAPHY

Gustavus Adolphus

DUPUY, T. N. The Military Life of Gustavus Adolphus, Father of Modern War. (7+) Watts, 1969. 160p. maps

Hammarskjöld

KELEN, EMERY (IMRE KELEN). Dag Hammarskjöld: A Biography. (5+) Meredith, 1969. 192p.

LEVINE, I. E. Champion of World Peace: Dag Hammarskjöld. (7+) Messner, 1962. 192p.

SIMON, C. M. Dag Hammarskjöld. (7+) Dutton, 1967. 158p. illus.

Linnaeus

DICKINSON, ALICE. Carl Linnaeus: Pioneer of Modern Botany. (7+) Watts, 1967. 224p. illus.

SILVERSTEIN, ALVIN AND SILVERSTEIN, VIRGINIA. Carl Linnaeus: The Man Who Put the World of Life in Order. (3-6) Day, 1969. 80p. illus.

STOUTENBURG, ADRIEN AND BAKER, L. N. Beloved Botanist. (7+) Scribner, 1961. 192p. illus.

Nobel

MEYER, E. P. Dynamite and Peace: Story of Alfred Nobel. (7+) Little, 1958. 298p.
Alfred Nobel works for peace.

Switzerland

NONFICTION

BRAGDON, L. J. The Land and People of Switzerland. (7-9) Lippincott, 1961. 128p. illus. maps

UNION OF SOVIET SOCIALIST REPUBLICS

BUFF, MARY. The Apple and the Arrow. (4-6) Houghton, 1951. 80p. illus.
> Retelling of William Tell story and the birth of free Switzerland.

EPSTEIN, SAMUEL AND EPSTEIN, BERYL. The First Book of Switzerland. (4-6) Watts, 1964. 94p. illus.

GEIS, DARLENE, ed. Let's Travel in Switzerland. (6+) Childrens, 1964. 88p. illus.

HÜRLIMANN, BETTINA. William Tell and His Son. (K-4) Harcourt, 1967. illus.

KUBLY, H. H. Switzerland; by [the author] and the editors of Life. (4+) Time-Life, 1964. 160p. illus. maps

LAUBER, PATRICIA. Getting to Know Switzerland. (3-5) Coward, 1960. 72p. illus.

SCHERMAN, KATHERINE. William Tell. (5-6) Random House, 1960. 64p. illus.

STERLING PUBLISHING COMPANY, EDITORS OF. Switzerland in Pictures. (6+) Sterling. 64p. illus.

BIOGRAPHY
Dunant

ROTHKOPF, CAROL. Jean Henri Dunant: Father of the Red Cross. (7+) Watts, 1969. 192p. illus.

STOIBER, R. M. Henri Dunant: Man in White. (5-10) Abelard, 1963. 160p.
> A Swiss humanitarian founds the Red Cross.

Union of Soviet Socialist Republics (USSR)

FICTION
Prehistory – A.D. 1900

ALMEDINGEN, E. M. (MARTHA EDITH VON ALMEDINGEN). The Knights of the Golden Table. (4-6) Lippincott, 1964. 192p. illus.
> Russian prince forms band to battle evil and villainy.

BARTOS-HÖPPNER, BARBARA. The Cossacks. (7+) Walck, 1963. 304p. illus.
>Excitement in sixteenth century Russia.

BARTOS-HÖPPNER, BARBARA. Hunters of Siberia. (7+) Walck, 1969. 256p.

BARTOS-HÖPPNER, BARBARA. Save the Khan. (7+) Walck, 1964. 248p. illus.

BARTOS-HÖPPNER, BARBARA. Storm Over the Caucasus. (7+) Walck, 1968. 288p.
>In 1800s, Caucasian tribes revolt against the Czar.

FAIRSERVIS, W. A. JR. Horsemen of the Steppes. (6+) World, 1962. 128p. illus.

MASEY, M. L. Story of the Steppes: Kazakh Folk Tales. (3-7) McKay, 1968. 160p. illus.

VERNE, JULES. Michael Strogoff. (7+) Scribner, 1927. 408p. illus.

WYNDHAM, LEE (pseud. of JANE ANDREWS LEE HYNDMAN). Tales the People Tell in Russia. (3-5) Messner, 1970. 96p. illus.

1900 – Present

ALMEDINGEN, E. M. (MARTHA EDITH VON ALMEDINGEN). Frossia: A Novel of Russia. (6+) Meredith, 1969. 320p.
>The fight for survival in postrevolutionary Russia.

BLOCH, M. H. The Two Worlds of Damyan. (4-6) Atheneum, 1966. 169p. illus.
>Conflict of Christianity and communism in a Russian boy.

ROSENFELD, SEMYON. The First Song. (7+) Doubleday, 1968. 288p.
>Tale of revolutionary Odessa in 1905.

NONFICTION

APPEL, BENJAMIN. Why the Russians Are the Way They Are. (7+) Little, 1966. 180p. maps

UNION OF SOVIET SOCIALIST REPUBLICS

Chubb, T. C. Slavic Peoples. (6+) World, 1962. 128p. illus.

Francini, Mario. Russia Invaded, from Genghis Khan to Hitler. (6+) Lion [c 1966]. 181p. illus.

Habberton, William. Russia: The Story of a Nation. (7+) Houghton, 1965. 288p. illus.

Hall, Elvajean. The Volga: Lifeline of Russia. (6+) Rand McNally, 1965. 112p. illus.

Hall, Elvajean and Criner, C. L. Picture Map Geography of Eastern Europe. (4-6) Lippincott, 1968. 160p. maps

Hoff, Rhoda. Russia: Adventures in Eyewitness History. (7-9) Walck, 1964. 208p.

Lawrence, J. W. Russia. (7+) Roy, 1965. 88p. illus.

Nazaroff, Alexander. The Land and People of Russia. (7-9) Lippincott, 1966. 192p. illus. maps

Popescu, Julian and Caldwell, J. C. Let's Visit Russia. (4-6) Day, 1968. 96p. illus. maps

Salisbury, H. E. The Key to Moscow. (4-6) Lippincott, 1963. 120p. illus. maps

Salisbury, H. E. Russia. (7+) Macmillan, 1965. 144p. photos; maps

Savage, Katharine. People and Power: The Story of Three Nations. (7-9) Walck, 1959. 250p. illus. maps
History of Germany, Russia, and Japan.

Seeger, Elizabeth. Pageant of Russian History. (7+) McKay, 1950. 448p. illus. maps

Sterling Publishing Company, Editors of. Russia in Pictures. (3-6) Sterling, 1966. 64p. illus.

Thayer, C. W. Russia. (4+) Time-Life, 1965. 160p. illus.

WALLACE, ROBERT. Rise of Russia. (7+) Time-Life, 1967. 200p. illus.

Prehistory – 1850

ALMEDINGEN, E. M. (MARTHA EDITH VON ALMEDINGEN). Retreat from Moscow. (7+) Warne, 1968. 91p. illus.

KOCHAN, MIRIAM. Life in Russia Under Catherine the Great. (7-11) Putnam, 1969. 182p.

MOSCOW, HENRY. Russia Under the Czars; by the editors of Horizon magazine; consultant: Cyril E. Black. Harper, 1962. 153p. illus.

MURPHY, ROBERT. The Haunted Journey. (7+) Farrar, 1969. 192p.
   Vitus Bering explores America for Peter the Great.

PRODANOVIC, N. C. Heroes of Siberia. (7+) Walck, 1964. 184p. illus.

RICE, T. T. Czars and Czarinas of Russia. (7+) Lothrop, 1968. 320p. illus.

RICE, T. T. Finding Out About the Early Russians. (6-10) Lothrop, 1964. 168p. illus.

TEALL, KAYE. From Tsars to Commissars: The Story of the Russian Revolution. (7+) Messner, 1966. 192p. illus. maps

WREN, M. C. Ancient Russia. (5+) Day, 1965. 112p. illus. maps

1850 – Present

CLAYTON, ROBERT. The U.S.S.R. (4-7) Day, 1970. 48p. maps

COOLIDGE, OLIVIA. Makers of the Red Revolution. (7+) Houghton, 1963. 240p. illus.

EDWARDS, L. F. Russia and Her Neighbors. (4-6) Watts, 1969. 96p. illus.

FOLSOM, FRANKLIN. The Soviet Union: A View from Within. (7+) Nelson, 1965. 224p. illus.

UNION OF SOVIET SOCIALIST REPUBLICS

FOOTMAN, DAVID. The Russian Revolutions. (6-8) Putnam, 1964. 128p. illus. maps

GEIS, DARLENE, ed. Let's Travel in the Soviet Union. (6+) Childrens, 1964. 88p. illus.

GOLDSTON, R. C. The Russian Revolution. (6+) Bobbs, 1966. 224p. illus. photos

GUNTHER, JOHN. Meet Soviet Russia. (7+) Harper, 1962. 2v. 246p. ea. illus.
> Book 1: Land, people, sights; Book 2: Leaders, politics, problems.

HALLIDAY, E. M. Russia in Revolution; by the editors of Horizon magazine [and the author]; consultant: Cyril E. Black. (6+) Harper, 1967. 153p. illus.

HELLER, DEANE AND HELLER, DAVID. The Cold War. (7+) Hawthorn, 1969. 160p. illus.

JOHNSON, G. W. Communism, an American's View. (7-9) Morrow, 1964. 160p. illus.
> Describes Marx, Lenin, the Russian Revolution and communism to the present.

KOCHAN, LIONEL. The Russian Revolution. (7-9) Day, 1970. 112p. illus. maps

LENSEN, G. A. The Soviet Union: An Introduction. (7+) Meredith, 1968. 182p.

MILLER, JACK. Life in Russia Today. (7-11) Putnam, 1969. 208p. illus.

RIEBER, A. J. AND NELSON, R. C. A Study of the USSR and Communism: An Historical Approach. (4-7) Putnam, 1964. 256p.

ROSSIF, FRÉDÉRIC AND CHAPSAL, MADELEINE. Portrait of a Revolution. (7+) Little, 1969. 160p. photos
> Pictorial history of the Russian Revolution from 1896 to 1924.

SAMMIS, E. R. Last Stand at Stalingrad: The Battle That Saved the World. (7+) Macmillan, 1966. 96p. photos; maps; chronology

SNYDER, L. L. The First Book of the Soviet Union. (7+) Watts, 1965. 96p. illus.

WALLACE, J. A. Getting to Know the Soviet Union. (3-5) Coward, 1964. 72p. illus.

WERSTEIN, IRVING. Ten Days in November. (7+) Macrae Smith, 1967. 192p. photos
Start of the Revolution.

BIOGRAPHY

COOLIDGE, OLIVIA. Makers of the Red Revolution. (7+) Houghton, 1963. 240p. illus.

Catherine the Great

ALMEDINGEN, E. M. (MARTHA EDITH VON ALMEDINGEN). Young Catherine the Great. (6-10) Roy [c 1965]. 141p. illus.

NOBLE, IRIS. Empress of All Russia: Catherine the Great. (7+) Messner, 1966. 192p.

SCHERMAN, KATHERINE. Catherine the Great. (7+) Random House, 1957. 192p. illus.

Khrushchev

HIRSCHFELD, BURT. Khrushchev. (7+) Hawthorn, 1969. 160p. illus.

Lenin

BAKER, N. B. Lenin. (7-9) Vanguard, 1945. 257p. illus.

CHARNOCK, J. T. Red Revolutionary: A Life of Lenin. (6+) Hawthorn, 1970. 138p.

LEVINE, I. E. Lenin: The Man Who Made a Revolution. (7+) Messner, 1969. 192p.

UNION OF SOVIET SOCIALIST REPUBLICS

LIVERSIDGE, DOUGLAS. Lenin: Genius of Revolution. (7+) Watts, 1969. 192p. map

ROBERTS, E. M. Lenin and the Downfall of Tsarist Russia. (7+) Roy, 1966. 100p. illus.

SHAPIRO, W. E. ed. Lenin and Trotsky. (7+) Watts, 1967. 66p. illus.

Peter the Great

BAKER, N. B. Peter the Great. (7+) Vanguard, 1943. 310p. illus.

JOSEPH, JOAN. Peter the Great. (7+) Messner, 1968. 192p.

LIVERSIDGE, DOUGLAS. Peter the Great. (7+) Watts, 1968. 160p. map

Razin

LAMB, HAROLD. Chief of the Cossacks. (5-6) Random House, 1959. 192p. illus.
    Stenka Razin fights to free Cossacks in 1600s.

Stalin

ARCHER, JULES. Man of Steel: Joseph Stalin. (7+) Messner, 1965. 192p.

KING-HALL, SIR STEPHEN. Three Dictators: Mussolini, Hitler, Stalin. (7+) Transatlantic, 1964. 132p.

LIVERSIDGE, DOUGLAS. Joseph Stalin. (7+) Watts, 1969. 192p. map

ROBERTS, E. M. Stalin: Man of Steel. (7+) Roy, 1968. 94p. illus. maps

Stravinsky

YOUNG, P. M. Stravinsky. (7+) White, 1970. 79p. illus.

Tchaikovsky

PURDY, C. L. Stormy Victory: The Story of Tchaikovsky. (7+) Messner, 1942. 256p.

WHEELER, OPAL. Peter Tschaikowsky and the Nutcracker Ballet. (3-7) Dutton, 1959. 95p. illus.

WHEELER, OPAL. Story of Peter Tschaikowsky. (3-7) Dutton, 1953. 119p. illus.

YOUNG, P. M. Tchaikovsky. (5-9) White, 1968. 76p. illus.

Tolstoy

PHILIPSON, M. H. The Count Who Wished He Were a Peasant. (7+) Pantheon, 1967. 192p. illus.
Life story of Tolstoy.

ROTHKOFF, CAROL. Leo Tolstoy. (7+) Watts, 1968. 160p. map

Trotsky

SHAPIRO, W. E. ed. Lenin and Trotsky. (7+) Watts, 1967. 66p. illus.

United Kingdom (UK)

FICTION

CORCORAN, JEAN. Folk Tales of England; editorial consultant: Jean Chall. (4+) Bobbs, 1963. 124p. illus.

Prehistory – A.D. 100

FAULKNER, NANCY. The Sacred Jewel. (7+) Doubleday, 1961. 213p.
Suspense story set in Britain at the time of Christ.

SNEDEKER, C. D. The White Isle. (7+) Doubleday, 1940. 271p. illus.
Patrician Roman girl goes to Britain.

SUTCLIFF, ROSEMARY. Eagle of the Ninth. (7+) Walck, 1954. 264p. illus.
Life in the Roman army occupying Britain.

UNITED KINGDOM

SUTCLIFF, ROSEMARY. The Mark of the Horse Lord. (7+) Walck, 1965. 305 p.
>Adventures of an ex-slave in second century Britain.

SUTCLIFF, ROSEMARY. Outcast. (7+) Walck, 1955. 240p. illus.
>Early Britain and Imperial Rome in conflict.

SUTCLIFF, ROSEMARY. Silver Branch. (7+) Walck, 1958. 228p. illus.
>Ancient Britons fight their Roman conquerors.

SUTCLIFF, ROSEMARY. Warrior Scarlet. (7+) Walck, 1958. 220p.
>Story of Bronze Age.

TREECE, HENRY. The Centurion. (7+) Meredith, 1967. 128p. illus.
>Roman soldier gets involved in Queen Boadicea's uprising.

TREECE, HENRY. War Dog. (6-10) Criterion, 1963. 120p. illus.
>Britain is invaded by the Romans in A.D. 43.

100 – 1000

BERRY, ERICK. The King's Jewel. (7+) Viking, 1957. 114p. illus.
>Alfred the Great struggles for England.

BOWERS, GWENDOLYN. Brother to Galahad. (7-9) Walck, 1963. 192p. illus.

BOWERS, GWENDOLYN. The Lost Dragon of Wessex. (7-9) Walck, 1957. 192p. illus.
>Adventure during the Anglo-Saxon era.

BULLA, C. R. The Sword in the Tree. (4-6) Crowell, 1956. 114p. illus.
>Realistic treatment of the Arthurian legend.

DISNEY (WALT) PRODUCTIONS. Stories from Other Lands. (4-6) Golden, 1965. 256p. illus.
>Stories feature some quasi-historical figures such as Robin Hood and King Arthur.

EUROPE

FINKEL, G. I. Watch Fires to the North. (7+) Viking, 1968. 124p.
> Roman Christians and Saxons clash in sixth century England.

FOSTER, HAROLD. Prince Valiant and the Golden Princess. (4-6) Hastings, 1968. 128p. illus.

FOSTER, HAROLD. Prince Valiant and the Three Challenges. (4-6) Hastings, 1960. 128p. illus.

FOSTER, HAROLD. Prince Valiant Fights Attila the Hun. (4-6) Hastings, 1953. 128p. illus.

FOSTER, HAROLD. Prince Valiant in the Days of King Arthur. (4-6) Hastings, 1969. 128p. illus.

FOSTER, HAROLD. Prince Valiant in the New World. (4-6) Hastings, 1968. 128p. illus.

FOSTER, HAROLD. Prince Valiant on the Inland Sea. (4-6) Hastings, 1968. 128p. illus.

FOSTER, HAROLD. Prince Valiant's Perilous Voyage. (4-6) Hastings, 1954. 128p. illus.

FRITH, HENRY. King Arthur and His Knights. (4-6) Doubleday, 1963. 416p. illus.

HADFIELD, A. M. King Arthur and the Round Table. (5-8) Dutton, 1953. 240p. illus.

HIEATT, CONSTANCE. The Knight of the Cart. (7+) Crowell, 1969. 85p. illus.
> Tale of King Arthur's knights.

HIEATT, CONSTANCE. Sir Gawain and the Green Knight. (7+) Crowell, 1967. 48p. illus.

HODGES, C. W. The Marsh King. (5-8) Coward, 1967. 256p. illus.
> Story involving Alfred the Great.

HODGES, C. W. The Namesake: A Story of King Alfred. (5-7) Coward, 1964. 225p. illus.

UNITED KINGDOM

LEIGHTON, MARGARET. Journey for a Princess. (7+) Farrar, 1960. 224p.
    Adventures of the youngest daughter of Alfred the Great.

MALORY, SIR THOMAS. Le Morte d'Arthur. (7+)
    Available in several editions, some modernized or adapted for younger readers.

NEWMAN, ROBERT. Merlin's Mistake. (5+) Atheneum, 1970. 237p. illus.
    Magic and adventure in the medieval England of Merlin's time.

PATON WALSH, GILLIAN (JILL PATON WALSH). Hengest's Tale. (7+) St. Martin's, 1967. 151p. illus.
    Adventure tale of fifth century warriors.

PATON WALSH, GILLIAN (JILL PATON WALSH) AND CROSSLEY-HOLLAND, KEVIN. Wordhoard. (7+) Farrar, 1970. 136p.
    Stories of Anglo-Saxon days.

PICARD, B. L. Hero-Tales from the British Isles. (6-10) Criterion, 1963. 159p. illus.
    Folk legends including King Arthur and Robin Hood.

PICARD, B. L. Stories of King Arthur and His Knights. (7+) Walck, 1955. 300p. illus.

PICARD, B. L. Tales of the British People. (6-10) Criterion, 1961. 159p. illus.

PYLE, HOWARD. Story of King Arthur and His Knights. (7-9)
    Originally published in 1903 and available in several editions.

PYLE, HOWARD. The Story of Sir Launcelot and His Companions. (7+) Scribner, 1907. 360p. illus.

PYLE, HOWARD. The Story of the Champions of the Round Table. (7+) Scribner, 1905. 352p. illus.

PYLE, HOWARD. The Story of the Grail and the Passing of Arthur. (7+) Scribner, 1910. 276p. illus.

ROBINSON, M. L. King Arthur and His Knights. (5-6) Random House, 1953. 192p. illus.

SCHNEIDER, ESTELLE, ed. King Arthur and the Knights of the Round Table. (K-3) Random House, 1954. 64p. illus.

STONE, EUGENIA. Page Boy for King Arthur. (4-6) Follett, 1949. 160p. illus.

STONE, EUGENIA. Squire for King Arthur. (4-6) Follett, 1955. 158p. illus.

SUTCLIFF, ROSEMARY. Dawn Wind. (7+) Walck, 1962. 248p. illus.
> Excitement in sixth century Britain.

SUTCLIFF, ROSEMARY. Lantern Bearers. (7+) Walck, 1959. 260p. illus.
> Tale of fifth century Britain.

TREASE, GEOFFREY. Escape to King Alfred. (6+) Vanguard, 1958. 251p.

WHITE, A. T. Knights of the Table Round. (4-7) Garrard, 1970. 96p. illus.

WILLIAMS, JAY. The Sword of King Arthur. (4-6) Crowell, 1968. 188p. illus.

1000 – 1400

CHAUCER, GEOFFREY. The Canterbury Tales. (7+)
> Available in several editions, some modernized or adapted for younger readers.

CHUTE, M. G. The Innocent Wayfaring. (7+) Dutton, 1955. 199p. illus.
> Two young people travel in fourteenth century England.

EAGER, E. M. Knight's Castle. (4-6) Harcourt, 1965. 183 p. illus.
> Modern children travel back in time to Ivanhoe's day.

FAULKNER, NANCY. The Yellow Hat. (7+) Doubleday, 1958. 212p.
> Story about Chaucer's serving maid.

GREENLEAF, M. F. Banner Over Me. (7-9) Follett, 1968. 288p. illus.
> Conflict between Normans and Saxons in eleventh century.

UNITED KINGDOM

JEWETT, E. M. Big John's Secret. (7+) Viking, 1962. 132p. illus.
>Boy joins Crusade in thirteenth century England.

JEWETT, E. M. The Hidden Treasure of Glaston. (7+) Viking, 1946. 133p. illus.
>Tale of England during the reign of Henry II.

LEWIS, H. W. Gentle Falcon. (4-7) Criterion, 1957. 256p.
>Tale revolving about Richard II.

PEART, HENDRY. Red Falcons of Trémoine. (5-6) Knopf, 1956. 256p. illus.
>Adventure in the twelfth century.

PICARD, B. L. Ransom for a Knight. (7+) Walck, 1956. 320p. illus.

SCOTT, SIR WALTER. Ivanhoe. (7+)
>Available in several editions.

SUTCLIFF, ROSEMARY. Knight's Fee. (7+) Walck, 1960. 248p. illus.
>Ragamuffin becomes knight in feudal England.

SUTCLIFF, ROSEMARY. Shield Ring. (7+) Walck, 1957. 288p. illus.
>Adventure after the Norman invasion.

TREECE, HENRY. Man With a Sword. (5-6) Pantheon, 1964. 160p. illus.
>Enmity flares between Hereward the Saxon and William the Conqueror.

WEBB, R. N. We Were There With Richard the Lionhearted in the Crusades; history consultant: Andre A. Beaumont. (4-6) Grosset, 1957. 182p. illus. maps

WEIR, ROSEMARY. High Courage. (7+) Farrar, 1967. 192p. illus.
>Castle life and adventure as Simon de Montfort opposes King Henry III.

WELCH, RONALD (pseud. of RONALD OLIVER FELTON). Bowman of Crécy. (7+) Criterion, 1967. 178p. illus.
>Outlaw leader joins King Edward against the French.

EUROPE

1400 – 1600

BILL, A. H. The Ring of Danger: A Tale of Elizabethan England. (7+) Knopf, 1948. 272p. illus.

COOKE, D. E. Men of Sherwood. (7+) Holt, 1961. 214p. illus.

CRESWICK, PAUL, ed. Robin Hood. (4-6) Scribner, 1917. illus.

DOLCH, E. W. and DOLCH, M. P. Robin Hood Stories. (3+) Garrard, 1957. 176p. illus.

DREWERY, MARY. Devil in Print. (8-12) McKay, 1966. 216p. illus.
> An apprentice faces religious persecution in printing English translation of the Bible.

FECHER, CONSTANCE. Heir to Pendarrow. (7+) Farrar, 1969. 192p.
> Plots and intrigue in 1558, pitting adherents of Princess Elizabeth against Queen Mary Tudor.

HAYCRAFT, M. C. The Reluctant Queen. (7-9) Lippincott, 1962. 256p.
> Historical novel about Mary Tudor.

HAYCRAFT, M. C. Too Near the Throne. (7-9) Lippincott, 1959. 240p.
> Fictionalized account of Lady Arbella Stuart (Arabella Stewart), cousin of Elizabeth I.

HOUSEHOLD, GEOFFREY. Prisoner of the Indies. (7+) Little, 1968. 203p. illus.
> A sailor's adventures in the New World during the Elizabethan age.

JOWETT, MARGARET. A Cry of Players. (4-6) Roy, 1963. 164p. illus.
> Elizabethan England through the eyes of a boy joining Shakespeare's Globe theatre.

KELLY, E. P. At the Sign of the Golden Compass. (7+) Macmillan, 1938. 208p. illus.
> Action with a printer's apprentice in sixteenth century England and Belgium.

UNITED KINGDOM

KENT, L. A. He Went With Drake. (7-9) Houghton, 1961. 256p. illus.

KINGSLEY, CHARLES. Westward Ho! (7+)
Available in several editions.

KNIGHT, FRANK. Remember Vera Cruz! (5+) Dial, 1966. 184p. illus.
Young boy sails to the New World with Hawkins and Drake.

KNIGHT, FRANK. They Told Mr. Hakluyt. (5-9) St. Martin's, 1964. 150p. illus. maps
Selections from Richard Hakluyt's The Principal Navigations, Voyages, Traffics, and Discoveries of the English Nation, with various explanatory notes.

LAMB, CHARLES AND LAMB, MARY. Tales from Shakespeare.
Available in several editions.

LEWIS, H. W. Here Comes Harry. (7+) Criterion, 1960. 261p. illus.
Henry VI befriends a goldsmith's apprentice.

McGOVERN, ANN. Robin Hood of Sherwood Forest. (4-6) Crowell, 1968. 164p. illus.

McSPADDEN, J. W. Robin Hood and His Merry Outlaws. (4-6) World, 1946. 285p. illus.

MAIDEN, CECIL. The Borrowed Crown. (4-6) Viking, 1968. 94p. illus.
Yorkists plot to regain the throne from Henry VII.

MALCOLMSON, ANNE. Song of Robin Hood. (7-9) Houghton, 1947. 128p. illus.

MANNING-SANDERS, RUTH. The Spaniards Are Coming. (2-4) Watts, 1970. 48p. illus.
Two children see the Spanish Armada defeated in 1588.

OLIVER, JANE. Queen Most Fair. (7+) St. Martin's, 1960. 247p. illus.
Story based on events in life of Mary, Queen of Scots.

OLIVER, JANE. Watch for the Morning. (7-9) St. Martin's, 1964. 185p. illus.
> Struggles for religious freedom in Henry VIII's reign.

OMAN, CAROLA. Robin Hood. (4-8) Dutton, 1951. 242p. illus.

PICARD, B. L. Lost John. (6-10) Criterion, 1963. 224p. illus.
> Outlaws keep boy in Forest of Arden.

PYLE, HOWARD. Men of Iron. (5+) Harper, 1892. 328p. illus.
> Story of the time of Henry IV.

PYLE, HOWARD. The Merry Adventures of Robin Hood of Great Renown in Nottinghamshire. (4-6)
> First published in 1883; available in several editions.

SERRAILLIER, IAN. Robin and His Merry Men. (7-9) Walck, 1970. 72p. illus.

STEPHENS, P. J. Battle for Destiny. (5-8) Atheneum, 1967. 300p. illus.
> A novel involving Henry VII, King of England in the fifteenth century.

STEVENSON, R. L. The Black Arrow. (5+)
> Available in several editions.

STONE, EUGENIA. Robin Hood's Arrow. (3-5) Follett, 1948. 164p. illus.

TREASE, GEOFFREY. Bows Against the Barons. (7+) Meredith, 1967. 154p. illus.
> Boy joins Robin Hood in fighting Normans.

TREASE, GEOFFREY. Cue for Treason. (7+) Vanguard, 1941. 281p. illus.
> Intrigue at the court of Elizabeth.

TWAIN, MARK (pseud. of SAMUEL LANGHORNE CLEMENS). The Prince and the Pauper. (4-6)
> Available in several editions.

VANCE, ELEANOR. Adventures of Robin Hood. (5-6) Random House, 1953. 64p. illus.

UNITED KINGDOM

WILLIAMSON, J. S. To Dream Upon a Crown. (7+) Knopf, 1967. 224p. illus.
    Shakespearean dialogue deals with England under Henry VI.

WOOD, J. P. The Queen's Most Honorable Pirate. (7+) Harper, 1961. 184p. illus.
    Adventures with Sir Francis Drake.

1600 – 1750

BEATTY, J. L. AND BEATTY, PATRICIA. Campion Towers. (7+) Macmillan, 1965. 208p.
    Puritan colonial girl visits England during the English Civil War.

BEATTY, J. L. AND BEATTY, PATRICIA. The Queen's Wizard. (6+) Macmillan, 1967. 192p.
    Astrologer's apprentice helps foil Guy Fawkes' Gunpowder Plot.

CAWLEY, WINIFRED. Down the Long Stairs. (7-9) Holt, 1965. 254p.
    Excitement in England's Puritan revolution.

CLARKE, M. S. Piper to the Clan. (7+) Viking, 1970. 240p.
    Scots fight Cromwell and suffer in defeat.

CRANDELL, M. C. Molly and the Regicides. (3-7) Simon & Schuster, 1968. 255p. illus.

DARINGER, H. F. Debbie of the Green Gate. (7-9) Harcourt, 1956. 232p. illus.
    A girl lives with Scrooby congregation in Holland in early 1600s.

DARINGER, H. F. Pilgrim Kate. (7-9) Harcourt, 1949. 252p. illus.
    Religious problems in Scrooby in early seventeenth century.

FECHER, CONSTANCE. Venture for a Crown. (7+) Farrar, 1968. 160p.
    Blacksmith's son helps Charles I in escape attempts in 1647.

HAWES, C. B. The Dark Frigate. (7+) Little, 1924. 247p. illus.
    Sea adventures in the 1600s.

HOLM, A. S. Peter. (7-9) Harcourt, 1968. 224p.
> Time-travel adventures of a boy in Ancient Greece, and in Norman and Cromwellian England.

HOPE-SIMPSON, JACYNTH. The Great Fire. (3-7) Dutton. 178p. illus.
> An orphan boy in London's great fire of 1666.

HUNT, M. L. Beggar's Daughter. (7-9) Lippincott, 1963. 192p.
> English orphan girl is raised in a Quaker family during reign of Charles II.

LATHAM, J. L. The Frightened Hero: A Story of the Siege of Latham House. (2-5) Chilton, 1965. 97p. illus.
> Roundheads fight Cavaliers in 1642.

MARRYAT, FREDERICK. The Children of the New Forest. (7+) Scribner, 1927. 372p. illus.
> Orphaned family struggles in Cromwell's England.

PEART, HENDRY. The Loyal Grenvilles. (5-6) Knopf, 1958. 224p. illus.
> Strife in Cromwell's England.

SOFTLY, BARBARA. Place Mill. (7+) St. Martin's, 1962. 190p. illus.
> Tale of English Civil War.

SOFTLY, BARBARA. Plain Jane. (7+) St. Martin's, 1961. 256p. illus.
> Tale of English Civil War.

SOFTLY, BARBARA. A Stone in a Pool. (7+) St. Martin's, 1964. 215p. illus.
> Royalists fight Roundheads.

WATSON, SALLY. Witch of the Glens. (7+) Viking, 1962. 147p. illus.
> Gypsy girl gets involved in clan activities in seventeenth century Scotland.

WEIR, ROSEMARY. The Lion and the Rose. (7+) Farrar, 1970. 192p. illus.
> Life in London after the Great Fire, as seen by a boy apprentice.

UNITED KINGDOM

WELCH, RONALD (pseud. of RONALD OLIVER FELTON). For the King. (7+) Criterion, 1962. 216p. illus.
: Roundheads battle Cavaliers in Civil War.

WILLARD, BARBARA. Flight to the Forest. (7+) Doubleday [c 1967]. 192p. illus.
: Family of actors become fugitives under Cromwell.

WILLIAMSON, H. R. Guy Fawkes. (7+) Roy, 1966. 160p. illus.
: Story of the Gunpowder Plot.

1750 – 1900

BARBARY, JAMES. The Engine and the Gun. (5-8) Meredith, 1967. 159p. illus.
: British boy witnesses interaction between Industrial Revolution and the revolt of the American colonies.

BEATTY, J. L. AND BEATTY, PATRICIA. At the Seven Stars. (6+) Macmillan, 1967. 288p. illus.
: Excitement in eighteenth century London.

BEATTY, J. L. AND BEATTY, PATRICIA. The Royal Dirk. (7-9) Morrow, 1966. 256p.
: Intrigue in eighteenth century Scotland and London.

BENTLEY, P. E. The Adventures of Tom Leigh. (4-6) Doubleday, 1964. 192p. illus.
: Struggles of a weaver's apprentice under stresses of the Industrial Revolution in eighteenth century Yorkshire.

BENTLEY, P. E. Oath of Silence. (4-6) Doubleday, 1967. 192p. illus.
: Strife during the Industrial Revolution (1812).

BEYER, A. W. Katharine Leslie. (7+) Knopf, 1963. 196p. illus.
: Young girl is unjustly sentenced to Newgate prison.

BEYER, A. W. The Sapphire Pendant. (7+) Knopf, 1961. 192p. illus.
: Intrigue and danger for a young girl in the Napoleonic era.

BROWN, ANTONY. Dangerfoot. (5+) Meredith, 1968. 188p. illus.
: Boy attempts to foil Napoleon's invasion of England.

EUROPE

BURTON, HESTER. Castors Away. (6+) World, 1963. 256p. illus.
>Adventures in Nelson's navy.

BURTON, HESTER. No Beat of Drums. (7+) World, 1966. 160p. illus.
>In 1830, an English family struggles against social injustices of the Industrial Revolution.

BURTON, HESTER. Time of Trial. (5-9) World, 1964. 224p. illus.
>Girl struggles for freedom of speech in early 1800s.

CROTHERS, S. M. ed. Children of Dickens. (7+) Scribner [c 1925]. 268p. illus.
>Example of children in Dickens' works.

DE WITT, JAMES. In Pursuit of the Spanish Galleon. (6+) Criterion, 1961. 189p. illus. map
>Englishman in 1740 sails around the world after Spanish gold.

EISENBERG, PHILIP. We Were There With Charles Darwin on H.M.S. Beagle; history consultant: Clyde R. Kluckhohn. (4-6) Grosset, 1960. 178p. illus.

FORESTER, C. S. Hornblower Goes to Sea; Extracts from Mr. Midshipman Hornblower, and Lieutenant Hornblower. (7+) Little, 1965. 191p. illus.
>Adventures in the English navy during the Napoleonic wars.

FORESTER, C. S. Hornblower in Captivity; Extracts from A Ship of the Line, and Flying Colours. (7+) Little, 1965. 224p. illus.

FORESTER, C. S. Hornblower Takes Command; Extracts from Hornblower and the Atropos, and Beat to Quarters (The Happy Return). (7+) Little, 1965. 223p. illus.

FORESTER, C. S. Hornblower's Triumph; Extracts from the Commodore, and Lord Hornblower. (7+) Little, 1965. 223p. illus.

GARFIELD, LEON. Devil in the Fog. (7+) Pantheon, 1966. 196p. illus.
>Family feuding in eighteenth century England.

UNITED KINGDOM

GARFIELD, LEON. Smith. (7+) Pantheon, 1967. 224p. illus.
> Tale of the eighteenth century London underworld.

GRAY, E. J. Adam of the Road. (7+) Viking, 1942. 317p. illus.

HUNTER, MOLLIE. A Pistol in Greenyards. (7+) Funk, 1968. 191p.
> Land problems in the Highlands in 1854.

HUNTER, MOLLIE. The Spanish Letters. (7+) Funk, 1967. 192p.
> Intrigue in Scotland in 1859.

HYDE, LAURENCE. Captain Deadlock. (4-6) Houghton, 1968. 192p. illus.
> Life with a highwayman in the nineteenth century.

LOBDELL, HELEN. Thread of Victory. (7-9) McKay, 1963. 160p.
> Robert Owen's industrial reforms.

NORDHOFF, C. B. AND HALL, J. N. The Bounty Trilogy. (7+) Little, 1946. 704p. illus.
> English seamen's life in the eighteenth century.

PICARD, B. L. The Young Pretenders. (6+) Criterion, 1966. 231p. illus.
> Adventures during the Jacobite rebellion.

PRIESTLEY, HAROLD. John Stranger. (7+) Roy, 1962. 176p. illus.
> Espionage in an England under threat of Napoleonic invasion.

STEVENSON, R. L. Kidnapped. (7+)
> Available in several editions.

STEVENSON, R. L. Treasure Island. (7+)
> Available in several editions.

STYLES, SHOWELL. Midshipman Quinn. (7+) Vanguard [c 1957]. 192p. illus.
> Sailing and sea battle with Britain's navy.

STYLES, SHOWELL. Midshipman Quinn and Denise, the Spy. (7+) Vanguard [c 1961]. 182p.

STYLES, SHOWELL. Quinn of the Fury. (5-8) Vanguard, 1961. 200p.

TAYLOR, DUNCAN. Fielding's England. (7+) Roy, 1965. 256p. illus.
> Eighteenth century England through the eyes of Fielding's characters.

TURNER, PHILIP. Steam on the Line. (5+) World, 1968. 192p. illus.
> Railway transforms rural life in 1800s.

WEBB, R. N. We Were There With Florence Nightingale in the Crimea; history consultant: Louis L. Snyder. (4-6) Grosset, 1958. 179p. illus.

WELCH, RONALD (pseud. of RONALD OLIVER FELTON). Nicholas Carey. (7+) Criterion, 1963. 212p. illus. maps
> British officer wins glory in mid-1800s in Crimea.

WIBBERLEY, LEONARD. Kevin O'Connor and the Light Brigade. (7+) Farrar, 1957. 192p.

WILLIAMSON, J. S. The Glorious Conspiracy. (5-6) Knopf, 1961. 224p.
> Life during the Industrial Revolution.

1900 – Present

KNIGHT, CLAYTON. We Were There at the Battle of Britain. (4-9) Grosset, 1959. 200p. illus.

KNIGHT, CLAYTON. We Were There at the Normandy Invasion. (4-9) Grosset, 1956. 200p. illus.

PATON WALSH, GILLIAN (JILL PATON WALSH). The Dolphin Crossing. (7+) St. Martin's, 1967. 134p.
> Two boys help evacuate Dunkirk in World War II.

NONFICTION

ASIMOV, ISAAC. The Shaping of England. (7+) Houghton, 1969. 288p. illus.

UNITED KINGDOM

BROWN, B. C. AND ARBUTHNOT, HELEN. Story of England. (4-6) Random House, 1943. 52p. illus.

BUCHANAN, F. M. The Land and People of Scotland. (7-9) Lippincott, 1962. 128p. illus. maps

BULLOCK, L. G. Children's Book of London. (5-7) Warne, 1960. 88p. illus. maps

BURTON, ELIZABETH. Here Is England. (7+) Farrar, 1965. 224p.

CLAYTON, ROBERT. British Isles. (4-7) Day, 1970. 48p. illus. maps

DE MARÉ, E. S. London's River—The Story of a City. (5+) McGraw, 1965. 128p. illus.

ELLACOTT, S. E. A History of Everyday Things in England. (6-8) Putnam, 1969. 224p. illus.

GEIS, DARLENE, ed. Let's Travel in England. (6+) Childrens, 1964. 88p. illus.

HAMPDEN, JOHN, ed. New Worlds Ahead. (7+) Farrar, 1968. 224p. illus.
 Fourteen voyages of discovery.

HUTTON, CLARKE. A Picture History of Britain. (4-6) Watts, 1959. 66p. illus.

JOHNSON, G. W. The British Empire, an American View of Its History from 1776 to 1945. (7-9) Morrow [1969]. 158p. illus.

JOY, C. R. Getting to Know England, Scotland, and Ireland. (3-5) Coward, 1966. 72p. illus.

LEYLAND, ERIC. For Valour: The Story of the Victoria Cross. (7+) Roy, 1961. 144p. illus.

LIVERSIDGE, DOUGLAS. The British Empire and Commonwealth of Nations. (4-6) Watts, 1971. 96p. illus.

MacVicar, Angus and Caldwell, J. C. Let's Visit Scotland. (4-6) Day, 1967. 96p. illus. maps

Marshall, H. E. Scotland's Story. (7+) rev. ed. Nelson, 1968. 236p. illus. maps

Maxey, Dale. Seeing London. (7+) Vanguard, 1967. 96p. illus.

Middleton, Drew. England. (7+) Macmillan, 1964. 144p. photos; maps

Moore, Marian (Marian Moore Taylor). United Kingdom: A New Britain. (7+) Nelson, 1966. 224p. illus.

Nic Leodhas, Sorche (Leclaire Alger). Claymore and Kilt; Tales of Scottish Kings and Castles. (4-7) Holt [c 1967]. 157p. illus.
  Scottish history highlights.

Osborne, John. Britain; by [the author and] the editors of Life. (4+) Time-Life, 1967. 176p. illus. maps

Reynolds, Q. J. The Battle of Britain. (5-6) Random House, 1953. 192p. illus.

Rosenbaum, Maurice. London. (5+) Rand McNally, 1963. 128p. illus.

Russ, Lavinia and Russ, Liza, eds. Forever England: Poetry and Prose About England and the English. (7+) Harcourt, 1969. 334p. illus.

Sasek, Miroslav. This Is Edinburgh. (3+) Macmillan, 1961. 64p. illus.

Sasek, Miroslav. This Is London. (6-10) Macmillan, 1959. 64p. illus.

Shuttlesworth, Dorothy. The Tower of London: Grim and Glamorous. (6+) Hastings, 96p. illus.

Sterling Publishing Company, Editors of. Scotland in Pictures. (3-6) Sterling, 1962. 64p. illus.

UNITED KINGDOM

STERLING PUBLISHING COMPANY, EDITORS OF. Wales in Pictures. (3+) Sterling, 1966. 64p. illus.

STREATFEILD, NOEL. The First Book of England. (4-6) Watts, 1958. 72p. illus.

STREATFEILD, NOEL. The Thames: London's River. (4-7) Garrard, 1964. 96p. illus.

STREET, ALICIA. The Land of the English People. (7-9) Lippincott, 1963. 162p. illus. maps

UNSTEAD, R. J. British Castles. (7+) Crowell, 1970. 96p. illus.

UNSTEAD, R. J. Looking at History. (6+) Macmillan, 1956. 364p. illus.
Social history of Britain.

UNSTEAD, R. J. The Story of Britain. (5+) Nelson, 1970. 328p. illus.

WHITE, D. M. Caesar to Churchill. (6+) Roy, 1969. 4v. illus.

Prehistory – A.D. 1000

BARKER, D. R. The Story of Roman Britain. (7+) St. Martin's, 1963. 64p. illus. maps

BIRLEY, ANTHONY. Life in Roman Britain. (7-9) Putnam, 1965. 176p. illus.

CRAMP, ROSEMARY AND GUMMER, JOAN. The Earliest English. (7+) St. Martin's, 1964. 64p. illus. maps
British history during the Dark Ages.

CRAMPTON, PATRICK. Stonehenge of the Kings: A People Appear. (7+) Day, 1968. 184p. illus. maps

FOX, AILEEN. Roman Britain. (7+) Dufour, 1968. 46p. illus.

NEURATH, MARIE. They Lived Like This in Ancient Britain. (3-5) Watts, 1969. 32p. illus.

QUENNELL, MARJORIE AND QUENNELL, C. H. Everyday Life in Roman and Anglo-Saxon Times. (7-11) Putnam, 1960. 225p. illus.

SELLMAN, R. R. The Anglo-Saxons. (7+) Roy, 1963. 76p. illus.

SELLMAN, R. R. Prehistoric Britain. (7+) Roy, 1964. 62p. illus.

SELLMAN, R. R. Roman Britain. (7+) Roy, 1963. 68p. illus.

1000 – 1400

ALDERMAN, C. L. Flame of Freedom: The Peasants' Revolt of 1381. (7+) Messner, 1969. 192p. illus. map

ALDERMAN, C. L. The Great Invasion: The Norman Conquest of 1066. (7+) Messner, 1969. 192p. illus. map

ALDERMAN, C. L. That Men Shall Be Free: The Story of the Magna Carta. (6+) Messner, 1964. 192p. illus. maps

DARTON, F. J. H. The Story of the Canterbury Pilgrims. (7-9) Lippincott, 1947. 310p. illus.

DAUGHERTY, J. H. Magna Carta. (7-9) Random House, 1956. 192p. illus.

DENNY, N. G. AND FILMER-SANKEY, JOSEPHINE. The Bayeux Tapestry; The Story of the Norman Conquest: 1066. (5-8) Atheneum, 1966. unp. illus.

DUGGAN, A. L. Growing Up in Thirteenth Century England. (7+) Pantheon, 1962. 192p. illus.

DUGGAN, A. L. Growing Up With the Norman Conquest. (7+) Pantheon, 1965. 224p. illus.

ELLACOTT, S. E. The Norman Invasion. (7+) Abelard, 1967. 160p. illus.

GRAY, PETER. The Battle of Hastings. (5+) McGraw, 1968. 64p. illus.

HAMILTON, FRANKLIN. Challenge for a Throne; The Wars of the Roses. (7+) Dial, 1967. 256p. illus. maps; genealogical tables

HAMILTON, FRANKLIN. 1066. (5+) Dial, 1964. 224p. illus.

UNITED KINGDOM

HODGES, C. W. Magna Carta: Story of Britain. (4-7) Coward, 1966. 32p. illus.

HODGES, C. W. The Norman Conquest: Story of Britain. (3-7) Coward, 1966. 32p. illus.

NEURATH, MARIE. They Lived Like This in Chaucer's England. (4-6) Watts, 1968. 32p. illus.

NORMAN, CHARLES. The Long Bows of Agincourt. (4+) Bobbs, 1963. 122p. illus.

SELLMAN, R. R. Medieval English Warfare. (7+) Roy, 1964. 78p. illus.

SELLMAN, R. R. Norman England. (7+) Roy, 1960. 66p. illus.

SWINDLER, W. F. Magna Carta. (7+) Grosset, 1968. 157p.

TAYLOR, DUNCAN. Chaucer's England: Living in England. (7+) Roy, 1960. 191p. illus.

1400 – 1600

BUEHR, WALTER. Spanish Armada. (3+) Putnam, 1962. 96p. illus.

DODD, A. H. Life in Elizabethan England. (7-9) Putnam, 1962. 224p. illus.

GARNETT, HENRY. Know About the Armada. (7+) Dufour, 1967. 60p. illus. maps

GRAY, E. J. I Will Adventure. (7+) Viking, 1962. 126p. illus.
Life (especially stage life) in Shakespeare's London.

GRAY, PETER. The Invincible Armada. (5+) McGraw, 1970. 64p. illus.

HIRSCHFELD, BURT. The Spanish Armada: The Story of a Glorious Defeat. (7+) Messner, 1966. 192p. illus. maps

HODGES, C. W. Shakespeare and the Players. (5-8) Coward, 1949. 100p. illus.

HODGES, C. W. Shakespeare's Theatre. (5-7) Coward, 1964. 103p. illus.

HODGES, C. W. The Spanish Armada. (3-7) Coward, 1968. 32p. illus.

HORIZON MAGAZINE, EDITORS OF. Shakespeare's England; in consultation with Louis B. Wright. (6+) Harper, 1964. 153p. illus.

KIRTLAND, G. B. One Day in Elizabethan England. (2-5) Harcourt, 1962. 40p. illus.

MARX, R. F. The Battle of the Spanish Armada, 1588. (4-9) World, 1965. 128p. illus. maps

NEURATH, MARIE. They Lived Like This in Shakespeare's England. (4-6) Watts, 1968. 32p. illus.

SANDERLIN, G. W. The Sea-Dragon: Journals of Francis Drake's Voyage Around the World. (6+) Harper, 1969. 243p. illus.

SELLMAN, R. R. Elizabethan Seamen. (7+) Roy, 1961. 70p. illus. maps

TAYLOR, DUNCAN. The Elizabethan Age: Living in England. (7+) Roy, 1954. 109p. illus.

WILLIAMS, JAY. The Spanish Armada; by [the author and] the editors of Horizon magazine; consultant: Lacey Baldwin Smith (6+) Harper, 1966. 153p. illus. maps

WILLIAMS, PENRY. Life in Tudor England. (7-9) Putnam, 1965. 176p. illus.

1600 – 1800

ALDERMAN, C. L. Death to the King: The Story of the English Civil War. (7+) Messner, 1968. 192p. illus. maps

ASHLEY, M. P. Life in Stuart England. (7-9) Putnam, 1964. 178p. illus.

GRAY, PETER. Plague and Fire. (5+) McGraw, 1968. 64p. illus.
London suffers twin disasters in 1660s.

UNITED KINGDOM

NOBLE, IRIS. Rivals in Parliament: William Pitt and Charles Fox. (7-12) Messner, 1970. 192p.

PRINGLE, PATRICK. Highwaymen. (7+) Roy, 1965. 192p. illus.
> The seventeenth century underworld forces the founding of the English police force.

ROSS, SUTHERLAND (pseud. of THOMAS HENRY CALLARD). The English Civil War. (5-9) Putnam, 1966. 158p. illus.

SELLMAN, R. R. Civil War and the Commonwealth. (7+) Roy, 1964. 82p. illus.

WEISS, D. A. Great Fire of London. (7+) Crown, 1968. 159p. illus.

WILLIAMS, E. N. Life in Georgian England. (7-9) Putnam, 1962. 168p. illus.

1800 – 1900

CAMMIADE, AUDREY. Victoria's Reign. (7+) Roy, 1960. 74p. illus.

CORBETT, SCOTT. Danger Point: The Wreck of the Birkenhead. (7+) Little, 1962. 141p.
> Tragic wreck of a troopship in 1852.

HEROLD, J. C. The Battle of Waterloo; by the editors of Horizon magazine [and the author]; consultant: Gordon Wright. (6+) Harper, 1967. 153p. illus. maps

KOMROFF, MANUEL. The Battle of Waterloo: One Hundred Days of Destiny. (6+) Macmillan, 1963. 96p. photos; maps; chronology

READER, W. J. Life in Victorian England. (7-9) Putnam, 1964. 176p. illus.

RIBBONS, IAN. Monday, 21 October 1805: The Day of Trafalgar. (5+) White, 1968. 80p. illus.

TENNYSON, ALFRED, LORD. Charge of the Light Brigade. (7+) Golden, 1964. 32p. illus.

VILLIERS, A. J. The Battle of Trafalgar. (6+) Macmillan, 1965. 96p. engravings; maps; chronology

WARNER, OLIVER. Nelson and the Age of Fighting Sail; by the editors of Horizon magazine [and the author]; consultant: Chester W. Nimitz. (6+) Harper, 1963. 153p. illus. maps

WHITE, R. J. Life in Regency England. (7+) Putnam, 1964. 176p. illus.

1900 – Present

BARNETT, CORRELLI. The Battle of El Alamein – Decision in the Desert. (6+) Macmillan, 1964. 96p. photos; maps

CARTER, HODDING. The Commandos of World War II. (7+) Random House, 1966. 192p. illus.

FORESTER, C. S. Last Nine Days of the Bismarck. (7+) Little, 1959. 138p. maps

GRAY, PETER. D-Day. (5+) McGraw, 1970. 64p. illus.
Story of D-Day told from points of view of an American and a British soldier.

MASON, H. M. The Commandos: British Raider Heroes of World War II. (5+) Meredith, 1966. 160p. photos; maps

NATHAN, A. G. Churchill's England. (7-9) Grosset, 1963. 92p. illus.

PUMPHREY, G. H. Conquering the English Channel. (7+) Abelard, 1965. 160p. illus. maps
Exciting stories of "first crossings" of the channel by various means.

SHIRER, W. L. The Sinking of the Bismarck. (5-6) Random House, 1962. 192p. illus. map

WILLIAMS, E. E. The Tunnel. (7+) Abelard, 1961. 192p. illus.
In World War II, British prisoners plot to escape from German prisoner-of-war camp.

WILLIAMS, E. E. The Wooden Horse. (7+) Abelard, 1958. 256p. illus.
RAF officers escape from World War II German prison camp.

UNITED KINGDOM

WILLIAMS, JAY. Battle for the Atlantic. (7-9) Random House, 1959. 178p. illus. maps
> German U-boats try to dominate the ocean in World War II.

BIOGRAPHY

CHURCHILL, SIR WINSTON. Heroes of History. (7+) Dodd, 1968. 192p. illus.
> Mainly English heroes from Alfred the Great to Queen Victoria.

PORTER, JANE. The Scottish Chiefs. (7+) Scribner, 1921. 520p. illus.

Queen Anne

HODGES, MARGARET. Lady Queen Anne. (7+) Farrar, 1969. 256p. photos

Baden-Powell

BLASSINGAME, WYATT. Baden-Powell: Chief Scout of the World. (2-5) Garrard, 1966. 80p. illus.

Becket

DUGGAN, A. L. The Falcon and the Dove: A Life of Thomas Becket of Canterbury. (7+) Pantheon, 1966. 224p. illus.

Bruce

BAKER, N. B. Robert Bruce: King of Scots. (7-9) Vanguard, 1948. 247p.

OLIVER, JANE. The Young Robert Bruce. (6-10) Roy, 1962. 144p. illus.

STEPHENS, P. J. Outlaw King: The Story of Robert the Bruce. (7-9) Atheneum, 1964. 199p. illus.

Sir Richard Burton

ORRMONT, ARTHUR. Fearless Adventurer: Sir Richard Burton. (7+) Messner, 1969. 192p. illus.

Edith Cavell

DE LEEUW, A. L. Edith Cavell: Nurse, Spy, Heroine. (5-7) Putnam, 1968. 128p. illus.

ELKON, JULIETTE. Edith Cavell: Heroic Nurse. (6+) Messner, 1956. 192p.

GREY, ELIZABETH. Friend Within the Gates, the Story of Nurse Edith Cavell. (7+) Houghton, 1961. 192p.

VINTON, IRIS. Story of Edith Cavell. (4-6) Grosset, 1959. 192p. illus.

Charles II

NORMAN, CHARLES. Flight and Adventures of Charles II. (7-9) Random House, 1958. 182p. illus.
Trials and tribulations of an exiled English king.

Chaucer

BREWER, D. S. Chaucer in His Time. (7+) Nelson, 1964. 243p. illus.

SERRAILLIER, IAN. Chaucer and His World. (7-9) Walck, 1968. 48p. illus.

Churchill

BOOTH, A. H. The True Story of Sir Winston Churchill. (5+) Childrens, 1964. 143p. illus.

CLARK, R. W. Sir Winston Churchill. (7+) Roy, 1962. 124p. illus.

COOLIDGE, OLIVIA. Winston Churchill and the Story of Two World Wars. (7+) Houghton, 1960. 288p. illus.

DOLAN, E. M. Churchill; adapted from text by Anthony Th. Mertens (4-6) McGraw [c 1968]. 28p. illus.

DUPUY, T. N. The Military Life of Winston Churchill of Britain. (7+) Watts, 1970. 207p. maps

UNITED KINGDOM

FARRELL, ALAN. Sir Winston Churchill. (5-9) Putnam, 1965. 160p. illus.

GILBERT, MARTIN. Winston Churchill. (6-9) Dial, 1967. 120p. illus.

MALKUS, A. S. Story of Winston Churchill. (4-6) Grosset, 1957. 192p. illus.

REYNOLDS, Q. J. Winston Churchill. (7+) Random House, 1963. 208p. illus.

RICHARDS, K. G. Sir Winston Churchill. (6+) Childrens, 1968. 95p. illus.

SMITH, N. D. Winston Churchill. (7+) Roy, 1964. 108p. illus.

WEBB, R. N. Winston Churchill: Man of the Century. (7+) Watts, 1969. 128p. map

WIBBERLEY, LEONARD. Life of Winston Churchill. (7+) Farrar, 1956. 224p. photos

Cockcroft

CLARK, R. W. Sir John Cockcroft. (7+) Roy, 1960. 109p. illus. Physicist heads Britain's atomic program.

Cromwell

LEVINE, I. E. Oliver Cromwell. (7+) Messner, 1966. 192p.

Cunard

GRANT, KAY. Samuel Cunard — Pioneer of the Atlantic Steamship. (5-10) Abelard, 1967. 192p. illus.

Darwin

DICKINSON, ALICE. Charles Darwin and Natural Selection. (7+) Watts, 1964. 212p.

GREENE, CARLA. Charles Darwin. (2-6) Dial, 1968. 64p. illus.

GREGOR, A. S. Charles Darwin. (5+) Dutton, 1966. 189p. illus.

EUROPE

Hope, Charlotte. Young Charles Darwin. (6-10) Roy, 1961. 127p. illus.

Riedman, S. R. Charles Darwin. (7-11) Holt, 1959. 192p.

Selsam, M. E. Around the World With Darwin. (2-5) Harper, 1960. 47p. illus.

Davy

Carrier, E. O. Humphry Davy and Chemical Discovery. (7+) Watts, 1965. 176p.

Dickens

Brown, I. J. C. Dickens and His World. (7-9) Walck, 1970. 48p. illus.

Brown, I. J. C. Dickens in His Time. (7+) Nelson, 1963. 248p.

Burton, H. M. Dickens and His Works. (7+) Roy, 1968. 91p. illus.

Cooper, L. U. Hand Upon Time: A Life of Charles Dickens. (7+) Pantheon, 1968. 192p. illus.

Haines, Charles. Charles Dickens. (7+) Watts, 1969. 192p. illus.

Kyle, Elisabeth (pseud. of Agnes Mary Robertson Dunlop). Great Ambitions: A Story of the Early Years of Charles Dickens. (7+) Holt, 1968. 217p.

Peare, C. O. Charles Dickens: His Life. (5-7) Holt, 1959. 125p. illus.

Pringle, Patrick. Young Dickens. (6-10) Roy, 1960. 159p. illus.

Wilkie, K. E. Charles Dickens, The Inimitable Boz. (5+) Abelard, 1970. 192p. illus.

Disraeli

Grant, Neil. Benjamin Disraeli: Prime Minister Extraordinary. (7+) Watts, 1969. 256p.

UNITED KINGDOM

KOMROFF, MANUEL. Disraeli. (7+) Messner, 1963. 192p.

Drake

FOSTER, J. T. Sir Francis Drake: A World Explorer. (3-6) Garrard, 1967. 96p. illus.

HOLWOOD, WILL (pseud. of WILSON HOLLINGSWORTH WOOD). The True Story of Sir Francis Drake, Privateer. (5+) Childrens, 1964. 139p. illus.

KNIGHT, FRANK. Young Drake. (6-10) Roy, 1962. 126p. illus.

LATHAM, J. L. Drake: The Man They Called a Pirate. (7+) Harper, 1960. 278p. illus.

SYME, RONALD. Francis Drake, Sailor of the Unknown Seas. (4-6) Morrow, 1961. 96p. illus.

Elizabeth I

BIGLAND, EILEEN. Queen Elizabeth I. (7+) Criterion, 1965. 151p.

CAMMIADE, AUDREY. Elizabeth the First. (7+) Roy, 1962. 79p. illus.

PLAIDY, JEAN. The Young Elizabeth. (6-10) Roy, 1961. 134p. illus.

STEARNS, MONROE. Elizabeth I of England. (7+) Watts, 1970. 256p. illus.

VANCE, MARGUERITE. Elizabeth Tudor, Sovereign Lady. (7+) Dutton, 1954. 156p. illus.

WINWAR, FRANCES. Queen Elizabeth and the Spanish Armada. (7-9) Random House, 1954. 192p. illus.

Elizabeth II

PARKER, ELINOR. Most Gracious Majesty. (7+) Crowell, 1962. 197p. illus.

Evans

SELDEN, GEORGE. Sir Arthur Evans: Discoverer of Knossos. (4-6) Macmillan, 1965. 48p. illus.
    Famous archaeologist uncovers history from Britain to Crete.

Faraday

HARVEY, TAD. The Quest of Michael Faraday. (7+) Garden City [c 1961]. 56p. illus.

MAY, C. P. Michael Faraday and the Electric Dynamo. (7+) Watts, 1961. 152p. illus.

Gilbert and Sullivan

HARRIS, PAULA. The Young Gilbert and Sullivan. (6-10) Roy, 1966. 128p. illus.

PURDY, C. L. Gilbert and Sullivan: Masters of Mirth and Melody. (6+) Messner, 1947. 276p. illus.

WYMER, N. G. Gilbert and Sullivan. (7-11) Dutton, 1963. 157p. illus.

Gordon

ORRMONT, ARTHUR. Chinese Gordon: Hero of Khartoum. (5-9) Putnam, 1966. 192p. illus.

Lady Jane Grey

VANCE, MARGUERITE. Lady Jane Grey, Reluctant Queen. (7-9) Dutton, 1952. 184p. illus.
    Tragedy of young claimant to the throne.

Harvey

HARRISON, W. C. Doctor William Harvey and the Discovery of Circulation. (4-6) Macmillan, 1967. 48p. illus.

MARCUS, R. B. William Harvey: Trailblazer of Scientific Medicine. (7+) Watts, 1962. 140p.

UNITED KINGDOM

Henry VIII

MALVERN, GLADYS. The Six Wives of Henry VIII. (7+) Vanguard, 1969. illus.

PITTENGER, W. N. Henry VIII of England. (7+) Watts, 1970. 160p.

VANCE, MARGUERITE. Six Queens: The Wives of Henry VIII. (7+) Dutton, 1965. 191p. illus.

Sir Julian Huxley

CLARK, R. W. Sir Julian Huxley. (7+) Roy, 1960. 128p. illus.

Jenner

EBERLE, IRMENGARDE. Edward Jenner and Smallpox Vaccination. (7+) Watts, 1962. 208p. illus.

Samuel Johnson

BROWN, I. J. C. Dr. Johnson and His World. (7+) Walck, 1966. 48p. illus.

Keats

GITTINGS, ROBERT AND MANTON, JO. Story of John Keats. (7-11) Dutton, 1963. 192p. illus.

Fanny Kemble

KERR, LAURA. Footlights to Fame: The Life of Fanny Kemble. (7+) Funk, 1962. 217p. illus.

RUSHMORE, ROBERT. Fanny Kemble. (7+) Macmillan, 1970. 216p.

WISE, WINIFRED. Fanny Kemble: Actress, Author, Abolitionist. (7-10) Putnam, 1966. 224p. illus.

Kipling

MANLEY, SEON. Rudyard Kipling: Creative Adventurer. (7+) Vanguard [1965]. 256p. illus.

EUROPE

Mary II

KYLE, ELISABETH (pseud. of AGNES MARY ROBERTSON DUNLOP). Princess of Orange. (7-9) Holt, 1966. 255p.
Biography of Mary II, Queen of Britain at the end of the seventeenth century.

Mary Stuart

HAHN, EMILY. Mary, Queen of Scots. (7+) Random House, 1953. 192p. illus.

KING, MARIAN. Young Mary Stuart: Queen of Scots. (7-9) Lippincott, 1954. 160p.

OLIVER, JANE. Queen Most Fair. (7+) St. Martin's, 1960. 247p. illus.
Tragic story of Mary, Queen of Scots.

PLAIDY, JEAN. Young Mary, Queen of Scots. (6-10) Roy, 1962. 144p. illus.

VANCE, MARGUERITE. Scotland's Queen; The Story of Mary Stuart. (5+) Dutton, 1962. illus.

Maxwell

MAY, C. P. James Clerk Maxwell and Electromagnetism. (7+) Watts, 1962. 160p. illus.

Milton

FULLER, EDMUND. John Milton. (7+) Seabury, 1967. 242p.

HOBBS, MARY. The Young Milton. (6-10) Roy, 1969. 138p. illus.

STROUSSE, FLORA. John Milton; Clarion Voice of Freedom. (7-11) Vanguard, 1962. 283p.

WEDGWOOD, C. V. Milton and His World. (7-9) Walck, 1969. 48p. illus.

Montgomery

CLARK, RONALD. Montgomery of Alamein. (7+) Roy, 1960. 109p. illus.

UNITED KINGDOM

Sir Thomas More

BRADY, C. A. Saint Thomas More of London Town. (4-6) St. Anthony, 1969. 56p. illus.

HAUGHTON, ROSEMARY. The Young Thomas More. (6-10) Roy, 1967. 128p. illus.

NEWELL, VIRGINIA. His Own Good Daughter. (6+) McKay, 1961. 151p. illus.
  Story of Sir Thomas More and his family.

STANLEY-WRENCH, MARGARET. The Conscience of a King: The Story of Thomas More. (5-9) Hawthorn [1962, c 1961]. 186p. illus.

Nelson

BELLIS, HANNAH. Admiral Nelson. (5+) McGraw, 1969. 60p. illus.

HOUGHTON, RICHARD. The True Story of Lord Nelson, Naval Hero. (5+) Childrens, 1964. 141p. illus.

SYME, RONALD. Young Nelson. (6-10) Roy, 1962. 121p. illus.

THOMPSON, JOHN. Nelson: Hero of Trafalgar. (6+) Putnam, 1968. 256p. illus.

Newton

HOUSTON, W. R. AND DEVAULT, M. V. Sir Isaac Newton. (3-7) Steck, 1960. 48p. illus.

KNIGHT, D. C. Isaac Newton: Mastermind of Science. (7+) Watts, 1961. 160p. illus.

MOORE, P. A. Isaac Newton. (5-8) Putnam, 1958. 128p. illus.

TANNENBAUM, BEULAH AND STILLMAN, MYRA. Isaac Newton: Pioneer of Space Mathematics. (7+) McGraw, 1959. 128p. illus.

Florence Nightingale

COLVER, ANNE. Florence Nightingale: War Nurse. (2-5) Garrard, 1961. 80p. illus.

COOPER, L. U. The Young Florence Nightingale. (6-10) Roy, 1961. 143p. illus.

HARMELINK, BARBARA. Florence Nightingale: Founder of Modern Nursing. (7+) Watts, 1969. 128p.

HUME, RUTH. Florence Nightingale. (7+) Random House, 1960. 192p. illus.

LEIGHTON, MARGARET. The Story of Florence Nightingale. (4-6) Grosset [1952]. 180p. illus.

NOLAN, J. C. Florence Nightingale. (7+) Messner, 1947. 192p. illus.

WEBB, R. N. The How and Why Wonder Book of Florence Nightingale. (4-6) Grosset [1962]. 48p. illus.

WYNDHAM, LEE (pseud. of JANE ANDREWS LEE HYNDMAN). Florence Nightingale, Nurse to the World. (7-10) World, 1958. illus.

Emmeline Pankhurst

KAMM, JOSEPHINE. The Story of Emmeline Pankhurst. (5+) Meredith, 1968. 170p. illus.

Fighting champion of women's rights.

Pepys

GUNSTON, DAVID. The Young Samuel Pepys. (5-7) Roy, 1966. 125p. illus.

Prince Philip

PEACOCKE, M. D. H.R.H. The Duke of Edinburgh. (7+) Roy, 1961. 128p. illus.

Story of Prince Philip, husband of Queen Elizabeth II.

Priestley

MARCUS, R. B. Joseph Priestley, Pioneer Chemist. (7+) Watts, 1961. 145p. illus.

UNITED KINGDOM

Raleigh

BAKER, N. B. Sir Walter Raleigh. (7+) Harcourt, 1950. 191p.

BUCKMASTER, HENRIETTA. Walter Raleigh: Man of Two Worlds. (7+) Random House, 1964. 192p. illus.

DE LEEUW, A. L. Sir Walter Raleigh: A World Explorer. (3-6) Garrard, 1964. 96p. illus.

SYME, RONALD. Walter Raleigh. (4-6) Morrow, 1962. 96p. illus.

Richard I

PITTENGER, W. N. Richard the Lionhearted: The Crusader King. (7+) Watts, 1970. 160p. map

POWER-WATERS, A. S. The Crusader: The Story of Richard the Lionheart. (5-9) Hawthorn, 1964. 185p. illus.

Richard III

VANCE, MARGUERITE. Song for a Lute. (7+) Dutton, 1958. 160p. illus.
> Romantic biography of Richard III and Anne.

Rutherford

KELMAN, PETER AND STONE, A. H. Ernest Rutherford: Architect of the Atom. (7+) Prentice-Hall, 1969. 72p. illus.

McKOWN, ROBIN. Giant of the Atom: Ernest Rutherford. (7+) Messner, 1962. 192p. illus.

ROWLAND, JOHN. Ernest Rutherford, Master of the Atom. (5-9) Dufour, 1964. 123p.

Scott

GRAY, E. J. Young Walter Scott. (7+) Viking [c 1935]. 239p. illus.

Selkirk

BALLARD, C. M. The Monarch of Juan Fernández. (7+) Scribner, 1968. 192p. illus.
> Fictionalized biography of Alexander Selkirk, eighteenth century castaway whose life on a desert island was the inspiration for Defoe's *Robinson Crusoe*.

Shakespeare

Bowers, Gwendolyn. At the Sign of the Globe. (7-9) Walck, 1966. 192p.
  Shakespeare and his times.

Brown, I. J. C. Shakespeare and His World. (7+) Walck, 1964. 48p. illus.

Brown, I. J. C. Shakespeare in His Time. (7+) Nelson, 1960. 238p. illus. maps

Haines, Charles. William Shakespeare and His Plays. (7+) Watts [c 1968]. 181p. illus.

Horizon Magazine, Editors of. Shakespeare's England; in consultation with Louis B. Wright. (6+) Harper, 1964. 153p. illus.

Noble, Iris. William Shakespeare. (7+) Messner, 1961. 192p.

Reese, M. M. William Shakespeare. (4-6) St. Martin's, 1963. 64p. illus.

Shirley, Jean. Shakespeare. (4-6) McGraw, 1969. [28p.] illus.

Sisson, Rosemary. Young Shakespeare. (6-10) Roy, 1960. 160p. illus.

White, A. T. Will Shakespeare and the Globe Theatre. (7-12) Random House, 1955. 192p. illus.

Shelley

Rush, Philip. The Young Shelley. (6-10) Roy, 1962. 135p. illus.

John Smith

Graves, C. P. John Smith: A World Explorer. (3-6) Garrard, 1965. 96p. illus.

Stevenson

Bailey, A. C. To Remember Robert Louis Stevenson. (7-10) McKay, 1966. 96p. illus.

UNITED KINGDOM

FINLAY, IAN. The Young Robert Louis Stevenson. (6-10) Roy, 1966. 124p. illus.

HOWARD, JOAN. Story of Robert Louis Stevenson. (4-6) Grosset, 1958. 192p. illus.

PEARE, C. O. Robert Louis Stevenson: His Life. (5-7) Holt, 1955. 128p. illus.

WILKIE, K. E. Robert Louis Stevenson: Storyteller and Adventurer. (4-6) Houghton [1961]. 189p. illus.

WOOD, J. P. The Lantern Bearer: A Life of Robert Louis Stevenson. (7+) Pantheon, 1965. 192p. illus.

Tennyson

HOPE, CHARLOTTE. The Young Tennyson. (6-10) Roy, 1965. 170p. illus.

Victoria

BOOTH, A. H. The True Story of Queen Victoria. (5+) Childrens, 1964. 143p. illus.

COOPER, L. U. The Young Victoria. (6-10) Roy, 1962. 144p. illus.

HAYCRAFT, M. C. Queen Victoria. (7+) Messner, 1956. 192p.

STREATFEILD, NOEL. Queen Victoria. (7-9) Random House, 1958. 192p. illus.

Watt

CRANE, W. D. The Man Who Transformed the World: James Watt. (7+) Messner, 1963. 192p.

WEBB, R. N. James Watt: Inventor of a Steam Engine. (6+) Watts, 1970. 128p. photos

Wesley

CLIFFORD, JOAN. The Young John Wesley. (6-10) Roy, 1967. 126p. illus.

McNeer, May and Ward, Lynd. John Wesley. (4-9) Abingdon [c 1951]. 95p. illus.

William I

Costain, T. B. William the Conqueror. (7+) Random House, 1959. 192p. illus.

Luckock, Elizabeth. William the Conqueror. (6-9) Putnam, 1966. 96p. illus.

Wren

Gould, Heywood. Sir Christopher Wren: Renaissance Architect, Philosopher, and Scientist. (7+) Watts, 1970. 224p. illus.

Vatican

NONFICTION

Deedy, John. First Book of the Vatican. (5+) Watts, 1970. 72p. photos

Kelen, Emery (Imre Kelen). Stamps Tell the Story of the Vatican. (5+) Hawthorn, 1969. 132p. illus.

MacGregor-Hastie, Roy. The Throne of Peter: A History of the Papacy. (7+) Criterion, 1966. 192p. illus.

Pepper, C. G. The Pope's Back Yard. (7+) Farrar, 1966. 192p. photos; map

BIOGRAPHY

Farjeon, Eleanor. Ten Saints. (4-6) Walck, 1936. 124p. illus.

Saint Augustine

Hansel, R. R. The Life of Saint Augustine. (7+) Watts, 1969. 192p.

Pope John XXIII

MacGregor-Hastie, Roy. Pope John XXIII. (7+) Criterion, 1962. 126p. illus.

VATICAN

RICHARDS, NORMAN. Pope John XXIII. (6+) Childrens, 1969. 95p. illus.

STRUCHEN, JEANETTE. Pope John XXIII: The Gentle Shepherd. (7+) Watts, 1969. 160p. illus.

St. Paul

FOSDICK, H. E. Life of St. Paul. (7-11) Random House, 1962. 192p. illus.

HAUGHTON, ROSEMARY. Paul and the World's Most Famous Letters. (5+) Abingdon, 1970. 110p. illus. maps

PITTENGER, W. N. The Life of St. Paul. (7+) Watts, 1968. 96p. maps

Pope Paul VI

MACGREGOR-HASTIE, ROY. Pope Paul VI. (7+) Criterion, 1965. 162p. illus.

PALLENBERG, CORRADO. Pope Paul VI. (7-11) Putnam, 1968. 224p.

SHAPIRO, W. E. ed. Pope Paul VI. (7+) Watts, 1967. 66p. illus.
Based on the CBS news television series The Twentieth Century.

St. Peter

PITTENGER, W. N. The Life of Saint Peter. (7+) Watts, 1971. 128p. maps

POLLAND, M. A. City of the Golden House. (7+) Doubleday, 1963. 190p. illus.
The last days of St. Peter in Nero's Rome.

THOMPSON, B. J. Peter and Paul: The Rock and the Sword. (4-10) Farrar, 1964. 192p. illus.

WOOD, K. M. The Holy Apostles Peter and Paul. (2-5) Kenedy, 1960. illus.

Pope Sylvester II

LATTIN, HARRIET. The Peasant Boy Who Became Pope. (5-10) Abelard, 1951. 192p.
> The biography of Gerbert who became Pope Sylvester II.

Wales
See United Kingdom (UK)

Yugoslavia

NONFICTION

AUTY, PHYLLIS. Yugoslavia. (5-9) Dufour, 1968. 144p. illus.

CALDWELL, J. C. AND POPESCU, JULIAN. Let's Visit Yugoslavia. (4-6) Day, 1969. 96p. illus.

HALL, ELVAJEAN AND CRINER, C. L. Picture Map Geography of Eastern Europe. (4-6) Lippincott, 1968. 160p. maps

KOSTICH, D. D. The Land and People of the Balkans. (7-9) Lippincott, 1962. 160p. illus. maps

PERL, LILA. Yugoslavia, Romania, Bulgaria: New Era in the Balkans. (6-9) Nelson, 1970. 224p. illus. maps

POPESCU, JULIAN. Let's Visit Yugoslavia. (4-6) Day, 1969. 96p. illus. maps

PRODANOVIC, N. C. Heroes of Serbia. (7-11) Walck, 1964. 184p. illus.

ROTHKOPF, CAROL. Yugoslavia. (7+) Watts, 1971. 72p. illus. maps

STERLING PUBLISHING COMPANY, EDITORS OF. Yugoslavia in Pictures. (3-6) Sterling, 1963. 64p. illus.

TILLYARD, ANGELA. The Land and People of Yugoslavia. (6+) Macmillan, 1963. 96p. photos; map

YUGOSLAVIA

UNDERWOOD, P. S. Getting to Know Eastern Europe. (3-5) Coward, 1966. 72p. illus.

BIOGRAPHY

Tito (Josip Broz)

ARCHER, JULES. Red Rebel: Tito of Yugoslavia. (7+) Messner, 1968. 192p.

II. MIDDLE EAST

General

BAINTON, R. H. The Church of Our Fathers. (7+) Scribner, 1950. 224p. illus.

CALDWELL, J. C. Let's Visit the Middle East. (4-6) Day, 1967. 96p. illus. maps

COPELAND, FRANCES. Land Between: The Middle East. (3-7) Abelard, 1958. 160p. illus.
> The people, traditions, and history of Lebanon, Syria, Jordan, and Iraq.

EISENBERG, AZRIEL. Voices from the Past: Stories of Great Biblical Discoveries. (7+) Abelard, 1959. 160p. illus.

EISENBERG, AZRIEL AND ELKINS, D. P. World's Lost and Found: Discoveries in Biblical Archaeology. (7+) Abelard, 1964. 192p. illus.

LOVEJOY, BAHIJA. Other Bible Lands. (5+) Abingdon, 1961. 176p. illus.

ROBINSON, C. A. JR. The First Book of Ancient Bible Lands. (4-6) Watts, 1962. 72p. illus.

Biblical

BOWIE, W. R. The Bible Story for Boys and Girls: New Testament. (4+) Abingdon, 1951. 224p. illus.

FRASER, EDITH. A Boy Hears Stories from the Old Testament. (1-3) Abingdon, 1965. 96p. illus.

HARTMAN, GERTRUDE. In Bible Days. (6+) Macmillan, 1948. 200p.

KRAUSE, J. E. AND OTHERS, eds. The Children's Bible. (2+) Golden [c 1965]. 509p. illus.
> Retelling of stories and poems from the Bible.

GENERAL

LAMPE, G. W. AND DANIELL, D. S. Discovering the Bible. (3-7) Abingdon, 1966. 160p. illus.

SMART, J. D. A Promise to Keep. (4-6) Westminster, 1949. illus.
A narrative story from Abraham to the Early Church.

SMITH, J. W. D. Bible Background. (7+) Roy [c 1959]. 73p. illus.

SMITHER, E. L. Early Old Testament Stories. (2-6) Abingdon [1954]. 79p. illus.

SMITHER, E. L. Later Old Testament Stories. (2-6) Abingdon [c 1956]. 80p. illus.

TERRIEN, SAMUEL. The Golden Bible Atlas. (7+) Golden, 1957. 96p. illus.

BIOGRAPHY

DE JONG, MEINDERT. The Mighty Ones: Great Men and Women of Early Bible Days. (5+) Harper [c 1959]. 282p. illus.

KOMROFF, MANUEL. Heroes of the Bible. (4-6) Golden [c 1966]. 138p. illus.
Stories of Old Testament figures such as Jacob, Moses, and Noah.

QUADFLIEG, JOSEF. The Book of The Twelve Apostles. (5-6) Pantheon [c 1961]. 168p. illus.

YATES, ELIZABETH. Children of the Bible. (2-5) Dutton, 1963. 92p. illus.
Retells the stories of the childhoods of favorite Bible characters.

Daniel

BOLLIGER, MAX. Daniel. (3-7) Delacorte, 1970. 128p. illus.
Biographical study of a slave boy who attained power at the Babylonian court of King Nebuchadnezzar.

David

DE REGNIERS, BEATRICE. David and Goliath. (K-3) Viking, 1965. 38p. illus.

HAZEN, B. S. David and Goliath. (K-2) Golden, 1968. 32p. illus.

Esther

MALVERN, GLADYS. Behold Your Queen. (6-9) McKay, 1951. 218p. illus.
>Biblical story of Esther, who became Queen of Persia.

Jesus Christ

BOWIE, W. R. The Story of Jesus: For Young People. (4-6) Scribner, 1937. 125p. illus.

CHUTE, M. G. Jesus of Israel. (7+) Dutton, 1961. 116p.

COLBY, J. P. Jesus and the World. (K-2) Hastings, 1968. 32p. illus.

DOANE, PELAGIE. The Boy Jesus. (4-6) Walck, 1953. 56p. illus.

FOSDICK, H. E. Jesus of Nazareth. (7+) Random House, 1959. 192p. illus.

LANGFORD, N. F. King Nobody Wanted. (4-6) Westminster, 1948. 192p. illus.
>Life of Christ.

PETERSHAM, MAUD AND PETERSHAM, MISKA. Story of Jesus. (2-4) Macmillan, 1967. 112p. illus.

PETERSON, E. C. AND PETERSON, B. N. To Find Jesus. (2-4) Abingdon, 1967. 112p. illus.

PITTENGER, W. N. The Life of Jesus Christ. (7+) Watts, 1968. 128p.

Joseph

BOLLIGER, MAX. Joseph. (3-7) Delacorte, 1969. 128p. illus.
>An adaptation of the Biblical story of Joseph and his brothers.

Moses

HAUGHTON, ROSEMARY. The Young Moses. (5-7) Roy, 1966. 136p. illus.

EGYPT

KLAGSBRUN, FRANCINE. The Story of Moses. (7+) Watts, 1968. 112p.

SHIPPEN, K. B. Moses. (7+) Harper, 1949. 132p.

WHEELER, OPAL. Moses. (3-6) Dutton [1962]. 94p. illus.

Samson

TASLITT, I. I. Young Samson. (3-7) Funk, 1968. 191p. illus.
Adventure tales of youthful Samson and a traveling companion.

Egypt

FICTION

BERRY, ERICK. Honey of the Nile. (7+) Viking, 1963. 114p.
Danger and suspense in ancient Egypt.

COOLIDGE, OLIVIA. Egyptian Adventures. (7+) Houghton, 1954. 224p. illus.
Twelve stories about real and fictional characters in Ancient Egypt.

JONES, R. F. Boy of the Pyramids. (5-6) Random House, 1952. 140p. illus.

MEADOWCROFT, ENID. Scarab for Luck: A story of Ancient Egypt. (4-6) Crowell, 1964. 229p. illus.
Youth aspires to be a chariot soldier under Thutmose III of Egypt.

PALMER, M. T. The Egyptian Necklace. (7+) Houghton, 1961. 144p. illus.

SCHLEIN, MIRIAM. Amuny, Boy of Old Egypt. (3-7) Abelard, 1961. 160p. illus.

SCHULTZ, BARBARA. The Secret of the Pharaohs. (5+) Bobbs, 1966. 231p.

NONFICTION

Prehistory – A.D. 1700

Asimov, Isaac. The Egyptians. (7+) Houghton, 1969. 288p. illus.

Baumann, Hans. The World of the Pharaohs. (7+) Pantheon, 1960. 256p. illus.

Burland, C. A. Ancient Egypt. (4-8) Dufour, 1962. 93p. illus.

Cottrell, Leonard. Land of the Pharaohs. (6+) World, 1960. 128p. illus.
  Life in Egypt under Tutankhamen.

Green, R. L. Ancient Egypt. (6-9) Day, 1964. 112p. illus. maps

Green, R. L. Tales of Ancient Egypt. (7+) Walck, 1968. 224p. illus.

Leacroft, Helen and Leacroft, R. V. B. Buildings of Ancient Egypt. (5-10) Scott, 1966. 40p. illus.

Mellersh, H. E. Finding Out About Ancient Egypt. (7+) Lothrop, 1961. 144p. illus.

Neurath, Marie. They Lived Like This in Ancient Egypt. (4-6) Watts, 1965. 32p. illus.

Ochsenschlager, Edward and Miller, Shane. The Egyptians in the Middle Kingdom. (5-8) Coward, 1963. 64p. illus.

Payne, Elizabeth. The Pharaohs of Ancient Egypt. (9-10) Random House, 1964. 192p. illus.

Pine, T. S. and Levine, Joseph. Egyptians Knew. (1-4) McGraw, 1964. 30p. illus.
  Aspects of Ancient Egypt.

Price, Christine. Made in Ancient Egypt. (7+) Dutton, 1969. 160p. illus.

Robinson, C. A. Jr. The First Book of Ancient Egypt. (4-6) Watts, 1960. 68p. illus.

EGYPT

SELLMAN, R. R. Ancient Egypt. (7+) Roy, 1962. 71p. illus.

SEWELL, BARBARA AND LYNCH, PATRICK. The Story of Ancient Egypt. (7+) St. Martin's, 1960. 64p. illus. maps

WHITE, J. M. Everyday Life in Ancient Egypt. (7-9) Putnam, 1964. 170p. illus.

WISE, WILLIAM. Two Reigns of Tutankhamen. (6+) Putnam, 1964. 160p.

1700 – Present

BURCHELL, S. C. Building the Suez Canal; by the editors of Horizon magazine; consultant: Charles Issawi. (6+) Harper, 1966. 153p. illus. maps

CHRISTIE, T. L. Legacy of a Pharaoh. (7-9) Lippincott, 1966. 128p. illus.
> Engineers work to save Egyptian temple from flooding by Aswan Dam.

DROWER, M. S. Nubia: A Drowning Land. (6+) Atheneum, 1970. 86p. illus. maps
> History and culture of a section of Egypt soon to be covered by the Aswan High Dam.

FAIRSERVIS, W. A. JR. Egypt, Gift of the Nile. (7+) Macmillan, 1963. 148p. photos

GLUBOK, SHIRLEY. Discovering the Royal Tombs at Ur. (7+) Macmillan, 1969. 128p. photos

GLUBOK, SHIRLEY. Discovering Tut-Ankh-Amen's Tomb. (5+) Macmillan, 1968. 144p. photos

HIRSCHFELD, BURT. The Vital Link: The Story of the Suez Canal. (7+) Messner, 1968. 192p. map

JOY, C. R. Island in the Desert: Challenge of the Nile. (6-8) Coward, 1959. 121p. illus.

MAHMOUD, Z. N. The Land and People of Egypt. (7-9) Lippincott, 1965. 128p. illus. maps

MEADOWCROFT, E. L. Gift of the River. (3-6) Crowell, 1937. 235p. illus.
> The story of Egypt.

MOOREHEAD, ALAN. The Story of the Blue Nile. (7+) Harper, 1966. 150p. engravings; photos; maps
> An abridgment by Lucy Moorehead of The Blue Nile.

RASWAN, C. R. Drinkers of the Wind. (6-9) Farrar, 1961. 160p. illus.
> Life among the Egyptians.

WALLACE, J. A. Getting to Know Egypt. (3-5) Coward, 1961. 72p. illus.

WARREN, RUTH. The Nile — The Story of Pharaohs, Farmers, and Explorers. (5+) McGraw, 1968. 128p. illus.

WATSON, J. W. Egypt: Child of the Nile. (3-6) Garrard, 1967. 112p. illus.

WEINGARTEN, VIOLET. The Nile: Lifeline of Egypt. (4-7) Garrard, 1964. 96p. illus.

BIOGRAPHY

COTTRELL, LEONARD. Five Queens of Ancient Egypt. (7+) Bobbs, 1969. 181p. illus.

COTTRELL, LEONARD. The Warrior Pharaohs. (6-8) Putnam, 1969. 144p. illus.

HAWKES, JACQUETTA. Pharaohs of Egypt; by the editors of Horizon magazine; consultant: Bernard V. Bottimer. (6+) Harper [1965]. 153p. illus. maps

Amenhotep

EDWARDS, M. D. Child of the Sun: A Pharaoh of Egypt. (4-7) Beacon, 1939. 111p. illus.
> Story of Ikhnaton, also known as Amenhotep IV, King of Egypt from 1388 to 1358 B.C.

EGYPT

Ankhsenamen

MORRISON, L. P. The Lost Queen of Egypt. (7-9) Lippincott, 1937. 367p. illus.

> True story of Ankhsenamen, who was King Tutankhamon's young bride.

Champollion

HONOUR, ALAN. The Man Who Could Read Stones: Champollion and the Rosetta Stone. (6-9) Hawthorn [1966]. 190p. illus.

Cleopatra

CRAYDER, TERESA (pseud.). Cleopatra. (6-8) Coward [1969]. 119p. illus.

HORNBLOW, LEONORA. Cleopatra of Egypt. (7+) Random House, 1961. 192p. illus.

LEIGHTON, MARGARET. Cleopatra: Sister of the Moon. (7+) Farrar, 1969. 256p. chronology

NOBLE, IRIS. Egypt's Queen: Cleopatra. (7+) Messner, 1963. 192p.

De Lesseps

LONG, LAURA. De Lesseps: Builder of Suez. (6-9) McKay, 1958. 154p.

Imhotep

CORMACK, MARIBELLE. Imhotep: Builder in Stone. (7+) Watts, 1965. 120p.

> Discovery of the principles leading to construction of pyramids.

Tutankhamon

BRUCKNER, KARL. The Golden Pharaoh. (7+) Pantheon, 1959. 192p. illus.

> Retelling of history and discovery of tomb of King Tutankhamon.

MIDDLE EAST

Iran

NONFICTION

BAHAR, HUSHANG. Getting to Know Iran and Iraq. (3-5) Coward, 1963. 64p. illus. maps

HINCKLEY, HELEN. The Land and People of Iran. (7-9) Lippincott, 1964. 160p. illus. maps

NEURATH, MARIE. They Lived Like This in Ancient Persia. (4-6) Watts, 1970. 32p. illus.

PAYNE, ROBERT. The Splendor of Persia. (7+) Knopf, 1957. 256p. illus.

PIKE, E. R. Ancient Persia. (4-8) Dufour, 1961. 144p.

SHEARMAN, JOHN. The Land and People of Iran. (7+) Macmillan, 1963. 96p. photos

STERLING PUBLISHING COMPANY, EDITORS OF. Iran in Pictures. (4-12) Sterling, 1968. 64p. illus.

WATSON, J. W. Iran: Crossroads of Caravans. (3-6) Garrard, 1966. 112p. illus.

Iraq

FICTION

FEAGLES, ANITA. He Who Saw Everything: The Epic of Gilgamesh. (4-6) Scott, 1966. 64p. illus.
> Legendary king, whose adventures were recorded in a Babylonian epic around 2000 B.C.

MORGAN, B. E. Hand of the King. (5-6) Random House, 1963. 192p. illus.
> In ancient Mesopotamia, a boy assists in a revolt against tyranny.

NONFICTION

BAUMANN, HANS. In the Land of Ur: The Discovery of Ancient Mesopotamia. (7+) Pantheon, 1969. 176p. illus.

IRAQ

BOYD, MILDRED. The Silent Cities—Civilizations Lost and Found. (7+) Criterion, 1967. 160p. illus.

COTTRELL, LEONARD. Land of the Two Rivers. (6+) World, 1962. 128p. illus.
> The development of southern Mesopotamian civilization.

FAIRSERVIS, W. A. JR. Mesopotamia: The Civilization That Rose Out of the Clay. (7+) Macmillan, 1963. 144p. photos; glossary

FALLS, C. B. The First 3000 Years: Ancient Civilizations of the Tigris, Euphrates, and Nile River Valleys, and the Mediterranean Sea. (7+) Viking, 1960. 124p. illus.

GREGOR, A. S. How The World's First Cities Began. (3+) Dutton [c 1967]. 64p. illus.

JOY, C. R. Getting to Know the Tigris and Euphrates. (3-5) Coward, 1956. 72p. illus.

KRAMER, S. N. Cradle of Civilization. (7+) Time-Life, 1967. 200p. illus.
> A survey of the Mesopotamian region.

LOVEJOY, BAHIJA. The Land and People of Iraq. (7-9) Lippincott, 1964. 160p. illus. maps

MELLERSH, H. E. Sumer and Babylon. (7+) Crowell, 1965. 85p. illus.

MILLS, DOROTHY. Book of the Ancient World. (5-9) Putnam, 1923. 219p. illus.

NEURATH, MARIE. They Lived Like This in Ancient Mesopotamia. (4-6) Watts, 1965. 32p. illus.

PALMER, GEOFFREY AND LLOYD, NOËL. Quest for Prehistory. (5-7) Day, 1966. 128p. illus.

ROBINSON, C. A. JR. The First Book of Ancient Mesopotomia and Persia. (4-6) Watts, 1962. 68p. illus.

UNSTEAD, R. J. Looking at Ancient History. (5-7) Macmillan, 1960. 112p. illus.

VLAHOS, OLIVIA. African Beginnings. (7+) Viking, 1969. 145p. illus.

WINER, BART. Life in the Ancient World. (7+) Random House, 1961. 216p. illus.

Israel

FICTION

COHEN, LENORE. Passover to Freedom. (6+) Ritchie [c 1967]. 90p.
> Fictionalized account of Moses and the Exodus.

DREWERY, MARY. Hamid and the Palm Sunday Donkey. (4-6) Hastings, 1968. 128p. illus.
> Story of Arab refugees in the Holy Land.

EDMONDS, I. G. Joel of the Hanging Gardens. (4-6) Lippincott, 1966, 160p.
> A young Hebrew slave helps his people escape from ancient Babylon.

FORMAN, JAMES. My Enemy, My Brother. (7+) Hawthorn [c 1969]. 224p.
> Concentration camp inmate faces challenges in Israel.

NURENBERG, THELMA. My Cousin, the Arab. (7+) Abelard, 1965. 224p.
> Seventeen-year-old Arab views Israel's fight for independence.

NONFICTION

COMAY, JOAN AND PEARLMAN, MOSHE. Israel. (7+) Macmillan, 1964. 128p. photos; maps

FEIGENBAUM, LAWRENCE AND SEIGEL, KALMAN. Israel: Crossroads of Conflict. (6+) Rand, 1968. 176p. illus.

GEIS, DARLENE, ed. Let's Travel in the Holy Land. (6+) Childrens, 1965. 88p. illus.

ISRAEL

GOLANN, C. P. Our World: The Taming of Israel's Negev. (4-6) Messner, 1970. 128p. photos

HIRSCHFELD, BURT. A State Is Born: The Story of Israel. (7+) Messner, 1967. 192p. illus. maps

HOFFMAN, GAIL. The Land and People of Israel. (7-9) Lippincott, 1963. 124p. illus. maps

HOLISHER, DESIDER. Growing Up in Israel. (7+) Viking, 1963. 180p. illus.

JOY, C. R. Getting to Know Israel. (3-5) Coward, 1961. 72p. illus.

KUBIE, N. B. First Book of Israel. (4-6) Watts, 1968. 96p. illus.

PALMER, GEOFFREY. Quest for the Dead Sea Scrolls. (5+) Day, 1965. 96p. illus.

RACHLEFF, O. S. Young Israel: A History of the Modern Nation. (7-12) Lion, 1968. 123p. illus.

RAPPAPORT, URIEL. The Story of the Dead Sea Scrolls. (5+) Harvey, 1967. 128p. illus.

SAMUEL, RINNA. Israel and the Holy Land. (7+) Golden, 1967. 160p. illus. photos
    Description of modern Israel with history of area and its religious sites.

SASEK, MIROSLAV. This Is Israel. (3+) Macmillan, 1962. 64p. illus.

SHAMIR, MAXIM AND SHAMIR, GABRIEL. The Story of Israel in Stamps. (3-7) Sabra, 1969. 75p. illus.

SMITHER, E. L. Picture Book of Palestine. (5-7) Abingdon, 1947. 64p. illus.

STERLING PUBLISHING COMPANY, EDITORS OF. Israel in Pictures. (4-12) Sterling, 1968. 64p. illus.

WATSON, SALLY. To Build a Land. (7-9) Holt, 1957. 255p. illus.
    Jews struggle to build Israel.

Prehistory – A.D. 1900

COHEN, LENORE. Came Liberty Beyond Our Hope, a Story of Hanukkah. (5+) Ritchie, 1963. illus.
> Gaining Jewish independence in ancient days.

COOLIDGE, OLIVIA. People in Palestine. (7+) Houghton, 1965. 240p. illus.
> Jewish, Greek, and Roman cultures clash in Palestine.

KAMM, JOSEPHINE. Hebrew People: A History of the Jews. (7+) McGraw, 1968. 224p. illus. maps

KOTKER, NORMAN. The Holy Land in the Time of Jesus; by the editors of Horizon magazine; consultant: Frederick C. Grant. (6+) Harper, 1967. 151p. illus. maps

MILLS, DOROTHY. The People of Ancient Israel. (7+) Scribner, 1932. 192p.

NEURATH, MARIE. They Lived Like This in Ancient Palestine. (4-6) Watts, 1966. 32p. illus.

PEARLMAN, MOSHE. The Zealots of Masada: Story of a Dig. (7+) Scribner, 1967. 224p. photos; maps

YADIN, YIGAEL. The Story of Masada. (9-10) Random House, 1959. 176p. illus.
> Jews defy Romans in mountain fortress.

1900 – Present

APPEL, BENJAMIN. Ben-Gurion's Israel. (7+) Grosset, 1965. 92p. illus.

BRAVERMAN, L. L. AND SILVER, S. M. The Six-Day Warriors. (5-10) Bloch, 1969. 165p. illus.
> The story of the 1967 Israel-Arab conflict.

IRVING, CLIFFORD. The Battle of Jerusalem: The Six-Day War of June, 1967. (5+) Macmillan, 1970. 96p. photos

MEEKER, ODEN. Israel Reborn. (7+) Scribner, 1964. 192p. photos; maps

WERSTEIN, IRVING. All the Furious Battles: The Saga of Israel's Army. (6+) Meredith [c 1969]. 160p.

BIOGRAPHY

KAMM, JOSEPHINE. Leaders of the People. (7+) Abelard, 1960. 200p.
> Biographies of Jewish leaders, from Biblical prophets to the founders of modern Israel.

Ben-Gurion

COMAY, JOAN. Ben-Gurion and the Birth of Israel. (7+) Random House, 1967. 192p. illus. map

SAMUELS, GERTRUDE. B-G. Fighter of Goliaths: The Story of David Ben-Gurion. (7+) Crowell, 1961. 275p. illus.

Dayan

TASLITT, ISRAEL. Soldier of Israel: The Story of General Moshe Dayan. (5+) Funk, 1969. 240p. illus.

Weizmann

BAKER, R. M. Chaim Weizmann: Builder of a Nation. (7+) Messner, 1950. 180p.

Yadin

MILLER, SHANE. Desert Fighter: The Story of General Yigael Yadin and the Dead Sea Scrolls. (5-9) Hawthorn, 1967. 178p. illus.

Jordan

NONFICTION

COPELAND, P. W. The Land and People of Jordan. (7-9) Lippincott, 1965. 160p. illus. maps

WEINGARTEN, VIOLET. The Jordan: River of the Promised Land. (4-7) Garrard, 1967. 96p. illus.

Lebanon

NONFICTION

BREETVELD, JIM. Getting to Know Lebanon. (3-5) Coward, 1958. 72p. illus.

STERLING PUBLISHING COMPANY, EDITORS OF. Lebanon in Pictures. (7+) Sterling, 1969. 64p. illus.

WINDER, V. H. The Land and People of Lebanon. (7-9) Lippincott, 1965. 160p. illus. maps

Saudi Arabia

FICTION

FRENCH, H. W. The Lance of Kanana. (4-6) Lothrop, 1932. 165p.
  Bedouin youth fights to free Arabia.

NONFICTION

ELLIS, H. B. The Arabs. (6+) World, 1958. 124p. illus.

GIDAL, SONIA AND GIDAL, TIM. Sons of the Desert. (5-6) Pantheon, 1960. 84p. illus.
  Survey of Bedouin life.

HOYT, OLGA. Bedouins. (2-6) Lothrop, 1969. 128p. illus.

PHILLIPS, TED. Getting to Know Saudi Arabia. (3-5) Coward, 1963. 72p. illus.

WARREN, RUTH. The First Book of the Arab World. (4-6) Watts, 1963. 72p. illus.

BIOGRAPHY

Lawrence

BARBARY, JAMES. Lawrence and His Desert Raiders. (4-7) Meredith, 1968. 96p. illus.

TURKEY

CADELL, JAMES (pseud. of R. W. THOMAS). Young Lawrence of Arabia. (6-10) Roy, 1961. 139p. illus.

MACLEAN, ALISTAIR. Lawrence of Arabia. (7+) Random House, 1962. 192p. illus.

THOMAS, JOHN. True Story of Lawrence of Arabia. (5+) Childrens, 1964. 141p. illus.

Muhammad

WARREN, RUTH. Muhammad: Prophet of Islam. (7+) Watts, 1965. 142p.

Syria

NONFICTION

COPELAND, P. W. The Land and People of Syria. (7-9) Lippincott, 1964. 160p. illus. maps

FICTION

MORGAN, B. E. Journey for Tobiyah. (5-6) Random House, 1966. 160p. illus.
   Trials of a Jewish slave in ancient Assyria.

WILLIAMSON, J. S. Hittite Warrior. (5-6) Knopf, 1960. 224p.

Turkey

FICTION

FAULKNER, NANCY. Knights Besieged. (7+) Doubleday [c 1964]. 188p.
   Adventures in Rhodes and at the court of Suleiman.

FORMAN, JAMES. The Shield of Achilles. (7+) Farrar, 1966. 224p.
   Contemporary conflict between Greek and Turkish Cypriotes.

GODDEN, RUMER. Operation Sippacik. (5+) Viking [c. 1969]. 96p. illus.
> A boy tries to keep peace between Greeks and Turks in modern Cyprus.

KELSEY, ALICE. Once the Hodja. (3-7) Longmans, 1943. 170p. illus.
> Turkish folk tales blending history and legend.

NONFICTION

CALDWELL, J. C. Let's Visit Turkey. (4-6) Day, 1969. 96p. illus. maps

CHUBB, T. C. The Byzantines. (6+) World, 1959. 126p. illus.

DAVIS, FANNY. Getting to Know Turkey. (3-5) Coward, 1957. 72p. illus.

DUPUY, T. N. AND HAYES, G. P. Campaigns on the Turkish Fronts. (7+) Watts, 1967. 96p. illus. maps

KIELTY, BERNARDINE. The Fall of Constantinople. (7+) Random House, 1957. 192p. illus.

LENGYEL, EMIL. First Book of Turkey. (5+) Watts, 1970. 96p. photos; map

RICE, T. T. Byzantium. (7-9) Day, 1970. 112p. illus. maps

RICE, T. T. Everyday Life in Byzantium. (7-9) Putnam, 1967. 176p. illus.

SPENCER, WILLIAM. The Land and People of Turkey. (7-9) Lippincott, 1964. 128p. illus. maps

STEWART, D. S. Turkey; by [the author] and the editors of Time-Life books. (4+) Time-Life, 1969. 160p. illus. maps

BIOGRAPHY
Ataturk

LENGYEL, EMIL. They Called Him Ataturk. (6-9) Day, 1962. 192p. illus. maps
> Biography of the father of modern Turkey.

Justinian

FITZGERALD, THOMAS. Justinian the Great: Roman Emperor of the East. (7+) Watts, 1970. 128p. map

III. ASIA
Afghanistan

NONFICTION

CALDWELL, J. C. Let's Visit Afghanistan. (4-6) Day, 1968. 96p. illus. maps

CRUIT, B. J. Land of the Afghans: A Book for Children. (3+) International Publications, 1968. 45p. illus.

WESTON, CHRISTINE. Afghanistan. (7+) Scribner, 1962. 176p. photos; maps

Burma
See also Southeast Asia

NONFICTION

LANDRY, LIONEL. The Land and People of Burma. (7-9) Lippincott, 1968. 160p. illus. maps

MAXWELL-LEFROY, CECIL. The Land and People of Burma. (6+) Macmillan, 1965. 96p. photos; map

TAYLOR, CARL. Getting to Know Burma. (3-5) Coward, 1962. 72p. illus.

Cambodia
See also Southeast Asia

NONFICTION

EDMONDS, I. G. The Khmers of Cambodia: The Story of a Mysterious People. (7+) Bobbs, 1970. 160p.

TOOZE, RUTH. Cambodia: Land of Contrasts. (7+) Viking, 1962. 145p. illus.

ASIA

Ceylon

NONFICTION

MAXWELL-LEFROY, CECIL. The Land and People of Ceylon. (7+) Macmillan, 1965. 96p. photos

STERLING PUBLISHING COMPANY, EDITORS OF. Ceylon in Pictures. (6+) Sterling, 1966. 64p. illus.

WESTON, CHRISTINE. Ceylon. (7+) Scribner, 1960. 162p. photos; maps

WILBER, D. N. The Land and People of Ceylon. (7-9) Lippincott [c 1963]. 157p. illus. maps

China

FICTION

ALEXANDER, ANNE. Little Foreign Devil. (4-6) Atheneum, 1970. 232p. illus.
> Adventures of an American girl in China following World War I.

ALEXANDER, FRANCES. Pebbles from a Broken Jar: Fables and Hero Stories from Old China. (5+) Bobbs [c 1967]. 29p. illus.

BAUMANN, HANS. Sons of the Steppe. (7+) Walck, 1958. 284p. illus.
> Novel about the grandsons of Genghis Khan.

BURLEIGH, D. R. Arrow Messenger. (4-6) Follett, 1962. 192p. illus.
> Mongol boy becomes a courier for Genghis Khan.

BURLEIGH, D. R. Messenger from K'itai. (4-6) Follett, 1964. 160p. illus.
> Adventures of young messenger for Genghis Khan.

GREEN, R. J. Whistling Sword. (7+) St. Martin's, 1962. 159p.
> Adventures of a boy serving Genghis Khan.

CHINA

JONES, ADRIENNE. Ride the Far Wind. (4-6) Little, 1964. 173p. illus.
  An adventure story in the Far East of the seventh century.

KENT, L. A. He Went With Marco Polo. (7-9) Houghton, 1935. 240p. illus.

RITCHIE, RITA. Golden Hawks of Genghis Khan. (7-9) Dutton, 1958. 191p. illus.

RITCHIE, RITA. Secret Beyond the Mountains. (7+) Dutton, 1960. 240p. illus.
  Boy uncovers plot against Genghis Khan.

RITCHIE, RITA. The Year of the Horse. (7+) Dutton, 1957. 191p. illus.
  Adventure with the Mongol armies.

WYNDHAM, LEE (pseud. of JANE ANDREWS LEE HYNDMAN), ed. Folk Tales of China. (4+) Bobbs, 1963. 126p. illus.

NONFICTION

APPEL, BENJAMIN. Why the Chinese Are the Way They Are. (7+) Little, 1968. 164p. maps

BRYAN, DEREK. The Land and People of China. (6+) Macmillan, 1965. 104p. photos; map

CALDWELL, J. C. Let's Visit China. (4-6) Day, 1963. 96p. illus. maps

GEIS, DARLENE, ed. Let's Travel in China. (5+) Childrens, 1965. 88p. illus.

HARRINGTON, LYN. The Grand Canal of China. (4+) Rand McNally, 1967. 112p. illus. maps

HOFF, RHODA. China: Adventures in Eyewitness History. (7-9) Walck, 1965. 192p.

JOY, C. R. Getting to Know the Two Chinas. (3-5) Coward, 1960. 72p. illus.

LIN YU-T'ANG. Chinese Way of Life. (6+) World, 1959. 127p. illus.

ASIA

QUINN, VERNON. Picture Map Geography of Asia. (4-6) Lippincott, 1963. 122p. maps

RAU, MARGARET. The Yangtze River. (4-6) Messner, 1970. 96p. photos

RAU, MARGARET. The Yellow River. (4-7) Messner, 1969. 96p. illus. maps

ROLAND, ALBERT. Profiles from the New Asia. (7+) Macmillan, 1970. 184p. illus.

SCOTT, JOHN. China, The Hungry Dragon. (7+) Parents, 1967. 208p. illus. maps
    Assessment of modern China.

SEEGER, ELIZABETH. The Pageant of Chinese History. (7+) McKay, 1962. 432p. illus. maps

SPENCER, CORNELIA. The Land of the Chinese People. (7-9) Lippincott, 1964. 128p. illus. maps

SPENCER, CORNELIA. Made in China. (7+) Knopf, 1952. 288p. illus.
    Presentation of China's contribution to world culture.

SPENCER, CORNELIA. The Yangtze: China's River Highway. (4-7) Garrard, 1963. 96p. illus.

Prehistory – A.D. 1800

BURLAND, C. A. Ancient China. (4-8) Dufour, 1961. 144p. illus.

LOEWE, MICHAEL. Everyday Life in Early Imperial China During the Han Period 202 B.C. - A.D. 220. (7-11) Putnam [1968]. 208p. illus.

NEURATH, MARIE. They Lived Like This in Ancient China. (4-6) Watts, 1967. 32p. illus.

PINE, T. S. AND LEVINE, JOSEPH. Chinese Knew. (1-4) McGraw, 1958. 32p. illus.

CHINA

PRICE, CHRISTINE. Cities of Gold and Isles of Spice. (7+) McKay, 1965. 224p. illus. maps
>Travelers' accounts of journeys to Near and Far East from the eighth to the fifteenth centuries.

SILVERBERG, ROBERT. Wonders of Ancient Chinese Science. (5+) Hawthorn [1969]. 96p. illus.

SPENCER, CORNELIA. Ancient China. (6-9) Day, 1965. 112p. illus. maps

WALKER, R. L. First Book of Ancient China. (7+) Watts, 1969. 72p. illus. maps

1800 – Present

BUELL, HAL. The World of Red China. (4-6) Dodd, 1967. 79p. illus.

DUPUY, T. N. The Military History of the Chinese Civil War. (7+) Watts, 1970. 110p. illus. maps

GOLDSTON, R. C. The Rise of Red China. (7+) Bobbs, 1967. 256p. illus.

HIRSCHFELD, BURT. Fifty-Five Days of Terror: The Story of the Boxer Rebellion. (7+) Messner, 1964. 192p. illus.

KINMOND, WILLIAM. The First Book of Communist China. (7+) Watts, 1962. 90p. illus. map

MARTIN, CHRISTOPHER. The Boxer Rebellion. (7+) Abelard, 1968. 176p. illus. maps

SPENCER, CORNELIA. Modern China. (6-9) Day, 1969. 112p. illus. maps

TOLAND, JOHN. Flying Tigers. (7-8) Random House, 1963. 192p. illus.
>American pilots battle Japanese in China before Pearl Harbor.

ASIA

BIOGRAPHY

SPENCER, CORNELIA. China's Leaders in Ideas and Action. (5+) Macrae Smith, 1966. 190p. maps
   China from Confucius to Chou En-lai.

Chiang Kai-shek

CURTIS, RICHARD. Chiang Kai-shek. (7+) Hawthorn, 1969. 176p. illus.

SPENCER, CORNELIA. Chiang Kai-shek: Generalissimo of Nationalist China. (7+) Day, 1968. 192p. illus.

Confucius

SIMS, B. B. Confucius. (7+) Watts, 1968. 150p. illus.

Genghis Khan

LAMB, HAROLD. Genghis Khan and the Mongol Horde. (7+) Random House, 1954. 192p. illus.

WEBB, R. N. Genghis Khan: Conqueror of the Medieval World. (7+) Watts, 1967. 128p. map

Kublai Khan

CHAPMAN, WALKER (pseud. of ROBERT SILVERBERG). Kublai Khan: Lord of Xanadu. (6+) Bobbs, 1966. 214p. illus.

Mao Tse-tung

ROBERTS, E. M. Mao Tse-tung and the Chinese Communist Revolution. (7+) Roy, 1970. 96p. illus. maps

Marco Polo

BUEHR, WALTER. The World of Marco Polo. (4-7) Putnam, 1961. 96p. illus.

GRAVES, C. P. Marco Polo. (3-6) Garrard, 1963. 96p. illus.

KOMROFF, MANUEL. Marco Polo. (7+) Messner, 1952. 192p. illus.

PRESTON, EDNA. Marco Polo: A Story of the Middle Ages. (4+) Crowell [1968]. 128p. illus.

PRICE, OLIVE. Story of Marco Polo. (4-6) Grossett, 1953. 179p. illus.

WALSH, R. J. The Adventures and Discoveries of Marco Polo. (5-6) Random House, 1953. 192p. illus.

WEBB, R. N. Marco Polo: The Great Traveler. (7+) Watts, 1967. 112p. maps

Ricci

POLLAND, M. A. Mission to Cathay. (7+) Doubleday [c 1965]. 240p. illus.
> Mathematician-priest Matteo Ricci builds first Christian church in China in sixteenth century.

Sun Yat-sen

BAKER, N. B. Sun Yat-sen. (4-6) Vanguard, 1946. 247p. illus.

BUCK, PEARL. The Man Who Changed China: The Story of Sun Yat-sen. (7+) Random House, 1953. 192p. illus.

SPENCER, CORNELIA. Sun Yat-sen: Founder of the Chinese Republic. (7+) Day, 1967. 192p. illus.

Hong Kong

NONFICTION

GEIS, DARLENE, ed. Let's Travel in Hong Kong. (6+) Childrens, 1965. 88p. illus.

JOY, C. R. Getting to Know Hong Kong. (3-5) Coward, 1962. 72p. illus.

SASEK, MIROSLAV. This Is Hong Kong. (3+) Macmillan, 1965. 64p. illus.

STERLING PUBLISHING COMPANY, EDITORS OF. Hong Kong in Pictures. (4-12) Sterling, 1963. 64p. illus.

VITTENGL, M. J. All Round Hong Kong. (5+) Dodd [1963]. 127p. illus.

India

FICTION

SEEGER, ELIZABETH. The Five Sons of King Pandu. (7+) Scott, 1969. 384p. illus.
   Hero tale of the Mahabharata of ancient India.

WYNDHAM, LEE (pseud. of JANE ANDREWS LEE HYNDMAN), ed. Folk Tales of India. (4+) Bobbs, 1963. 127p.

NONFICTION

BOTHWELL, JEAN. The First Book of India. (4-6) Watts, 1966. 72p. illus.

BOTHWELL, JEAN. Omen for a Princess: The Story of Jahanara, Royal Poet of the Seventeenth Century. (5-10) Abelard, 1963. 192p.
   A princess struggles for the right to marry.

BOTHWELL, JEAN. Story of India. (7-9) Harcourt, 1952. 180p. illus.

BRYCE, L. W. India: Land of Rivers. (7+) Nelson, 1966. 222p. illus.

CALDWELL, J. C. Let's Visit India. (4-6) Day, 1960. 96p. illus. maps

CALDWELL, J. C. AND CALDWELL, E. F. Our Neighbors in India. (2-4) Day, 1960. 48p. illus.

FAIRSERVIS, W. A. JR. India. (6+) World, 1961. 128p. illus.

GEIS, DARLENE, ed. Let's Travel in India. (6+) Childrens, 1965. 88p. illus.

HAMPDEN, JOHN. A Picture History of India. (4-6) Watts, 1966. 64p. illus.

INDIA

KATZ, ELIZABETH. India in Pictures. (4-9) rev. ed. Sterling, 1968. 64p. illus.

LAMB, B. L. P. India. (7+) Macmillan, 1965. 144p. photos; maps

LASCHEVER, B. D. Getting to Know India. (3-5) Coward, 1961. 72p. illus.

MODAK, MANORAMA. The Land and People of India. (7-9) Lippincott, 1960. 128p. illus. maps

NEURATH, MARIE. They Lived Like This in Ancient India. (4-6) Watts, 1967. 32p. illus.

PIKE, E. R. Ancient India. (4-8) Weidenfeld, 1961. 135p.

SEN, GERTRUDE. Pageant of India's History. (7+) McKay, 1964. 448p. illus.

SONI, W. H. Getting to Know the River Ganges. (3-5) Coward, 1964. 72p. illus.

WATSON, J. W. India: Old Land, New Nation. (3-6) Garrard, 1966. 112p. illus.

WATSON, J. W. The Indus: South Asia's Highway of History. (4-7) Garrard, 1970. 96p. illus.

WEINGARTEN, VIOLET. Ganges: Sacred River of India. (5+) Garrard, 1969. 96p. illus.

ZINKIN, TAYA. India and Her Neighbors. (4-6) Watts, 1968. 96p. illus.

BIOGRAPHY

Asoka the Great

LENGYEL, EMIL. Asoka the Great: India's Royal Missionary. (7+) Watts, 1969. 160p. map
  Indian emperor spreads the teaching of Buddha.

Buddha

COHEN, J. L. Buddha. (3-7) Delacorte, 1969. 96p. illus.

KELEN, BETTY. Gautama Buddha, in Life and Legend. (7+) Lothrop, 1967. 192p. illus.

SERAGE, NANCY. The Prince Who Gave up a Throne: A Story of the Buddha. (4-6) Crowell, 1966. 62p.

Clive

RUSSELL, JACK. Clive of India. (6-10) Putnam, 1965. 255p. maps

Indira Gandhi

GARNETT, EMMELINE. Madame Prime Minister: The Story of Indira Gandhi. (7+) Farrar, 1967. 144p. photos

HUTHEESING, K. N. Dear to Behold: An Intimate Portrait of Indira Gandhi. (7+) Macmillan, 1969. 224p.

Mahatma Gandhi

EATON, JEANETTE. Gandhi: Fighter Without a Sword. (7-9) Morrow, 1950. 256p. illus.

JACOB, H. P. A Garland for Gandhi. (2-5) Parnassus, 1968. 47p. illus.

KYTLE, CALVIN. Gandhi, Soldier of Nonviolence: His Effect on India and the World Today. (7+) Grosset, 1969. 194p. illus.

LENGYEL, EMIL. Mahatma Gandhi: The Great Soul. (7+) Watts, 1967. 216p. illus.

MASANI, SHAKUNTALA. Gandhi's Story. (4-6) Oxford, 1950. 101p. illus.

MONTGOMERY, E. R. Gandhi: Peaceful Fighter. (5-9) Garrard, 1970. 80p. illus.

PEARE, C. O. Mahatma Gandhi: The Father of Nonviolence. (7+) Hawthorn, 1969. 208p. illus.

REYNOLDS, REGINALD. The True Story of Gandhi, Man of Peace. (5+) Childrens, 1964. 141p. illus.

TORGERSEN, D. A. Gandhi. (6+) Childrens, 1969. 96p. illus.

JAPAN

ZINKIN, TAYA. The Story of Gandhi. (7+) Criterion, 1966. 190p. illus.

Nehru

APSLER, ALFRED. Fighter for Independence: Jawaharlal Nehru. (7+) Messner, 1963. 192p.

LAMB, B. L. P. The Nehrus of India: Three Generations of Leadership. (7+) Macmillan, 1967. 288p. photos

LENGYEL, EMIL. Jawaharlal Nehru: the Brahman from Kashmir. (7+) Watts, 1968. 224p. illus.

Ross

KAMM, JOSEPHINE. Malaria Ross: A Story Biography. (3-7) Criterion, 1964. 179p. illus.
English doctors stationed in India research the cause of malaria.

Japan

FICTION

CARLSON, DALE. Warlord of the Genji. (4-7) Atheneum, 1970. 184p. illus.
Story of Japanese hero, Yoshitsune, in the twelfth century.

LEWIS, MILDRED. The Honorable Sword. (4-6) Houghton, 1960. 192p. illus.
Youthful adventures in feudal Japan.

NEWMAN, S. P. Folk Tales of Japan. (4+) Bobbs, 1963. 111p. illus.

NONFICTION

BOARDMAN, G. R. Living in Tokyo. (5-8) Nelson, 1970. 128p. illus.

CALDWELL, J. C. Let's Visit Japan. (4-6) Day, 1959. 96p. illus. maps

ASIA

CALDWELL, J. C. AND CALDWELL, E. F. Our Neighbors in Japan. (2-4) Day, 1960. 48p. illus.

CARR, R. E. The Picture Story of Japan. (4-6) McKay, 1962. 61p. illus.

DILTS, M. M. Pageant of Japanese History. (7+) McKay, 1961. 368p. illus.

EDELMAN, LILY. Japan in Story and Pictures. (4-6) Harcourt, 1953. 56p. illus.

GALLANT, KATHRYN. Mountains in the Sea: Challenge of Crowded Japan. (6-8) Coward, 1957. 121p. illus.

GEIS, DARLENE, ed. Let's Travel in Japan. (6+) Childrens, 1965. 88p. illus.

JAKEMAN, ALAN. Getting to Know Japan. (3-5) Coward, 1966. 72p. illus.

KIRK, RUTH. Japan: Crossroads of East and West. (7+) Nelson, 1966. 223p. illus.

MILLER, E. K. Tell Me About Tokyo. (1-4) Tuttle, 1964. 39p. illus.

MILLER, R. J. AND KATOH, LYNN. First Book of Japan. (4-6) Watts, 1969. 96p. illus.

NEWMAN, ROBERT. The Japanese: People of the 3 Treasures. (7+) Atheneum, 1964. 187p. illus.

POWELL, BRIAN. Modern Japan: A Brief History from 800 A.D. to the Present Day. (6+) Day, 1969. 112p. illus. maps

SAVAGE, KATHARINE. People and Power: The Story of 3 Nations. (7-9) Walck, 1959. 250p. illus. maps
   Panorama of Japanese history.

SHELDON, W. J. The Key to Tokyo. (4-6) Lippincott, 1962. 128p. illus. maps

STEINBERG, RAFAEL. Japan. (7+) Macmillan, 1969. 144p. photos; map

JAPAN

STORRY, RICHARD. Japan. (5-9) White, 1970. 127p. illus.

VAUGHAN, J. B. The Land and People of Japan. (7-9) Lippincott, 1962. 128p. illus. maps

WATSON, JANE. Japan: Islands of the Rising Sun. (3-6) Garrard, 1968. 112p. illus.

Prehistory – A.D. 1900

KIDDER, J. E. Ancient Japan. (6-9) Day, 1965. 112p. illus. maps

LEONARD, J. N. Early Japan. (7+) Time-Life, 1968. 200p. illus.

NEURATH, MARIE. They Lived Like This in Old Japan. (4-6) Watts, 1967. 32p. illus.

REYNOLDS, R. L. Commodore Perry in Japan; consultant: Douglas MacArthur, 2d. (6+) Harper, 1963. 153p. illus.

1900 – Present

BRUCKNER, KARL. The Day of the Bomb. (6+) Van Nostrand, 1963. 189p.
History of the Hiroshima catastrophe.

DUPUY, T. N. Air War in the Pacific: Air Power Leads the Way. (7+) Watts, 1964. 96p. illus. maps

DUPUY, T. N. Air War in the Pacific: Victory in the Air. (7+) Watts, 1964. 96p. illus. maps

DUPUY, T. N. Asian and Axis Resistance Movements. (7+) Watts, 1965. 96p. illus.

DUPUY, T. N. Asiatic Land Battles: Allied Victories in China and Burma. (7+) Watts, 1963. 96p. illus. maps

DUPUY, T. N. Asiatic Land Battles: Japanese Ambitions in the Pacific. (7+) Watts, 1963. 96p. illus. maps

DUPUY, T. N. Naval War in the Pacific: On to Tokyo. (7+) Watts, 1964. 96p. illus. maps

DUPUY, T. N. Naval War in the Pacific: Rising Sun of Nippon. (7+) Watts, 1964. 96p. illus. maps

ASIA

HERSEY, J. R. Hiroshima. (6+) Knopf, 1946. 117p.

HIRSCHFELD, BURT. A Cloud Over Hiroshima: The Story of the Atomic Bomb. (7+) Messner, 1967. 191p. illus. maps

LIFTON, B. J. Return to Hiroshima. (6+) Atheneum, 1970. 90p. illus.

MARTIN, CHRISTOPHER. The Russo-Japanese War. (7+) Abelard, 1967. 256p. illus. maps

NAKAMOTO, HIROKO. My Japan, 1930-1951. (5+) McGraw, 1970. 160p. illus.

VINING, E. G. Windows for the Crown Prince. (7-9) Lippincott, 1952. 320p. illus.
    A Quaker woman tutors Japan's Crown Prince.

BIOGRAPHY

Akihito

SIMON, C. M. The Sun and the Birch: The Story of Crown Prince Akihito and Crown Princess Michiko. (7+) Dutton, 1960. 192p. illus.
    Japanese royalty weds a merchant's daughter.

Korea

NONFICTION

CALDWELL, J. C. Let's Visit Korea. (4-6) Day, 1959. 96p. illus. maps

CALDWELL, J. C. AND CALDWELL, E. F. Our Neighbors in Korea. (2-4) Day, 1961. 48p. illus.

EVANS, M. F. The Land and People of Korea. (6+) Macmillan, 1963. 96p. photos; map

FEHRENBACH, T. R. Fight for Korea: From the War of 1950 to the Pueblo Incident. (7+) Grosset, 1970. 165p. illus.

GOSFIELD, FRANK AND HURWOOD, B. J. Korea: Land of the 38th Parallel. (7+) Parents, 1968. 256p.

JOHNSTON, RICHARD. Getting to Know the Two Koreas. (3-5) Coward, 1965. 63p. illus.

LECKIE, ROBERT. The War in Korea: 1950-1953. (7+) Random House, 1963. 192p. illus.

MARSHALL, S. L. A. The Military History of the Korean War. (7+) Watts, 1963. 96p. illus. maps

WERSTEIN, IRVING. Trespassers: Korea, June, 1871. (5+) Dutton, 1969. 158p. illus.

Malaysia
See also Southeast Asia

NONFICTION

CALDWELL, J. C. Let's Visit Malaysia. (4-6) Day, 1968. 96p. illus. maps

KING, SETH. Getting to Know Malaysia and Singapore. (3-5) Coward, 1964. 72p. illus.

Nepal and the Himalayas

NONFICTION

DOUGLAS, W. O. Exploring the Himalayas. (7-9) Random House, 1958. 192p. illus.

REDFORD, L. B. Getting to Know the Central Himalayas: Nepal, Sikkim, Bhutan. (3-5) Coward, 1964. 72p. illus.

REDFORD, L. B. Getting to Know the Northern Himalayas: Kashmir, Tibet, Assam. (3-5) Coward [1964]. 64p. illus.

WIBBERLEY, LEONARD. Epics of Everest. (7+) Farrar, 1954. 256p. illus.

BIOGRAPHY

Hillary

STYLES, SHOWELL. First Up Everest. (3-7) Coward, 1969. 38p. illus.

Edmund Hillary reaches the top of the world.

SUFRIN, MARK. To the Top of the World: Sir Edmund Hillary and the Conquest of Everest. (7+) Platt, 1966. 94p. illus.

Leigh-Mallory

STYLES, SHOWELL. Mallory of Everest. (7+) Macmillan, 1968. 192p. illus.

Pakistan

FICTION

KALISH, B. M. Eleven: Time to Think of Marriage, Farhut. (4-6) Atheneum, 1970. 248p. illus.

Life in Bengal (Pakistan) for an eleven-year-old girl just before World War I.

NONFICTION

CALDWELL, J. C. Let's Visit Pakistan. (4-6) Day, 1960. 96p. illus. maps

FELDMAN, HERBERT. The Land and People of Pakistan. (6+) Macmillan, 1958. 96p. photos; map

LANG, R. P. The Land and People of Pakistan. (7-9) Lippincott, 1968. 160p. illus. maps

LASCHEVER, B. D. Getting to Know Pakistan. (3-5) Coward, 1961. 72p. illus.

STERLING PUBLISHING COMPANY, EDITORS OF. Pakistan in Pictures. (4-12) Sterling, 1969. 64p. illus.

Southeast Asia

See also Burma, Cambodia, Malaysia, Thailand, Vietnam

NONFICTION

BUELL, HAL. Main Streets of Southeast Asia. (7+) Dodd, 1962. 126p. illus.

CALDWELL, J. C. Let's Visit Southeast Asia. (4-6) rev. ed. Day, 1967. 96p. illus. maps

LISS, HOWARD. The Mighty Mekong. (5-8) Hawthorn, 1967. 112p. illus.
> History and importance of a mighty river.

POOLE, F. K. First Book of Southeast Asia. (4-6) Watts, 1968. 96p. illus.

Taiwan

NONFICTION

CALDWELL, J. C. Let's Visit Formosa. (4-6) Day, 1956. 96p. illus. maps

Thailand

See also Southeast Asia

NONFICTION

AYER, MARGARET. Getting to Know Thailand. (3-5) Coward, 1959. 72p. illus.

AYER, MARGARET. Made in Thailand. (7-8) Knopf, 1964. 244p. illus.

CALDWELL, J. C. Let's Visit Thailand. (4-6) Day, 1967. 96p. illus. maps

CALDWELL, J. C. AND CALDWELL, E. F. Our Neighbors in Thailand. (2-4) Day, 1968. 48p. illus.

ASIA

EXELL, F. K. The Land and People of Thailand. (6+) Macmillan, 1961. 96p. photos; map

GEIS, DARLENE, ed. Let's Travel in Thailand. (6+) Childrens, 1966. 88p. illus.

MATTHEW, E. S. The Land and People of Thailand. (7-9) Lippincott, 1964. 160p. illus. maps

STERLING PUBLISHING COMPANY, EDITORS OF. Thailand in Pictures. (6+) Sterling, 1963. 64p. illus.

WATSON, JANE. Thailand: Rice Bowl of Asia. (3-6) Garrard, 1966. 112p. illus.

Vietnam

See also Southeast Asia

NONFICTION

BUELL, HAL. Viet Nam: Land of Many Dragons. (7+) Dodd [1968]. 142p. illus. map

CALDWELL, J. C. Let's Visit Viet Nam. (4-6) Day, 1966. 96p. illus. maps

DAREFF, HAL. The Story of Vietnam: A Background Book for Young People. (7+) Parents [1966]. 256p.

NGUYEN CAO DAM AND TRAN CAO LINH. Vietnam, Our Beloved Land. (5+) Tuttle, 1968. 124p. illus.

O'DANIEL, J. W. Vietnam Today: The Challenge of a Divided Nation. (6-8) Coward, 1962. 121p. illus.

SHELDON, W. J. Tiger in the Rice: A Short History of Vietnam. (7+) Macmillan, 1969. 160p. photos; maps; chronology

WEST, FRED. Getting to Know the Two Vietnams. (3-5) Coward, 1963. 72p. illus.

IV. AFRICA

General

FICTION

BEYER, A. W. Dark Venture. (7+) Knopf, 1968. 224p. illus.
A novel of the slave trade.

HARMAN, HUMPHREY. African Samson. (7+) Viking, 1966. 128p.
African legend akin to Biblical tale of Samson.

HENNESSEY, M. N. AND SAUTER, EDWIN, JR. A Crown for Thomas Peters. (6-8) Washburn [c 1964]. 160p.
Englishman John Hawley Glover leads West African regiment in mid-1800s.

HENNESSEY, M. N. AND SAUTER, EDWIN, JR. Soldier of Africa. (6-8) Washburn, 1965. 150p.
African soldier fights in World War I and World War II.

HENNESSEY, M. N. AND SAUTER, EDWIN, JR. Sword of the Hausas. (6-8) Washburn, 1964. 142p.
African chief's son escapes English slavery to return to Sierra Leone.

SEED, JENNY. The Voice of the Great Elephant. (5+) Pantheon, 1968. 178p. illus.
Novel of life in the great Zulu Kingdom of Chaka (1787-1828).

STERNE, E. G. The Long Black Schooner. (4-6) Follett, 1968. 192p. illus.
In 1839, African slaves seize ship sailing them to Cuba and redirect it to the United States.

WOLFE, LOUIS. Ifrikiya: Stories About Africa and Africans. (5-8) Putnam, 1964. 160p. illus.

NONFICTION

ADDONA, A. F. Organization of African Unity. (7+) World, 1969. 256p. illus.

BAYLISS, JOHN, ed. Exploits in Africa. (7-10) N.Y. Graphic Society, 1964. 140p.

BERNHEIM, MARC AND BERNHEIM, EVELYNE. From Bush to City: A Look at the New Africa. (7+) Harcourt, 1968. 96p. illus.

BOND, J. C. A Is for Africa. (K-3) Watts, 1969. 64p. illus.

BONTEMPS, ARNA. The Story of the Negro. (7+) Knopf, 1958. 256p. illus.

CALDWELL, J. C. Let's Visit Middle Africa. (4-6) Day, 1958. 96p. illus. maps

CALDWELL, J. C. Let's Visit West Africa. (4-6) revised ed. Day, 1969. 96p. illus. maps

CALDWELL, J. C. AND CALDWELL, E. F. Our Neighbors in Africa. (2-4) Day, 1961. 48p. illus.

CHU, DANIEL AND SKINNER, ELLIOTT. A Glorious Age in Africa: The Story of Three Great African Empires. (6+) Doubleday, 1965. 128p. illus.

CLEMENTS, FRANK. Getting to Know Southern Rhodesia, Zambia, and Malawi. (3-5) Coward, 1964. 72p. illus.

DAVIDSON, BASIL. Africa in History. (7+) Macmillan, 1969. 320p.

DAVIDSON, BASIL. A Guide to African History. (6+) Doubleday, [c 1969]. 128p. illus.

DAVIS, RUSSELL AND ASHABRANNER, BRENT. Land in the Sun: The Story of West Africa. (4-6) Little, 1963. 92p. illus.
   Emphasizes importance of the new African countries.

FRITZ, JEAN. Animals of Doctor Schweitzer. (3-5) Coward, 1958. unp. illus.

GATTI, ATTILIO AND GATTI, ELLEN. The New Africa. (7+) Scribner, 1960. 224p. illus. maps

GRIFFIN, ELLA. Continent in a Hurry: The Challenge of Africa Today. (6-10) Coward, 1962. 121p. illus.

GENERAL

GUNTHER, JOHN. Meet the Congo and Its Neighbors. (7+) Harper, 1959. 260p. illus.

HILLYER, V. M. AND HUEY, E. G. Africa and Asia. (5+) Meredith [1966]. 127p. illus. maps
> New edition designed and revised by Childrens Press; consultants: William T. Nichol, John R. Lee.

HOBLEY, L. F. Opening Africa. (7+) Roy [1956]. 76p. illus.

HOFF, RHODA. Africa: Adventures in Eyewitness History. (7-9) Walck, 1963. 192p.

HUGHES, LANGSTON. The First Book of Africa. (4-6) Watts, 1964. 96p. illus.

KAULA, E. M. First Book of the Bantu Africans. (4-6) Watts, 1968. 90p. illus.

KIRBY, C. P. East Africa: Kenya, Uganda and Tanzania. (5+) Benn, 1968. 127p. illus.

LACY, LESLIE. Black Africa on the Move. (5+) Watts, 1969. 63p. illus.

LAUBER, PATRICIA. The Congo: River Into Central Africa. (4-7) Garrard, 1964. 96p. illus.

LENS, SIDNEY. Africa: Awakening Giant. (5-7) Putnam, 1962. 192p. illus.

LOBSENZ, N. M. The First Book of East Africa. (4-6) Watts, 1964. 96p. illus.

MACGREGOR-HASTIE, ROY. Africa: Background for Today. (7+) Criterion, 1968. 193p. illus. maps

MCKOWN, ROBIN. The Congo—River of Mystery. (5+) McGraw [c 1968]. 144p. illus.

MOOREHEAD, ALAN. The Story of the White Nile. (7+) Harper, 1967. 159p. photos; drawings; maps
> An abridgment by Lucy Moorehead of The White Nile.

NEURATH, MARIE. They Lived Like This in Ancient Africa. (4-6) Watts, 1967. 32p. illus.

NEVINS, A. J. Away to East Africa. (7+) Dodd, 1959. 96p. illus. map

NOLEN, BARBARA, ed. Africa Is People: Firsthand Accounts from Contemporary Africa. (7+) Dutton, 1967. 288p. illus.

OLDEN, SAM. Getting to Know Africa's French Community. (3-5) Coward, 1961. 72p. illus.

PINE, T. S. AND LEVINE, JOSEPH. Africans Knew. (1-4) McGraw, 1967. 28p. illus.
   Tools and techniques known to early Africans.

QUINN, VERNON. Picture Map Geography of Africa. (4-6) Lippincott, 1964. 128p. maps

ROBINS, ERIC. Getting to Know the Congo River. (3-5) Coward, 1965. 72p. illus.

SAVAGE, KATHARINE. Story of Africa: South of the Sahara. (7+) Walck, 1961. 184p. photos; maps

SPENCER, CORNELIA. Claim to Freedom: The Rise of the Afro-Asian Peoples. (6-9) Day, 1962. 192p. illus. maps

STERLING, T. L. Exploration of Africa; consultant: George H. T. Kimble. (6+) Harper, 1963. 153p. illus.

STINETORF, L. A. Children of Africa. (4-6) Lippincott, 1964. 160p. illus.

THOMPSON, E. B. Africa: Past and Present. (7+) Houghton, 1966. 320p. illus.

TURNBULL, C. M. The Peoples of Africa. (6+) World, 1962. 128p. illus.

BIOGRAPHY

DOBLER, LAVINIA AND BROWN, WILLIAM. Great Rulers of the African Past. (6+) Doubleday, 1965. 128p. illus.

KAULA, E. M. Leaders of the New Africa. (7+) World, 1966. 160p. illus.

GENERAL

MITCHISON, N. M. H. African Heroes. (7+) Farrar, 1969. 192p. illus.

POLATNICK, F. T. AND SALETAN, A. L. Shapers of Africa. (7+) Messner, 1969. 224p. illus. map

Chaka

KEATING, BERN. Chaka: King of the Zulus. (7+) Putnam, 1968. 128p.

SEED, JENNY. Voice of the Great Elephant. (5+) Pantheon, 1968. 178p.
  Life of Zulu Chief Chaka, 1787-1828.

Kingsley

SYME, RONALD. African Traveler: The Story of Mary Kingsley. (7-9) Morrow, 1962. 192p. illus.
  First Englishwoman to explore Africa.

Livingstone

ARNOLD, RICHARD. True Story of David Livingstone. (5+) Childrens, 1964. 139p. illus.

EATON, JEANETTE. David Livingstone: Foe of Darkness. (7-9) Morrow, 1947. 256p. illus.
  Missionary explores Africa.

PRINGLE, PATRICK. Young Livingstone. (6-10) Roy, 1962. 136p. illus.

PURTON, R. W. Doctor Livingstone. (5+) McGraw, 1970. 56p. illus.

Schweitzer

DANIEL, ANITA. The Story of Albert Schweitzer. (7+) Random House, 1957. 192p. illus.

FRANCK, FREDERICK. My Friend in Africa. (2-6) Bobbs, 1960. 94p. illus.
  Story of Albert Schweitzer.

GOLLOMB, JOSEPH. Albert Schweitzer: Genius in the Jungle. (7-9) Vanguard, 1949. 249p. illus.

MANTON, JO. The Story of Albert Schweitzer. (5-10) Abelard, 1955. 224p. illus.
A great musician devotes his life to doctoring African natives.

MERRETT, JOHN. True Story of Albert Schweitzer, Humanitarian. (5+) Childrens, 1964. 143p. illus.

NORTHCOTT, CECIL. Forest Doctor: The Story of Albert Schweitzer. (4-6) Roy, 1957. 93p.

PAYNE, P. S. R. Three Worlds of Albert Schweitzer. (7+) Nelson, 1957. 252p.

RICHARDS, K. G. Albert Schweitzer. (6+) Childrens, 1968. 94p. illus.

SIMON, C. M. All Men Are Brothers: A Portrait of Albert Schweitzer. (7-10) Dutton, 1956. 192p. illus.

THOMAS, M. Z. (pseud. of THOMAS MICHAEL ZOTTMANN). Albert Schweitzer; tr. by James Thin. (5-10) Knox, 1965. 166p. illus.

Stanley

ALTER, R. E. Henry Stanley. (5-9) Putnam, 1967. 192p.

GRAVES, C. P. Henry Morton Stanley. (3-6) Garrard, 1967. 96p. illus.

HALL-QUEST, O. W. With Stanley in Africa. (7+) Dutton [c 1961]. 157p. illus.

SMITH, FREDRIKA. Stanley: African Explorer. (7+) Rand McNally, 1968. 240p. illus.

Algeria
See North Africa

The Congo and Zaïre

FICTION

SAVORY, PHYLLIS. Congo Fireside Tales. (4-6) Hastings, 1962. 96p. illus.

NONFICTION

BLEEKER, SONIA. The Pygmies; Africans of the Congo Forest. (4-6) Morrow [c 1968]. 160p. illus.

KITTLER, G. D. Let's Travel in the Congo. (6+) Childrens, 1965. 88p. illus.

BIOGRAPHY

Brazza

CARBONNIER, JEANNE. Congo Explorer. (7+) Scribner, 1960. 224p. illus. maps
> Pierre Savorgnan de Brazza colonizes the French Congo peacefully.

Ethiopia

FICTION

BRADLEY, DUANE. Meeting With a Stranger. (4-6) Lippincott, 1964. 128p. illus.
> Ethiopian boy's ways clash with American ideas.

COATSWORTH, ELIZABETH. The Princess and the Lion. (3-7) Pantheon, 1963. 88p. illus.
> Abyssinian princess sets out to rescue her imprisoned brother.

NONFICTION

KAULA, E. M. The Land and People of Ethiopia. (7-9) Lippincott, 1965. 160p. illus. maps

NOLEN, BARBARA. Ethiopia. (4-6) Watts, 1971. 96p. illus.

WATSON, JANE. Ethiopia: Mountain Kingdom. (3-6) Garrard, 1966. 112p. illus.

BIOGRAPHY

Haile Selassie

GORHAM, C. O. Lion of Judah: The Story of Haile Selassie I, Emperor of Ethiopia. (7+) Farrar, 1966. 160p.

Ghana

FICTION

KAYE, GERALDINE. Great Day in Ghana; Gwasi Goes to Town. (1-4) Abelard, 1962. 32p. illus.
  Life in Ghana for a young boy on Independence Day.

NONFICTION

BLEEKER, SONIA. The Ashanti of Ghana. (4-6) Morrow, 1966. 160p. illus.

SALE, J. K. The Land and People of Ghana. (7-9) Lippincott, 1963. 160p. illus. maps

Kenya

NONFICTION

BLEEKER, SONIA. The Masai; Herders of East Africa. (4-6) Morrow, 1963. 160p. illus.

FOSTER, F. B. First Book of Kenya. (7+) Watts, 1969. 72p. illus. map

GRUNDY, KENNETH. The Lands and Peoples of Kenya, Tanzania and Uganda. (6+) Macmillan, 1968. 96p. photos; map

INGALLS, LEONARD. Getting to Know Kenya. (3-5) Coward, 1963. 72p. illus.

KAULA, E. M. The Land and People of Kenya. (7-9) Lippincott, 1968. 160p. illus. maps

KENWORTHY, LEONARD. Profile of Kenya. (7+) Doubleday [c 1963]. 128p. illus.

KIRBY, C. P. East Africa: Kenya, Uganda and Tanzania. (5+) Benn, 1968. 127p. illus.

STERLING PUBLISHING COMPANY, EDITORS OF. Kenya: In Pictures. (7+) Sterling, 1969. 64p. illus.

BIOGRAPHY

Kenyatta

ARCHER, JULES. African Firebrand: Kenyatta of Kenya. (7+) Messner, 1969. 192p.

Liberia

NONFICTION

STERLING PUBLISHING COMPANY, EDITORS OF. Liberia in Pictures. (6+) Sterling, 1971. 64p. illus.

BIOGRAPHY

Ashmun

ORRMONT, ARTHUR. Fighter Against Slavery: Jehudi Ashmun. (7+) Messner, 1966. 192p. illus.
  Colonial agent fights for freedom in Liberia.

Libya
See North Africa

Morocco
See North Africa

AFRICA

Nigeria

NONFICTION

BLEEKER, SONIA. The Ibo of Biafra. (4-6) Morrow, 1969. 160p. illus.

FORMAN, BRENDA-LU AND FORMAN, HARRISON. The Land and People of Nigeria. (7-9) Lippincott, 1964. 160p. illus. maps

FREVILLE, NICHOLAS AND CALDWELL, J. C. Let's Visit Nigeria. (4-8) Day, 1970. 96p. illus. map

KENWORTHY, LEONARD. Profile of Nigeria. (7+) Doubleday, 1960. 95p. illus.

KITTLER, G. D. ed. Let's Travel in Nigeria and Ghana. (6+) Childrens, 1965. 88p. illus.

OLDEN, SAM. Getting to Know Nigeria. (3-5) Coward, 1960. 72p. illus.

WATSON, JANE. Nigeria: Republic of a Hundred Kings. (3-6) Garrard, 1967. 112p. illus.

BIOGRAPHY

Slessor

SYME, RONALD. Nigerian Pioneer, the Story of Mary Slessor. (7-9) Morrow, 1964. 192p. illus.

North Africa (Algeria, Libya, Morocco, Tunisia)

FICTION

FROST, KELMAN. Stallion of the Desert. (5-10) Abelard, 1966. 168p. illus.
    An Arab boy outwits deserters from the French Foreign Legion.

HOLDING, JAMES. The King's Contest and Other North African Tales. (1-4) Abelard, 1964. 128p. illus.
    Fables and folklore of North Africa.

NORTH AFRICA

NONFICTION

BLEEKER, SONIA. The Tuareg, Nomads and Warriors of the Sahara. (4-6) Morrow, 1964. 160p. illus.
 Introduction to Berber nomads who roam the Sahara Desert.

CAVANNA, BETTY (ELIZABETH CAVANNA HEADLEY). First Book of Morocco. (4+) Watts, 1970. photos

COPELAND, P. W. The Land and People of Libya. (7-9) Lippincott, 1967. 160p. illus. maps

DEMING, ANGUS. Getting to Know Algeria. (3-5) Coward, 1963. 72p. illus.

FORESTER, C. S. The Barbary Pirates. (7+) Random House, 1953. 192p. illus.

GOTTLIEB, GERALD. The First Book of the Mediterranean. (4-6) Watts, 1960. 68p. illus.

GUNTHER, JOHN, AND OTHERS. Meet North Africa. (7+) Harper, 1957. 244p. illus.

JOY, C. R. Desert Caravans: Challenge of the Changing Sahara. (6-8) Coward, 1960. 121p. illus.

JOY, C. R. Getting to Know the Sahara. (3-5) Coward, 1963. 72p. illus.

KITTLER, G. D. Mediterranean Africa; Four Muslim Nations. (7+) Nelson, 1969. 224p. illus.

MARTIN, RUPERT. The Land and People of Morocco. (6+) Macmillan, 1968. 96p. photos; map

SEARS, S. W. Desert War in North Africa; by [the author and] the editors of Horizon magazine; consultant: I.S.O. Playfair. (6+) Harper, 1967. Illus.

SPENCER, WILLIAM. The Land and People of Morocco. (7-9) Lippincott, 1965. 160p. illus. maps

SPENCER, WILLIAM. The Land and People of Tunisia. (7-9) Lippincott, 1967. 160p. illus. maps

AFRICA

Rhodesia

NONFICTION

CLEMENTS, FRANK. Getting to Know Southern Rhodesia, Zambia, and Malawi. (3-5) Coward, 1964. 72p. illus.

KAULA, E. M. The Land and People of Rhodesia. (7-9) Lippincott, 1967. 160p. illus. maps

Tanzania

NONFICTION

BLEEKER, SONIA. The Masai; Herders of East Africa. (4-6) Morrow, 1963. 160p. illus.

JOY, C. R. Getting to Know Tanzania. (3-5) Coward, 1966. 64p. illus.

KAULA, E. M. The Land and People of Tanganyika. (7-9) Lippincott, 1963. 160p. illus. maps

KIRBY, C. P. East Africa: Kenya, Uganda and Tanzania. (5+) Benn, 1968. 127p. illus.

Tunisia
See North Africa

Union of South Africa

FICTION

GOLDIE, FAY. Zulu Boy. (7+) St. Martin's, 1968. 178p. illus.
A tribal boy encounters change in modern Africa.

MANZI, ALBERTO. White Boy. (7+) Macmillan, 1963. 208p.
Conflict in South Africa between natives and Boer settlers.

UNION OF SOUTH AFRICA

NONFICTION

BARBARY, JAMES. The Boer War. (5+) Meredith, 1969. 210p. illus.

BLEEKER, SONIA. The Zulu of South Africa; Cattlemen, Farmers, and Warriors. (4-6) Morrow, 1970. 160p. illus. maps

CALDWELL, J. C. AND NEWMAN, BERNARD. Let's Visit South Africa. (4-6) Day, 1968. 96p. illus. maps

GUNTHER, JOHN, AND OTHERS. Meet South Africa. (7+) Harper, 1958. 232p. illus.

INGALLS, LEONARD. Getting to Know South Africa. (3-5) Coward, 1965. 72p. illus.

LEGUM, COLIN AND LEGUM, MARGARET. The Bitter Choice: Eight South Africans' Resistance to Racial Tyranny. (7+) World, 1968. 208p. illus.

MARTIN, CHRISTOPHER (pseud. of EDWIN PALMER HOYT). Boer War. (7-12) Abelard, 1969. 192p. illus. maps

PATON, ALAN. The Land and People of South Africa. (7-9) Lippincott, 1964. 160p. illus. maps

STERLING PUBLISHING COMPANY, EDITORS OF. South Africa in Pictures. (4-12) Sterling, 1968. 64p. illus.

BIOGRAPHY

Smuts

JOSEPH, JOAN. South African Statesman: Jan Christiaan Smuts. (7+) Messner, 1969. 192p.

V. NORTH AMERICA
Canada

FICTION

APPEL, BENJAMIN. We Were There in the Klondike Gold Rush. (4-9) Grosset, 1956. 200p. illus.

CORCORAN, JEAN, ed. Folk Tales of North America. (4+) Bobbs, 1962. 123p.

DWIGHT, ALLAN (pseud. of ALLAN TAYLOR AND LOIS DWIGHT COLE). Drums in the Forest. (7+) Macmillan, 1936. 270p. illus.

Tale of the French in early Quebec.

DWIGHT, ALLAN (pseud. of ALLAN TAYLOR AND LOIS DWIGHT COLE). Guns at Quebec. (7-9) Macmillan, 1963. 241p.

Colonial battles at Quebec in 1760.

HAYS, WILMA. Drummer Boy for Montcalm. (4-6) Viking, 1959. 88p. illus.

KENT, L. A. He Went With Champlain. (7-9) Houghton, 1959. 256p. illus.

MACARTHUR, D. W. Traders North. (7+) Knopf, 1952. 246p. illus.

The first two voyages of the Hudson's Bay Company recounted.

MALKUS, A. S. Outpost of Peril. (7+) Day, 1961. 192p.

A novel about Madeleine de La Verchères, Canada's Joan of Arc.

NORTH, STERLING. Captured by the Mohawks. (7-11) Houghton, 1960. 192p. illus.

RIDLE, J. B. Mohawk Gamble. (7+) Harper, 1963. 209p.

Tale of the North American wilderness in the time of Radisson (1636-1710).

WOLFE, LOUIS. Let's Go to the Klondike Gold Rush. (3-6) Putnam, 1964. 48p. illus.

CANADA

NONFICTION

BARCLAY, ISABEL. O Canada! (4-6) Doubleday [c 1964]. 96p. illus.

BONNER, M. G. Canada and Her Story. (7+) Knopf, 1950. 200p. illus.

BRAITHWAITE, MAX. Canada: Wonderland of Surprises. (4-7) Dodd, 1967. 63p. illus. maps

CALDWELL, J. C. Let's Visit Canada. (4-6) Day, 1964. 96p. illus. maps

DOWNING, JOAN AND DYRA, FRANCES, eds. Let's Travel in Canada. (6+) Childrens, 1968. 85p. illus.

FIELD, J. L. AND DENNIS, L. A. From Sea to Sea: The Story of Canada in the Nineteenth and Twentieth Centuries. (7-9) Abelard, 1965. 310p. illus. maps

GORDON, R. L. The Land and People of Canada. (5-7) Macmillan, 1954. 96p. illus. maps

HEATON, P. R. Canada. (5-8) Rockliff, 1957. 335p. illus. maps

HILLYER, V. M. AND HUEY, E. G. Americas [Canada, Mexico and South America]. (5+) Childrens, 1966. 127p. illus.

HOLBROOK, SABRA. Taming the Columbia River: The Challenge of American-Canadian Cooperation. (6-8) Coward, 1967. 121p. illus.

HOWARD, R. W. First Book of Niagara Falls. (4-6) Watts, 1969. 96p. illus. map

JUDSON, C. I. Saint Lawrence Seaway. (7-9) Follett, 1964. 160p. illus.

LAMBIE, B. R. The MacKenzie: River to the Top of the World. (4-7) Garrard, 1967. 96p. illus.

LAUBER, PATRICIA. Changing the Face of North America: Challenge of the St. Lawrence Seaway. (6-8) Coward [c 1959]. 96p. illus.

LEITCH, ADELAIDE. Canada, Young Giant of the North. (7+) Nelson, 1968. 223p. illus.

LINEAWEAVER, C. P. Canada. (4-6) Watts, 1967. 68p. illus. maps

LINDSAY, SALLY AND MCAULAY, J. D. This Is Canada. (4-6) Grosset, 1965. 61p. illus.

MCNEER, MAY. The Canadian Story. (7+) Farrar, 1958. 96p. lithographs

MAY, C. P. Great Cities of Canada. (5-10) Abelard, 1968. 192p. illus.

MEYER, E. P. Friendly Frontier. (6-9) Little, 1962. 296p. illus.
Canadian history and society.

NEUBERGER, R. L. Royal Canadian Mounted Police. (7+) Random House, 1953. 192p. illus.

PECK, A. M. The Pageant of Canadian History. (7+) McKay, 1963. 400p. illus.

PLACE, M. T. The Yukon. (6+) Washburn, 1967. 211p.

QUINN, VERNON. Picture Map Geography of Canada and Alaska. (4-6) Lippincott, 1960. 120p. maps

ROLLINS, FRANCES. Getting to Know Canada. (3-5) Coward, 1966. 72p. illus.

Ross, F. A. The Land and People of Canada. (7-9) Lippincott, 1964. 152p. illus. maps

STERLING PUBLISHING COMPANY, EDITORS OF. Canada in Pictures. Sterling, 1966. 64p. illus.

STERLING PUBLISHING COMPANY, EDITORS OF. French Canada in Pictures. (6+) Sterling, 1970. 64p. illus.

TOYE, WILLIAM. St. Lawrence. (7-9) Walck, 1959. 300p. illus.
A river's influence on national life.

WATSON, J. W. Canada: Giant Nation of the North. (3-6) Garrard, 1968. 112p. illus.

CANADA

WHITE, A. T. The St. Lawrence: Seaway of North America. (4-7) Garrard, 1961. 96p. illus.

WOOD, DOROTHY. Enchantment of Canada. (4+) Childrens, 1964. 96p. illus.

Prehistory – A.D. 1750

DOUVILLE, RAYMOND AND CASANOVA, J. D. Daily Life in Early Canada. (7+) Macmillan, 1968. 256p.

FIELD, J. L. AND DENNIS, L. A. Land of Promise: The Story of Early Canada. (7-10) House of Grant, 1960. 375p. illus. maps

MORENUS, RICHARD. The Hudson's Bay Company. (5-6) Random House, 1956. 192p. illus.

THARP, L. H. Company of Adventurers; The Story of the Hudson's Bay Company. (7+) Little, 1946. 301p. illus.
  Canadian voyageurs build the Hudson's Bay Company.

YATES, ELIZABETH. With Pipe, Paddle, and Song: A Story of the French-Canadian Voyageurs, circa 1750. (5+) Dutton, 1968. 256p. illus.

1750 – Present

BERTON, PIERRE. Stampede for Gold: The Story of the Klondike. (7-9) Knopf, 1955. 192p. illus.

FIELD, J. L. AND DENNIS, L. A. From Sea to Sea: The Story of Canada in the Nineteenth and Twentieth Centuries. (7-9) Abelard, 1965. 310p. illus. maps

HENTY, G. A. With Wolfe in Canada; ed. by Nancy Faulkner. (6-8) Walker, 1961. 249p. illus.
  Originally published at the turn of the century.

LONGSTREETH, T. M. The Scarlet Force: Making of the Mounted Police. (7+) St. Martin's, 1953. 182p. illus.
  The first twenty years of the Royal Canadian Mounted Police.

MASON, F. V. Battle for Quebec. (7+) Houghton, 1965. 192p. illus.

NORTH AMERICA

SCHULL, JOSEPH. Battle for the Rock: The Story of Wolfe and Montcalm. (4-6) St. Martin's, 1960. 158p. illus.

WENTWORTH, ELAINE. Mission to Metlakatla. (4-6) Houghton, 1968. 256p. illus.
> In 1857, William Duncan establishes a mission in fierce Indian country of British Columbia.

WILLIAMS, BARRY. Struggle for North America. (5+) McGraw, 1969. 96p. illus.
> French and British contend for Canada.

BIOGRAPHY

ABODAHER, D. J. The French Explorers of North America. (4-6) Messner, 1970. 96p. illus.

BUEHR, WALTER. French Explorers in America. (4-6) Putnam, 1961. 96p. illus.

GRANT, NEIL. English Explorers of North America. (3-6) Messner, 1970. 96p. illus.

HARRIS, J. N. Knights of the Air: Canadian Aces of World War I. (5-9) St. Martin's, 1959. 156p. illus.

MEREDITH, R. K. AND SMITH, E. B. Exploring the Great River: Early Voyagers on the Mississippi from De Soto to La Salle. (7+) Little, 1969. 184p. illus.

Brock

ADAMS, S. H. General Brock and Niagara Falls. (7+) Random House, 1957. 192p. illus.

Cabot

HILL, KAY. And Tomorrow the Stars: The Story of John Cabot. (7+) Dodd, 1968. 363p. illus.

Cartier

AVERILL, ESTHER. Cartier Sails the St. Lawrence. (4+) Harper, 1956. 108p. illus.
> First published in 1937.

CANADA

FERGUSON, R. D. Man from St. Malo. (5+) St. Martin's, 1959. 160p. illus.
　　Explorations of Jacques Cartier.

SYME, RONALD. Cartier: Finder of the St. Lawrence. (4-6) Morrow, 1958. 96p. illus.

TOYE, WILLIAM. Cartier Discovers the St. Lawrence. (4-6) Walck, 1970. 32p. illus.

Champlain

EDWARDS, C. P. Champlain; Father of New France. (3+) Abingdon, 1955. 128p. illus.

SYME, RONALD. Champlain of the St. Lawrence. (7-9) Morrow, 1952. 192p. illus.

THARP, L. H. Champlain: Northwest Voyager. (7+) Little, 1944. 250p. illus.

WILSON, C. M. Wilderness Explorer: The Story of Samuel de Champlain. (5-9) Hawthorn [c 1963]. 188p. illus.

Frontenac

SYME, RONALD. Frontenac of New France. (7-9) Morrow, 1969. 192p. illus.

Hudson

BAKER, N. B. Henry Hudson. (5-6) Knopf, 1958. 160p. illus.

CARMER, CARL. Henry Hudson: Captain of the Icebound Sea. (2-5) Garrard, 1960. 80p. illus. maps

GERSON, N. B. Passage to the West: The Great Voyages of Henry Hudson. (7+) Messner, 1968. 192p. illus. map

POLKING, KIRK. Let's Go on the Half Moon With Henry Hudson. (4-7) Putnam, 1964. 47p. illus.

RACHLIS, EUGENE. The Voyages of Henry Hudson. (5-6) Random House, 1962. 192p. illus.

SNOW, D. J. Henry Hudson, Explorer of the North. (4-6) Houghton, 1962. 190p. illus. maps

SYME, RONALD. Henry Hudson. (7-9) Morrow, 1955. 192p. illus.

La Salle

BUCHHEIMER, NAOMI. Let's Go Down the Mississippi with La Salle. (3-5) Putnam, 1962. 48p. illus.

GRAHAM, A. P. La Salle, River Explorer. (4+) Abingdon, 1954. 127p. illus.

NOLAN, J. C. La Salle and the Grand Enterprise. (6+) Messner, 1951. 178p. map

SYME, RONALD. La Salle of the Mississippi. (7-9) Morrow, 1953. 184p. illus.

Marquette and Joliet

KELLY, R. Z. Marquette and Joliet. (5+) Follett, 1965. 144p. illus.

KJELGAARD, J. A. Explorations of Pere Marquette. (4-6) Random House, 1951. 181p. illus.

Mackenzie

O'MEARA, WALTER. First Northwest Passage. (7+) Houghton, 1960. 192p. illus.
> Sir Alexander Mackenzie crosses Canada.

SYME, RONALD. Alexander Mackenzie, Canadian Explorer. (4-6) Morrow, 1964. 96p. illus.
> Struggle to find overland fur route to Pacific in 1788.

Radisson

RITCHIE, C. T. Runner of the Woods: Story of Young Radisson. (4-6) St. Martin's, 1964. 160p. illus.

SYME, RONALD. Bay of the North: The Story of Pierre Radisson. (5-8) Morrow, 1950. 192p. illus.

MEXICO

Vancouver

SYME, RONALD. Vancouver, Explorer of the Pacific Coast. (4-6) Morrow, 1970. 96p. illus.

Mexico

FICTION

BEALS, CARLETON. Stories Told by the Aztecs: Before the Spaniards Came. (7+) Abelard, 1970. 208p. illus.

BRUCKNER, KARL. Viva Mexico. (6-10) Roy, 1962. 190p. illus.
> Two boys participate in the Mexican Revolution of 1910.

CAMPBELL, CAMILLA. Star Mountain and Other Legends of Mexico. (3-6) McGraw, 1968. 92p.

CESCO, FREDERICA DE. The Prince of Mexico. (7-9) Day, 1970. 224p.
> Guatemoc, last of the Aztec rulers, battles the Spanish.

HALLER, ADOLPH. He Served Two Masters. (7+) Pantheon, 1962. 256p. illus.
> Young boy serves both Cortez and Montezuma.

KIDWELL, CARL. The Angry Earth. (7+) Viking [c 1964]. 133p. illus.
> A story of ancient Mexico.

LAMPMAN, E. S. The Tilted Sombrero. (7+) Doubleday, 1966. 264p. illus.
> Mexican revolt against Spanish rule in 1810.

MANTEL, S. G. The Youngest Conquistador. (7+) McKay, 1963. 192p.
> Young boy helps capture Aztec Empire.

NONFICTION

CALDWELL, J. C. Let's Visit Mexico. (4-6) Day, 1965. 96p. illus. maps

NORTH AMERICA

CHAMBERS, BRADFORD. Aztecs of Mexico, the Lost Civilization. (4-6) Grosset [1965]. 61p. illus.

COY, HAROLD. Mexicans. (7-9) Little, 1970. 326p. illus. maps

CREDLE, ELLIS. Mexico: Land of Hidden Treasure. (7+) Nelson, 1967. 224p.

EPSTEIN, SAM AND EPSTEIN, BERYL. The First Book of Mexico. Watts, 1955. 80p. illus.

GEIS, DARLENE, ed. Let's Travel in Mexico. (6+) Childrens, 1965. 88p. illus.

GÓMEZ, BARBARA. Getting to Know Mexico. (3-5) Coward, 1959. 72p. illus.

GRANT, CLARA. Mexico: Land of the Plumed Serpent. (3-6) Garrard, 1968. 112p. illus.

HANCOCK, RALPH. Mexico. (5-7) Macmillan, 1964. 128p. illus. maps

HILLYER, V. M. AND HUEY, E. G. Americas [Canada, Mexico and South America]. (5+) Childrens, 1966. 127p. illus.

LARRALDE, ELSA. The Land and People of Mexico. (7-9) Lippincott, 1964. 160p. illus. maps

McCLARREN, J. K. Mexican Assignment. (7+) Funk, 1957. 247p. illus.

Medical and cultural problems in rural Mexico in modern times.

McNEER, MAY. The Mexican Story. (7+) Farrar, 1953. 96p. lithographs

NEVINS, A. J. Away to Mexico. (7+) Dodd, 1966. 96p. illus.

NORMAN, JAMES. Charro: Mexican Horseman. (6-9) Putnam, 1969. 128p. illus.

ROSS, BETTY. Mexico: Land of Eagle and Serpent. (7+) Roy, 1965. 104p. illus.

TREVIÑO, E. B. DE. Here Is Mexico. (7+) Farrar, 1970. 256p. illus.

MEXICO

VON HAGEN, V. W. Maya: Land of the Turkey and the Deer. (6+) World, 1960. 128p. illus.

WITTON, DOROTHY. Our World: Mexico. (4-6) Messner, 1969. 128p. illus.

WOOD, F. E. Enchantment of Mexico. (4+) Childrens, 1964. 96p. illus.

WORCESTER, D. E. Three Worlds of Latin America: Mexico, Central America, South America. (7+) Dutton, 1963. 189p. illus. maps

Pre-Columbian Period

BEALS, CARLETON. Land of the Mayas; Yesterday and Today. (7+) Abelard [1967, c 1966]. 192p. illus.

BECK, B. L. The First Book of the Ancient Maya. (4-6) Watts, 1965. 94p. illus.

BECK, B. L. The First Book of the Aztecs. (4-6) Watts, 1966. 88p. illus.

BLEEKER, SONIA. The Aztec, Indians of Mexico. (4-6) Morrow, 1963. 160p. illus.

BLEEKER, SONIA. The Maya, Indians of Central America. (4-6) Morrow, 1961. 160p. illus.

BRAY, WARWICK. Everyday Life of the Aztecs. (7-11) Putnam, 1969. 240p. illus.

BURLAND, C. A. Aztecs. (4+) Weidenfeld, 1961. 144p. illus.

BURLAND, C. A. The Ancient Maya. (6-9) Day, 1967. 112p. illus. maps

GLUBOK, SHIRLEY, ed. The Fall of the Aztecs; Illustrations by the Conquered, Text by the Conquerors. (7+) St. Martin's, 1965. 114p. illus.
> Based on the text of The Discovery and Conquest of Mexico, 1517-1521, by Bernal Diaz del Castillo.

HALL-QUEST, O. W. Conquistadors and Pueblos: The Story of the American Southwest, 1540-1848. (7+) Dutton, 1969. 256p. illus.

KEATING, BERN. The Life and Death of the Aztec Nation. (5-9) Putnam, 1964. 192p. illus.

KIRTLAND, G. B. One Day in Aztec Mexico. (2-5) Harcourt, 1963. 40p. illus.

MCDONALD, L. S. AND ROSS, Z. L. For Glory and the King. (5+) Meredith, 1969. 149p.
> Mexican boy joins Spanish explorers of the Pacific coast in the late 1700s.

NEURATH, MARIE. They Lived Like This: The Ancient Maya. (4-6) Watts, 1967. 32p. illus.

POWELL, G. E. Latest Aztec Discoveries; Origin and Untold Riches. (7+) Naylor, 1970. 79p. illus. maps

VON HAGEN, V. W. The Sun Kingdom of the Aztecs. (6+) World, 1958. 126p. illus.

YOUNG, BOB AND YOUNG, JAN. The Last Emperor: The Story of Mexico's Fight for Freedom. (7+) Messner, 1969. 192p. drawings; map

BIOGRAPHY

ROSENBLUM, MORRIS. Heroes of Mexico. (7+) Fleet [c 1969]. 144p. illus.

Carlota

VANCE, MARGUERITE. Ashes of Empire: Carlota and Maximilian of Mexico. (7+) Dutton [c 1959]. 159p. illus.

Coronado

CAMPBELL, CAMILLA. Coronado and His Captains. (5+) Follett, 1958. 176p. illus.

MEXICO

Garst, Shannon. Three Conquistadors: Cortes, Coronado, Pizarro. (7+) Messner [c 1947]. 227p. illus.

Knoop, F. Y. A World Explorer; Francisco Coronado. (3-6) Garrard [c 1967]. 96p. illus.

Meredith, R. K. and Smith, E. B. Riding With Coronado. (6+) Little, 1964. 107p. illlus.

Syme, Ronald. Francisco Coronado and the Seven Cities of Gold. (7-9) Morrow, 1965. 192p. illus.

Cortes

Appel, Benjamin. We Were There With Cortes and Montezuma. (4-6) Grosset, 1959. 179p. illus.

Blacker, I. R. Cortes and the Aztec Conquest; by the editors of Horizon magazine [and the author] in consultation with Gordon Eckholm. (6+) Harper, 1965. 153p. illus.

Coleman, E. S. The Cross and the Sword of Cortes. (7+) Simon & Schuster [c 1968]. 191p.

Garst, Shannon. Three Conquistadors: Cortes, Coronado, Pizarro. (7+) Messner [c 1947]. 227p. illus.

Graff, Stewart. Hernando Cortes. (3-6) Garrard, 1970. 96p. illus.

Johnson, W. W. Captain Cortes Conquers Mexico. (7+) Random House, 1960. 186p. illus.

Strousse, Flora. Friar and the Knight: Bartolomé de Olmedo and Cortez. (5-8) Kenedy, 1957. 190p. illus.

Syme, Ronald. Cortes of Mexico. (7-9) Morrow, 1951. 192p. illus.

Juarez

Baker, N. B. Juarez, Hero of Mexico. (7-9) Vanguard, 1942. 316p. illus.

STERNE, E. G. Benito Juarez: Builder of a Nation. (6+) Knopf, 1967. 224p. illus.

Maximilian

VANCE, MARGUERITE. Ashes of Empire: Carlota and Maximilian of Mexico. (7+) Dutton [c 1959]. 159p. illus.

Stephens

O'CONNOR, RICHARD. John Lloyd Stephens: Explorer of Lost Worlds. (7+) McGraw [c 1968]. 126p. illus.
  Archaeologist uncovers the Maya civilization.

SUTTON, ANN AND SUTTON, MYRON. Among the Maya Ruins: The Adventures of John Lloyd Stephens and Frederick Catherwood. (7+) Rand McNally, 1967. 222p. illus. maps

VI. SOUTH AMERICA
General

FICTION

NEWMAN, S. P. Folk Tales of Latin America. (4+) Bobbs, 1962. 123p. illus.

NONFICTION

BAITY, E. C. Americans Before Columbus. (7+) Viking [1961]. 272p. illus. maps

GOETZ, DELIA. Half a Hemisphere: The Story of Latin America. (7-9) Harcourt, 1943. 278p. illus.
> A history of Latin America from its earliest days to national independence.

GOETZ, DELIA. Neighbors to the South. (7-9) rev. ed. Harcourt, 1956. 179p. illus.

HILLYER, V. M. AND HUEY, E. G. Americas [Canada, Mexico and South America]. (5+) Childrens, 1966. 127p. illus.

HOBLEY, L. F. Exploring the Americas. (7+) Roy, 1962. 76p. illus.

JOHNSON, W. W. Andean Republics. (4+) Time-Life, 1965. 160p. illus.

NEVINS, A. J. Away to the Lands of the Andes. (7+) Dodd, 1962. 96p. illus. maps

PECK, A. M. Pageant of South American History. (7+) McKay, 1962. 432p. illus.

PRAGO, ALBERT. The Revolution in Spanish America: The Independence Movements of 1808-1825. (7+) Macmillan, 1970. 256p. photos

QUINN, VERNON. Picture Map Geography of South America. (4-6) Lippincott, 1966. 112p. maps

SOUTH AMERICA

VLAHOS, OLIVIA. New World Beginnings: Indian Cultures in the Americas. (7+) Viking, 1971. 320p. illus.

WHITNEY, D. C. Latin America. (4-6) Golden, 1968. 62p. photos; diagrams; maps
> Concise discussion of each South and Central American country.

WORCESTER, D. E. Three Worlds of Latin America: Mexico, Central America, South America. (7+) Dutton, 1963. 189p. illus. maps

BIOGRAPHY

BAILEY, BERNADINE. Famous Latin-American Liberators. (7+) Dodd, 1960. 158p. photos

WORCESTER, D. E. Makers of Latin America. (7+) Dutton, 1966. 224p. illus.

YOUNG, BOB AND YOUNG, JAN. Liberators of Latin America. (7+) Lothrop, 1970. 224p. illus. maps

Bolívar

BAKER, N. B. He Wouldn't Be King: The Story of Simon Bolivar. (7-9) Vanguard, 1941. 305p. illus.

RINK, PAUL. Quest for Freedom; Bolivar and the South American Revolution. (7+) Messner, 1968. 188p. illus. maps

SYME, RONALD. Bolivar: The Liberator. (7-9) Morrow, 1968. 192p. illus.

WEBB, R. N. Simón Bolívar: The Liberator. (7+) Watts, 1966. 128p.

WHITRIDGE, ARNOLD. Simon Bolivar: The Great Liberator. (7+) Random House, 1954. 192p. illus.

YOUNG, BOB AND YOUNG, JAN. Simon Bolivar: The George Washington of South America. (5-9) Hawthorn, 1968. 192p. illus.

BOLIVIA

Humboldt

THOMAS, M. Z. (pseud. of THOMAS MICHAEL ZOTTMANN). Alexander von Humboldt: Scientist, Explorer, Adventurer. (7+) Pantheon [c 1960]. 192p. illus.

Vespucci

BAKER, N. B. Amerigo Vespucci. (5-6) Knopf, 1956. 160p. illus.

KNOOP, F. Y. Amerigo Vespucci. (3-6) Garrard, 1966. 96p. illus.

SYME, RONALD. Amerigo Vespucci, Scientist and Sailor. (4-6) Morrow, 1969. 96p. illus.

Argentina

NONFICTION

CALDWELL, J. C. Let's Visit Argentina. (4-6) Day, 1961. 96p. illus. maps

CARPENTER, ALLAN. Argentina. (5+) Childrens, 1969. 96p. illus.

HALL, ELVAJEAN. The Land and People of Argentina. (7-9) Lippincott, 1962. 128p. illus. maps

HORNOS, AXEL. Argentina, Paraguay and Uruguay. (7+) Nelson, 1969. 224p. illus.

OLDEN, SAM. Getting to Know Argentina. (3-5) Coward, 1961. 65p. illus.

PENDLE, GEORGE. The Land and People of Argentina. (5-7) Macmillan, 1957. 96p. illus. maps

Bolivia

NONFICTION

CARPENTER, ALLAN AND LYON, J. C. Bolivia; consulting editor: Alicia F. de Taendier. (5+) Childrens [c 1970]. 95p. illus.

CARTER, W. E. The First Book of Bolivia. (4-6) Watts, 1963. 96p. illus.

MACEOIN, GARY. Colombia and Venezuela and the Guianas. (4+) Time-Life, 1965. 160p. illus.

MAY, C. P. Peru, Bolivia, Ecuador: The Indian Andes. (6+) Nelson, 1969. 224p. illus.

Brazil

NONFICTION

BREETVELD, JIM. Getting to Know Brazil. (3-5) Coward, 1960. 72p. illus.

BROWN, ROSE. The Land and People of Brazil. (7-9) Lippincott, 1960. 128p. illus. maps

CALDWELL, J. C. Let's Visit Brazil. (4-6) Day, 1961. 96p. illus. maps

CALDWELL, J. C. AND CALDWELL, E. F. Our Neighbors in Brazil. (2-4) Day, 1962. 48p. illus.

CARPENTER, ALLAN. Enchantment of South America: Brazil. (5+) Childrens [c 1968]. 96p. illus.

CLARK, LEONARD. The Rivers Ran East. (7+) Funk, 1953. 366p. illus. maps
> Leonard Clark explores the Amazon jungles in search of Inca treasure.

JOY, C. R. Getting to Know the River Amazon. (3-5) Coward, 1963. 72p. illus.

MACDONALD, NORMAN. Land and People of Brazil. (5+) Macmillan, 1959. 96p. illus.

MALKUS, A. S. The Amazon — River of Promise. (5+) McGraw, 1970. 128p. illus.

SEEGERS, KATHLEEN. Brazil: Awakening Giant. (7+) Nelson, 1967. 224p.

COLOMBIA

SHEPPARD, SALLY. The First Book of Brazil. (4-6) Watts, 1962. 90p. illus.

SPERRY, ARMSTRONG. The Amazon: River Sea of Brazil. (4-7) Garrard, 1961. 96p. illus.

Chile

NONFICTION

BOWEN, J. D. The Land and People of Chile. (7-9) Lippincott, 1966. 160p. illus. maps

BREETVELD, JIM. Getting to Know Chile. (3-5) Coward, 1960. 72p. illus.

CALDWELL, J. C. Let's Visit Chile. (4-6) Day, 1963. 96p. illus. maps

CARPENTER, ALLAN. Chile. (5+) Childrens, 1969. 96p. illus.

MAY, C. P. Chile: Progress on Trial. (7+) Nelson, 1968. 224p.

PENDLE, GEORGE. The Land and People of Chile. (5-7) Macmillan, 1960. 96p. illus. maps

STERLING PUBLISHING COMPANY, EDITORS OF. Chile in Pictures. (4-12) Sterling, 1962. 64p. illus.

Colombia

NONFICTION

BECK, B. L. First Book of Colombia. (4-6) Watts, 1968. 72p. illus. map

CALDWELL, J. C. Let's Visit Colombia. (4-6) Day [1962]. 96p. illus. maps

CARPENTER, ALLAN AND LYON, J. C. Enchantment of South America: Colombia. (5+) Childrens, 1969. 96p. illus.

HALSELL, GRACE. Getting to Know Colombia. (3-5) Coward, 1969. 72p. illus.

MacEoin, Gary. Colombia and Venezuela and the Guianas. (4+) Time-Life, 1965. 160p. illus.

BIOGRAPHY

Quesada

Syme, Ronald. Quesada of Colombia. (7-9) Morrow, 1966. 192p. illus.
> Spanish conquistador fights the jungle.

Ecuador

NONFICTION

May, C. P. Peru, Bolivia, Eduador: The Indian Andes. (6+) Nelson, 1969. 224p. illus.

Sterling Publishing Company, Editors of. Ecuador in Pictures. (7+) Sterling, 1969. 64p. illus.

Guianas

NONFICTION

Fletcher, A. M. The Land and People of the Guianas. (7-9) Lippincott, 1966. 160p. illus. maps

Hoke, John. The First Book of the Guianas. (7+) Watts, 1965. 70p. illus.

MacEoin, Gary. Colombia and Venezuela and the Guianas. (4+) Time-Life, 1965. 160p. illus.

Paraguay

NONFICTION

Carpenter, Allan and Balow, Tom. Enchantment of South America: Paraguay. (5+) Childrens, 1970. 96p. photos

HORNOS, AXEL. Argentina, Paraguay, and Uruguay. (7+) Nelson, 1969. 224p. illus.

PENDLE, GEORGE. The Lands and Peoples of Paraguay and Uruguay. (5+) Macmillan, 1958. 96p. illus. map

Peru

FICTION

BENNETT, ROWEN. Runner for the King. (3-5) Follett, 1945. 48p. illus.
   Thrill of Inca adventures.

MALKUS, A. S. Young Inca Prince. (7+) Knopf, 1957. 256p. illus.

NONFICTION

BOWEN, J. D. The Land and People of Peru. (7-9) Lippincott [c 1963]. 160p. illus. maps

CALDWELL, J. C. Let's Visit Peru. (4-6) Day, 1962. 96p. illus. maps

CALDWELL, J. C. AND CALDWELL, E. F. Our Neighbors in Peru. (2-4) Day, 1962, 48p. illus.

CARPENTER, ALLAN. Enchantment of South America: Peru. Childrens, 1970. 96p. photos

CROSBY, A. L. The Rimac: River of Peru. (4-7) Garrard, 1966. 96p. illus.

HALSELL, GRACE. Getting to Know Peru. (3-5) Coward, 1964. 72p. illus.

HALSELL, GRACE. Peru. (7+) Macmillan, 1969. 128p. photos; map

MAY, C. P. Peru, Bolivia, Ecuador: The Indian Andes. (6+) Nelson, 1969. 224p. illus.

PENDLE, GEORGE. The Land and People of Peru. (5-7) Macmillan, 1968. 96p. illus.

WATSON, JANE. Peru: Land Astride the Andes. (3-6) Garrard, 1967. 112p. illus.

Inca Period

APPEL, BENJAMIN. Shepherd of the Sun. (5+) Obolensky, 1961. 87p. illus.

    A story of Inca life.

BAUMANN, HANS. Gold and Gods of Peru; tr. by Stella Humphries. (7+) Pantheon, 1963. 224p. illus.

BECK, B. L. First Book of the Incas. (4-6) Watts, 1966. 96p. illus.

BLEEKER, SONIA. The Inca, Indians of the Andes. (4-6) Morrow, 1960. 160p. illus.

BURLAND, C. A. Inca Peru. (4-8) Dufour, 1962. 93p. illus.

DESCOLA, JEAN. Daily Life in Peru in the Time of the Spaniards. (7+) Macmillan, 1968. 256p.

GLUBOK, SHIRLEY. The Fall of the Incas. (5+) Macmillan, 1967. 128p. illus.

KERBY, E. P. The Conquistadors. (6-8) Putnam, 1969. 96p. illus.

MCKOWN, ROBIN. The Story of the Incas: Mightiest Empire of the Early Americas. (5-9) Putnam [1966]. 223p.

NEURATH, MARIE. They Lived Like This in Ancient Peru. (4-6) Watts, 1967. 32p. illus.

NORMAN, JAMES. The Riddle of the Incas: The Story of Hiram Bingham and Macchu Picchu. (5-9) Hawthorn, 1968. 192p. illus.

    Archaeologist discovers lost Inca cities.

PINE, T. S. AND LEVINE, JOSEPH. Incas Knew. (K-3) McGraw, 1968. 32p. illus.

VON HAGEN. V. W. The Incas: People of the Sun. (6+) World, 1961. 128p. illus.

BIOGRAPHY

Pizzaro

DUVOISIN, ROGER. The Four Corners of the World. (5-6) Knopf, 1948. 128p. illus.
> Francisco Pizarro conquers Peru.

GARST, SHANNON. Three Conquistadors: Cortes, Coronado, Pizarro. (7+) Messner [c 1947]. 227p. illus.

HOWARD, CECIL. Pizarro and the Conquest of Peru; by [the author] and the editors of Horizon magazine; consultant: J. H. Parry. (6+) Harper, 1968. 153p. illus. maps

SYME, RONALD. Francisco Pizarro, Finder of Peru. (4-6) Morrow, 1963. 96p. illus.

Uruguay

NONFICTION

DOBLER, LAVINIA. The Land and People of Uruguay. (7-9) Lippincott, 1965. 160p. illus. maps

HORNOS, AXEL. Argentina, Paraguay, and Uruguay. (7+) Nelson, 1969. 224p. illus.

PENDLE, GEORGE. The Lands and Peoples of Paraguay and Uruguay. (5+) Macmillan, 1958. 96p. illus. map

Venezuela

NONFICTION

BECK, B. L. First Book of Venezuela. (4-6) Watts, 1969. 72p. illus.

CALDWELL, J. C. Let's Visit Venezuela. (4-6) Day, 1962. 96p. illus. maps

SOUTH AMERICA

CARPENTER, ALLAN AND HAAN, E. R. Enchantment of South America: Venezuela. (5+) Childrens [1970]. 95p. photos

LASCHEVER, B. D. Getting to Know Venezuela. (3-5) Coward, 1962. 82p. illus.

MACEOIN, GARY. Colombia and Venezuela and the Guianas. (4+) Time-Life, 1965. 160p. illus.

NEVINS, A. J. Away to Venezuela. (7+) Dodd, 1970. 96p. illus. map

STERLING PUBLISHING COMPANY, EDITORS OF. Venezuela in Pictures. (3-6) Sterling, 1965. 64p. illus.

WOHLRABE, R. A. AND KRUSCH, WERNER. The Land and People of Venezuela. (7-9) Lippincott, 1963. 128p. illus. maps

VII. CENTRAL AMERICA

FICTION

DUNCOMBE, F. R. The Quetzal Feather. (4-6) Lothrop, 1967. 256p. illus.
> A Spanish boy views the conquest of Guatemala by Pedro Alvarado in 1523.

NONFICTION

CALDWELL, J. C. Let's Visit Central America. (4-6) Day, 1964. 96p. illus. maps

CALDWELL, J. C. AND CALDWELL, E. F. Our Neighbors in Central America. (2-4) Day, 1967. 48p. illus.

COLVIN, GERARD. Central America. (5-7) Macmillan, 1962. 96p. illus.

DAY, DEE. Getting to Know Panama. (3-5) Coward, 1958. 72p. illus.

HALSELL, GRACE. Getting to Know Guatemala and the Two Honduras. (3-5) Coward, 1964. 72p. illus.

JOY, C. R. Getting to Know Costa Rica, El Salvador, and Nicaragua. (3-5) Coward, 1964. 72p. illus.

KAREN, RUTH. The Land and People of Central America. (7-9) Lippincott, 1965. 160p. illus. maps

LATHAM, J. L. The Chagres: Power of the Panama Canal. (4-7) Garrard, 1964. 96p. illus.

MARKUN, P. M. The First Book of Central America and Panama. (4-6) Watts, 1963. 90p. illus.

MARKUN, P. M. First Book of the Panama Canal. (4-6) Watts, 1958. 70p. illus.

MAY, C. P. Central America: Lands Seeking Unity. (7+) Nelson, 1966. 224p. illus. maps

CENTRAL AMERICA

NEVINS, A. J. Away to Central America. (7+) Dodd, 1967. 96p. illus.

PECK, A. M. Pageant of Middle American History. (7+) McKay, 1947. 508p. illus.

QUINN, VERNON. Picture Map Geography of Mexico, Central America, and the West Indies. (4-6) Lippincott, 1963. 114p. maps

STERLING PUBLISHING COMPANY, EDITORS OF. Honduras in Pictures. (5-10) Sterling, 1968. 64p. illus.

STERLING PUBLISHING COMPANY, EDITORS OF. Panama and the Canal Zone in Pictures. (7+) Sterling, 1969. 64p. illus.

WHITNEY, D. C. Latin America. (4-6) Golden, 1968. 62p. photos; diagrams; maps
    Concise discussion of each South and Central American country.

WORCESTER, D. E. Three Worlds of Latin America: Mexico, Central America, South America. (7+) Dutton, 1963. 189p. illus. maps

BIOGRAPHY

Balboa

KNOOP, F. Y. Vasco Nunez de Balboa. (3-6) Garrard, 1969. 96p. illus.

MIRSKY, JEANETTE. Balboa: Discoverer of the Pacific. (5+) Harper, 1964. 164p. illus.

NOBLE, IRIS. The Honor of Balboa. (7+) Messner, 1970. 192p.

RIESENBERG, FELIX. Balboa: Swordsman and Conquistador. (7+) Random House, 1956. 192p. illus.

STERNE, E. G. Vasco Nuñez de Balboa. (7+) Knopf, 1961. 160p. illus.

SYME, RONALD. Balboa, Finder of the Pacific. (4-6) Morrow, 1952. 96p. illus.

VIII. THE CARIBBEAN
General

FICTION

BARBARY, JAMES. Student Buccaneer. (7+) Roy, 1965. 140p. illus.
> English student joins Sir Henry Morgan.

DIEKMANN, MIEP. Slave Doctor. (7+) Morrow, 1970. 288p.
> Slavers and freebooters in seventeenth century West Indies.

MIERS, E. S. Pirate Chase. (7-9) Colonial Williamsburg [distributed by Holt], 1965. 129p. illus.
> Saga of the capture of Edward Teach ("Blackbeard").

STAHL, BEN. Blackbeard's Ghost. (4-6) Houghton, 1965. 192p. illus.

NONFICTION

BOTHWELL, JEAN. By Sail and Wind: The Story of the Bahamas. (5-10) Abelard, 1946. 144p. illus. maps
> History and geography of the Bahamas.

BRIGGS, PETER. Buccaneer Harbor. (7+) Simon & Schuster, 1970. 128p. maps
> History of Port Royal, Jamaica, from its Spanish origins to its destruction by earthquake in 1692.

CALDWELL, J. C. Let's Visit the West Indies. (4-6) Day, 1963. 96p. illus. maps

CARTEY, WILFRED. West Indies: Islands in the Sun. (7+) Nelson, 1967. 223p. illus.

MARX, R. F. Following Columbus: The Voyage of the Nina II. (4-6) World, 1964. 80p. illus.

MARX, R. F. Pirate Port: The Story of the Sunken City of Port Royal. (5+) World, 1967. 192p. illus. maps

THE CARIBBEAN

MARX, R. F. Treasure Fleets of the Spanish Main. (5+) World, 1968. 128p. illus.

QUINN, VERNON. Picture Map Geography of Mexico, Central America, and the West Indies. (4-6) Lippincott, 1963. 114p. maps

SAUNDERS, F. W. Crossroads of Conquerors: The West Indies. (4-6) Little, 1962. 88p. illus.

SHERLOCK, PHILIP. The Land and People of the West Indies. (7-9) Lippincott, 1967. 176p. illus. maps

STERLING PUBLISHING COMPANY, EDITORS OF. Caribbean—The English-Speaking Islands in Pictures. (4-12) Sterling, 1968. 64p. illus.

STERLING PUBLISHING COMPANY, EDITORS OF. Jamaica in Pictures. (4-12) Sterling, 1967. 64p. illus.

BIOGRAPHY

BOYD, MILDRED. Black Flags and Pieces of Eight. (5+) Criterion [1965]. 136p. illus.

COCHRAN, HAMILTON. Pirates of the Spanish Main; in consultation with Robert I. Nesmith. (5+) Golden, 1961. 153p. illus.

DAVIDSON, MICKIE. Pirate Book. (2-4) Random House, 1965. 64p. illus.

HYDE, LAURENCE. Under the Pirate Flag. (4-6) Houghton, 1965. 208p. illus.

JENKINS, A. C. Pirates and Highwaymen. (4-6) Walck, 1965. 56p. illus.

MCCALL, E. S. Pirates and Privateers. (3+) Childrens, 1963. 128p. illus.

PYLE, HOWARD. Howard Pyle's Book of Pirates. (5+) Harper, 1921. 246p. illus.

STOCKTON, F. R. Buccaneers and Pirates of Our Coasts. (7+) Random House, 1960. 320p. illus.

WHIPPLE, A. B. Famous Pirates of the New World. (5-6) Random House, 1958. 192p. illus.

YOLEN, JANE. Pirates in Petticoats. (7-9) McKay, 1963. 224p. illus.

Morgan

BEATTY, J. L. AND BEATTY, PATRICIA. Pirate Royal. (6+) Macmillan, 1969. 224p. illus. map
Henry Morgan ravages the Caribbean.

SYME, RONALD. Sir Henry Morgan, Buccaneer. (4-6) Morrow, 1965. 96p. illus.

Ponce de León

BAKER, N. B. Juan Ponce de León. (5-6) Knopf, 1957. 160p. illus.

BLASSINGAME, WYATT. Ponce de León. (3-6) Garrard, 1965. 96p. illus.

Toussaint L'Ouverture

GRIFFITHS, ANN. Black Patriot and Martyr: Toussaint of Haiti. (7+) Messner, 1970. 192p. map

SCHERMAN, KATHERINE. The Slave Who Freed Haiti: The Story of Toussaint L'Ouverture. (5-6) Random House, 1954. 192p. illus.

Cuba

FICTION

DWIGHT, ALLAN (pseud. of ALLAN TAYLOR AND LOIS DWIGHT COLE). The Silver Dagger. (7+) Macmillan, 1959. 252p. illus.

NONFICTION

GOLDSTON, R. C. The Cuban Revolution. (7+) Bobbs, 1970. 224p. drawings; photos; maps

LASCHEVER, B. D. Getting to Know Cuba. (3-5) Coward, 1962. 72p. illus.

MARSHALL, S. L. A. The Military History of the Spanish-American War: The War to Free Cuba. (7+) Watts, 1966. 79p. illus. maps

MATTHEWS, H. L. Cuba. (7+) Macmillan, 1964. 144p. photos; maps

WILLIAMS, BYRON. Cuba, the Continuing Revolution. (7+) Parents, 1969. 256p. maps

IX. THE PACIFIC AREA
General

NONFICTION

DAY, A. G. They Peopled the Pacific. (5+) Duell [c 1964]. 180p. illus.

HILLYER, V. M. AND HUEY, E. G. The Orient—Australia and the South Sea Islands. (5+) Childrens, 1966. 127p. illus.

HOBLEY, L. F. Exploring the Pacific. (7+) Roy [1961]. 71p. illus.

QUINN, VERNON. Picture Map Geography of the Pacific Islands. (4-6) Lippincott, 1964. 120p. maps

SPERRY, ARMSTRONG. Pacific Islands Speaking. (7+) Macmillan, 1955. 228p. illus.

SUGGS, R. C. Lords of the Blue Pacific. (7+) N.Y. Graphic Society, 1962. 151p. illus. maps

BIOGRAPHY

DAY, A. G. Explorers of the Pacific. (6+) Duell, 1967. 180p. illus. maps

DAY, A. G. Pirates of the Pacific. (5+) Meredith, 1968. 160p. illus.

Cook

BELLIS, HANNAH. Captain Cook. (5+) McGraw [1968]. 60p. illus. map

BORDEN, CHARLES. He Sailed With Captain Cook. (5+) Macrae Smith, 1968. 192p. illus.

CARRISON, D. J. Captain James Cook: Genius Afloat. (7+) Watts, 1967. 256p. maps

DE LEEUW, A. L. James Cook. (3-6) Garrard, 1963. 96p. illus.

KNIGHT, FRANK. Young Captain Cook. (6-10) Roy, 1966. 127p. illus.

LATHAM, J. L. Far Voyager: The Story of James Cook. (5+) Harper, 1970. 256p. maps

MERRETT, JOHN. Captain James Cook. (6-9) Criterion, 1957. 192p. illus.

SELSAM, M. E. The Quest of Captain Cook. (7+) Doubleday [1962]. 128p. illus.

SPERRY, ARMSTRONG. Captain Cook Explores the South Seas. (7+) Random House, 1955. 192p. illus.

SYME, RONALD. Captain Cook, Pacific Explorer. (4-6) Morrow, 1960. 96p. illus.

WARNER, OLIVER. Captain Cook and the South Pacific; by the editors of Horizon magazine and [the author]; consultant: J. C. Beaglehole. (6+) American Heritage, 1963. 153p. illus. maps

Australia

FICTION

KEESING, NANCY. By Gravel and Gum: Story of a Pioneer Family. (3-7) St. Martin's, 1963. 168p. illus.
   Struggles in New South Wales.

WILTON, ELIZABETH. Riverboat Family. (7+) Farrar, 1969. 224p.
   Family pioneering in Australia (1897).

NONFICTION

BLUNDEN, GODFREY. The Land and People of Australia. (7-9) Lippincott, 1963. 128p. illus. maps

CAIRNS, G. O. The Land and People of Australia. (6+) Macmillan, 1954. 96p. photos; map

AUSTRALIA

CALDWELL, J. C. Let's Visit Australia. (4-6) Day, 1963. 96p. illus. maps

CALDWELL, J. C. AND CALDWELL, E. F. Our Neighbors in Australia and New Zealand. (2-4) Day, 1967. 48p. illus.

CURRIE, GORDON. Let's Travel in Australia. (5+) Childrens, 1968. 88p. illus.

DAY, A. G. The Story of Australia. (5-6) Random House, 1960. 192p. illus.

HARRINGTON, LYN. Australia and New Zealand: Pacific Community. (7+) Nelson, 1969. 224p. illus.

HILLYER, V. M. AND HUEY, E. G. The Orient—Australia and the South Sea Islands. (5+) Childrens, 1966. 127p. illus.

HOYT, OLGA. Aborigines of Australia. (7+) Lothrop, 1969. 128p. illus.

KAULA, E. M. The First Book of Australia. (4-6) Watts, 1960. 68p. illus.

MACINNES, COLIN. Australia and New Zealand. (4+) Time-Life, 1969. 160p. illus. maps

MONYPENNY, KATHLEEN. Young Traveler in Australia. (7-10) Dutton, 1954. 223p.

PARKE, M. B. Getting to Know Australia. (3-5) Coward, 1962. 72p. illus.

PLACE, M. J. Gold Down Under: The Story of the Australian Gold Rush. (7+) Macmillan, 1969. 176p. photos

POWNALL, EVE. Exploring Australia. (7+) Roy, 1961. 74p. illus.

RITCHIE, PAUL. Australia. (6+) Macmillan, 1968. 128p. photos; maps

WILSON, B. K. Australia: Wonderland Down Under. (4-6) Dodd, 1969. 80p. illus.

THE PACIFIC AREA

BIOGRAPHY

Kenny

THOMAS, HENRY. Sister Elizabeth Kenny. (7-10) Putnam, 1958. 128p.

Indonesia

NONFICTION

POOLE, F. K. Indonesia. (4-6) Watts, 1971. 72p. illus.

SMITH, D. C. JR. The Land and People of Indonesia. (7-9) Lippincott, 1968. 128p. illus. maps

TAYLOR, CARL. Getting to Know Indonesia. (3-5) Coward, 1961. 72p. illus.

The Islands (Melanesia, Micronesia, Polynesia)

FICTION

EDMONDS, I. G. Bounty's Boy. (6-10) Bobbs, 1962. 189p. illus.
Adventures aboard the mutinous H.M.S. Bounty.

HILL, W. M. Tales of Maui. (4-6) Dodd, 1964. 74p. illus.
Tales of legendary folk-hero of the Polynesians.

NORDHOFF, C. B. AND HALL, J. N. Men Against the Sea. (7+) Little, 1934. 251p.
Captain Bligh navigates a small boat to safety after losing the Bounty in a mutiny.

NORDHOFF, C. B. AND HALL, J. N. Mutiny on the Bounty. (7+) Little, 1932. 396p.

NONFICTION

BERRY, ERICK AND BEST, HERBERT. The Polynesian Triangle. (7+) Funk, 1969. 128p. illus.
Polynesian life and customs.

NEW ZEALAND

CALDWELL, J. C. Let's Visit Micronesia: Guam (USA), and Trust Territory of the Pacific Islands. (4-6) Day, 1969. 96p. illus.

CALDWELL, J. C. Let's Visit the South Pacific. (4-6) Day, 1963. 96p. illus. maps

CAVANNA, BETTY (ELIZABETH CAVANNA HEADLEY). The First Book of Fiji. (4-6) Watts, 1969. 72p. illus.

GEIS, DARLENE, ed. Let's Travel in the South Seas. (6+) Childrens, 1965. 88p. illus.

HEYERDAHL, THOR. Aku-Aku: The Secret of Easter Island. (7+) Rand McNally, 1958. 384p. illus.

HEYERDAHL, THOR. Kon-Tiki; a special Rand McNally Color Edition for Young People. (4+) Rand McNally, 1960. 165p. illus.

   Modern Norsemen raft across the Pacific.

JOY, C. R. Getting to Know the South Pacific. (3-5) Coward, 1961. 72p. illus.

NEWTON, DOUGLAS. Seafarers of the Pacific. (6+) World, 1964. 128p. illus.

   A portrait of Polynesian civilization.

STERLING PUBLISHING COMPANY, EDITORS OF. Tahiti and the French Islands of the Pacific—in Pictures. (6+) Sterling, 1967. 64p. illus.

New Zealand

FICTION

MANSON, CECIL AND MANSON, CELIA. The Adventures of Johnny Van Bart. (4-6) Roy, 1966. 202p. illus.

   Twelve-year-old boy finds excitement in New Zealand in 1830s.

NONFICTION

CALDWELL, J. C. Let's Visit New Zealand. (4-6) Day, 1963. 96p. illus. maps

CALDWELL, J. C. AND CALDWELL, E. F. Our Neighbors in Australia and New Zealand (2-4) Day, 1967. 48p. illus.

HARRINGTON, LYN. Australia and New Zealand: Pacific Community. (7+) Nelson, 1969. 224p. illus.

KAULA, E. M. The Land and People of New Zealand. (7-9) Lippincott [c 1964]. 160p. illus. maps

LONGLEY, JOHN (pseud. of JOHN DENTON). New Zealand. (2-4) Putnam, 1965. unp. illus.

McGUIRE, EDNA. The Maoris of New Zealand. (5-7) Macmillan, 1968. 192p. photos; map; glossary of Maori words

MACINNES, COLIN. Australia and New Zealand. (4+) Time-Life, 1969. 160p. illus. maps

MARSH, NGAIO. New Zealand. (7+) Macmillan, 1964. 128p. photos; maps

The Philippines

NONFICTION

ARCHER, JULES. Philippines' Fight for Freedom. (7-12) Crowell Collier, 1970. 230p. illus. maps

BROOKS, P. K. The Philippines: Wonderland of Many Cultures. (4-6) Dodd, 1968. 64p. illus.

CALDWELL, J. C. Let's Visit the Philippines. (4-6) Day, 1961. 96p. illus. maps

CALDWELL, J. C. AND CALDWELL, E. F. Our Neighbors in the Philippines. (2-4) Day, 1961. 48p. illus.

GEIS, DARLENE, ed. Let's Travel in the Philippines. (6+) Childrens, 1966. 88p. illus.

POOLE, F. K. The Philippines. (7+) Watts, 1971. 96p. illus. maps

THE PHILIPPINES

ROLAND, ALBERT. The Philippines. (7+) Macmillan, 1967. 144p. photos; maps

TOR, REGINA. Getting to Know the Philippines. (3-5) Coward, 1958. 72p. illus.

VAUGHAN, J. B. The Land and People of the Philippines. (7-9) Lippincott, 1960. 128p. illus. maps

WISE, WILLIAM. Secret Mission to the Philippines: The Story of the "Spyron" and the American-Filipino Guerrillas of World War II. (7-10) Dutton [c 1968]. 160p. illus.

BIOGRAPHY

Magsaysay

GRAY, MARVIN. Island Hero: The Story of Ramón Magsaysay. (4-9) Hawthorn [c 1965]. 188p. illus.

Quezon

GOETTEL, ELINOR. Eagle of The Philippines: President Manuel Quezon. (7+) Messner, 1970. 224p. map

X. THE POLAR REGIONS
General

NONFICTION

BLEEKER, SONIA. The Eskimo, Arctic Hunters and Trappers. (4-6) Morrow, 1959. 160p. illus.

GLINES, C. V. ed. Polar Aviation. (6-12) Watts, 1964. 289p. illus.

NEURATH, MARIE. Wonder World of Snow and Ice. (K-3) Lothrop, 1963. 36p. illus.

OWEN, RUSSELL. Conquest of the North and South Poles. (5-6) Random House, 1952. 192p. illus.

ROBBIN, IRVING. How and Why Wonder Book of Polar Regions. (4-6) Wonder, 1965. 48p. illus.

SPERRY, ARMSTRONG. All About the Arctic and Antarctic. (4-6) Random House, 1957. 160p. illus.

BIOGRAPHY

ANDRIST, R. K. Heroes of Polar Exploration; by the editors of Horizon magazine [and the author]; in consultation with George J. Dufek. (6+) Harper, 1962. 153p. illus.

DOLAN, E. F. JR. Explorers of the Arctic and Antarctic. (7+) Macmillan, 1968. 160p. photos; map

Antarctic

FICTION

STRONG, C. S. We Were There With Byrd at the South Pole. (4-9) Grosset, 1956. 200p. illus.

ANTARCTIC

NONFICTION

BAUM, A. Z. Antarctica: The Worst Place in the World. (7+) Macmillan, 1967. 160p. photos

BERRILL, JACQUELYN. Wonders of the Antarctic. (4-6) Dodd, 1958. 96p. illus.

CHAPMAN, WALKER (pseud. of ROBERT SILVERBERG). Loneliest Continent: The Story of Antarctic Discovery. (7-10) N.Y. Graphic Society, 1964. 279p. illus.

DUFEK, G. J. Through the Frozen Frontier. (7-9) Harcourt, 1959. 192p. illus.

DUKERT, J. M. This Is Antarctica. (5-8) Coward, 1965. 191p. illus.

EULLER, JOHN. Antarctic World. (5-10) Abelard, 1960. 222p. illus. maps

EULLER, JOHN. Our Navy Explores Antarctica. (5-10) Abelard [c 1966]. 127p. illus. maps

FRANCIS, HENRY AND SMITH, PHILIP. Defrosting Antarctic Secrets. (5-8) Coward, 1962. 121p. illus.

FRANK, R. JR. Ice Island: The Story of Antarctica. (7+) Crowell, 1957. 218p. illus.

ICENHOWER, J. B. The First Book of the Antarctic. (4-6) Watts, 1971. 72p. illus.

SCARF, MAGGIE. Antarctica: Exploring the Frozen Continent. (3-6) Random House, 1970. 82p. illus. maps

BIOGRAPHY

Amundsen

DE LEEUW, CATEAU. Roald Amundsen. (3-6) Garrard, 1965. 96p. illus.

KUGELMASS, J. A. Roald Amundsen: A Saga of the Polar Seas. (7+) Messner, 1955. 192p.

VAETH, J. G. To the Ends of the Earth: The Explorations of Roald Amundsen. (7+) Harper, 1962. 219p. illus. maps

Byrd

DE LEEUW, A. L. Richard E. Byrd: Adventurer to the Poles. (2-5) Garrard, 1963. 80p. illus.

GLADYCH, MICHAEL. Admiral Byrd of Antarctica. (6+) Messner, 1960. 192p.

OLDS, H. D. Richard E. Byrd. (2-4) Putnam [c 1969]. 62p. illus.

VAN RIPER, GUERNSEY. Richard Byrd: Boy Who Braved the Unknown. (3-7) Bobbs, 1958. 190p. illus.

Fuchs

LARSEN, EGON (pseud. of EGON LEHRBURGER). Sir Vivian Fuchs. (7+) Roy, 1960. 110p. illus.
  First man across Antarctica.

Scott

HOLWOOD, WILL (pseud. of WILLIAM HOLLINGSWORTH WOOD). True Story of Captain Scott at the South Pole. (5+) Childrens, 1964. 141p. illus.

PURTON, R. W. Captain Scott. (5+) McGraw, 1970. 56p. illus.

Shackleton

BIXBY, WILLIAM. The Impossible Journey of Sir Ernest Shackleton. (7+) Little, 1960. 207p.
  English explorer fights for survival in Antarctica in early 1900s.

BROWN, MICHAEL. Shackleton's Epic Voyage. (3-7) Coward, 1969. 40p. illus.

Wilkes

SILVERBERG, ROBERT. Stormy Voyager: The Story of Charles Wilkes. (7-9) Lippincott, 1968. 192p. illus.
  Basis of US claims on Antarctica laid by 1838 naval expedition which circumnavigated the globe.

Arctic

NONFICTION

ANDERSON, W. R. First Under the North Pole: The Voyage of the Nautilus. (4-6) World, 1959. 64p. illus.

BERRILL, JACQUELYN. Wonders of the Arctic. (4-6) Dodd, 1959. 94p. illus.

EULLER, JOHN. Arctic World. (5-10) Abelard, 1958. 144p. illus. maps

EULLER, JOHN. Ice, Ships, and Men. (5-10) Abelard, 1964. 208p. illus. maps
   The story of Arctic exploration.

GOETZ, DELIA. Arctic Tundra. (4-6) Morrow, 1958. 64p. illus.

HALL, D. W. (b. 1841). Arctic Rovings; or, The Adventures of a New Bedford Boy on Sea and Land. (7+) Scott, 1968. 144p. illus.

HOGG, GARRY. Airship Over the Pole: The Story of the Italia. (7-12) Abelard, 1969. 160p. illus.

LIVERSIDGE, DOUGLAS. The First Book of the Arctic. (4-6) Watts, 1967. 72p. illus.

LIVERSIDGE, DOUGLAS. First Book of Arctic Exploration. (4-6) Watts, 1970. 96p. illus.

OGLE, ED. Getting to Know the Arctic. (3-5) Coward, 1961. 72p. illus.

OSMOND, EDWARD. People of the Arctic. (4-9) Transatlantic, 1964. 45p. illus.

SMITH, F. C. The World of the Arctic. (7-9) Lippincott, 1960. 128p. illus. maps

STEFANSSON, EVELYN. Here Is the Far North. (7+) Scribner, 1957. 160p. illus.
   Information on Iceland, Greenland, and the Soviet sector of the New North.

SUTTON, ANN AND SUTTON, MYRON. Journey Into Ice: John Franklin and the Northwest Passage. (6+) Rand McNally, 1965. 272p. illus.
> Sailing with Lord Nelson, exploring the Arctic and circumnavigating Australia.

TOLBOOM, WANDA. People of the Snow: Eskimos of Arctic Canada. (6-8) Coward, 1956. 96p. illus. maps

BIOGRAPHY

Bernier

FAIRLEY, T. C. AND ISRAEL, C. E. True North: Story of Captain Joseph Bernier. (5-9) St. Martin's, 1957. 160p. illus.
> Explorations in the Arctic.

Hearne

SYME, RONALD. On Foot to the Arctic: The Story of Samuel Hearne. (7-9) Morrow, 1959. 192p. illus.

Henson

HENSON, M. A. Black Explorer at the North Pole: An Autobiographical Report by the Negro Who Conquered the Top of the World With Admiral Robert E. Peary. (7+) Walker, 1969. 224p. illus.

RIPLEY, S. N. Matthew Henson: Arctic Hero. (4-6) Houghton, 1966. 192p. illus.

Nansen

BERRY, ERICK. Fridtjof Nansen. (3-6) Garrard, 1969. 96p. illus.

DENZEL, J. F. Adventure North: The Story of Fridtjof Nansen. (5-10) Abelard, 1968. 176p. illus.

NOEL-BAKER, F. E. Fridtjof Nansen: Arctic Explorer. (5-9) Putnam, 1958. 128p. illus.

ARCTIC

Peary

ANGELL, P. K. To the Top of the World: the Story of Peary and Henson. (7+) Rand McNally, 1964. 288p. illus. maps

BERRY, ERICK. Robert E. Peary: North Pole Conqueror. (2-5) Garrard, 1963. 80p. illus.

CLARK, ELECTA. Robert Peary: Boy of the North Pole. (3-7) Bobbs, 1963. 200p. illus.

LORD, WALTER. Peary to the Pole. (5+) Harper, 1963. 141p. illus.

SIMON, TONY. North Pole: The Story of Robert E. Peary. (7-9) Doubleday, 1961. 143p. illus.

STAFFORD, M. P. Discoverer of the North Pole, the Story of Robert E. Peary. (7-9) Morrow, 1959. 224p. illus.

Stefansson

BERRY, ERICK. Mister Arctic: An Account of Vilhjalmur Stefansson. (8-12) McKay, 1966. 192p. illus.

MYERS, HORTENSE AND BURNETT, RUTH. Vilhjalmur Stefansson: Young Arctic Explorer. (3-7) Bobbs, 1966. 200p. illus.

XI. HISTORY OF MANKIND: POLITICAL, CULTURAL, AND TECHNOLOGICAL

General

NONFICTION

Ansley, Delight. The Good Ways. (7+) Crowell, 1959. 214p. illus.
> Origin and history of the world's great religions.

Boardman, F. W. History and Historians. (7-9) Walck, 1965. 144p.

Boesch, M. J. The World of Rice. (5-9) Dutton [1967]. 160p. illus.
> Effects of rice on world civilization.

Caldwell, J. C. Communism in Our World. (7+) rev. ed. Day, 1968. 128p. illus. maps

Caldwell, W. E. and Merrill, E. H. The New Popular History of the World; The Story of Mankind from Earliest Times to the Present Day. (7+) Greystone [1964]. 2v (912p.) illus. maps

Cheney, L. J. History of the Western World. (7+) Pitman, 1959. 335p. illus. maps

De Witt, W. A. History's Hundred Greatest Events. (7+) Grosset, 1970. 149p. illus.

Duché, Jean. The Great Trade Routes. (5+) McGraw, 1969. 128p. illus.

Edmonds, I. G. Revolts and Revolutions. Hawthorn [1969]. 164p. illus.
> From Oliver Cromwell to Fidel Castro.

Elting, Mary and Folsom, Franklin. Answer Book of History. (4-6) Grosset, 1966. 154p. illus.

GENERAL

ELTING, MARY AND FOLSOM, FRANKLIN. Flags of All Nations and the People Who Live Under Them. (4+) Grosset, 1970. 157p. illus.

EVANS, E. K. All About Us. (4-7) Western, 1947, 95p. illus.
History of man, stressing commonality of origin and importance of all peoples.

FOSTER, GENEVIEVE. Abraham Lincoln's World. (5-11) Scribner, 1944. 360p. illus.
World events during Lincoln's lifetime.

FOSTER, GENEVIEVE. Augustus Caesar's World. (5-11) Scribner, 1949. 352p. illus.
World events during the Emperor's lifetime.

FOSTER, GENEVIEVE. Birthdays of Freedom, II. (7+) Scribner, 1957. 64p. charts; maps
Great events in freedom from the fall of Rome to 1776.

FOSTER, GENEVIEVE. George Washington's World. (7+) Scribner, 1941. 360p. illus.
World events during the American Revolution.

FOSTER, GENEVIEVE. The World of Captain John Smith. (5-11) Scribner, 1959. 416p. illus.
World events in the lifetime of Captain John Smith.

FOSTER, GENEVIEVE. Year of Columbus, 1492. (4+) Scribner, 1969. 64p. illus.

FOSTER, GENEVIEVE. Year of the Pilgrims, 1620. (7+) Scribner, 1969. 64p. illus.

GELINAS, P. J. AND SCHARFF, ROBERT. History of the World for Young Readers. (4-8) Grosset, 1965. 380p. illus. maps

HARTMAN, GERTRUDE. The World We Live In and How It Came to Be. (6+) Macmillan, 1939. 366p. illus.

HEAPS, W. A. Assassination: A Special Kind of Murder. (6+) Meredith, 1969. 218p.

JOY, C. R. Race Between Food and People: The Challenge of a Hungry World. (6-8) Coward [c 1961]. 121p. illus.

HISTORY OF MANKIND

Jupo, F. J. Walls, Gates, and Avenues: The Story of the Town. (3-6) Prentice-Hall, 1964. 64p. illus.

Leaf, Munro. History Can Be Fun. (K-3) Lippincott, 1950. 64p. illus.

Linton, Ralph and Linton, A. S. B. H. Man's Way: From Cave to Skyscraper. (7-9) Harper, 1947. 185p. illus.

Mellersh, H. E. Boys' Book of the Wonders of Man and His Achievements. (6-10) Roy, 1964. 144p.

Meltzer, Milton. Slavery: From the Rise of Western Civilization to the Renaissance. (7+) Cowles, 1971. 255p. illus. maps

Montgomery, E. R. Toward Democracy: Great Documents of History. (6+) Washburn [1967]. 243p.

Morgan, Edmund. So What About History? (7+) Atheneum, 1969. 95p.
   The reasons for studying history.

Morris, R. W. Town Life Through the Ages. (5-8) Allen [1952]. 40p. illus.

Morris, R. W. Transport, Trade, and Travel Through the Ages. (5-8) Allen [1955]. 32p.

Paradis, A. A. Trade: The World's Lifeblood. (4-6) Messner, 1969. 94p. illus.

Popescu, Julian and others. Rivers of the World, v 1: Danube, Amazon, Niger, Ganges. (4-6) Walck, 1962. 128p. illus. maps

Roesch, R. F. World's Fairs: Yesterday, Today, Tomorrow. (4-6) Day, 1967. 96p. illus.

Rogers, W. G. Mightier Than the Sword; Cartoon, Caricature, Social Comment. (7+) Harcourt, 1969. 287p. illus.
   Social and political cartooning through the years.

GENERAL

SAVAGE, KATHARINE. The Story of Marxism and Communism. (7+) Walck, 1969. 224p. illus.

SAVAGE, KATHARINE. Story of World Religions. (7+) Walck, 1967. 288p. photos; maps

SEVERN, BILL. Free But Not Equal: How Women Won the Right to Vote. (7+) Messner, 1967. 192p. photos

SILVERBERG, ROBERT. The Seven Wonders of the Ancient World. (6+) Crowell Collier, 1970. 120p. illus. maps

SULLIVAN, GEORGE. Seven Wonders of the Modern World. (7-9) Putnam, 1968. 128p. illus.

TAYLOR, DUNCAN AND COCHRANE, LOUISE. The World of Nations. (4+) Whitman, 1963. 104p. illus.
Information on world history, geography, and customs.

WEISGARD, LEONARD. Beginnings of Cities. (5-8) Coward, 1968. 64p. illus.

WHITTAM, GEOFFREY AND OTHERS. Rivers of the World, v2: Rhine, Murray, Nile, St. Lawrence. (4-6) Walck, 1963. 132p. illus.

WOLCOTT, LEONARD AND WOLCOTT, CAROLYN. Religions Around the World. (6+) Abingdon, 1967. 208p. illus.

BIOGRAPHY

ARCHER, JULES. Dictators. (7+) Hawthorn, 1967. 179p. illus.

BARTLETT, R. M. They Stand Invincible; the Men Who Are Reshaping Our World. (7+) Crowell, 1959. 261p.

BENSON, SALLY. Stories of the Gods and Heroes. (3-7) Dial, 1940. 256p. illus.

BERRY, ERICK AND BEST, HERBERT. Men Who Changed the Map. (7+) Funk, 1968. 170p. maps
World history from A.D. 400 to 1914.

HISTORY OF MANKIND

BOYD, MILDRED. Rulers in Petticoats. (7+) Criterion, 1967. 224p. illus.
> Accounts of eighteen sovereigns from Hatshepsut to Elizabeth II.

COFFMAN, R. P. AND GOODMAN, N. G. Famous Kings and Queens for Young People. (7+) Dodd, 1945. 136p. illus.

COTTLER, JOSEPH AND JAFFE, HAYM. Heroes of Civilization. (7+) Little, 1969. 408p.
> Short biographies of many nations' heroes in exploration, science, invention, and medicine.

COTTLER, JOSEPH AND JAFFE, HAYM. More Heroes of Civilization. (5-8) Little, 1969. 320p.
> Short biographies emphasizing scientific and humanitarian figures of all nations.

DONOVAN, F. R. Famous Twentieth Century Leaders. (7+) Dodd, 1964. 160p. illus.

FARJEON, ELEANOR AND MAYNE, WILLIAM, eds. A Cavalcade of Kings. (4-6) Walck, 1965. 238p. illus.

FARJEON, ELEANOR AND MAYNE, WILLIAM, eds. A Cavalcade of Queens. (4-6) Walck, 1965. 238p. illus.

FARMER, L. H. A Book of Famous Queens. (7+) Crowell, 1964. 246p.

FRIEDMAN, ROSE. Freedom Builders: Great Teachers from Socrates to John Dewey. (7+) Little, 1968. 271p.

HILL, F. E. Famous Historians. (7+) Dodd, 1966. 160p. illus.

KENWORTHY, LEONARD. Twelve Citizens of the World. (7+) Doubleday, 1953. 286p. illus.
> Biographies of famous people.

KENWORTHY, LEONARD AND FERRARI, ERMA. Leaders of New Nations. (7+) Doubleday, 1968. 384p. illus.
> Sixteen men lead their nations to independence after World War II.

LARSEN, EGON (pseud. of EGON LEHRBURGER). Men Who Fought for Freedom. (7+) Roy, 1958. 191p. illus.

COMMUNICATION

LOEPER, J. J. Men of Ideas. (5+) Atheneum, 1970. 120p. illus.
   Brief biographies and discussion of philosophers from Socrates to Santayana.

MCNEER, MAY. Armed With Courage. (4+) Abingdon, 1957. 112p.

MAYNE, WILLIAM, ed. William Mayne's Book of Heroes; Stories and Poems. (2-6) Dutton [c 1967]. 230p. illus.
   Stories and poems of heroes of all nations.

MEYER, E. P. Champions of the Four Freedoms. (7+) Little, 1966. 301p. illus.
   People and institutions who have upheld basic human freedoms.

QUADFLIEG, JOSEF. The Saints and Your Name. (5-6) Pantheon, 1958. 160p. illus.

SUFRIN, MARK. Brave Men: Twelve Portraits of Courage. (6+) Platt, 1967. 306p. illus.

SUTCLIFF, ROSEMARY. Heroes and History. (4-9) Putnam, 1966. 176p. illus.

WEBB, R. N. Leaders of Our Time: v3. (7+) Watts, 1966. 160p. illus.
   Brief biographies of American and world leaders.

WEBB, R. N. Leaders of Our Time: v4. (7+) Watts, 1969. 128p. illus.

Communication

NONFICTION

ADLER, IRVING AND ADLER, RUTH. Communication. (3-5) Day, 1967. 48p. illus.

BATCHELOR, J. F. Communication: From Cave Writing to Television. (4-6) Harcourt, 1953. 116p. illus.

BROWN, ANTONY. Great Ideas in Communications. (6+) White, 1969. 174p.

BUEHR, WALTER. Sending the Word: The Story of Communications. (4-6) Putnam, 1959. 96p. illus.

FLOHERTY, J. J. Men Against Distance: The Story of Communications. (7-9) Lippincott, 1954. 160p. illus.

FOSTER, G. A. Communication: From Primitive Tom-Toms to Telstar. (7+) Criterion, 1965. illus.

HARTMAN, GERTRUDE. Machines and the Men Who Made the World of Industry. (6+) Macmillan, 1939. 288p. illus. photos

HOSKEN, F. P. The Language of Cities. (7+) Macmillan, 1968. 128p.

MINER, IRENE. True Book of Communication. (K-5) Childrens, 1961. 48p. illus.

NEAL, H. E. Communication: From Stone Age to Space Age. (6+) Messner, 1960. 192p. illus.

OSMOND, EDWARD. From Drumbeat to Tickertape. (5-10) Hutchinson, 1960. 127p. illus.

ROGERS, FRANCES AND BEARD, ALICE. Heels, Wheels and Wire: The Story of Messages and Signals. (7-9) Lippincott, 1967. 265p. illus.

WISE, WILLIAM. From Scrolls to Satellites. (2-4) Parents, 1970. 64p. illus.

Exploration and Adventure

NONFICTION

ALTER, R. E. Who Goes Next: True Stories of Strange Escapes. (5-9) Putnam, 1966. 192p. illus.

BARKER, E. J. AND HAMMER, C. L. Seeking New Lands. (2-6) Verry, 1962. 80p. illus.

EXPLORATION AND ADVENTURE

BERNA, PAUL. They Didn't Come Back; tr: by John Buchanan-Brown. (7+) Pantheon, 1969.
    Stories of unsuccessful explorations.

BRINDZE, RUTH. All About Sailing the Seven Seas. (4-6) Random House, 1962. 160p. illus.

BRINDZE, RUTH. All About Undersea Exploration. (5-9) Random House, 1960. 160p. illus.

CAMPBELL, A. B. Great Moments at Sea. (5-10) Roy, 1957. 128p. illus.

CLARK, R. W. Great Moments in Escaping. (7+) Roy, 1959. 126p. illus.

CLARK, R. W. Great Moments in Mountaineering. (7+) Roy [1956]. 128p. illus.

CLARK, R. W. Great Moments in Rescue Work. (7+) Roy, 1959. 128p. illus.

COGGINS, JACK. By Star and Compass: The Story of Navigation. (5+) Dodd, 1967. 96p. illus.

DAUGHERTY, C. M. Searchers of the Sea: Pioneers in Oceanography. (7+) Viking, 1961. 121p. illus.

EVANS, I. O. Exploring the Earth. (7+) Roy [1961]. 224p. illus.

HEATTER, BASIL. Against Odds. (7+) Farrar, 1970. 160p. photos
    Tales of courage in a world-wide setting.

HEWES, A. D. Spice Ho! A Story of Discovery. (3-7) 2d. ed. enl. [Knopf, 1947.] 207p. illus.
    Tales of early explorations.

HILLARY, EDMUND, ed. Challenge of the Unknown. (7+) Dutton, 1958. 221p. illus.
    Twelve first-hand accounts of exploration.

HOPKINS, KENNETH. Great Moments in Exploration. (7+) Roy, 1957. 128p. illus.

HISTORY OF MANKIND

ICENHOWER, J. B. Man Against the Unknown. (7-9) Winston, 1957. 117p. illus.

KNIGHT, FRANK. They Told Mister Hakluyt. (7+) St. Martin's [1964]. 150p. illus.

LARSEN, EGON (pseud. of EGON LEHRBURGER). Men Under the Sea. (7+) Roy [1956]. 223p. illus.

LAWRENCE, M. W. Rockets' Red Glare: Challenge of Outer Space. (6-8) Coward, 1960. 121p. illus.

McFALL, CHRISTIE. Maps Mean Adventure. (7+) Dodd [1961]. 128p. illus.

MACMILLAN, NORMAN. Great Flights and Air Adventures: From Balloons to Spacecraft. (7+) St. Martin's, 1965. 236p.

MANLEY, SEON AND LEWIS, GOGO, eds. Teen-Age Treasury of Imagination and Discovery. (6-10) Funk, 1962. 332p.

MASON, H. M. Famous Firsts in Exploration. (5+) Putnam, 1967. 72p. illus.

MERRETT, JOHN. Famous Voyages in Small Boats. (6-10) Criterion, 1957. 188p. illus.

MOORE, P. A. Exploring the World. (4-6) Watts, 1968. 96p. illus.

PINNEY, ROY. Quest for the Unknown: Explorers of Today. (7-9) Lippincott, 1965. 128p. photos
> Expeditions of mountain climbers, spelunkers, and other adventurers.

SCOGGIN, MARGARET, ed. Escapes and Rescues. (7+) Knopf, 1960. 256p.

STAMBLER, IRWIN. Wonders of Underwater Exploration. (5+) Putnam, 1962. 128p. illus.

WRIGHT, HELEN AND RAPPORT, S. B. eds. Great Undersea Adventures. (7+) Harper, 1966. 381p.

BIOGRAPHY

APPELL, CLAUDE. Great Adventurers. (4-6) Follett, 1968. 72p. illus.
> From Alexander the Great to modern astronauts.

BAILEY, BERNARDINE. Famous Modern Explorers. (7+) Dodd, 1963. 160p. illus.

BARCLAY, ISABEL. Worlds Without End. (7+) Doubleday, 1956. 352p. maps
> Stories of explorers.

CLARK, L. F. Explorers' Digest. (7+) Houghton [1955]. 256p. illus.
> Six stories of modern explorers.

CLARK, R. W. Explorers of the World. (7+) Doubleday. 256p. illus.

COFFMAN, R. P. AND GOODMAN, N. G. Famous Explorers for Young People. (7+) Dodd, 1942. 166p. illus.

DUGAN, JAMES. Undersea Explorer: The Story of Captain Cousteau. (5+) Harper, 1957. 143p. illus.

DUVOISIN, ROGER. They Put Out to Sea. (5-6) Knopf, 1944. 192p. illus.
> Early traders and explorers from the Phoenicians to Magellan.

HOBLEY, L. F. Early Explorers to A.D. 1500. (7+) Roy [1956]. 76p. illus.

HOFF, RHODA AND DE TERRA, HELMUT. They Explored. (7-9) Walck, 1959. 128p. maps

JACOBS, J. K. Against All Odds. (7+) Crowell Collier [1967]. 160p. photos
> Ten historical figures who made dramatic escapes to freedom.

KNIGHT, FRANK (FRANCIS EDGAR KNIGHT). Stories of Famous Explorers by Sea. (4-7) Oliver, 1964. 160p. illus.

RITTENHOUSE, MIGNON. Seven Women Explorers. (7-9) Lippincott, 1964. 160p.

Geography and Maps

NONFICTION

BACON, PHILLIP, ed. The Children's Picture Atlas of the World. (4-8) rev. ed. Golden, 1966. 544p. illus.

CARLISLE, NORMAN AND CARLISLE, MADELYN. True Book of Maps. (2-4) Childrens, 1969. 48p. illus.

DUCHÉ, JEAN. The Great Trade Routes. (5+) McGraw, 1969. 128p. illus.

DUVOISIN, ROGER. They Put Out to Sea. (5-6) Knopf, 1944. 192p. illus.
> Story of the map.

EPSTEIN, SAM AND EPSTEIN, BERYL. The First Book of Maps and Globes. (4-6) Watts, 1959. 72p. illus.

MCFALL, CHRISTIE. Maps Mean Adventure. (7+) Dodd [1961]. 128p.

MARSH, SUSAN. All About Maps and Mapmaking. (5-9) Random House [1963]. 143p. illus.

MATKIN, R. B. Your Book of Maps and Map Reading. (7+) Faber, 1970. 96p. illus. maps

MOORE, P. A. AND BRINTON, HENRY. Exploring Maps. (4-6) Hawthorn [1967]. 95p. illus.

NEAL, H. E. Of Maps and Men. (7+) Funk, 1970. 179p. illus.

POPESCU, JULIAN AND OTHERS. Rivers of the World, v 1: Danube, Amazon, Niger, Ganges. (4-6) Walck, 1962. 128p. illus. maps

TANNENBAUM, BEULAH AND STILLMAN, MYRA. Understanding Maps; Charting the Land, Sea and Sky. (5+) McGraw, 1969. 159p. illus.

WHITTAM, GEOFFREY, AND OTHERS. Rivers of the World, v2: Rhine, Murray, Nile, St. Lawrence. (4-6) Walck, 1963. 132p. illus.

International Organizations

NONFICTION

BECKEL, GRAHAM AND LEE, FELICE. Workshops for the World: The United Nations Family of Agencies. (7+) Abelard, 1962. 288p. illus.

BREETVELD, JIM. Getting to Know United Nations Crusaders: How UNICEF Saves Children. (3-5) Coward, 1970. 72p. illus.

COATSWORTH, ELIZABETH. The Lucky Ones. (4-6) Macmillan, 1968. 96p. illus.
> Refugee children from five different cultures ranging from Chinese to Watusi are helped by UN.

COCHRANE, JOANNA. Let's Go to the United Nations Headquarters. (4-6) Putnam, 1958. 48p. illus.

COMAY, JOAN. The U.N. in Action. (7+) Macmillan, 1965. 160p. photos; maps

DEMING, RICHARD. Heroes of the International Red Cross. (5+) Meredith, 1969. 196p. illus.

EPSTEIN, BERYL AND EPSTEIN, SAM. Story of the International Red Cross. (7+) Nelson [1963]. 183p. illus.

FEHRENBACH, T. R. The United Nations in War and Peace. (7+) Random House, 1968. 192p. illus. cartoons; maps

FISHER, D. C. Fair World for All. (5+) McGraw, 1952. 159p. illus.
> Meaning of the Declaration of Human Rights.

FISHER, LOIS. You and the United Nations. (5-10) Childrens, 1958. 64p. illus.

GALT, TOM. How the United Nations Works. (5+) Crowell, 1965. 246p. illus.

GRIFFIN, ELLA. Getting to Know UNESCO: How U.N. Crusaders Fight Ignorance. (3-5) Coward, 1962. 72p. illus.

HAVERSTOCK, NATHAN. Organization of American States: The Challenge of the Americas. (6-8) Coward, 1966. 121p. illus.

JOYCE, J. A. Decade of Development: The Challenge of the Underdeveloped Nations. (6-8) Coward, 1966. 121p. illus.

KELEN, EMERY (IMRE KELEN). Peace Is an Adventure: The Men and Women of the U.N. in Action Around the World. (5+) Meredith [1967]. 87p.

KELEN, EMERY (IMRE KELEN). Stamps Tell the Story of the United Nations. (5+) Meredith, 1968. 96p. photos

LEAF, MUNRO. Three Promises to You. (K-6) Lippincott, 1957. 48p. illus.
  Aims of the UN.

PAULI, H. E. Toward Peace: The Nobel Prizes and the Struggle for Peace. (6+) Washburn [c 1969]. 119p.

PIERSON, SHERLEIGH. What Does a U.N. Soldier Do? (4-6) Dodd, 1964. 64p. illus.

ROTHKOPF, CAROL. The Red Cross. (4-6) Watts, 1971. 72p. illus.

ROWE, JEANNE. United Nations Workers: Their Jobs, Their Goals, Their Triumphs. (4-6) Watts, 1970. 72p. illus.

SAVAGE, KATHARINE. Story of the United Nations. (7+) Walck, 1970. 224p. photos; maps

SCHLINING, PAULA. United Nations and What It Does. (4-6) Lothrop, 1961. 61p. illus.

SHIPPEN, K. B. Pool of Knowledge: How the United Nations Share Their Skills. (7+) Harper, 1965. 99p.

SMITH, R. L. Getting to Know the World Health Organization. (3-5) Coward, 1963. 72p. illus.

SPEISER, JEAN. UNICEF and the World. (6-9) Day, 1965. 96p. illus. map

INTERNATIONAL ORGANIZATIONS

Sterling, Dorothy. United Nations, N.Y. (7+) Doubleday [c 1961]. 80p. illus.

Yates, Elizabeth. Rainbow Round the World: A Story of UNICEF. (7+) Bobbs [1954]. 174p.
Work done by the UN is extolled.

BIOGRAPHY

Meyer, E. P. Champions of Peace: Winners of the Nobel Peace Prize. (7+) Little, 1959. 216p. illus.

Wintterle, John and Cramer, R. S. Portraits of Nobel Laureates in Peace. (7+) Abelard, 1971. 256p. illus.

Prehistory

FICTION

Behn, Harry. The Faraway Lurs. (7-11) World, 1963. 192p. illus.
A Stone Age tribe clashes with a Bronze Age culture.

Osborne, C. G. The First Bow and Arrow. (4-6) Follett, 1951. 88p. illus.

Osborne, C. G. The First Lake Dwellers. (4-6) Follett, 1956. 128p. illus.

Osborne, C. G. The First Wheel. (4-6) Follett, 1959. 128p. illus.

NONFICTION

Anthropology: The Story of Early Man

Ames, Gerald and Wyler, Rose. First People in the World. (3-5) Harper, 1958. 48p. illus.

Baldwin, G. C. The World of Prehistory. (5+) Putnam, 1963. 192p. illus.

Barker, E. J. and Hammer, C. L. People of Long Ago. (2-6) Verry, 1962. 80p. illus.

HISTORY OF MANKIND

BARR, DONALD. How and Why Wonder Book of Primitive Man. (4-6) Grosset [1961]. 47p. illus.

BATEMAN, W. L. How Man Began. (4-6) Benefic [1966]. 96p.

BAUMANN, HANS. The Caves of the Great Hunters. (5+) Pantheon, 1962. 184p. illus. maps

BURRELL, R. E. C. Early Days of Man. (5+) McGraw, 1968. 169p. illus. maps

DICKINSON, ALICE. The First Book of Stone Age Man. (4-6) Watts, 1962. 86p. illus.

EDEL, MAY. Story of Our Ancestors. (7-10) Little, 1955. 199p. illus.

EPSTEIN, SAM AND EPSTEIN, BERYL. All About Prehistoric Cave Men. (5-9) Random House, 1959. 160p. illus.

FOLSOM, FRANKLIN. Science and the Secret of Man's Past. (7+) Harvey, 1966. 192p. illus.

FRIEDMAN, ESTELLE. Man in the Making. (5-9) Putnam, 1960. 192p. illus.

GOLDMAN, HANNAH AND GOLDMAN, IRVING. First Men: The Story of Human Beginnings. (7+) Abelard [1955]. 180p. illus.

GREGOR, A. S. Adventure of Man. (7+) Macmillan, 1966. 192p. illus.

HOWELL, F. C. Early Man. (4+) Time-Life, 1965. 200p. illus.

JACOBSON, DANIEL. A Story of Man. (4-8) Parents, 1963. 56p. illus.

KRAMER, B. L. About Cave Men of the Old Stone Age. (2-6) Melmont, 1955. unp. illus.

LISITZKY, G. H. Four Ways of Being Human. (7+) Viking, 1956. 303p. illus.

PREHISTORY

Lucas, J. M. Man's First Million Years. (7-11) Harcourt, 1941. 277p. illus.

Marcus, R. B. Prehistoric Cave Paintings. (7+) Watts, 1968. 88p. illus.

Martin, Christopher (pseud. of Edwin Palmer Hoyt). Wonders of Prehistoric Man. (5-9) Putnam, 1964. 128p. illus.

May, Julian. First Men. (1-4) Holiday, 1968. 40p. illus.

Mead, Margaret. People and Places. (7+) World, 1959. 318p. illus. maps

Morrow, S. S. There Was a Time: The Story of Evolution. (K-3) Dutton [1965]. 40p. illus.

Napier, John. The Origins of Man. (3-7) McGraw, 1969. 32p. illus.

Neurath, Marie. They Lived Like This in the Old Stone Age. (4-6) Watts, 1971. 32p. illus.

Perkins, C. M. The Shattered Skull: A Safari to Man's Past. (4-6) Atheneum, 1965. 59p. illus.
   Investigations into the origins of man.

Pfeiffer, J. E. The Search for Early Man; by [the author] and the editors of Horizon magazine; consultant: Carleton S. Coon. (6+) American Heritage, 1963. 153p. illus.

Powers, R. M. Cave Dwellers: In the Old Stone Age. (5-8) Coward, 1963. 64p. illus.

Quennell, Marjorie and Quennell, C. H. Everyday Life in Prehistoric Times. (6-10) Putnam, 1960. 206p. illus.

Scheele, W. E. Cave Hunters. (4-6) World, 1959. 63p. illus.

Scheele, W. E. Mound Builders. (4-6) World, 1960. 69p. illus.

Scheele, W. E. Prehistoric Man and the Primates. (7+) World, 1957. 121p. illus.

STILWELL, HART. Looking at Man's Past. (3-7) Steck, 1965. 48p. illus.

VLAHOS, OLIVIA. Human Beginnings. (7+) Viking, 1966. 255p. illus.

WEISGARD, LEONARD. First Farmers: In the Stone Age. (5-8) Coward, 1966. 64p. illus.

WHITE, A. T. First Men in the World. (7-9) Random House, 1953. 192p. illus.

Archaeology: The Search for Yesterday

BRAIDWOOD, R. J. Archaeologists and What They Do. (7+) Watts, 1960. 256p.

BRENNAN, L. A. The Buried Treasure of Archaeology. (7+) Random House, 1964. 256p. illus.

BURLAND, C. A. Adventuring in Archaeology. (4-8) Warne, 1963. 64p. illus. photos

CLEATOR, P. E. Exploring the World of Archaeology. (6+) Odhams, 1967. 141p. maps

COHEN, DANIEL. Secrets from Ancient Graves. (7+) Dodd, 1968. 158p. illus.

COTTRELL, LEONARD. Digs and Diggers. (7-10) World [1964]. 288p. illus.
  A comprehensive review of the great archaeological discoveries.

ELTING, MARY AND FOLSOM, FRANKLIN. The Story of Archaeology in the Americas. (4+) Harvey, 1960. 160p. illus.

FLETCHER, H. J. Adventures in Archaeology. (5-9) Bobbs, 1962. 216p. illus.

FREEMAN, M. B. Finding Out About the Past. (4-8) Random House, 1967. 96p. illus.

FRIEDMAN, ESTELLE. Digging Into Yesterday. (5-8) Putnam, 1958. 160p. illus.

SCIENCE AND TECHNOLOGY

GARNETT, HENRY. Treasures of Yesterday. (5-8) Doubleday, 1965. 256p. illus.

HALL, JENNIE. Buried Cities. (5+) Macmillan, 1964. 128p. illus.

HUME, I. N. Great Moments in Archaeology. (7+) Roy [1958]. 127p. illus.

KUBIE, N. B. The First Book of Archaeology. (4-6) Watts, 1957. 65p. illus.

PALMER, GEOFFREY AND LLOYD, NOEL. Quest for Prehistory. (5-7) Day, 1966. 128p. illus.

SAMACHSON, DOROTHY AND SAMACHSON, JOSEPH. Good Digging: The Story of Archaeology. (6-9) Rand McNally, 1960. 224p. illus. maps

SHIPPEN, K. B. Portals to the Past: The Story of Archaeology (7+) Viking, 1963. 255p. illus.

WHITE, A. T. All About Archaeology. (5-9) Random House, 1959. 160p. illus.

WHITE, A. T. Lost Worlds: The Romance of Archaeology. (7+) Random House [1941]. 316p. illus.

BIOGRAPHY

CLARK, R. W. Sir Mortimer Wheeler. (7+) Roy, 1960. 106p. illus.
> Archaeologist uncovers history.

DAUGHERTY, C. M. The Great Archaeologists. (7+) Crowell, 1962. 140p. illus.

MULVEY, M. W. Digging Up Adam: The Story of L.S.B. Leakey. (7+) McKay, 1969. 224p. photos
> Anthropologist studies early man.

Science and Technology
See also Communication, Transportation.

NONFICTION

ADLER, IRVING. Fire in Your Life. (5-9) Day, 1955. 128p. illus.
> Importance of fire in civilization.

ASIMOV, ISAAC. Breakthroughs in Science. (5+) Houghton, 1960. 224p. illus.

ASIMOV, ISAAC. Great Ideas of Science. (7+) Houghton, 1969. 140p. illus.

ASIMOV, ISAAC. Words of Science and the History Behind Them. (6-12) Houghton [1959]. 266p. illus.

BERGER, MELVIN. Triumphs of Modern Science. (7+) McGraw, 1964. 189p. illus.

BURNS, W. A. Man and His Tools. (5+) McGraw, 1956. 158p. illus.

COGGINS, JACK. By Star and Compass: The Story of Navigation. (5+) Dodd, 1967. 96p. illus.

COOKE, D. C. Inventions That Made History. (5+) Putnam, 1969. 72p. illus.

ESTERER, A. K. Tools: Shapers of Civilization. (7+) Messner, 1966. 192p. illus.

FOLSOM, FRANKLIN. Science and the Secret of Man's Past. (7+) Harvey, 1966. 192p. illus.

GOLDSTEIN, K. K. The World of Tomorrow. (5+) McGraw, 1969. 128p. illus.
> Projections of effects of today's technology on tomorrow's history.

GREGOR, A. S. Short History of Science. (5-9) Macmillan, 1963. 240p. illus.

HALACY, D. S. Science and Serendipity; Great Discoveries by Accident. (7+) Macrae Smith, 1967. 155p. illus.

HAMILTON, RUSSEL. Science, Science, Science. (7+) Watts [1960]. 210p. illus.
> An anthology of scientific achievement from Archimedes to Einstein.

HOYT, E. P. A Short History of Science, v 1: Ancient Science. (7+) Day, 1965. 256p. illus.

SCIENCE AND TECHNOLOGY

Hoyt, E. P. A Short History of Science, v2: Modern Science. (7+) Day, 1966. 288p. illus.
   Scientific discoveries from the Middle Ages to the present.

Larsen, Egon (pseud. of Egon Lehrburger). A History of Invention. (7+) Roy, 1961. 382p. illus.

Ludovici, L. J. Great Moments in Medicine. (7+) Roy, 1960. 128p. illus.

Meyer, J. S. Great Accidents in Science That Changed the World. (7+) Arco, 1967. 80p. illus.

Meyer, J. S. World Book of Great Inventions. (7-9) World, 1956. 270p. illus.

Montgomery, E. R. The Story Behind Great Inventions. (7+) Dodd, 1953. 263p. illus.

Montgomery, E. R. The Story Behind Great Medical Discoveries. (7+) Dodd, 1945. 247p. illus.

Peet, Creighton. The First Book of Bridges. (4-6) Watts, 1966. 72p. illus.

Roy, A. E. Great Moments in Astronomy. (7+) Roy, 1963. 128p. illus.

Salter, R. J. Great Moments in Engineering. (7+) Roy, 1964. 116p. illus.

Scheib, Ida. What Happened: The Science Stories Behind the News. (4-8) McKay, 1955. 128p. illus.

Spencer, Cornelia. Keeping Ahead of Machines: The Human Side of the Automation Revolution. (6-9) Day, 1965. 128p. illus.

Wright, Helen and Rapport, S. B. eds. Great Adventures in Science. (7+) Harper, 1956. 338p.

BIOGRAPHY

Blow, Michael. Men of Science and Invention; in consultation with Robert P. Multhauf. (5+) Golden, 1961. 153p. illus.

HISTORY OF MANKIND

BOLTON, SARAH. Famous Men of Science. (7+) Crowell, 1960. 326p.

CANE, PHILIP. Giants of Science. (7+) Grosset, 1959. 159p. illus.

CHANDLER, C. A. Famous Men of Medicine. (7-9) Dodd, 1950. 140p. illus.

EBERLE, IRMENGARDE. Famous Inventors for Young People. (6-10) Dodd, 1953. 130p. illus.

EVANS, I. O. Engineers of the World. (5-9) Warne, 1963. 207p. illus.

EVANS, I. O. Inventors of the World. (5-9) Warne, 1962. 191p. illus.

HALACY, D. S. They Gave Their Names to Science. (5-9) Putnam, 1967. 160p.
> Brief biographies of ten famous natural scientists.

LARSEN, EGON (pseud. of EGON LEHRBURGER). Men Who Changed the World. (7+) 2d ed. Roy [1953]. 224p. illus.
> Lives of famous inventors and scientists.

LARSEN, EGON (pseud. of EGON LEHRBURGER). Men Who Shaped the Future. (7+) Roy, 1954. 223p. illus.
> Inventors who affected social history.

MCGRADY, MIKE. Jungle Doctors. (7-9) Lippincott, 1962. 192p. photos

MANCHESTER, HARLAND. Trail Blazers of Technology. (7-11) Scribner, 1962. 256p. illus.

MANN, A. L. AND VIVIAN, A. C. Famous Physicists. (5-7) Day [c 1963]. 159p. illus.

PICKERING, J. S. Famous Astronomers. (7+) Dodd, 1968. 128p. illus.

PRATT, FLETCHER. All About Famous Inventors and Their Inventions. (4-6) Random House, 1955. 160p. illus.

TRANSPORTATION

RIEDMAN, S. R. Men and Women Behind the Atom. (7+) Abelard [c 1958]. 228p. illus.

ROBBIN, IRVING. Giants of Medicine. (7+) Grosset, 1962. 141p. illus.

SIEDEL, FRANK AND SIEDEL, J. M. Pioneers in Science. (7+) Houghton, [1968]. 160p. illus.

STEVENS, W. O. Famous Scientists. (7+) Dodd, 1952. 162p. illus.

STONAKER, F. B. Famous Mathematicians. (7-9) Lippincott, 1966. 118p.
    Lives of ten mathematicians from Euclid to Weiner.

Transportation

NONFICTION

AYLESWORTH, T. G. Traveling Into Tomorrow: Transportation for the Future. (5+) World, 1970. 164p. illus.

BENDICK, JEANNE. The First Book of Ships. (4-6) Watts, 1959. 72p. illus.

BETHERS, RAY. Ships of Adventure. (4-6) Hastings, 1961. 48p. illus.
    History of famous ships of the world.

BOTHWELL, JEAN. The First Book of Roads. (4-6) Watts, 1954. 72p. illus.

BUEHR, WALTER. Galleys and Galleons. (4-7) Putnam, 1964. 96p. illus.

COGGINS, JACK. By Star and Compass: The Story of Navigation. (5+) Dodd, 1967. 96p. illus.

HISTORY OF MANKIND

Cooke, D. C. Dirigibles That Made History. (4-6) Putnam, 1963. 72p. illus.

Cooke, D. C. Flights That Made History. (4-8) Putnam [c 1961]. 70p. illus.

Cooke, D. C. Helicopters That Made History. (5+) Putnam, 1963. 72p. illus.

Cooke, D. C. Racing Cars That Made History. (5-9) Putnam, 1960. 72p. illus.

Cooke, D. C. Seaplanes That Made History. (5+) Putnam, 1963. 72p. illus.

Coombs, C. I. Wheels, Wings, and Water: The Story of Cargo Transport. (6-10) World, 1963. 222p.

De Leeuw, Hendrik. From Flying Horse to Man in the Moon: History of Flight from Its Earliest Beginnings to the Conquest of Space. (7-9) St. Martin's, 1963. 310p. illus.

Fleming, Alice. Wheels: From Ox Carts to Sports Cars. (7-9) Lippincott, 1960. 192p. illus.

Friskey, Margaret. Caveman to Spaceman. (4+) Childrens, 1961. 64p. illus.

Transportation through history.

Gramet, Charles. Highways Across Waterways. (5-10) Abelard, 1966. 160p. illus.

Hellman, Hal. Navigation: Land, Sea and Sky. (3-6) Prentice-Hall, 1965. 65p. illus.

Hirsch, S. C. On Course! Navigating in Sea, Air, and Space. (7+) Viking, 1967. 156p. illus.

Hoag, Edwin. Roads of Man. (7-10) Putnam, 1967. 192p. illus.

Hogg, Garry. Orient Express: The Birth, Life, and Death of a Great Train. (7+) Walker [1969]. 175p. illus. map

Ingraham, Joseph. Friendship Road: Challenge of the Pan American Highway. (6-8) Coward, 1961. 121p. illus.

WARFARE

KNIGHT, FRANK. Stories of Famous Ships. (4-7) Westminster, 1967. 151p. illus.

MACMILLAN, NORMAN. Great Flights and Air Adventures: From Balloons to Spacecraft. (7+) St. Martin's, 1965. 236p.

MELLIN, JEANNE. Horses Across the Ages. (4+) Dutton, 1954. 91p. illus.

MORRIS, R. W. Transport, Trade, and Travel Through the Ages. (5-8) Allen [1955]. 32p.

PEET, CREIGHTON. The First Book of Bridges. (4-6) Watts, 1966. 72p. illus.

TAYLOR, J. W. Great Moments in Flying. (7+) Roy, 1957. 126p. illus.

TUNIS, EDWIN. Oars, Sails, and Steam. (6+) World, 1952. 78p. illus.

TUNIS, EDWIN. Wheels: A Pictorial History. (6+) World, 1955. 96p. illus.

BIOGRAPHY

WALLHAUSER, H. T. Pioneers of Flight. (7+) Hammond, 1969. 93p. illus. maps

Warfare

NONFICTION

BELFIELD, EVERSLEY. Defy and Endure: Great Sieges of Modern History. (7+) Crowell Collier, 1968. 96p. illus.

BUEHR, WALTER. Heraldry: The Story of Armorial Bearings. (4-7) Putnam, 1964. 96p. illus.

CARR, A. H. Z. Matter of Life and Death: How Wars Get Started —or Are Prevented. (7+) Viking, 1966. 256p. illus. maps

CLARK, R. W. Great Moments in Espionage. (5-10) Roy, 1963. 126p. illus.

HISTORY OF MANKIND

Colby, C. B. Fighter Parade: Headliners in Fighter Plane History. (4-6) Coward, 1960. 48p. illus.

Cooke, D. C. Bomber Planes That Made History. (4-6) Putnam, 1959. 72p. illus.

Cooke, D. C. Fighter Planes That Made History. (4-7) Putnam, 1958. 72p. illus.

Cooke, D. C. Transport Planes That Made History. (4-6) Putnam, 1959. 72p. illus.

Daniell, D. S. (pseud. of Albert Scott Daniell). Sea Fights. (5+) Batsford, 1966. 96p. illus. maps

Ellacott, S. E. Conscripts on the March: The Story of the Soldier from Napoleon to the Nuclear Age. (7+) Abelard, 1966. 160p. illus.

Ellacott, S. E. Guns. (7+) Roy [1956]. 76p. illus.

Ellacott, S. E. Spearman to Minuteman: The Story of the Soldier: 2000 b.c. to 1783 a.d. (7+) Abelard, 1966. 160p. illus.

Fenner, P. R. ed. Danger Is the Password: Stories of Wartime Spies. (7-9) Morrow, 1965. 224p. illus.

Fenner, P. R. ed. No Time for Glory: Stories of World War II. (7-11) Morrow, 1962. 224p. illus.

Funderburk, T. R. Early Birds of War; The Daring Pilots and Fighter Airplanes of World War I. (7+) Grosset [1968]. 156p.

Hoyt, E. P. Deadly Craft: Fire Ships to PT Boats. (5+) Little, 1968. 159p. illus.

Icenhower, J. B. The First Book of Submarines. (4-6) Watts, 1957. 70p. illus.

Knight, Frank. Stories of Famous Sea Fights. (4-7) Westminster, 1967. 133p. illus. maps

WARFARE

KOMROFF, MANUEL. True Adventures of Spies. (7+) Little, 1954. 220p. illus.

LAFFIN, JOHN. Boys in Battle. (7+) Abelard, 1967. 192p. illus.
Youngsters in all eras exhibit audacity in war.

LAFFIN, JOHN. Codes and Ciphers: Secret Writing Through the Ages. (7+) Abelard, 1964. 144p. illus.

LAFFIN, JOHN. The Face of War. (7+) Abelard, 1963. 191p. illus.
Ten land battles that revolutionized military thinking.

LISTON, R. A. The Dangerous World of Spies and Spying. (6+) Platt [1967]. 274p.

LLOYD, CHRISTOPHER. Sea Fights Under Sail. (5+) Collins, 1970. 128p. illus. maps

MACINTYRE, D. G. Fighting Ships and Seamen. (7+) St. Martin's, 1963. 195p. illus.
Sea battles of World War I and World War II.

MORRISON, SEAN. Armor. (7+) Crowell, 1963. 261p. illus.

NICKEL, HELMUT. Warriors and Worthies; Arms and Armor Through the Ages. (7+) Atheneum, 1969. 122p. photos

ORBAAN, ALBERT. Powder and Steel: Notable Battles of the 1800s from New Orleans to the Zulu War. (6-8) Day [1963]. 191p. illus.

PETERSON, H. L. A History of Body Armor. (4-6) Scribner, 1968. 64p. illus.

PETERSON, H. L. A History of Firearms. (7+) Scribner, 1961. 64p. illus.

SETH, RONALD. Spies: Their Trade and Tricks. (7+) Hawthorn, 1969. 144p. illus.

SILVERBERG, ROBERT. Fifteen Battles That Changed the World. (6+) Putnam, 1963. 192p. illus.

SLINKMAN, JOHN. Duel to the Death: Eyewitness Accounts of Great Battles at Sea; comp. by John Slinkman and the editors of Navy Times. (4-7) Harcourt, 1969. 191p. illus.

SULLY, FRANÇOIS. Age of the Guerrilla: A Background Book for Young People on Modern Guerrilla Warfare. (7+) Parents, 1968. 256p.
   Story of guerrilla warfare from ancient times to today.

TIBBETS, A. B. comp. Salute to the Brave: Stories of World War II. (7+) Little, 1960. 274p.

TUCKER, E. E. Soldiers and Armies. (4-6) Lothrop, 1965. 256p. illus.

TUCKER, E. E. The Story of Fighting Ships. (4-6) Lothrop, 1962. 256p. illus.

TUNIS, EDWIN. Weapons: A Pictorial History. (6+) World, 1954. 160p. illus.

VAUGHAN-JACKSON, GENEVIEVE. Animals and Men in Armor. (6-9) Hastings [1958]. 88p. illus.

WELLER, GEORGE. Story of Submarines. (5-8) Random House, 1962. 224p. illus.

WIDDER, ARTHUR. Action in Submarines. (6+) Harper, 1967. 213p. illus.

WIDDER, ARTHUR. Adventures in Black. (7+) Harper, 1962. 180p.
   Tales of espionage.

WILKINSON, BURKE. Cry Spy: True Stories of Twentieth Century Spies and Spy Catchers. (6+) Bradbury [1969]. 271p.

WILKINSON, FREDERICK. Arms and Armour. (6-9) Dufour, 1963. 64p. illus.

BIOGRAPHY

COFFMAN, R. P. AND GOODMAN, N. G. Famous Generals and Admirals for Young People. (7+) Dodd, 1948. 160p. illus.

HOOD, ROBERT. Twelve at War: Great Photographers Under Fire. (6-10) Putnam, 1967. 160p. illus.

DIRECTORY OF PUBLISHERS AND DISTRIBUTORS

Abelard. Abelard-Schuman Limited, 257 Park Ave. S., New York 10010
Abingdon. Abingdon Press, 201 Eighth Ave. S., Nashville, Tn. 37202
Allen. George Allen & Unwin Ltd., 40 Museum St., London, W.C. 1A 1LU
American Heritage. American Heritage Publishing Co., Inc., 551 Fifth Ave., New York 10017
American Israeli. American-Israeli Book Co., 38 W. 32d St., New York 10001
Arco. Arco Publishing Co., Inc., 219 Park Ave. S., New York 10003
Astor. Astor-Honor, Inc., 67 Southfield Ave., Stamford, Ct. 06904
Atheneum. Atheneum Publishers, 122 E. 42d St., New York 10017

Batsford. B. T. Batsford Ltd., 4 Fitzhardinge St., London W1H 0AH
Beacon. Beacon Press, 25 Beacon St., Boston 02108
Benefic. Benefic Press, 10300 W. Roosevelt Rd., Westchester, Il. 60153
Benn. Ernest Benn Ltd., Bouverie House, 154 Fleet St., London E.C. 4
Biblo. Biblo & Tannen Booksellers & Publishers, Inc., 63 Fourth Ave., New York 10003
Bloch. Bloch Publishing Co., Inc., 915 Broadway, New York 10010
Bobbs. The Bobbs-Merrill Co., Inc., 4300 W. 62d St., Indianapolis, In. 46268
Bradbury. Bradbury Press, Inc., 2 Overhill Rd., Scarsdale, N.Y. 10583
Branford. Charles T. Branford Company, 28 Union St., Newton Centre, Ma. 02159

Cambridge. Cambridge University Press, 32 E. 57th St., New York 10022
Childrens. Childrens Press, 1224 W. Van Buren St., Chicago 60607
Chilton. Chilton Book Company, 401 Walnut St., Philadelphia 19106
Collins. William Collins Sons & Co., Ltd., 215 Park Ave. S., New York 10003
Colonial Williamsburg. The Colonial Williamsburg Foundation, Williamsburg, Va. 23185
Concordia. Concordia Publishing House, 3558 S. Jefferson Ave., St. Louis 63118

DIRECTORY OF PUBLISHERS AND DISTRIBUTORS

Coward. Coward, McCann & Geoghegan, Inc., 200 Madison Ave., New York 10016
Cowles. See Regnery
Criterion. Criterion Books, 257 Park Ave. S., New York 10010
Crowell. Thomas Y. Crowell Company, 666 Fifth Ave., New York 10019
Crowell Collier. Crowell Collier and Macmillan, Inc. See Macmillan
Crown. Crown Publishers, Inc. 419 Park Ave. S., New York 10016

Day. The John Day Company, Inc., 257 Park Ave. S., New York 10010
Delacorte. The Delacorte Press. See Dell Publishing Co., Inc.
Dell. Dell Publishing Co., Inc., 750 Third Ave., New York 10017
Dial. The Dial Press, 750 Third Ave., New York 10017
Dodd. Dodd, Mead & Company, 79 Madison Ave., New York 10016
Doubleday. Doubleday & Company, Inc., Garden City, N.Y. 11530
Duell. Duell, Sloan & Pearce, Inc. See Meredith
Dufour. Dufour Editions, Inc., Chester Springs, Pa. 19425
Dutton. E. P. Dutton & Co., Inc., 201 Park Ave. S., New York 10003

Faber. Faber & Faber Ltd., 3 Queen Sq., London WC1N 3AU
Farrar. Farrar, Strauss & Giroux, Inc., 19 Union Square W., New York 10003
Fleet. Fleet Press Corporation, 156 Fifth Ave., New York 10010
Follett. Follett Publishing Company, 1010 W. Washington Blvd., Chicago 60607
Funk. Funk & Wagnalls, Inc., c/o Thomas Y. Crowell Company, 666 Fifth Ave., New York 10019

Garden City. Garden City Books. See Doubleday
Garrard. Garrard Publishing Company, 1607 N. Market St., Champaign, Il. 61820
Golden. Golden Press. See Western
Greystone. Greystone Corporation, 225 Park Ave. S., New York 10003
Grosset. Grosset & Dunlap, Inc., 51 Madison Ave., New York 10010

Hale. E. M. Hale and Company, Pubs., 1201 S. Hasting Way, Eau Claire, Wi. 54701
Hammond. Hammond Incorporated, Maplewood, N.J. 07040
Harcourt. Harcourt Brace Jovanovich, Inc., 757 Third Ave., New York 10017
Harper. Harper & Row, Publishers, 10 E. 53d St., New York 10022
Harvey. Harvey House, Inc., Publishers, Irvington-on-Hudson, N.Y. 10533

WORLD HISTORY IN JUVENILE BOOKS

Hastings. Hastings House, Publishers, Inc. 10 E. 40th St., New York 10016

Hawthorn. Hawthorn Books, Inc., 70 Fifth Ave., New York 10011

Holiday. Holiday House, Inc., 18 E. 56th St., New York 10022

Holt. Holt, Rinehart and Winston, Inc., 383 Madison Ave., New York 10017

Houghton. Houghton Mifflin Company, 2 Park St., Boston 02107

House of Grant. The House of Grant, Ltd., 91-93 Union St., Glasgow C.1

Hutchinson. The Hutchinson Publishing Group Ltd., 178-202 Great Portland St., London W1N 6AQ

International Publications. International Publications Service, 114 E. 32d St., New York 10016

Kenedy. P. J. Kenedy & Sons, 866 Third Ave., New York 10022

Knopf. Alfred A. Knopf, Inc., 201 E. 50th St., New York 10022

Knox. John Knox Press, 801 E. Main St., Box 1176, Richmond, Va. 23209

Lantern. Lantern Press, Inc., 354 Hussey Rd., Mt. Vernon, N.Y. 10552

Lion. Lion Books, 52 Park Ave., New York 10016

Lippincott. J. B. Lippincott Company, E. Washington Sq., Philadelphia 19105

Little. Little, Brown and Company, 34 Beacon St., Boston 02106

Longmans. Longman Group Ltd., Longman House, Burnt Mill, Harlow, Essex

Lothrop. Lothrop, Lee & Shepard Company, 105 Madison Ave., New York 10016

Macrae Smith. Macrae Smith Company, 225 S. 15th St., Philadelphia 19102

McGraw. McGraw-Hill Book & Education Services Group, 1221 Avenue of the Americas, New York 10020

McKay. David McKay Co., Inc., 750 Third Ave., New York 10017

Macmillan. The Macmillan Company, 866 Third Ave., New York 10022

Melmont. Melmont Publishers. See Childrens

Meredith. Meredith Corporation, 1716 Locust St., Des Moines, Ia. 50336

Messner. Julian Messner, 1 W. 39th St., New York 10018

Morrow. William Morrow & Co., Inc., 105 Madison Ave., New York 10016

DIRECTORY OF PUBLISHERS AND DISTRIBUTORS

Naylor. Naylor Company, 1015 Culebra Ave., San Antonio, Tx. 78201
Nelson. Thomas Nelson, Inc., Copewood and Davis Sts., Camden, N.J. 08103
N.Y. Graphic Society. New York Graphic Society Ltd., 140 Greenwich Ave., Greenwich, Ct. 06830
Norton. W. W. Norton & Company, Inc., 55 Fifth Ave., New York 10003

Obolensky. Obolensky Books. See Astor-Honor
Odhams. Odhams Books Ltd., 40 Long Acre, London, W.C. 2
Oliver. Oliver & Boyd Ltd., Tweeddale Court, 14 High St., Edinburgh EH1 1YL
Oxford. Oxford University Press, Inc., 200 Madison Ave., New York 10016

Pantheon. Pantheon Books, Inc., 201 E. 50th St., New York 10022
Parents. Parents' Magazine Press, 52 Vanderbilt Ave., New York 10017
Parnassus. Parnassus Press, 2721 Parker St., Berkeley, Ca. 94704
Phillips. S. G. Phillips, Inc., 305 W. 86th St., New York 10024
Pitman. Pitman Publishing Corporation, 6 E. 43d St., New York 10017
Platt. Platt & Munk, 1055 Bronx River Ave., Bronx, N.Y. 10472
Prentice-Hall. Prentice-Hall, Inc., Englewood Cliffs, N.J. 07632
Putnam. G. P. Putnam's Sons, 200 Madison Ave., New York 10016

Rand McNally. Rand McNally & Company, Box 7600, Chicago 60680
Random House. Random House, Inc., 201 E. 50th St., New York 10022
Regnery. Henry Regnery Company, 114 W. Illinois St., Chicago 60610
Ritchie. The Ward Ritchie Press, 3044 Riverside Dr., Los Angeles 90039
Rockliff. Rockliff Publishing Corporation, 1 Dorset Bldgs., Salisbury Sq., Fleet St., London E.C. 4
Roy. Roy Publishers, Inc., 30 E. 74th St., New York 10021

Sabra. Sabra Books. See American-Israeli
St. Anthony. St. Anthony Guild Press, 508 Marshall St., Paterson, N.J. 07503
St. Martin's. St. Martin's Press, Inc., 175 Fifth Ave., New York 10010
Schocken. Schocken Books Inc., 200 Madison Ave., New York 10016
Scott. Young Scott Books, 333 Avenue of the Americas, New York 10014

Scribner. Charles Scribner's Sons, 597 Fifth Ave., New York 10017
Seabury. The Seabury Press, Inc., 815 Second Ave., New York 10017
Simon & Schuster. Simon & Schuster, Inc., 630 Fifth Ave., New York 10020
Steck. Steck-Vaughn Company, Box 2028, Austin, Tx. 78767
Sterling. Sterling Publishing Co., Inc., 419 Park Ave. S., New York 10016

Time-Life. Time-Life Books, a division of Time Inc., Time & Life Bldg., Rockefeller Center, New York 10020
Transatlantic. Transatlantic Arts, Inc., North Village Green, Levittown, N.Y. 11756
Tuttle. Charles E. Tuttle Co., Inc., 28 S. Main St., Rutland, Vt. 05701

Vanguard. Vanguard Press, Inc., 424 Madison Ave., New York 10017
Van Nostrand. Van Nostrand Reinhold Company, 450 W. 33d St., New York 10001
Verry. Lawrence Verry, Inc., River Rd., Mystic, Ct. 06355
Viking. The Viking Press, Inc., 625 Madison Ave., New York 10022

Walck. Henry Z. Walck, Inc., 19 Union Sq. W., New York 10003
Walker. Walker & Company, 720 Fifth Ave., New York 10019
Warne. Frederick Warne & Co., Inc., 101 Fifth Ave., New York 10003
Washburn. Ives Washburn, Inc., 750 Third Ave., New York 10017
Watts. Franklin Watts, Inc., 845 Third Ave., New York 10022
Webster. Webster Publishing. See McGraw
Weidenfeld. George Weidenfeld & Nicolson Ltd., 5 Winsley St., Oxford Circus, London W.1
Western. Western Publishing Company, Inc., 1220 Mound Ave., Racine, Wi. 53404
Westminster. The Westminster Press, Witherspoon Bldg., Philadelphia 19107
White. David White Company, 60 E. 55th St., New York 10022
Whitman. Albert Whitman & Company, 560 W. Lake St., Chicago 60606
Winston. John C. Winston Company. See Holt
Wonder. Wonder-Treasure Books. See Grosset
World. World Publishing Company, 110 E. 59th St., New York 10022

AUTHOR INDEX

Abodaher, D. J. *Freedom Fighter: Casimir Pulaski*, 59; *The French Explorers of North America*, 170; *Warrior on Two Continents: Thaddeus Kosciuszko*, 59

Absolem, R. *Mussolini and the Rise of Italian Fascism*, 53

Adams, S. H. *General Brock and Niagara Falls*, 170

Addona, A. F. *Organization of African Unity*, 153

Adler, I. *Fire in Your Life*, 225

—and Adler, R. *Communication*, 213

Adler, R. *See* Adler, I. jt. auth.

Agle, N. H. *Makon and the Dauphin*, 18

Alderman, C. L. *Death to the King: The Story of the English Civil War*, 98; *Flame of Freedom: The Peasants' Revolt of 1381*, 96; *The Great Invasion: The Norman Conquest of 1066*, 96; *Liberty, Equality, Fraternity: The Story of the French Revolution*, 21; *That Men Shall Be Free: The Story of the Magna Carta*, 96

Alexander, Albert. *Karl Marx: The Father of Modern Socialism*, 34

Alexander, Anne. *Little Foreign Devil*, 136

Alexander, B. *Famous Myths of the Golden Age*, 35

Alexander, F. *Pebbles from a Broken Jar: Fables and Hero Stories from Old China*, 136

Alger, L. *See* Nic Leodhas, S.

Allen, A. *The Story of Michelangelo*, 53

Almedingen, E. M. *A Candle at Dusk*, 17; *Frossia: A Novel of Russia*, 72; *The Knights of the Golden Table*, 71; *Retreat from Moscow*, 74; *The Treasure of Siegfried*, 27; *Young Catherine the Great*, 76; *Young Leonardo da Vinci*, 52

Almedingen, M. E. von. *See* Almedingen, E. M.

Alter, R. E. *Henry Stanley*, 158; *Who Goes Next: True Stories of Strange Escapes*, 214

Ames, G. and Wyler, R. *First People in the World*, 221

Anderson, H. J. *Henry the Navigator, Prince of Portugal*, 61

Anderson, P. L. *Pugnax, the Gladiator*, 45; *Slave of Catiline*, 45; *With the Eagles*, 46

Anderson, W. R. *First Under the North Pole: The Voyage of the Nautilus*, 205

Andrews, F. E. *For Charlemagne*, 17

Andrews, M. E. *Hostage to Alexander*, 37

Andrist, R. K. *Heroes of Polar Exploration*, 202

Angell, P. K. *To the Top of the World: the Story of Peary and Henson*, 207

Ansley, D. *The Good Ways*, 1, 208

Appel, B. *Ben-Gurion's Israel*, 130; *Hitler: From Power to Ruin*, 32; *Illustrated Book of Knights*, 1;

Shepherd of the Sun, 186; *We Were There in the Klondike Gold Rush*, 166; *We Were There With Cortes and Montezuma*, 177; *Why the Chinese Are the Way They Are*, 137; *Why the Russians Are the Way They Are*, 72

Appell, C. *Great Adventurers*, 217

Apsler, A. *Fighter for Independence: Jawaharlal Nehru*, 145; *Iron Chancellor: Otto von Bismarck*, 31; *Prophet of Revolution: Karl Marx*, 34; *The Sun King: Louis XIV of France*, 25

Arbuthnot, H. See Brown, B. C. jt. auth.

Archer, J. *African Firebrand: Kenyatta of Kenya*, 161; *Colossus of Europe: Metternich*, 12; *Dictators*, 211; *Man of Steel: Joseph Stalin*, 77; *Philippines' Fight for Freedom*, 200; *Red Rebel: Tito of Yugoslavia*, 117; *Twentieth Century Caesar: Benito Mussolini*, 53

Arkin, D. *The Twenty Children of Johann Sebastian Bach*, 30

Army Times, Editors of the. *Famous Fighters of World War I*, 9

Arnold, E. *A Kind of Secret Weapon*, 15

Arnold, R. *True Story of David Livingstone*, 157

Asbjørnsen, P. *Norwegian Folk Tales*, 56

Ashabranner, B. See Davis, R. jt. auth.

Ashby, G. M. *Looking at Norway*, 57

Ashley, M. P. *Life in Stuart England*, 98

Asimov, I. *Breakthroughs in Science*, 226; *Dark Ages*, 1; *The Egyptians*, 122; *Great Ideas of Science*, 226; *Greeks: A Great Adventure*, 39; *The Roman Empire*, 49; *Roman Republic*, 48; *The Shaping of England*, 92; *Words of Science and the History Behind Them*, 226

Aulaire, E. P. d'. See Aulaire, I. M. d', jt. auth.

Aulaire, I. M. d' and Aulaire, E. P. d'. *Columbus*, 67; *Ingri and Edgar Parin d'Aulaire's Book of Greek Myths*, 35; *Leif the Lucky*, 58; *Norse Gods and Giants*, 62

Auty, P. *Yugoslavia*, 116

Averill, E. *Cartier Sails the St. Lawrence*, 170

Ayer, M. *Getting to Know Thailand*, 151; *Made in Thailand*, 151

Aylesworth, T. G. *Traveling Into Tomorrow: Transportation for the Future*, 229

Bacon, P. ed. *The Children's Picture Atlas of the World*, 218

Bahar, H. *Getting to Know Iran and Iraq*, 126

Bailey, A. and Reit, S. *The West in the Middle Ages*, 2

Bailey, A. C. *To Remember Robert Louis Stevenson*, 112

Bailey, B. *Christopher Columbus: Sailor and Dreamer*, 67; *Denmark: Wonderland of Work and Play*, 15; *Famous Latin-American Liberators*, 180; *Famous Modern Explorers*, 217

Bainton, R. H. *The Church of Our Fathers*, 118

Baity, E. C. *Americans Before Columbus*, 179

AUTHOR INDEX

Baker, F. E. N. *See* Noel-Baker, F. E.

Baker, L. N. *See* Stoutenburg, A. jt. auth.

Baker, N. B. *Amerigo Vespucci,* 181; *He Wouldn't Be King: The Story of Simon Bolivar,* 180; *Henry Hudson,* 171; *Juan Ponce de León,* 193; *Juarez, Hero of Mexico,* 177; *Lenin,* 76; *Peter the Great,* 77; *Robert Bruce: King of Scots,* 101; *Sir Walter Raleigh,* 111; *Story of Christopher Columbus,* 67; *Sun Yatsen,* 141; *William the Silent,* 56

Baker, R. M. *Chaim Weizmann: Builder of a Nation,* 131

Balderson, M. *When Jays Fly to Bárbmo,* 57

Baldwin, G. C. *The World of Prehistory,* 221

Baldwin, J. *The Story of Siegfried,* 27

Ballard, C. M. *The Monarch of Juan Fernández,* 111

Balow, T. *See* Carpenter, A. jt. auth.

Barbary, J. *The Boer War,* 165; *The Engine and the Gun,* 89; *Lawrence and His Desert Raiders,* 132; *Student Buccaneer,* 191; *Ten Thousand Heroes,* 39; *Young Cicero,* 51

Barclay, I. *O Canada!* 167; *Worlds Without End,* 217

Barker, D. R. *The Story of Ancient Athens,* 39; *The Story of Roman Britain,* 95; *The Vikings at Home and Abroad,* 63

Barker, E. J. and Hammer, C. L. *People of Long Ago,* 221; *Seeking New Lands,* 214

Barker, S. *The Trojan Horse,* 35

Barnett, C. *The Battle of El Alamein — Decision in the Desert,* 100

Barnouw, A. J. *The Land and People of Holland,* 55

Barr, D. *How and Why Wonder Book of Primitive Man,* 222

Barry, J. *France,* 19

Bartlett, R. M. *They Stand Invincible; the Men Who Are Reshaping Our World,* 211

Bartlett, V. and Caldwell, J. C. *Let's Visit Italy,* 47

Bartos-Höppner, B. *The Cossacks,* 72; *Hunters of Siberia,* 72; *Save the Khan,* 72; *Storm Over the Caucasus,* 72

Batchelor, J. F. *Communication: From Cave Writing to Television,* 213

Bateman, W. L. *How Man Began,* 222

Baum, A. Z. *Antarctica: The Worst Place in the World,* 203

Baumann, H. *Alexander's Great March,* 37; *Barque of the Brothers,* 60; *The Caves of the Great Hunters,* 222; *Gold and Gods of Peru,* 186; *I Marched With Hannibal,* 46; *In the Land of Ur: The Discovery of Ancient Mesopotamia,* 126; *Lion Gate and Labyrinth,* 38; *Sons of the Steppe,* 136; *The World of the Pharaohs,* 122

Bayliss, J. ed. *Exploits in Africa,* 154

Beals, C. *Land of the Mayas; Yesterday and Today,* 175; *Stories Told by the Aztecs: Before the Spaniards Came,* 173

Beard, A. *See* Rogers, F. jt. auth.

Beatty, J. L. and Beatty, P. *At the Seven Stars,* 89; *Campion Tow-*

ers, 87; *Pirate Royal*, 193; *The Queen's Wizard*, 87; *The Royal Dirk*, 89; *Witch Dog*, 14

Beatty, P. See Beatty, J. L. jt. auth.

Beck, B. L. *First Book of Colombia*, 183; *The First Book of the Ancient Maya*, 175; *The First Book of the Aztecs*, 175; *First Book of the Incas*, 186; *First Book of Venezuela*, 187

Beckel, G. and Lee, F. *Workshops for the World: The United Nations Family of Agencies*, 219

Becker, B. *Jules Verne*, 27

Behn, H. *The Faraway Lurs*, 221; *Omen of the Birds*, 46

Belfield, E. *Defy and Endure: Great Sieges of Modern History*, 231

Bell, G. *The Crusaders*, 2

Bellis, H. *Admiral Nelson*, 109; *Captain Cook*, 195

Benary-Isbert, M. *The Ark*, 28; *A Time to Love*, 28

Bendick, J. *Archimedes and the Door of Science*, 41; *The First Book of Ships*, 229

Bennett, R. *Runner for the King*, 185

Benson, S. *Stories of the Gods and Heroes*, 211

Bentley, P.E. *The Adventures of Tom Leigh*, 89; *Oath of Silence*, 89

Berger, M. *Triumphs of Modern Science*, 226

Berk, P. L. *Duke's Command*, 32

Berna, P. *They Didn't Come Back*, 215

Bernhardsen, C. *Fight in the Mountains*, 57

Bernheim, E. See Bernheim, M. jt. auth.

Bernheim, M. and Bernheim, E. *From Bush to City: A Look at the New Africa*, 154

Berrill, J. *Wonders of the Antarctic*, 203; *Wonders of the Arctic*, 205

Berry, E. *Fridtjof Nansen*, 206; *Honey of the Nile*, 121; *The King's Jewel*, 79; *The Land and People of Finland*, 17; *Land and People of Iceland*, 44; *Leif the Lucky: Discoverer of America*, 58; *Men, Moss, and Reindeer: Challenge of Lapland*, 64; *Mister Arctic: An Account of Vilhjalmur Stefansson*, 207; *Robert E. Peary: North Pole Conqueror*, 207

—and Best, H. *Men Who Changed the Map*, 211; *The Polynesian Triangle*, 198

Berton, P. *Stampede for Gold: The Story of the Klondike*, 169

Best, H. See Berry, E. jt. auth.

Bethers, R. *Ships of Adventure*, 229

Beyer, A. W. *Dark Venture*, 153; *Katharine Leslie*, 89; *The Sapphire Pendant*, 89

Bigland, E. *Queen Elizabeth I*, 105

Bill, A. H. *The Ring of Danger: A Tale of Elizabethan England*, 84

Birley, A. *Life in Roman Britain*, 95

Bishop, C. H. *French Roundabout*, 20; *Here Is France*, 20; *Lafayette: French-American Hero*, 24; *Mozart: Music Magician*, 12; *Twenty and Ten*, 19

Bixby, W. *The Impossible Journey of Sir Ernest Shackleton*, 204; *The Universe of Galileo and Newton*, 4

AUTHOR INDEX

Black, I. S. *Castle, Abbey and Town: How People Lived in the Middle Ages,* 2

Blacker, I. R. *Cortes and the Aztec Conquest,* 177

Blassingame, W. *Baden-Powell: Chief Scout of the World,* 101; *The French Foreign Legion,* 21; *Ponce de León,* 193

Bleeker, S. *The Ashanti of Ghana,* 160; *The Aztec, Indians of Mexico,* 175; *The Eskimo, Arctic Hunters and Trappers,* 202; *The Ibo of Biafra,* 162; *The Inca, Indians of the Andes,* 186; *The Masai, Herders of East Africa,* 160, 164; *The Maya, Indians of Central America,* 175; *The Pygmies; Africans of the Congo Forest,* 159; *The Tuareg, Nomads and Warriors of the Sahara,* 163; *The Zulu of South Africa; Cattlemen, Farmers, and Warriors,* 165

Bliven, B. *Story of D-Day: June 6, 1944,* 7

Bloch, M. H. *The Two Worlds of Damyan,* 72

Blow, M. *Men of Science and Invention,* 227

Blunden, G. *The Land and People of Australia,* 196

Boardman, F. W. *Castles,* 2; *History and Historians,* 208

Boardman, G. R. *Living in Tokyo,* 145

Boesch, M. J. *The World of Rice,* 208

Bolliger, M. *Daniel,* 119; *Joseph,* 120

Bolton, S. *Famous Men of Science,* 228

Bond, J. C. *A Is for Africa,* 154

Bonner, M. G. *Canada and Her Story,* 167

Bontemps, A., *The Story of the Negro,* 154

Booth, A. H. *The True Story of Queen Victoria,* 113; *The True Story of Sir Winston Churchill,* 102

Borden, C. *He Sailed With Captain Cook,* 195

Born, F. *Jules Verne: The Man Who Invented the Future,* 27

Borski, L. *Good Sense and Good Fortune, and Other Polish Folk Tales,* 58

Borton, E. *See* Treviño, E. B. de

Bothwell, J. *By Sail and Wind: The Story of the Bahamas,* 191; *The First Book of India,* 142; *The First Book of Roads,* 229; *Omen for a Princess: The Story of Jahanara, Royal Poet of the Seventeenth Century,* 142; *Story of India,* 142

Boucher, A. *The Land Seekers,* 43; *The Sword of the Raven,* 43

Bourliaguet, L. *The Guns of Valmy,* 18

Bowen, J. D. *The Land and People of Chile,* 183; *The Land and People of Peru,* 185

Bowen, R. S. *They Flew to Glory,* 22

Bowers, G. *At the Sign of the Globe,* 112; *Brother to Galahad,* 79; *The Lost Dragon of Wessex,* 79

Bowie, W. R. *The Bible Story for Boys and Girls: New Testament,* 118; *The Story of Jesus: For Young People,* 120

Bowman, J. *The Age of Enlightenment,* 4

WORLD HISTORY IN JUVENILE BOOKS

Boyce, B. *The Emperor's Arrow*, 17

Boyd, M. *Black Flags and Pieces of Eight*, 192; *Rulers in Petticoats*, 212; *The Silent Cities—Civilizations Lost and Found*, 127

Bradley, D. *Meeting With a Stranger*, 159

Brady, C. A. *Saint Thomas More of London Town*, 109

Bragdon, L. J. *The Land and People of France*, 20; *The Land and People of Switzerland*, 70

Braidwood, R. J. *Archaeologists and What They Do*, 224

Braithwaite, M. *Canada: Wonderland of Surprises*, 167

Braverman, L. L. and Silver, S. M. *The Six-Day Warriors*, 130

Bray, W. *Everyday Life of the Aztecs*, 175

Braymer, M. *Walls of Windy Troy: A Biography of Heinrich Schliemann*, 42

Breetveld, J. *Getting to Know Brazil*, 182; *Getting to Know Chile*, 183; *Getting to Know Lebanon*, 132; *Getting to Know United Nations Crusaders: How UNICEF Saves Children*, 219

Brennan, L. A. *The Buried Treasure of Archaeology*, 224

Brewer, D. S. *Chaucer in His Time*, 102

Briggs, P. *Buccaneer Harbor*, 191

Brindze, Ruth. *All About Sailing the Seven Seas*, 215; *All About Undersea Exploration*, 215

Brinton, H. *Spain*, 65

—See Moore, P. A. jt. auth.

Brogan, D. W. *France*, 20

Brooks, P. K. *The Philippines: Wonderland of Many Cultures*, 200

Brooks, P. S. and Walworth, N. Z. *The World Awakes: The Renaissance in Western Europe*, 10; *The World of Walls: The Middle Ages in Western Europe*, 10

Brown, A. *Dangerfoot*, 89; *Great Ideas in Communications*, 213

Brown, B. C. and Arbuthnot, H. *Story of England*, 93

Brown, D. *World of Velázquez, 1599-1660*, 69

Brown, I. J. C. *Dickens and His World*, 104; *Dickens in His Time*, 104; *Dr. Johnson and His World*, 107; *Shakespeare and His World*, 112; *Shakespeare in His Time*, 112

Brown, I. M. See Snyder, L. L. jt. auth.

Brown, M. *Shackleton's Epic Voyage*, 204

Brown, R. *The Land and People of Brazil*, 182

Brown, W. See Dobler, L. jt. auth.

Browne, H. *Hitler and the Rise of Nazism*, 32

Bruckner, K. *The Day of the Bomb*, 147; *The Golden Pharaoh*, 125; *Viva Mexico*, 173

Bryan, D. *The Land and People of China*, 137

Bryce, L. W. *India: Land of Rivers*, 142

Buchanan, F. M. *The Land and People of Scotland*, 93

Buchheimer, N. *Let's Go Down the Mississippi with La Salle*, 172

Buck, P. *The Man Who Changed China: The Story of Sun Yat-sen*, 141

AUTHOR INDEX

Buckley, P. *Spanish Plateau: Challenge of a Dry Land*, 65

Buckmaster, H. *Walter Raleigh: Man of Two Worlds*, 111

Buehr, W. *Chivalry and the Mailed Knight*, 2; *The Crusaders*, 2; *French Explorers in America*, 170; *Galleys and Galleons*, 229; *Heraldry: The Story of Armorial Bearings*, 231; *Knights and Castles and Feudal Life*, 2; *The Portuguese Explorers*, 60, 61; *Sending the Word: The Story of Communications*, 214; *Spanish Armada*, 97; *Viking Explorers*, 64; *The World of Marco Polo*, 140

Buell, H. *Main Streets of Southeast Asia*, 151; *Viet Nam: Land of Many Dragons*, 152; *The World of Red China*, 139

Buff, M. *The Apple and the Arrow*, 71

Bull, G. A. *The Renaissance*, 4

Bulla, C. R. *The Sword in the Tree*, 79

Bullock, L. G. *Children's Book of London*, 93

Burch, G. *Modern Composers for Young People*, 10

—and Wolcott, J. *Famous Composers for Young People*, 10

Burchell, S. C. *Building the Suez Canal*, 123

Burland, C. A. *Adventuring in Archaeology*, 224; *Ancient China*, 138; *Ancient Egypt*, 122; *Ancient Greece*, 39; *The Ancient Maya*, 175; *Ancient Rome*, 48; *Aztecs*, 175; *Inca Peru*, 186; *The Vikings*, 64

Burleigh, D. R. *Arrow Messenger*, 136; *Messenger from K'itai*, 136

Burnett, R. *See* Myers, H. jt. auth.

Burns, W. A. *Man and His Tools*, 226

Burrell, R. E. C. *Early Days of Man*, 222

Burt, O. *Our World: Bulgaria*, 14

Burton, E. *Here Is England*, 93

Burton, H. *Castors Away*, 90; *No Beat of Drums*, 90; *Time of Trial*, 90

Burton, H. M. *Dickens and His Works*, 104

Burton, M. J. *Louis Pasteur: Founder of Microbiology*, 26

Busoni, R. *The Man Who Was Don Quixote: The Story of Miguel Cervantes*, 66

Butler, M. A. *Twice Queen of France: Anne of Britany*, 22; *Ward of the Sun King*, 18

Cadell, J. *Young Lawrence of Arabia*, 133

Cairns, G. O. *The Land and People of Australia*, 196

Caldwell, E. F. *See* Caldwell, J. C. jt. auth.

Caldwell, J. C. *Communism in Our World*, 208; *Let's Visit Afghanistan*, 135; *Let's Visit Argentina*, 181; *Let's Visit Australia*, 197; *Let's Visit Brazil*, 182; *Let's Visit Canada*, 167; *Let's Visit Central America*, 189; *Let's Visit Chile*, 183; *Let's Visit China*, 137; *Let's Visit Colombia*, 183; *Let's Visit Formosa*, 151; *Let's Visit India*, 142; *Let's Visit Japan*, 145; *Let's Visit Korea*, 148; *Let's Visit Malaysia*, 149; *Let's Visit Mexico*, 173; *Let's Visit Micronesia: Guam (USA), and Trust Territory of the Pacific Islands*, 199; *Let's Visit Middle Africa*, 154;

Let's Visit New Zealand, 199; *Let's Visit Pakistan*, 150; *Let's Visit Peru*, 185; *Let's Visit Southeast Asia*, 151; *Let's Visit Thailand*, 151; *Let's Visit the Middle East*, 118; *Let's Visit the Philippines*, 200; *Let's Visit the South Pacific*, 199; *Let's Visit Turkey*, 134; *Let's Visit Venezuela*, 187; *Let's Visit Viet Nam*, 152; *Let's Visit West Africa*, 154; *Let's Visit the West Indies*, 191

—See Bartlett, V.; Freville, N.; MacVicar, A.; Moore, J.; Newman, B. jt. auths.

—and Caldwell, E. F. *Our Neighbors in Africa*, 154; *Our Neighbors in Australia and New Zealand*, 197, 200; *Our Neighbors in Brazil*, 182; *Our Neighbors in Central America*, 189; *Our Neighbors in India*, 142; *Our Neighbors in Japan*, 146; *Our Neighbors in Korea*, 148; *Our Neighbors in Peru*, 185; *Our Neighbors in Thailand*, 151; *Our Neighbors in the Philippines*, 200

—and Newman, B. *Let's Visit South Africa*, 165

—and others. *Let's Visit Ireland*, 44

Caldwell, W. E. and Merrill, E. H. *The New Popular History of the World: The Story of Mankind from Earliest Times to the Present Day*, 208

Callard, T. H. See Ross, S. pseud.

Cammiade, A. *Elizabeth the First*, 105; *Napoleon*, 25; *Victoria's Reign*, 99

Campbell, A. B. *Great Moments at Sea*, 215

Campbell, C. *Coronado and His Captains*, 176; *Star Mountain and Other Legends of Mexico*, 173

Cane, P. *Giants of Science*, 228

Carbonnier, J. *Congo Explorer*, 159

Carew, D. *The Netherlands*, 55; *Portugal*, 60

Carlisle, M. See Carlisle, N. jt. auth.

Carlisle, N. and Carlisle, M. *True Book of Maps*, 218

Carlson, D. *Warlord of the Genji*, 145

Carmer, C. *Henry Hudson: Captain of the Icebound Sea*, 171

Carmichael, J. *Karl Marx: The Passionate Logician*, 34

Carpenter, A. *Argentina*, 181; *Chile*, 183; *Enchantment of South America: Brazil*, 182; *Enchantment of South America: Peru*, 185

—and Balow, T. *Enchantment of South America: Paraguay*, 184

—and Haan, E. R. *Enchantment of South America: Venezuela*, 188

—and Lyon, J. C. *Bolivia*, 181; *Enchantment of South America: Colombia*, 183

Carr, A. H. Z. *Matter of Life and Death: How Wars Get Started —or Are Prevented*, 231

Carr, R. E. *The Picture Story of Japan*, 146

Carrier, E. O. *Humphry Davy and Chemical Discovery*, 104

Carrison, D. J. *Captain James Cook: Genius Afloat*, 195; *Christopher Columbus: Navigator to the New World*, 67

Carter, H. *The Commandos of*

AUTHOR INDEX

World War II, 100; *The Marquis de Lafayette*, 24

Carter, W. E. *The First Book of Bolivia*, 182

Cartey, W. *West Indies: Islands in the Sun*, 191

Cary, S. *Volcanoes and Glaciers: Challenge of Iceland*, 44

Casanova, J. D. See Douville, R. jt. auth.

Cassiday, B. *Guerrilla Scout*, 47

Cavanna, B. *The First Book of Fiji*, 199; *First Book of Morocco*, 163

Cawley, W. *Down the Long Stairs*, 87

Cellini, B. *Autobiography*, 51

Cervantes Saavedra, M. de. *Don Quixote of La Mancha*, 65

Cesco, Frederica de. *The Prince of Mexico*, 173

Chambers, B. *Aztecs of Mexico, the Lost Civilization*, 174

Chandler, C. A. *Famous Men of Medicine*, 228

Chapman, W. *Kublai Khan: Lord of Xanadu*, 140; *Loneliest Continent: The Story of Antarctic Discovery*, 203

Chapsal, M. See Rossif, F. jt. auth.

Charnock, J. T. *The Land and People of Poland*, 59; *Red Revolutionary: A Life of Lenin*, 76

Chaucer, G. *The Canterbury Tales*, 82

Cheney, L. J. *History of the Western World*, 208

Chissell, J. *Chopin*, 59

Christie, T. L. *Legacy of a Pharaoh*, 123

Chu, D. and Skinner, E. *A Glorious Age in Africa: The Story of Three Great African Empires*, 154

Chubb, M. A. *An Alphabet of Ancient Greece; Book 1: Early Days*, 39; *An Alphabet of Ancient Greece; Book 2: The Golden Years*, 39

Chubb, T. C. *The Byzantines*, 134; *The Northmen*, 64; *Prince Henry the Navigator and the Highways of the Sea*, 61; *Slavic Peoples*, 73; *The Venetians: Merchant Princes*, 50

Church, A. J. *Lucius: Adventures of a Roman Boy*, 46

Church, R. J. *Looking at France*, 20

Churchill, Sir Winston. *Heroes of History*, 101; *Joan of Arc*, 23

Chute, M.G. *The Innocent Wayfaring*, 82; *Jesus of Israel*, 120

Clark, E. *Robert Peary: Boy of the North Pole*, 207

Clark, L. *The Rivers Ran East*, 182

Clark, L. F. *Explorers' Digest*, 217

Clark, R. W. *Explorers of the World*, 217; *Great Moments in Escaping*, 215; *Great Moments in Espionage*, 231; *Great Moments in Mountaineering*, 215; *Great Moments in Rescue Work*, 215; *Montgomery of Alamein*, 108; *Sir John Cockcroft*, 103; *Sir Julian Huxley*, 107; *Sir Mortimer Wheeler*, 225; *Sir Winston Churchill*, 102

Clark, W. R. pseud. See Clark, R. W.

Clarke, M. S. *Piper to the Clan*, 87

Clayton, R. *British Isles*, 93; *The U.S.S.R.*, 74

Cleator, P. E. *Exploring the World of Archaeology*, 224

Clemens, S. L. *See* Twain, M. pseud.
Clement, M. *In France*, 20
Clements, F. *Getting to Know Southern Rhodesia, Zambia, and Malawi*, 154, 164
Clifford, J. *The Young John Wesley*, 113
Coatsworth, E. *The Hand of Apollo*, 37; *The Lucky Ones*, 219; *The Princess and the Lion*, 159
Cochran, H. *Pirates of the Spanish Main*, 192
Cochrane, J. *Let's Go to the United Nations Headquarters*, 219
Cochrane, L. *See* Taylor, D. jt. auth.
Coffman, R. P. and Goodman, N. G. *Famous Explorers for Young People*, 217; *Famous Generals and Admirals for Young People*, 235; *Famous Kings and Queens for Young People*, 212
Coggins, J. *By Star and Compass: The Story of Navigation*, 215, 226, 229
Cohen, D. *Secrets from Ancient Graves*, 224
Cohen, J. L. *Buddha*, 143
Cohen, L. *Came Liberty Beyond Our Hope, a Story of Hanukkah*, 130; *Passover to Freedom*, 128
Cohn, A. *The First Book of the Netherlands*, 55
Colby, C. B. *Aircraft of World War I: Fighters, Scouts, Bombers, and Observation Planes*, 5; *Fighter Parade: Headliners in Fighter Plane History*, 232
Colby, J. P. *Jesus and the World*, 120
Coleman, E. S. *The Cross and the Sword of Cortes*, 177

Collin, H. *Young Hans Christian Andersen*, 16
Colum, P. *Children of Odin*, 62; *The Golden Fleece and the Heroes Who Lived Before Achilles*, 35
Colver, A. *Florence Nightingale: War Nurse*, 109
Colvin, G. *Central America*, 189
Comay, J. *Ben-Gurion and the Birth of Israel*, 131; *The U.N. in Action*, 219
—and Pearlman, M. *Israel*, 128
Cone, M. *Green, Green Sea: A Story of Greece*, 38
Constable, G. *The Warrior Knights*. *See* Williams, Paul, il.
Cooke, D. C. *Bomber Planes That Made History*, 232; *Dirigibles That Made History*, 230; *Fighter Planes That Made History*, 232; *Flights That Made History*, 230; *Helicopters That Made History*, 230; *Inventions That Made History*, 226; *The Planes the Allies Flew in World War II*, 7; *The Planes They Flew in World War I*, 5; *Racing Cars That Made History*, 230; *Seaplanes That Made History*, 230; *Transport Planes That Made History*, 232
Cooke, D. E. *Men of Sherwood*, 84
Coolidge, O. *Caesar's Gallic War*, 49; *Egyptian Adventures*, 121; *The Golden Days of Greece*, 39; *Greek Myths*, 35; *Legends of the North*, 62; *Lives of Famous Romans*, 50; *Makers of the Red Revolution*, 74, 76; *Marathon Looks on the Sea*, 35; *Men of Athens*, 39; *People in Palestine*, 130; *Roman People*, 48; *Trojan*

AUTHOR INDEX

War, 35; *Winston Churchill and the Story of Two World Wars,* 102

Coombs, C. I. *Wheels, Wings, and Water: The Story of Cargo Transport,* 230

Cooper, L. *Young Napoleon,* 25

Cooper, L. U. *Hand Upon Time: A Life of Charles Dickens,* 104; *The Twig of Cypress,* 47; *The Young Florence Nightingale,* 110; *The Young Victoria,* 113

Cooper, M. *Inventions of Leonardo da Vinci,* 52

Copeland, F. *Land Between: The Middle East,* 118

Copeland, P. W. *The Land and People of Jordan,* 131; *The Land and People of Libya,* 163; *The Land and People of Syria,* 133

Corbett, S. *Danger Point: The Wreck of the Birkenhead,* 99

Corcoran, J. *Folk Tales of England,* 78; (ed.) *Folk Tales of North America,* 166

Cordell, A. *The White Cockade,* 44

Corley, A. *True Story of Napoleon,* 26

Cormack, M. *Imhotep: Builder in Stone,* 125

Corney, L. C. *The Story of Rome,* 48

Costain, T. B. *William the Conqueror,* 114

Cottler, J. and Jaffe, H. *Heroes of Civilization,* 212; *More Heroes of Civilization,* 212

Cottrell, L. *Crete: Island of Mystery,* 38; *Digs and Diggers,* 224; *Five Queens of Ancient Egypt,* 124; *Great Leaders of Greece and Rome,* 50; *Land of the Pharaohs,* 122; *Land of the Two Rivers,* 127; *The Warrior Pharaohs,* 124

Coughlan, R. *World of Michelangelo,* 53

Cowan, L. *Children of the Resistance,* 7

Cowell, F. R. *Everyday Life in Ancient Rome,* 49

Cowie, L. W. *The Reformation,* 10

Cowley, R. *1918: Gamble for Victory — the Greatest Attack of World War I,* 5

Coy, H. *Mexicans,* 174

Cramer, R. S. *See* Wintterle, J. jt. auth.

Cramp, R. and Gummer, J. *The Earliest English,* 95

Crampton, P. *Stonehenge of the Kings: A People Appear,* 95

Crandell, M. C. *Molly and the Regicides,* 87

Crane, W. D. *The Man Who Transformed the World: James Watt,* 113

Crayder, T. pseud. *Cleopatra,* 125

Craz, A. *Getting to Know Italy,* 48

Credle, E. *Mexico: Land of Hidden Treasure,* 174

Creswick, P. ed. *Robin Hood,* 84

Crick, J. *See* Dupuy, T. N. jt. auth.

Criner, C. L. *See* Hall, E. jt. auth.

Criss, M. *Isabella, Young Queen of Spain,* 69

Crosby, A. L. *The Rimac: River of Peru,* 185

Crossley-Holland, K. *Havelok the Dane,* 16

—*See* Paton Walsh, G. jt. auth.

Crothers, S. M. ed. *Children of Dickens,* 90

Cruit, B. J. *Land of the Afghans: A Book for Children,* 135

Csicsery-Rónay, I. *The First Book*

of Hungary, 43

Curren, P. *Folk Tales of France,* 17; (ed.) *Folk Tales of Scandinavia,* 62

Currie, G. *Let's Travel in Australia,* 197

Curtis, R. *Chiang Kai-shek,* 140

Dalgliesh, A. *The Columbus Story,* 67

Daly, M. *The Small War of Sergeant Donkey,* 47; *Spain: Wonderland of Contrasts,* 65

Daniel, A. *The Story of Albert Schweitzer,* 157

Daniell, A. S. *See* Daniell, D. S. pseud.

Daniell, D. S. *Sea Fights,* 232

—*See* Lampe, G. W. jt. auth.

Dareff, H. *The Story of Vietnam: A Background Book for Young People,* 152

Daringer, H. F. *Debbie of the Green Gate,* 87; *Pilgrim Kate,* 87; *Yesterday's Daughter,* 35

Darton, F. J. H. *The Story of the Canterbury Pilgrims,* 96

Daugherty, C. M. *The Great Archaeologists,* 225; *Searchers of the Sea: Pioneers in Oceanography,* 215

Daugherty, J. H. *Magna Carta,* 96

Davenport, M. *Garibaldi: Father of Modern Italy,* 52

Davenport, W. *The Seine — from Its Source to the Sea,* 20

David, P. *Julius Caesar,* 50

Davidson, B. *Africa in History,* 154; *A Guide to African History,* 154

Davidson, M. *Pirate Book,* 192

Davis, F. *Getting to Know Turkey,* 134

Davis, R. and Ashabranner, B. *Land in the Sun: The Story of West Africa,* 154

Day, A. G. *Explorers of the Pacific,* 195; *Pirates of the Pacific,* 195; *The Story of Australia,* 197; *They Peopled the Pacific,* 195

Day, D. *Getting to Know Panama,* 189; *Getting to Know Spain,* 65

Deedy, J. *First Book of the Vatican,* 114

De Jong, D. *The Level Land,* 54

De Jong, M. *The Mighty Ones: Great Men and Women of Early Bible Days,* 119

De Kay, O., Jr. *Meet Christopher Columbus,* 67

De Lacy, E. A. *Euclid and Geometry,* 42

De Leeuw, A. L. *Edith Cavell: Nurse, Spy, Heroine,* 102; *James Cook,* 196; *Richard E. Byrd: Adventurer to the Poles,* 204; *Sir Walter Raleigh: A World Explorer,* 111

De Leeuw, C. *Roald Amundsen,* 203

De Leeuw, H. *From Flying Horse to Man in the Moon: History of Flight from Its Earliest Beginnings to the Conquest of Space,* 230

De Maré, E. S. *London's River — The Story of a City,* 93

Deming, A. *Getting to Know Algeria,* 163

Deming, R. *Heroes of the International Red Cross,* 219

Dennis, L. A. *See* Field, J. L. jt. auth.

Denny, N. G. and Filmer-Sankey, J. *The Bayeux Tapestry; The Story of the Norman Conquest: 1066,* 96

AUTHOR INDEX

Denton, J. See Longley, J. pseud.

Denzel, J. F. *Adventure North: The Story of Fridtjof Nansen*, 206

De Regniers, B. *David and Goliath*, 119

Derleth, A. *Columbus and the New World*, 67

Descola, J. *Daily Life in Peru in the Time of the Spaniards*, 186

De Terra, H. See Hoff, R. jt. auth.

Deucher, S. *Edvard Grieg, Boy of the Northland*, 58; *The Young Brahms*, 31

—See Wheeler, O. jt. auth.

Deutsch, B. *Heroes of the Kalevala*, 17

DeVault, M. V. See Houston, W. R. jt. auth.

De Vivanco, M. *Siegfried, the Mighty Warrior*, 27

De Witt, J. *In Pursuit of the Spanish Galleon*, 90

De Witt, W. A. *History's Hundred Greatest Events*, 208

Dibner, B. *Alessandro Volta and the Electric Battery*, 54; *Wilhelm Conrad Röntgen and the Discovery of X-Rays*, 34

Dickens, C. *A Tale of Two Cities*, 18

Dickinson, A. *Carl Linnaeus: Pioneer of Modern Botany*, 70; *Charles Darwin and Natural Selection*, 103; *The First Book of Stone Age Man*, 222

Diekmann, M. *Slave Doctor*, 191

Dillon, E. *The Seals*, 44

Dilts, M. M. *Pageant of Japanese History*, 146

Disney (Walt) Productions. *Stories from Other Lands*, 79

Doane, P. *The Boy Jesus*, 120

Dobler, L. *The Land and People of Uruguay*, 187

—and Brown, W. *Great Rulers of the African Past*, 156

Dobrin, A. *Italy: Modern Renaissance*, 50

Dodd, A. H. *Life in Elizabethan England*, 97

Dolan, E. F. Jr. *Explorers of the Arctic and Antarctic*, 202

Dolan, E. M. *Churchill*, 102

Dolch, E. W. and Dolch, M. P. *Greek Stories*, 35; *Robin Hood Stories*, 84

Dolch, M. P. See Dolch, E. W. jt. auth.

Domjan, J. *Hungarian Heroes and Legends*, 42

Donauer, F. *Swords Against Carthage*, 46

Donovan, F. R. *Famous Twentieth Century Leaders*, 212; *The Vikings*, 64

Doorly, E. *Microbe Man*, 26

Douglas, M. S. *The Key to Paris*, 20

Douglas, W. O. *Exploring the Himalayas*, 149

Douville, R. and Casanova, J. D. *Daily Life in Early Canada*, 169

Dowd, D. L. *The French Revolution*, 21

Downey, G. *Aristotle: Dean of Early Science*, 41; *Stories from Herodotus*, 40

Downing, J. and Dyra, F. eds. *Let's Travel in Canada*, 167

Drewery, M. *Devil in Print*, 84; *Hamid and the Palm Sunday Donkey*, 128

Drower, M. S. *Nubia: A Drowning Land*, 123

Duché, J. *The Great Trade Routes*, 208, 218

253

WORLD HISTORY IN JUVENILE BOOKS

Dufek, G. J. *Through the Frozen Frontier*, 203

Dugan, J. *Undersea Explorer: The Story of Captain Cousteau*, 217

Duggan, A. L. *The Castle Book*, 2; *The Falcon and the Dove: A Life of Thomas Becket of Canterbury*, 101; *Growing Up in Thirteenth Century England*, 96; *Growing Up With the Norman Conquest*, 96; *The Romans*, 49

Dukert, J. M. *This Is Antarctica*, 203

Dumas, A. *The Three Musketeers*, 18

Duncombe, F. R. *The Quetzal Feather*, 189

Dunlop, A. M. R. *See* Kyle, E. pseud.

Dupuy, T. N. *Air War in the Pacific: Air Power Leads the Way*, 147; *Air War in the Pacific: Victory in the Air*, 147; *The Air War in the West: June 1941-April 1945*, 7; *The Air War in the West: September 1939-May 1941*, 7; *Asian and Axis Resistance Movements*, 8, 147; *Asiatic Land Battles: Allied Victories in China and Burma*, 147; *Asiatic Land Battles: Japanese Ambitions in the Pacific*, 147; *The Battle of Austerlitz: Napoleon's Greatest Victory*, 21; *Chronological Military History of World War II*, 8; *Combat Leaders of World War II*, 10; *European Land Battles, 1939-1943*, 8; *European Land Battles, 1944-1945*, 8; *European Resistance Movements*, 8; *Land Battles: North Africa, Sicily, and Italy*, 8; *The Military History of the Chinese Civil War*, 139; *The Military Life of Adolph Hitler, Führer of Germany*, 32; *The Military Life of Alexander the Great of Macedon*, 41; *The Military Life of Frederick the Great of Prussia*, 32; *The Military Life of Gustavus Adolphus, Father of Modern War*, 70; *The Military Life of Hannibal, Father of Strategy*, 52; *The Military Life of Julius Caesar, Imperator*, 50; *The Military Life of Napoleon, Emperor of the French*, 26; *The Military Life of Winston Churchill of Britain*, 102; *The Military Lives of Hindenburg and Ludendorff of Imperial Germany*, 32, 33; *Naval and Overseas War, 1914-1915*, 5; *Naval War in the Pacific: On to Tokyo*, 147; *Naval War in the Pacific: Rising Sun of Nippon*, 147; *The Naval War in the West: The Raiders*, 5; *The Naval War in the West: The Wolf Packs*, 5; *1914: The Battles in the East*, 5; *1914: The Battles in the West*, 6; *Stalemate in the Trenches*, 6; *Strategic Direction of World War II*, 8; *Summation: Strategic and Combat Leadership*, 6; *Triumphs and Tragedies in the East*, 6; *The War in the Air*, 6

—and Crick, J. *1918: Decision in the West*, 6; *1918: The German Offensives*, 6

—and Hayes, G. P. *Campaigns on the Turkish Fronts*, 134; *Naval and Overseas War, 1916-1918*, 6

—and Mayo, M. R. *Campaigns in Southern Europe*, 8

AUTHOR INDEX

Duvoisin, R. *The Four Corners of the World,* 187; *They Put Out to Sea,* 217, 218

Dwight, A. *Drums in the Forest,* 166; *Guns at Quebec,* 166; *The Silver Dagger,* 193

Dyra, F. ed. *Let's Travel in West Germany,* 29

—*See* Downing, J. jt. ed.

Eager, E. M. *Knight's Castle,* 82

Eaton, J. *David Livingstone: Foe of Darkness,* 157; *Gandhi: Fighter Without a Sword,* 144

Eberle, I. *Edward Jenner and Smallpox Vaccination,* 107; *Famous Inventors for Young People,* 228

Ecke, W. *Flight Toward Home,* 28

Edel, M. *Story of Our Ancestors,* 222

Edelman, L. *Japan in Story and Pictures,* 146

Edmonds, I. G. *Bounty's Boy,* 198; *Joel of the Hanging Gardens,* 128; *The Khmers of Cambodia: The Story of a Mysterious People,* 135; *Revolts and Revolutions,* 208

Edwards, C. P. *Champlain; Father of New France,* 171

Edwards, H. *Scandinavia: The Challenge of Welfare,* 64

Edwards, L. F. *Russia and Her Neighbors,* 74

Edwards, M. D. *Child of the Sun: A Pharaoh of Egypt,* 124

Eimerl, S. *Revolution: France 1789-1794,* 21

Eisenberg, A. *Voices from the Past: Stories of Great Biblical Discoveries,* 118

—and Elkins, D. P. *World's Lost and Found: Discoveries in Biblical Archaeology,* 118

Eisenberg, P. *We Were There With Charles Darwin on H.M.S. Beagle,* 90

Elder, M. *The Young Martin Luther,* 33

Elkin, S. *Search for a Lost City,* 42

Elkins, D. P. *See* Eisenberg, A. jt. auth.

Elkon, J. *Edith Cavell: Heroic Nurse,* 102

Ellacott, S. E. *Conscripts on the March: The Story of the Soldier from Napoleon to the Nuclear Age,* 232; *Guns,* 232; *A History of Everyday Things in England,* 93; *The Norman Invasion,* 96; *Spearman to Minuteman: The Story of the Soldier: 2000 B.C. to 1783 A.D.,* 232

Ellis, H. B. *The Arabs,* 132; *The Common Market,* 8

Elting, M. and Folsom, F. *Answer Book of History,* 208; *Flags of All Nations and the People Who Live Under Them,* 209; *The Story of Archaeology in the Americas,* 224

Epstein, B. and Epstein, S. *Story of the International Red Cross,* 219

—*See* Epstein, S. jt. auth.

Epstein, B. W. *See* Epstein, B.

Epstein, S. and Epstein, B. *All About Prehistoric Cave Men,* 222; *The First Book of Italy,* 48; *The First Book of Maps and Globes,* 218; *The First Book of Mexico,* 174

—and Williams, B. *European Folk Festivals,* 1; *The First Book of Switzerland,* 71

—See Epstein, B. jt. auth.
Erdoes, R. *Ireland: Bewitching Wonderland,* 45; *A Picture History of Ancient Rome,* 49
Esterer, A. K. *Tools: Shapers of Civilization,* 226
Esterházy, C. *Young Traveler in Austria,* 11
Estes, E. *Miranda the Great,* 46
Euller, J. *Antarctic World,* 203; *Arctic World,* 205; *Ice, Ships, and Men,* 205; *Our Navy Explores Antarctica,* 203
Evans, E. K. *All About Us,* 209
Evans, I. O. *Engineers of the World,* 228; *Exploring the Earth,* 215; *Inventors of the World,* 228
Evans, M. F. *The Land and People of Korea,* 148
Exell, F. K. *The Land and People of Thailand,* 152

Fadiman, C. *Adventures of Hercules,* 35; *The Voyages of Ulysses,* 35
Fairley, T. C. and Israel, C. E. *True North: Story of Captain Joseph Bernier,* 206
Fairservis, W. A. Jr. *Egypt, Gift of the Nile,* 123; *Horsemen of the Steppes,* 72; *India,* 142; *Mesopotamia: The Civilization That Rose Out of the Clay,* 127
Falls, C. B. *The First 3000 Years: Ancient Civilizations of the Tigris, Euphrates, and Nile River Valleys, and the Mediterranean Sea,* 127
Farjeon, E. *Ten Saints,* 114
—and Mayne, W. eds. *A Cavalcade of Kings,* 212; *A Cavalcade of Queens,* 212
Farmer, L. H. *A Book of Famous Queens,* 212
Farrell, A. *Sir Winston Churchill,* 103
Faulkner, N. *Knights Besieged,* 133; *The Sacred Jewel,* 78; *The Yellow Hat,* 82;
Feagles, A. *He Who Saw Everything: The Epic of Gilgamesh,* 126
Fecher, C. *Heir to Pendarrow,* 84; *Venture for a Crown,* 87
Fehrenbach, T. R. *Fight for Korea: From the War of 1950 to the Pueblo Incident,* 148; *The United Nations in War and Peace,* 219
Feigenbaum, L. and Seigel, K. *Israel: Crossroads of Conflict,* 128
Feldman, H. *The Land and People of Pakistan,* 150
Felton, R. O. See Welch, R. pseud.
Fenner, P. R. ed. *Danger Is the Password: Stories of Wartime Spies,* 232; *No Time for Glory: Stories of World War II,* 232
Fenton, S. H. *Greece: A Book to Begin On,* 38
Ferguson, R. D. *Man from St. Malo,* 171
Ferrari, E. See Kenworthy, L. jt. auth.
Field, G. L. *The Minoans of Ancient Crete,* 39
Field, J. L. and Dennis, L. A. *From Sea to Sea: The Story of Canada in the Nineteenth and Twentieth Centuries,* 167, 169; *Land of Promise: The Story of Early Canada,* 169
Filmer-Sankey, J. See Denny, N. G. jt. auth.
Finger, C. J. *Courageous Companions,* 60, 61

AUTHOR INDEX

Finkel, G. I. *The Long Pilgrimage,* 17; *Watch Fires to the North,* 80

Finlay, I. *The Young Robert Louis Stevenson,* 113

Firoozi, E. and Klein, I. N. *The Age of Great Kings,* 10

Fisher, A. *Jeanne d'Arc,* 23

Fisher, D. C. *Fair World for All,* 219

Fisher, L. *You and the United Nations,* 219

Fisk, N. *Richthofen, the Red Baron,* 34

FitzGerald, T. *Justinian the Great: Roman Emperor of the East,* 134

Fleming, A. *Wheels: From Ox Carts to Sports Cars,* 230

Fletcher, A. M. *The Land and People of the Guianas,* 184

Fletcher, H. J. *Adventures in Archaeology,* 224

Floherty, J. J. *Men Against Distance: The Story of Communications,* 214

Folsom, F. *Science and the Secret of Man's Past,* 222, 226; *The Soviet Union: A View from Within,* 74

—See Elting, M. jt. auth.

Footman, D. *The Russian Revolutions,* 75

Forester, C. S. *The Barbary Pirates,* 163; *Hornblower Goes to Sea,* 90; *Hornblower in Captivity,* 90; *Hornblower Takes Command,* 90; *Hornblower's Triumph,* 90; *Last Nine Days of the Bismarck,* 100

Forman, B.-L. and Forman, H. *The Land and People of Nigeria,* 162

Forman, H. See Forman, B.-L. jt. auth.

Forman, J. *Horses of Anger,* 28; *My Enemy, My Brother,* 128; *Ring the Judas Bell,* 35; *The Shield of Achilles,* 133; *The Skies of Crete,* 36; *The Traitors,* 28

Fosdick, H. E. *Jesus of Nazareth,* 120; *Life of St. Paul,* 115; *Martin Luther,* 33

Foster, F. B. *First Book of Kenya,* 160

Foster, G. *Abraham Lincoln's World,* 209; *Augustus Caesar's World,* 49, 209; *Birthdays of Freedom, I,* 40; *Birthdays of Freedom, II,* 209; George Washington's *World,* 209; *World of Captain John Smith,* 10, 209; *The World of Columbus and Sons,* 4; *Year of Columbus, 1492,* 4, 209; *Year of the Pilgrims, 1620,* 209

Foster, G. A. *Communication: From Primitive Tom-Toms to Telstar,* 214

Foster, H. *The Medieval Castle,* 2; *Prince Valiant and the Golden Princess,* 80; *Prince Valiant and the Three Challenges,* 80; *Prince Valiant Fights Attila the Hun,* 80; *Prince Valiant in the Days of King Arthur,* 80; *Prince Valiant in the New World,* 80; *Prince Valiant on the Inland Sea,* 80; *Prince Valiant's Perilous Voyage,* 80

Foster, J. T. *Napoleon's Marshal: The Life of Michel Ney,* 26; *Sir Francis Drake: A World Exlorer,* 105

Foster, M. S. *Red Carpet for Lafayette,* 18

Fox, A. *Roman Britain*, 95
Francini, M. *Russia Invaded, from Genghis Khan to Hitler*, 73
Francis, H. and Smith, P. *Defrosting Antarctic Secrets*, 203
Franck, F. *My Friend in Africa*, 157
Frank, R. Jr. *Ice Island: The Story of Antarctica*, 203
Fraser, E. *A Boy Hears Stories from the Old Testament*, 118
Freeman, M. B. *Finding Out About the Past*, 224
Fremantle, A. J. *Age of Faith*, 2
French, H. W. *The Lance of Kanana*, 132
Freville, N. and Caldwell, J. C. *Let's Visit Nigeria*, 162
Friedman, E. *Digging Into Yesterday*, 224; *Man in the Making*, 222
Friedman, R. *Freedom Builders: Great Teachers from Socrates to John Dewey*, 212
Friskey, M. *Caveman to Spaceman*, 230
Frith, H. *King Arthur and His Knights*, 80
Fritz, J. *Animals of Doctor Schweitzer*, 154
Frost, K. *Stallion of the Desert*, 162
Fuller, E. *John Milton*, 108
Funderburk, T. R. *Early Birds of War; The Daring Pilots and Fighter Airplanes of World War I*, 232

Gage, J. *Life in Italy at the Time of the Medici*, 50
Gail, M. *Life in the Renaissance*, 4
Gale, E. *Julia Valeria*, 46

Gallant, K. *Mountains in the Sea: Challenge of Crowded Japan*, 146
Galt, T. *How the United Nations Works*, 219
Gardner, M. *Archimedes: Mathematician and Inventor*, 41
Garfield, L. *Devil in the Fog*, 90; *Smith*, 91
Garnett, E. *Madame Prime Minister: The Story of Indira Gandhi*, 144
Garnett, H. *Know About the Armada*, 97; *The Red Bonnet*, 18; *Treasures of Yesterday*, 225
Garrison, W. B. See Webster, G. pseud.
Garst, Mrs. Doris Shannon. See Garst, S.
Garst, S. *Three Conquistadors: Cortes, Coronado, Pizarro*, 177, 187
Garthwaite, M. H. *The Locked Crowns*, 15
Gass, I. *Mozart: Child Wonder, Great Composer*, 12
Gatti, A. and Gatti, E. *The New Africa*, 154
Gatti, E. See Gatti, A. jt. auth.
Geis, D. ed. *Let's Travel in China*, 137; *Let's Travel in England*, 93; *Let's Travel in France*, 20; *Let's Travel in Greece*, 38; *Let's Travel in Hong Kong*, 141; *Let's Travel in India*, 142; *Let's Travel in Italy*, 48; *Let's Travel in Japan*, 146; *Let's Travel in Mexico*, 174; *Let's Travel in Spain*, 65; *Let's Travel in Switzerland*, 71; *Let's Travel in Thailand*, 152; *Let's Travel in the Holy Land*, 128; *Let's Travel in the Philippines*, 200; *Let's Travel in the South Seas*, 199;

AUTHOR INDEX

Let's Travel in the Soviet Union, 75
Gelinas, P. J. and Scharff, R. *History of the World for Young Readers,* 209
Gerson, N. B. *Belgium,* 13; *Passage to the West: The Great Voyages of Henry Hudson,* 171
Gianakoulis, T. *The Land and People of Greece,* 38
Gidal, S. and Gidal, T. *Sons of the Desert,* 132
Gidal, T. *See* Gidal, S. jt. auth.
Gilbert, M. *Winston Churchill,* 103
Gillette, H. S. *Leonardo da Vinci: Pathfinder of Science,* 52; *Raphael: Painter of the Renaissance,* 53
Gimpel, H. J. *Beethoven: Master Composer,* 31; *Napoleon, Man of Destiny,* 26
Gittings, R. and Manton, J. *Story of John Keats,* 107
Gladych, M. *Admiral Byrd of Antarctica,* 204
Glines, C. V. ed. *Polar Aviation,* 202
Glubok, S. *Discovering the Royal Tombs at Ur,* 123; *Discovering Tut-Ankh-Amen's Tomb,* 123; (ed.) *The Fall of the Aztecs,* 175; *The Fall of the Incas,* 186; *Knights in Armor,* 2
Godden, R. *Operation Sippacik,* 134
Goettel, E. *Eagle of The Philippines: President Manuel Quezon,* 201
Goetz, D. *Arctic Tundra,* 205; *Half a Hemisphere: The Story of Latin America,* 179; *Neighbors to the South,* 179
Golann, C. P. *Our World: The Taming of Israel's Negev,* 129
Goldberg, H. S. *Hippocrates: Father of Medicine,* 42
Golden, G. B. *Made in Iceland,* 44
Goldie, F. *Zulu Boy,* 164
Goldman, H. and Goldman, I. *First Men: The Story of Human Beginnings,* 222
Goldman, I. *See* Goldman, H. jt. auth.
Goldstein, K. K. *The World of Tomorrow,* 226
Goldston, R. C. *The Civil War in Spain,* 66; *The Cuban Revolution,* 193; *The Legend of the Cid,* 66; *The Life and Death of Nazi Germany,* 29; *The Rise of Red China,* 139; *The Russian Revolution,* 75; *Spain,* 66
Goldthwait, P. *Night of the Wall,* 28
Gollomb, J. *Albert Schweitzer: Genius in the Jungle,* 158
Gómez, B. *Getting to Know Mexico,* 174
Goodman, N. G. *See* Coffman, R. P. jt. auth.
Gordon, R. L. *The Land and People of Canada,* 167
Gorham, C. O. *Lion of Judah: The Story of Haile Selassie I, Emperor of Ethiopia,* 160
Gosfield, F. and Hurwood, B. J. *Korea: Land of the 38th Parallel,* 149
Goss, M. B. *Beethoven: Master Musician,* 31
Gottlieb, G. *The First Book of the Mediterranean,* 38, 48, 163
Gottschalk, F. *The Youngest General: A Story of Lafayette,* 24
Gough, C. *Boyhoods of Great Composers, Book 1,* 10; *Boy-*

hoods of Great Composers, Book II, 10
Gould, H. *Sir Christopher Wren: Renaissance Architect, Philosopher, and Scientist*, 114
Graff, S. *Hernando Cortes*, 177
Graham, A. P. *Christopher Columbus, Discoverer*, 67; *Lafayette: Friend of America*, 24; *La Salle, River Explorer*, 172
Graham, F. *Austria*, 11
Gramet, C. *Highways Across Waterways*, 230
Granberg, W. J. *Let's Go Exploring With Magellan*, 61
Grant, C. *Mexico: Land of the Plumed Serpent*, 174
Grant, K. *Samuel Cunard — Pioneer of the Atlantic Steamship*, 103
Grant, N. *Benjamin Disraeli: Prime Minister Extraordinary*, 104; *Charles V, Holy Roman Emperor*, 31; *English Explorers of North America*, 170; *The Renaissance*, 4
Graves, C. P. *Henry Morton Stanley*, 158; *John Smith: A World Explorer*, 112; *Marco Polo*, 140
Graves, R. *Greek Gods and Heroes*, 36; *The Siege and Fall of Troy*, 36
Gray, E. J. *Adam of the Road*, 91; *I Will Adventure*, 97; *Young Walter Scott*, 111
Gray, M. *Island Hero: The Story of Ramón Magsaysay*, 201
Gray, P. *The Battle of Hastings*, 96; *D-Day*, 100; *The Invincible Armada*, 97; *Plague and Fire*, 98
Green, R. J. *Whistling Sword*, 136
Green, R. L. *Ancient Egypt*, 122; *Ancient Greece*, 40; *Heroes of Greece and Troy*, 36; *Tales of Ancient Egypt*, 122
Greene, C. *Charles Darwin*, 103; *Gregor Mendel*, 12
Greenleaf, M. F. *Banner Over Me*, 82
Gregor, A. S. *Adventure of Man*, 222; *Charles Darwin*, 103; *How The World's First Cities Began*, 127; *Short History of Science*, 226
Grey, E. *Friend Within the Gates, the Story of Nurse Edith Cavell*, 102
Griffin, E. *Continent in a Hurry: The Challenge of Africa Today*, 154; *Getting to Know UNESCO: How U.N. Crusaders Fight Ignorance*, 219
Griffiths, A. *Black Patriot and Martyr: Toussaint of Haiti*, 193
Groh, L. *A World Explorer: Ferdinand Magellan*, 61
Grundy, K. *The Lands and Peoples of Kenya, Tanzania and Uganda*, 160
Gummer, J. *See* Cramp, R. jt. auth.
Gunston, D. *The Young Samuel Pepys*, 110
Gunther, J. *Alexander the Great*, 41; *Julius Caesar*, 50; *Meet Soviet Russia*, 75; *Meet the Congo and Its Neighbors*, 155
—and others. *Meet North Africa*, 163; *Meet South Africa*, 165
Gurney, G. *Flying Aces of World War I*, 6

Haan, E. R. *See* Carpenter, A. jt. auth.
Habberton, W. *Russia: The Story of a Nation*, 73
Hadas, M. *Imperial Rome*, 49

AUTHOR INDEX

Hadfield, A. M. *King Arthur and the Round Table,* 80

Hahn, E. *Leonardo da Vinci,* 52; *Mary, Queen of Scots,* 108

Haines, C. *Charles Dickens,* 104; *William Shakespeare and His Plays,* 112

Halacy, D. S. *Science and Serendipity; Great Discoveries by Accident,* 226; *They Gave Their Names to Science,* 228

Hall, D. W. *Arctic Rovings,* 205

Hall, E. *The Land and People of Argentina,* 181; *The Land and People of Czechoslovakia,* 15; *The Land and People of Norway,* 57; *The Volga: Lifeline of Russia,* 73

—and Criner, C L. *Picture Map Geography of Eastern Europe,* 14, 15, 43, 59, 62, 73, 116

Hall, G. L. *William, Father of the Netherlands,* 56

Hall, J. *Buried Cities,* 225

Hall, J. N. *See* Nordhoff, C. B. jt. auth.

Hall, S. K. *See* King-Hall, S.

Hall-Quest, O. W. *Conquistadors and Pueblos: The Story of the American Southwest, 1540-1848,* 176; *With Stanley in Africa,* 158

Haller, A. *He Served Two Masters,* 173

Halliday, E. M. *Russia in Revolution,* 75

Halsell, G. *Getting to Know Colombia,* 183; *Getting to Know Guatemala and the Two Honduras,* 189; *Getting to Know Peru,* 185; *Peru,* 185

Hamilton, E. *Roman Way,* 49

Hamilton, F. *Challenge for a Throne; The Wars of the Roses,* 96; *The Crusades,* 2; *1066,* 96

Hamilton, R. *Science, Science, Science,* 226

Hammer, C. L. *See* Barker, E. J. jt. auth.

Hammond-Innes, R. *See* Innes, H. pseud.

Hamori, L. *Dangerous Journey,* 42

Hampden, J. ed. *New Worlds Ahead,* 93; *A Picture History of India,* 142

Hancock, R. *Mexico,* 174

Hansel, R. R. *The Life of Saint Augustine,* 114

Harman, H. *African Samson,* 153

Harmelink, B. *Florence Nightingale: Founder of Modern Nursing,* 110

Harrington, L. *Australia and New Zealand: Pacific Community,* 197, 200; *The Grand Canal of China,* 137

Harris, J. N. *Knights of the Air: Canadian Aces of World War I,* 170

Harris, P. *Introducing Beethoven,* 31; *The Young Gilbert and Sullivan,* 106

Harrison, W. C. *Doctor William Harvey and the Discovery of Circulation,* 106

Hartman, G. *In Bible Days,* 118; *Machines and the Men Who Made the World of Industry,* 214; *Medieval Days and Ways,* 2; *The World We Live In and How It Came to Be,* 209

—and Saunders, L. S. *Builders of the Old World,* 2

Harvey, T. *The Quest of Michael Faraday,* 106

Hastie, R. M. *See* MacGregor-Hastie, R.

Haugaard, E. C. *Hakon of Rogen's Saga*, 56; *A Slave's Tale*, 62

Haughton, R. *Paul and the World's Most Famous Letters*, 115; *Therese Martin*, 27; *The Young Moses*, 120; *The Young Thomas More*, 109

Hautzig, E. *The Endless Steppe: Growing Up in Siberia*, 58

Haverstock, N. *Organization of American States: The Challenge of the Americas*, 220

Hawes, C. B. *The Dark Frigate*, 87

Hawkes, J. *Pharaohs of Egypt*, 124

Haycraft, M. C. *Queen Victoria*, 113; *The Reluctant Queen*, 84; *Too Near the Throne*, 84

Hayes, G. P. *See* Dupuy, T. N. jt. auth.

Hays, W. *Drummer Boy for Montcalm*, 166

Hazen, B. S. *David and Goliath*, 120

Headley, E. C. *See* Cavanna, B.

Heaps, W. A. *Assassination: A Special Kind of Murder*, 209; *The Wall of Shame*, 29

Heaton, P. R. *Canada*, 167

Heatter, B. *Against Odds*, 215

Heller, David. *See* Heller, Deane, jt. auth.

Heller, Deane and Heller, David. *The Cold War*, 75

Hellman, H. *Navigation: Land, Sea and Sky*, 230

Hennessey, M. N. and Sauter, E. Jr. *A Crown for Thomas Peters*, 153; *Soldier of Africa*, 153; *Sword of the Hausas*, 153

Henson, M. A. *Black Explorer at the North Pole: An Autobiographical Report by the Negro Who Conquered the Top of the World With Admiral Robert E. Peary*, 206

Henty, G. A. *With Wolfe in Canada*, 169

Herold, J. C. *Age of Napoleon*, 26; *The Battle of Waterloo*, 99

Hersey, J. R. *Hiroshima*, 148

Hewes, A. D. *A Boy of the Lost Crusade*, 18; *Spice and the Devil's Cave*, 60; *Spice Ho! A Story of Discovery*, 215

Heyerdahl, T. *Aku-Aku: The Secret of Easter Island*, 199; *Kon-Tiki*, 199

Hieatt, C. *The Knight of the Cart*, 80; *Sir Gawain and the Green Knight*, 80

Hill, F. E. *Famous Historians*, 212

Hill, K. *And Tomorrow the Stars: The Story of John Cabot*, 170

Hill, W. M. *Tales of Maui*, 198

Hillary, E. ed. *Challenge of the Unknown*, 215

Hillyer, V. M. and Huey, E. G. *Africa and Asia*, 155; *Americas [Canada, Mexico and South America]*, 167, 174, 179; *Europe*, 1; *The Orient — Australia and the South Sea Islands*, 195, 197

Hinckley, H. *The Land and People of Iran*, 126

Hine, A. *D-Day: The Invasion of Europe*, 8

Hirsch, S. C. *On Course! Navigating in Sea, Air, and Space*, 230

Hirschfeld, B. *A Cloud Over Hiroshima: The Story of the Atomic Bomb*, 148; *Fifty-Five Days of Terror: The Story of the Boxer Rebellion*, 139; *Khrushchev*, 76; *The Spanish Armada: The Story of a Glorious Defeat*, 97; *A State Is Born: The Story of Israel*,

AUTHOR INDEX

129; *The Vital Link: The Story of the Suez Canal,* 123
Hoag, E. *Roads of Man,* 230
Hobbs, M. *The Young Milton,* 108
Hobley, L. F. *Early Explorers to A.D. 1500,* 217; *Exploring the Americas,* 179; *Exploring the Pacific,* 195; *Opening Africa,* 155
Hodges, C. W. *Columbus Sails,* 67; *Magna Carta: Story of Britain,* 97; *The Marsh King,* 80; *The Namesake: A Story of King Alfred,* 80; *The Norman Conquest: Story of Britain,* 97; *Shakespeare and the Players,* 97; *Shakespeare's Theatre,* 98; *The Spanish Armada,* 98
Hodges, M. *Lady Queen Anne,* 101
Hoff, R. *Africa: Adventures in Eyewitness History,* 155; *China: Adventures in Eyewitness History,* 137; *Russia: Adventures in Eyewitness History,* 73
—and De Terra, H. *They Explored,* 217
Hoffman, G. *The Land and People of Israel,* 129
Hogeboom, A. *Christopher Columbus and His Brothers,* 67
Hogg, B. T. *See* Grey, E. pseud.
Hogg, G. *Airship Over the Pole: The Story of the Italia,* 205; *Orient Express: The Birth, Life, and Death of a Great Train,* 230
Hoke, J. *The First Book of the Guianas,* 184
Holbrook, S. *Bruno and Karen of Berlin,* 28; *Capital Without a Country,* 29; *Germany: East and West,* 29; *Getting to Know the Two Germanys,* 29; *Sir Tristan of All Time,* 28; *Taming the Columbia River: The Challenge of American-Canadian Cooperation,* 167
Holding, J. *The King's Contest and Other North African Tales,* 162
Holisher, D. *Growing Up in Israel,* 129
Holland, C. *The King's Road,* 28
Holland, K. C. *See* Crossley-Holland, K.
Holm, A. S. *North to Freedom,* 15; *Peter,* 88
Holst, I. *Bach,* 30
Holwood, W. *True Story of Captain Scott at the South Pole,* 204; *The True Story of Sir Francis Drake, Privateer,* 105
Homer. *The Iliad,* 36; *The Odyssey,* 36
Homze, A. and Homze, E. L. *Germany: The Divided Nation,* 29
Homze, E. L. *See* Homze, A. jt. auth.
Honour, A. *The Man Who Could Read Stones: Champollion and the Rosetta Stone,* 125; *Tormented Genius: The Struggles of Vincent Van Gogh,* 56
Hood, R. *Twelve at War: Great Photographers Under Fire,* 235
Hope, C. *Young Charles Darwin,* 104; *The Young Tennyson,* 113
Hope-Simpson, J. *The Great Fire,* 88
Hopkins, K. *Great Moments in Exploration,* 215
Hopp, S. M. B. *See* Hopp, Z.
Hopp, Z. *Great Day in Norway: the 17th of May,* 57
Höppner, B. B. *See* Bartos-Höppner, B.
Horizon Magazine, Editors of. *Shakespeare's England,* 98, 112

Hornblow, L. *Cleopatra of Egypt,* 125

Hornos, A. *Argentina, Paraguay and Uruguay,* 181, 185, 187

Hosken, F. P. *The Language of Cities,* 214

Houghton, R. *The True Story of Lord Nelson, Naval Hero,* 109

Household, G. *Prisoner of the Indies,* 84

Houston, W. R. and DeVault, M. V. *Sir Isaac Newton,* 109

Howard, C. *Pizarro and the Conquest of Peru,* 187

Howard, J. *Story of Robert Louis Stevenson,* 113

Howard, R. W. *First Book of Niagara Falls,* 167

Howarth, D. A. *D-Day, the Sixth of June, 1944,* 8; *We Die Alone,* 57

Howell, F. C. *Early Man,* 222

Hoyt, E. P. *Deadly Craft: Fire Ships to PT Boats,* 232; *He Freed the Minds of Men: René Descartes,* 23; *A Short History of Science, v 1: Ancient Science,* 226; *A Short History of Science, v2: Modern Science,* 227; *Swan of the East: The Life and Death of the German Cruiser Emden in World War I,* 29

—See also Martin, C. pseud.

Hoyt, O. *Aborigines of Australia,* 197; *Bedouins,* 132

Huey, E. G. See Hillyer, V. M. jt. auth.

Hughes, L. *The First Book of Africa,* 155

Hume, I. N. *Great Moments in Archaeology,* 225

Hume, P. and Hume, R. *The Lion of Poland: The Story of Paderewski,* 59

Hume, R. *Florence Nightingale,* 110

—See Hume, P. jt. auth.

Hummel, R. S. *Little Martin Luther,* 33

Hunt, M. L. *Beggar's Daughter,* 88

Hunter, M. *A Pistol in Greenyards,* 91; *The Spanish Letters,* 91

Hürlimann, B. *William Tell and His Son,* 71

Hurwood, B. J. See Gosfield, F. jt. auth.

Hutheesing, K. N. *Dear to Behold: An Intimate Portrait of Indira Gandhi,* 144

Hutton, C. *A Picture History of Britain,* 93

Hyde, L. *Captain Deadlock,* 91; *Under the Pirate Flag,* 192

Hyndman, J. A. L. See Wyndham, L. pseud.

Icenhower, J. B. *The First Book of Submarines,* 232; *The First Book of the Antarctic,* 203; *Man Against the Unknown,* 216

Ingalls, L. *Getting to Know Kenya,* 160; *Getting to Know South Africa,* 165

Ingraham, J. *Friendship Road: Challenge of the Pan American Highway,* 230

Innes, H. *Scandinavia,* 64

Irving, C. *The Battle of Jerusalem: The Six-Day War of June, 1967,* 130; *Spy: The Story of Modern Espionage,* 8

Irving, W. *Legends of the Alhambra,* 66

Irwin, T. ed. *Let's Travel in Holland,* 55

Isbert, M. B. See Benary-Isbert, M.

AUTHOR INDEX

Isenberg, I. *Caesar,* 51
Ish-Kishor, S. *A Boy of Old Prague,* 14
Israel, C. E. *Five Ships West — The Story of Magellan,* 61
—*See* Fairley, T. C. jt. auth.

Jablonski, E. *Warriors With Wings,* 22
Jackson, G. V. *See* Vaughan-Jackson, G.
Jacob, H. P. *A Garland for Gandhi,* 144
Jacobs, J. K. *Against All Odds,* 217
Jacobson, D. *A Story of Man,* 222
Jaffe, H. *See* Cottler, J. jt. auth.
Jakeman, A. *Getting to Know Japan,* 146
Janeway, E. *The Vikings,* 64
Janssen, P. *A Moment of Silence,* 54
Jantzen, S. *Hooray for Peace, Hurrah for War,* 6
Jenkins, A. *The Young Mozart,* 13
Jenkins, A. C. *Pirates and Highwaymen,* 192
Jewett, E. M. *Big John's Secret,* 83; *The Hidden Treasure of Glaston,* 83
Johnson, D. M. *Farewell to Troy,* 36; *Greece: Wonderland of the Past and Present,* 38
Johnson, G. W. *The British Empire, an American View of Its History from 1776 to 1945,* 93; *Communism, an American's View,* 75
Johnson, W. W. *Andean Republics,* 179; *Captain Cortes Conquers Mexico,* 177
Johnston, J. and Steffensen, J. L. *Reformation and Exploration,* 4
Johnston, R. *Getting to Know the Two Koreas,* 149

Jonas, A. *Archimedes and His Wonderful Discoveries,* 41
Jones, A. *Ride the Far Wind,* 137
Jones, R. F. *Boy of the Pyramids,* 121
Joseph, J. *Peter the Great,* 77; *South African Statesman: Jan Christiaan Smuts,* 165
Jowett, M. *A Cry of Players,* 84
Joy, C. R. *Desert Caravans: Challenge of the Changing Sahara,* 163; *Getting to Know Costa Rica, El Salvador, and Nicaragua,* 189; *Getting to Know England, Scotland, and Ireland,* 45, 93; *Getting to Know Hong Kong,* 141; *Getting to Know Israel,* 129; *Getting to Know Tanzania,* 164; *Getting to Know the River Amazon,* 182; *Getting to Know the Sahara,* 163; *Getting to Know the South Pacific,* 199; *Getting to Know the Tigris and Euphrates,* 127; *Getting to Know the Two Chinas,* 137; *Island in the Desert: Challenge of the Nile,* 123; *Race Between Food and People: The Challenge of a Hungry World,* 209
Joyce, J. A. *Decade of Development: The Challenge of the Underdeveloped Nations,* 220
Judson, C. I. *Christopher Columbus,* 67; *Saint Lawrence Seaway,* 167
Jupo, F. J. *People and Things in Early Greece,* 40; *Walls, Gates, and Avenues: The Story of the Town,* 210

Kalish, B. M. *Eleven: Time to Think of Marriage, Farhut,* 150
Kamm, J. *Hebrew People: A History of the Jews,* 130; *Leaders*

of the People, 131; *Malaria Ross: A Story Biography*, 145; *The Story of Emmeline Pankhurst*, 110

Karen, R. *The Land and People of Central America*, 189

Katoh, L. See Miller, R. J. jt. auth.

Katz, E. *India in Pictures*, 143

Kaufman, M. D. *Christopher Columbus*, 67

Kaufmann, H. L. *Anvil Chorus: The Story of Giuseppe Verdi*, 54; *Story of Beethoven*, 31; *The Story of Haydn*, 12; *Story of Mozart*, 13

Kaula, E. M. *The First Book of Australia*, 197; *First Book of the Bantu Africans*, 155; *The Land and People of Ethiopia*, 159; *The Land and People of Kenya*, 161; *The Land and People of New Zealand*, 200; *The Land and People of Rhodesia*, 164; *The Land and People of Tanganyika*, 164; *Leaders of the New Africa*, 156

Kaye, G. *Great Day in Ghana; Gwasi Goes to Town*, 160

Keary, A. and Keary, E. *Heroes of Asgard: Tales from Scandinavian Mythology*, 62

Keary, E. See Keary, A. jt. auth.

Keating, B. *Chaka: King of the Zulus*, 157; *The Invaders of Rome*, 49; *The Life and Death of the Aztec Nation*, 176

Keesing, N. *By Gravel and Gum: Story of a Pioneer Family*, 196

Kelen, B. *Gautama Buddha, in Life and Legend*, 144

Kelen, E. *Dag Hammarskjöld: A Biography*, 70; *Peace Is an Adventure: The Men and Women of the U.N. in Action Around the World*, 220; *Stamps Tell the Story of the United Nations*, 220; *Stamps Tell the Story of the Vatican*, 114

Kelen, I. See Kelen, E.

Kelly, E. P. *At the Sign of the Golden Compass*, 84; *The Trumpeter of Krakow*, 58

—and Kostich, D. D. *The Land and People of Poland*, 59

Kelly, R. Z. *Marquette and Joliet*, 172

Kelman, P. and Stone, A. H. *Ernest Rutherford: Architect of the Atom*, 111

Kelsey, A. *Once the Hodja*, 134

Kent, L. A. *He Went With Champlain*, 166; *He Went With Christopher Columbus*, 65; *He Went With Drake*, 85; *He Went With Hannibal*, 46; *He Went With Magellan*, 60; *He Went With Marco Polo*, 137; *He Went With Vasco da Gamma*, 60

Kenworthy, L. *Profile of Kenya*, 161; *Profile of Nigeria*, 162; *Twelve Citizens of the World*, 212

—and Ferrari, E. *Leaders of New Nations*, 212

Kerby, E. P. *The Conquistadors*, 186

Kerr, L. *Footlights to Fame: The Life of Fanny Kemble*, 107

Kidder, J. E. *Ancient Japan*, 147

Kidwell, C. *The Angry Earth*, 173; *Granada, Surrender!* 65

Kielty, B. *The Fall of Constantinople*, 134; *Marie Antoinette*, 25

Kimball, G. *Puzzle of the Lost Dauphin*, 18

King, M. *Young Mary Stuart:*

AUTHOR INDEX

Queen of Scots, 108

King, S. *Getting to Know Malaysia and Singapore*, 149

King-Hall, Sir S. *Three Dictators: Mussolini, Hitler, Stalin*, 33, 53, 77

Kingsley, C. *Heroes*, 36; *Westward Ho!* 85

Kinmond, W. *The First Book of Communist China*, 139

Kirby, C. P. *East Africa: Kenya, Uganda and Tanzania*, 155, 161, 164

Kirk, R. *Japan: Crossroads of East and West*, 146

Kirtland, G. B. *One Day in Ancient Rome*, 49; *One Day in Aztec Mexico*, 176; *One Day in Elizabethan England*, 98

Kishor, S. I. *See* Ish-Kishor, S.

Kittler, G. D. (ed.) *Let's Travel in Nigeria and Ghana*, 162; *Let's Travel in the Congo*, 159; *Mediterranean Africa; Four Muslim Nations*, 163

Kjelgaard, J. A. *Explorations of Père Marquette*, 172

Klagsbrun, F. *Sigmund Freud*, 12; *The Story of Moses*, 121

Klein, I. N. *See* Firoozi, E. jt. auth.

Knight, C. *We Were at the Battle of Britain*, 92; *We Were There at the Normandy Invasion*, 92

—and Knight, K. S. *We Were There With the Lafayette Escadrille*, 19

Knight, D. C. *Copernicus: Titan of Modern Astronomy*, 51; *The First Book of Berlin: Tale of a Divided City*, 29; *Isaac Newton: Mastermind of Science*, 109; *Johannes Kepler and Planetary Motion*, 33; *Robert Koch: Father of Bacteriology*, 33

Knight, F. *Olaf's Sword*, 63; *Remember Vera Cruz!* 85; *Stories of Famous Explorers by Sea*, 217; *Stories of Famous Sea Fights*, 232; *Stories of Famous Ships*, 231; *They Told Mr. Hakluyt*, 85, 216; *Young Captain Cook*, 196; *Young Columbus*, 67; *Young Drake*, 105

Knight, F. E. *See* Knight, F.

Knight, K. S. *See* Knight, C. jt. auth.

Knoop, F. Y. *Amerigo Vespucci*, 181; *Vasco Nunez de Balboa*, 190; *A World Explorer; Francisco Coronado*, 177

Kochan, L. *The Russian Revolution*, 75

Kochan, M. *Life in Russia Under Catherine the Great*, 74

Komroff, M. *The Battle of Waterloo: One Hundred Days of Destiny*, 99; *Charlemagne*, 23; *Disraeli*, 105; *Heroes of the Bible*, 119; *Julius Caesar*, 51; *Marco Polo*, 140; *Mozart*, 13; *Napoleon*, 26; *Talleyrand*, 27; *True Adventures of Spies*, 233

—and Komroff, O. *Marie Antoinette*, 25

Komroff, O. *See* Komroff, M. jt. auth.

Koningsberger, H. *The World of Vermeer, 1632-1675*, 56

Kostich, D. D. *The Land and People of the Balkans*, 14, 62, 116

—*See* Kelly, E. P. jt. auth.

Kotker, N. *The Holy Land in the Time of Jesus*, 130

Kramer, B. L. *About Cave Men of the Old Stone Age*, 222

Kramer, S. N. *Cradle of Civilization,* 127

Krause, J. E. and others, eds. *The Children's Bible,* 118

Krusch, W. See Wohlrabe, R. A. jt. auth.

Kubie, N. B. *The First Book of Archaeology,* 225; *First Book of Israel,* 129

Kubly, H. H. *Switzerland,* 71

Kugelmass, J. A. *Roald Amundsen: A Saga of the Polar Seas,* 203

Kullman, H. *Under Secret Orders,* 11

Kyle, E. *Duet:* The *Story of Clara and Robert Schumann,* 34; *Great Ambitions: A Story of the Early Years of Charles Dickens,* 104; *Princess of Orange,* 108; *Song of the Waterfall: The Story of Edvard and Nina Grieg,* 58

Lacy, L. *Black Africa on the Move,* 155

Laffin, J. *Boys in Battle,* 233; *Codes and Ciphers: Secret Writing Through The Ages,* 233; *The Face of War,* 233

Lamb, B. L. P. *India,* 143; *The Nehrus of India: Three Generations of Leadership,* 145

Lamb, C. and Lamb, M. *Tales from Shakespeare,* 85

Lamb, H. *Chief of the Cossacks,* 77; *Genghis Khan and the Mongol Horde,* 140

Lamb, M. See Lamb, C. jt. auth.

Lambie, B. R. *The MacKenzie: River to the Top of the World,* 167

Lampe, G. W. and Daniell, D. S. *Discovering the Bible,* 119

Lampman, E. S. *The Tilted Sombrero,* 173

Lamprey, L. *Children of Ancient Rome,* 49

Lancelot, M. See Whitehouse, A. jt. auth.

Land, B. *The Quest of Johannes Kepler, Astronomer,* 33

Landry, L. *The Land and People of Burma,* 135

Lang, A. *Tales of Troy and Greece,* 36

Lang, R. P. *The Land and People of Pakistan,* 150

Langford, N. F. *King Nobody Wanted,* 120

Larralde, E. *The Land and People of Mexico,* 174

Larsen, E. *A History of Invention,* 227; *Men Under the Sea,* 216; *Men Who Changed the World,* 228; *Men Who Fought for Freedom,* 212; *Men Who Shaped the Future,* 228; *Sir Vivian Fuchs,* 204

Laschever, B. D. *Getting to Know Cuba,* 194; *Getting to Know India,* 143; *Getting to Know Pakistan,* 150; *Getting to Know Venezuela,* 188

Latham, J. L. *The Chagres: Power of the Panama Canal,* 189; *Drake: The Man They Called a Pirate,* 105; *Far Voyager: The Story of James Cook,* 196; *The Frightened Hero: A Story of the Siege of Latham House,* 88

Lattin, H. *The Peasant Boy Who Became Pope,* 116

Lauber, P. *Battle Against the Sea: How the Dutch Made Holland,* 55; *Changing the Face of North America: Challenge of the St. Lawrence Seaway,* 167; *The*

AUTHOR INDEX

Congo: River Into Central Africa, 155; Getting to Know Switzerland, 71; The Quest of Louis Pasteur, 26

Lauritzen, J. *Blood, Banners and Wild Boars: Tales of Early Spain,* 66

Lawrence, J. W. *Russia,* 73

Lawrence, M. W. *Rockets' Red Glare: Challenge of Outer Space,* 216

Lawson, D. ed. *Great Air Battles: World Wars I and II,* 6

Lawson, R. *I Discover Columbus,* 65

Leacroft, H. and Leacroft, R. V. B. *Buildings of Ancient Egypt,* 122; *The Buildings of Ancient Greece,* 40

Leacroft, R. V. B. *See* Leacroft, H. jt. auth.

Leaf, M. *History Can Be Fun,* 210; *Three Promises to You,* 220

Leckie, R. *The Story of World War I,* 6; *Story of World War II,* 8; *The War in Korea: 1950-1953,* 149

Lee, F. *See* Beckel, G. jt. auth.

Lefroy, C. M. *See* Maxwell-Lefroy, C.

Legum, C. and Legum, M. *The Bitter Choice: Eight South Africans' Resistance to Racial Tyranny,* 165

Legum, M. *See* Legum, C. jt. auth.

Lehrburger, E. *See* Larsen, E. pseud.

Leighton, M. *Cleopatra: Sister of the Moon,* 125; *Journey for a Princess,* 81; *The Story of Florence Nightingale,* 110; *Voyage to Coromandel,* 63

Leitch, A. *Canada, Young Giant of the North,* 168

Lengyel, E. *Asoka the Great: India's Royal Missionary,* 143; *First Book of Turkey,* 134; *Ignace Paderewski: Musician and Statesman,* 59; *Jawaharlal Nehru: the Brahman from Kashmir,* 145; *Lajos Kossuth: Hungary's Great Patriot,* 43; *The Land and People of Hungary,* 43; *Mahatma Gandhi: The Great Soul,* 144; *They Called Him Ataturk,* 134

Lens, S. *Africa: Awakening Giant,* 155

Lensen, G. A. *The Soviet Union: An Introduction,* 75

Leonard, J. N. *Early Japan,* 147

Lester, J. *De Gaulle: King Without a Crown,* 23

Levin, J. W. *Star of Danger,* 15

Levine, I. E. *Champion of World Peace: Dag Hammarskjöld,* 70; *Lenin: The Man Who Made a Revolution,* 76; *Oliver Cromwell,* 103

Levine, J. *See* Pine, T. S. jt. auth.

Levinger, E. *Galileo: First Observer of Marvelous Things,* 51

Levitin, S. *Journey to America,* 28

Levron, J. *Daily Life at Versailles in the 17th and 18th Centuries,* 21

Lewellen, J. B. *True Book of Knights,* 2

Lewis, G. *See* Manley, S. jt. ed.

Lewis, H. W. *Gentle Falcon,* 83; *Here Comes Harry,* 85

Lewis, M. *The Honorable Sword,* 145

Lexau, J. *Archimedes Takes a Bath,* 40

Leyland, E. *For Valour: The Story of the Victoria Cross,* 93

Lifton, B. J. *Return to Hiroshima*, 148

Lin Yu-t'ang. *Chinese Way of Life*, 137

Lindquist, W. *The Age of Revolution*, 6; *Industrial Revolution and Nationalism*, 6

Lindsay, S. and McAulay, J. D. *This Is Canada*, 168

Lineaweaver, C. P. *Canada*, 168

Linton, A. S. B. H. See Linton, R. jt. auth.

Linton, R. and Linton, A. S. B. H. *Man's Way: From Cave to Skyscraper*, 210

Lisitzky, G. H. *Four Ways of Being Human*, 222

Liss, H. *The Mighty Mekong*, 151

Liston, R. A. *The Dangerous World of Spies and Spying*, 233

Liversidge, D. *The British Empire and Commonwealth of Nations*, 93; *First Book of Arctic Exploration*, 205; *The First Book of the Arctic*, 205; *Ignatius of Loyola: The Soldier Saint*, 69; *Joseph Stalin*, 77; *Lenin: Genius of Revolution*, 77; *Peter the Great*, 77; *Saint Francis of Assisi*, 51

Lloyd, C. *Sea Fights Under Sail*, 233

Lloyd, N. See Palmer, G. jt. auth.

Lobdell, H. *Thread of Victory*, 91

Lobsenz, N. M. *First Book of Denmark*, 16; *The First Book of East Africa*, 155; *The First Book of West Germany*, 30

Loder, D. H. *Land and People of Belgium*, 13; *The Land and People of Spain*, 66

Loeper, J. J. *Men of Ideas*, 213

Loewe, M. *Everyday Life in Early Imperial China During the Han Period 202 B.C. - A.D. 220*, 138

Loman, A. *Looking at Holland*, 55

Long, L. *De Lesseps: Builder of Suez*, 125

Longley, J. *France: A First-Look-At-Geography Book*, 20; *New Zealand*, 200

Longstreeth, T. M. *The Scarlet Force: Making of the Mounted Police*, 169

Lord, W. *Peary to the Pole*, 207

Lovejoy, B. *The Land and People of Iraq*, 127; *Other Bible Lands*, 118

Lownsbery, E. *The Boy Knight of Reims*, 18

Lowrey, J. S. *In the Morning of the World*, 36

Lucas, J. M. *Man's First Million Years*, 223

Luckock, E. *William the Conqueror*, 114

Ludovici, L. J. *Great Moments in Medicine*, 227

Lynch, P. See Sewell, B. jt. auth.

Lyon, J. C. See Carpenter, A. jt. auth.

MacArthur, D. W. *Traders North*, 166

McAulay, J. D. See Lindsay, S. jt. auth.

McCall, E. S. *Pirates and Privateers*, 192

McClarren, J. K. *Mexican Assignment*, 174

McDonald, L. S. and Ross, Z. L. *For Glory and the King*, 176

MacDonald, N. *Land and People of Brazil*, 182

MacEoin, G. *Colombia and Venezuela and the Guianas*, 182, 184, 188

AUTHOR INDEX

McFall, C. *Maps Mean Adventure*, 216, 218

McGovern, A. *Robin Hood of Sherwood Forest*, 85; *The Story of Christopher Columbus*, 67

McGrady, M. *Jungle Doctors*, 228

MacGregor-Hastie, R. *Africa: Background for Today*, 155; *Pope John XXIII*, 114; *Pope Paul VI*, 115; *The Throne of Peter: A History of the Papacy*, 114

McGuire, E. *The Maoris of New Zealand*, 200

MacInnes, C. *Australia and New Zealand*, 197, 200

MacIntyre, D. G. *Fighting Ships and Seamen*, 233

McKendrick, M. *Ferdinand and Isabella*, 68, 69

McKinney, R. J. *Famous Old Masters of Painting*, 10

McKown, R. *The Congo—River of Mystery*, 155; *Giant of the Atom: Ernest Rutherford*, 111; *Marie Curie*, 23; *She Lived for Science: Irène Joliot-Curie*, 23; *The Story of the Incas: Mightiest Empire of the Early Americas*, 186

McLanathan, R. B. K. *Images of the Universe: Leonardo da Vinci, the Artist as Scientist*, 52; *The Pageant of Medieval Art and Life*, 3

MacLean, A. *Lawrence of Arabia*, 133

Macmillan, N. *Great Flights and Air Adventures: From Balloons to Spacecraft*, 216, 231

McNeer, M. *Armed With Courage*, 213; *The Canadian Story*, 168; *The Mexican Story*, 174

—and Ward, L. *John Wesley*, 114; *Martin Luther*, 33

Mac Orlan, P. *The Anchor of Mercy*, 19

McSpadden, J. W. *Robin Hood and His Merry Outlaws*, 85

McSwigan, M. *All Aboard for Freedom!*, 15; *Snow Treasure*, 57

MacVicar, A. and Caldwell, J. C. *Let's Visit Scotland*, 94

Madden, D. M. *Spain & Portugal: Iberian Portrait*, 60, 66

Mahmoud, Z. N. *The Land and People of Egypt*, 123

Maiden, C. *The Borrowed Crown*, 85

Malcolmson, A. *Song of Robin Hood*, 85

Malkus, A. S. *The Amazon—River of Promise*, 182; *Outpost of Peril*, 166; *Story of Louis Pasteur*, 26; *Story of Winston Churchill*, 103; *Young Inca Prince*, 185

Malory, Sir T. *Le Morte d'Arthur*, 81

Malvern, G. *Behold Your Queen*, 120; *The Six Wives of Henry VIII*, 107; *Tamar*, 46

Manchester, H. *Trail Blazers of Technology*, 228

Manley, S. *Rudyard Kipling: Creative Adventurer*, 107

—and Lewis, G. eds. *Teen-Age Treasury of Imagination and Discovery*, 216

Mann, A. L. and Vivian, A. C. *Famous Physicists*, 228

Mann, J. H. *Louis Pasteur, the Germ Killer*, 26

Manning-Sanders, R. *The Spaniards Are Coming*, 85; *Story of Hans Andersen: Swan of Denmark*, 16

Manson, Cecil and Manson, Celia. *The Adventures of Johnny Van Bart,* 199

Manson, Celia. See Manson, Cecil, jt. auth.

Mantel, S. G. *The Youngest Conquistador,* 173

Manton, J. *Portrait of Bach,* 30; *The Story of Albert Schweitzer,* 158

—See Gittings, R. jt. auth.

Manz, P. *Life in the Age of Charlemagne,* 3

Manzi, A. *White Boy,* 164

Marcus, R. B. *Antoine Lavoisier and the Revolution in Chemistry,* 25; *Galileo and Experimental Science,* 51; *Joseph Priestley, Pioneer Chemist,* 110; *Prehistoric Cave Paintings,* 223; *William Harvey: Trailblazer of Scientific Medicine,* 106

Markun, P. M. *The First Book of Central America and Panama,* 189; *First Book of the Panama Canal,* 189

Marryat, F. *The Children of the New Forest,* 88

Marsh, N. *New Zealand,* 200

Marsh, S. *All About Maps and Mapmaking,* 218

Marshall, H. E. *Scotland's Story,* 94

Marshall, S. L. A. *The Military History of the Korean War,* 149; *The Military History of the Spanish-American War: The War to Free Cuba,* 194

Martin, C. *Boer War,* 165; *The Boxer Rebellion,* 139; *The Russo-Japanese War,* 148; *Wonders of Prehistoric Man,* 223

—See also Hoyt, E. P.

Martin, R. *The Land and People of Morocco,* 163; *Looking at Italy,* 48

Marx, R. F. *The Battle of Lepanto 1571,* 5; *The Battle of the Spanish Armada, 1588,* 98; *Following Columbus: The Voyage of the Nina II,* 191; *Pirate Port: The Story of the Sunken City of Port Royal,* 191; *Treasure Fleets of the Spanish Main,* 192

Masani, S. *Gandhi's Story,* 144

Masefield, J. *Shepherdess of France: Remembrances of Jeanne d'Arc,* 23

Masey, M. L. *Story of the Steppes: Kazakh Folk Tales,* 72

Mason, F. V. *Battle for Quebec,* 169

Mason, H. M. *The Commandos: British Raider Heroes of World War II,* 100; *Duel for the Sky: Fighter Planes and Fighting Pilots of World War II,* 8; *Famous Firsts in Exploration,* 216

Matkin, R. B. *Your Book of Maps and Map Reading,* 218

Matthew, E. S. *The Land and People of Thailand,* 152

Matthews, H. L. *Cuba,* 194

Maurois, A. *Lafayette in America,* 24

Maxey, D. *Seeing London,* 94

Maxwell-Lefroy, C. *The Land and People of Burma,* 135; *The Land and People of Ceylon,* 136

May, C. P. *Central America: Lands Seeking Unity,* 189; *Chile: Progress on Trial,* 183; *Great Cities of Canada,* 168; *James Clerk Maxwell and Electromagnetism,* 108; *Michael Faraday and the Electric Dynamo,* 106; *Peru, Bolivia, Ecua-*

AUTHOR INDEX

dor: *The Indian Andes*, 182, 184, 185

May, J. *First Men*, 223

Mayne, W. ed. *William Mayne's Book of Heroes; Stories and Poems*, 213

—See Farjeon, E. jt. ed.

Mayo, M. R. *See* Dupuy, T. N. jt. auth.

Mead, M. *People and Places*, 223

Meadowcroft, E. L. *Gift of the River*, 124; *Scarab for Luck: A Story of Ancient Egypt*, 121

Meeker, O. *Israel Reborn*, 130

Mellersh, H. E. *Boys' Book of the Wonders of Man and His Achievements*, 210; *Finding Out About Ancient Egypt*, 122; *Imperial Rome*, 49; *Sumer and Babylon*, 127

Mellin, J. *Horses Across the Ages*, 231

Meltzer, M. *Slavery: From the Rise of Western Civilization to the Renaissance*, 210

Mercer, C. *Alexander the Great*, 41; *Let's Go to Europe*, 1

Meredith, R. K. and Smith, E. B. *Exploring the Great River: Early Voyagers on the Mississippi from De Soto to La Salle*, 170; *Quest of Columbus*, 67; *Riding With Coronado*, 177

Merrett, J. *Captain James Cook*, 196; *Famous Voyages in Small Boats*, 216; *True Story of Albert Schweitzer, Humanitarian*, 158

Merrick, H. H. *The First Book of Norway*, 57

Merrill, E. H. *See* Caldwell, W. E. jt. auth.

Meyer, E. P. *Champions of Peace: Winners of the Nobel Peace Prize*, 221; *Champions of the Four Freedoms*, 213; *Dynamite and Peace: Story of Alfred Nobel*, 70; *Friendly Frontier*, 168

Meyer, J. S. *Great Accidents in Science That Changed the World*, 227; *World Book of Great Inventions*, 227

Middleton, D. *England*, 94

Miers, E. S. *Pirate Chase*, 191

Miller, E. K. *Tell Me About Tokyo*, 146

Miller, H. H. *Greece*, 38

Miller, J. *Life in Russia Today*, 75

Miller, R. J. and Katoh, L. *First Book of Japan*, 146

Miller, S. *Desert Fighter: The Story of General Yigael Yadin and the Dead Sea Scrolls*, 131; *The Romans in the Days of the Empire*, 49

—See Ochsenschlager, E. jt. auth.

Mills, D. *Book of the Ancient World*, 127; *The People of Ancient Israel*, 130; *Renaissance and Reformation Times*, 5

Miner, I. *True Book of Communications*, 214

Mirsky, J. *Balboa: Discoverer of the Pacific*, 190

Mirsky, R. P. *Beethoven*, 31; *Brahms*, 31; *Haydn*, 12; *Johann Sebastian Bach*, 30; *Mozart*, 13

Mitchison, N. M. H. *African Heroes*, 157; *The Young Alexander the Great*, 41

Modak, M. *The Land and People of India*, 143

Montgomery, E. R. *Gandhi: Peaceful Fighter*, 144; *Hans Christian Andersen: Immortal Storyteller*, 16; *Hernando de Soto*, 68; *The Story Behind Great Inventions*, 227; *The Story Behind Great Medical Discoveries*, 227;

Toward Democracy: Great Documents of History, 210

Monypenny, K. *Young Traveler in Australia*, 197

Moore, J. and Caldwell, J. C. *Let's Visit Germany*, 30

Moore, M. *United Kingdom: A New Britain*, 94

Moore, P. A. *Exploring the World*, 216; *Isaac Newton*, 109

—and Brinton, H. *Exploring Maps*, 218

Moorehead, A. *The Story of the Blue Nile*, 124; *The Story of the White Nile*, 155

Morenus, R. *The Hudson's Bay Company*, 169

Morgan, B. E. *Hand of the King*, 126; *Journey for Tobiyah*, 133

Morgan, E. *So What About History?* 210

Morris, R. W. *Town Life Through the Ages*, 210; *Transport, Trade, and Travel Through the Ages*, 210, 231

Morrison, L. P. *The Lost Queen of Egypt*, 125

Morrison, S. *Armor*, 233

Morrow, S. S. *There Was a Time: The Story of Evolution*, 223

Moscow, H. *Russia Under the Czars*, 74

Mott, M. *The Blind Cross: A Novel of the Children's Crusade*, 1

Mulvey, M. W. *Digging Up Adam: The Story of L.S.B. Leakey*, 225

Murphy, R. W. *World of Cézanne*, 22

Murphy, Robert. *The Haunted Journey*, 74

Myers, H. and Burnett, R. *Vilhjalmur Stefansson: Young Arctic Explorer*, 207

Nakamoto, H. *My Japan, 1930-1951*, 148

Nano, F. C. *The Land and People of Sweden*, 69

Napier, J. *The Origins of Man*, 223

Nathan, A. G. *Churchill's England*, 100

Nazaroff, A. *The Land and People of Russia*, 73

Neal, H. E. *Communication: From Stone Age to Space Age*, 214; *Of Maps and Men*, 218

Nelson, R. C. *See* Rieber, A. J. jt. auth.

Nettel, R. *Great Moments in Music*, 10

Neuberger, R. L. *Royal Canadian Mounted Police*, 168

Neurath, M. *They Lived Like This in Ancient Africa*, 155; *They Lived Like This in Ancient Britain*, 95; *They Lived Like This in Ancient China*, 138; *They Lived Like This in Ancient Crete*, 39; *They Lived Like This in Ancient Egypt*, 122; *They Lived Like This in Ancient India*, 143; *They Lived Like This in Ancient Mesopotamia*, 127; *They Lived Like This in Ancient Palestine*, 130; *They Lived Like This in Ancient Persia*, 126; *They Lived Like This in Ancient Peru*, 186; *They Lived Like This in Ancient Rome*, 49; *They Lived Like This in Chaucer's England*, 97; *They Lived Like This in Old Japan*, 147; *They Lived Like This in Shakespeare's England*, 98; *They Lived Like This in the Old Stone Age*, 223; *They Lived Like This: The Ancient*

AUTHOR INDEX

Maya, 176; *They Lived Like This: The Vikings*, 64; *Wonder World of Snow and Ice*, 202

Nevins, A. J. *Away to Central America*, 190; *Away to East Africa*, 156; *Away to Mexico*, 174; *Away to the Lands of the Andes*, 179; *Away to Venezuela*, 188

Newcomb, C. *Leonardo da Vinci, Prince of Painters*, 52

Newell, V. *His Own Good Daughter*, 109

Newman, B. and Caldwell, J. C. *Let's Visit France*, 20
—See Caldwell, J. C. jt. auth.

Newman, R. *Grettir the Strong*, 63; *The Japanese: People of the 3 Treasures*, 146; *Merlin's Mistake*, 81

Newman, S. P. *Folk Tales of Japan*, 145; *Folk Tales of Latin America*, 179

Newton, D. *Seafarers of the Pacific*, 199

Nguyen Cao Dam and Tran Cao Linh. *Vietnam, Our Beloved Land*, 152

Nic Leodhas, S. *Claymore and Kilt; Tales of Scottish Kings and Castles*, 94

Nickel, H. *Warriors and Worthies; Arms and Armor Through the Ages*, 10, 233

Noble, I. *Egypt's Queen: Cleopatra*, 125; *Empress of All Russia: Catherine the Great*, 76; *The Honor of Balboa*, 190; *Rivals in Parliament: William Pitt and Charles Fox*, 99; *Spain's Golden Queen Isabella*, 69; *William Shakespeare*, 112

Noel-Baker, F. E. *Fridtjof Nansen: Arctic Explorer*, 206; *Looking at Greece*, 38

Nolan, J. C. *Florence Nightingale*, 110; *La Salle and the Grand Enterprise*, 172; *Story of Joan of Arc*, 24

Nolen, B. (ed.) *Africa Is People: Firsthand Accounts from Contemporary Africa*, 156; *Ethiopia*, 159

Nordhoff, C. B. and Hall, J. N. *The Bounty Trilogy*, 91; *Falcons of France*, 22; *Men Against the Sea*, 198; *Mutiny on the Bounty*, 198

Norman, C. *Flight and Adventures of Charles II*, 102; *The Long Bows of Agincourt*, 97

Norman, G. *A Man Named Columbus*, 68

Norman, J. *Charro: Mexican Horseman*, 174; *The Riddle of the Incas: The Story of Hiram Bingham and Macchu Picchu*, 186

North, S. *Captured by the Mohawks*, 166

Northcott, C. *Forest Doctor: The Story of Albert Schweitzer*, 158

Nowlan, N. *The Shannon: River of Loughs and Legends*, 45; *The Tiber: The Roman River*, 48

Nurenberg, T. *My Cousin, the Arab*, 128

Oakeshott, R. E. *A Knight and His Armor*, 3; *A Knight and His Horse*, 3; *A Knight and His Weapons*, 3

O'Brien, E. *The Land and People of Ireland*, 45

Ochsenschlager, E. and Miller, S. *The Egyptians in the Middle Kingdom*, 122

O'Connor, R. *John Lloyd Stephens: Explorer of Lost Worlds*, 178

O'Daniel, J. W. *Vietnam Today: The Challenge of a Divided Nation*, 152

Ogle, E. *Getting to Know the Arctic*, 205

Olden, S. *Getting to Know Africa's French Community*, 156; *Getting to Know Argentina*, 181; *Getting to Know Nigeria*, 162

Olds, H. D. *Christopher Columbus*, 68; *Richard E. Byrd*, 204

Oliver, J. *Queen Most Fair*, 85, 108; *Watch for the Morning*, 86; *The Young Robert Bruce*, 101

Oman, C. *Robin Hood*, 86

O'Meara, W. *First Northwest Passage*, 172

O'Neill, H. *The Picture Story of Denmark*, 16

O'Neill, M. *Saints: Adventures in Courage*, 11

Orbaan, A. *Duel in the Shadows*, 29; *Powder and Steel: Notable Battles of the 1800s from New Orleans to the Zulu War*, 233

Orczy, Emmuska, baroness. *The Scarlet Pimpernel*, 19

Orrmont, A. *Chinese Gordon: Hero of Khartoum*, 106; *Fearless Adventurer: Sir Richard Burton*, 101; *Fighter Against Slavery: Jehudi Ashmun*, 161

Osborne, C. G. *The First Bow and Arrow*, 221; *The First Lake Dwellers*, 221; *The First Wheel*, 221

Osborne, J. *Britain*, 94

Osmond, E. *From Drumbeat to Tickertape*, 214; *People of the Arctic*, 205

Owen, R. *Conquest of the North and South Poles*, 202

Paine, A. B. *The Girl in White Armor*, 24

Pallenberg, C. *Pope Paul VI*, 115

Palmer, G. *Quest for the Dead Sea Scrolls*, 129

—and Lloyd, N. *Quest for Prehistory*, 127, 225

Palmer, M. T. *At the Lion Gate*, 36; *The Egyptian Necklace*, 121

Paloheimo, L. and Watson, J. W. *Finland: Champion of Independence*, 17

Paradis, A. A. *Trade: The World's Lifeblood*, 210

Parke, M. B. *Getting to Know Australia*, 197

Parker, E. *Most Gracious Majesty*, 105

Paton, A. *The Land and People of South Africa*, 165

Paton Walsh, G. *The Dolphin Crossing*, 92; *Hengest's Tale*, 81

—and Crossley-Holland, K. *Wordhoard*, 81

Patton, W. *The Florentine Giraffe: A Tale of the Italian Renaissance*, 47

Pauli, H. E. *America's First Christmas*, 65; *Toward Peace: The Nobel Prizes and the Struggle for Peace*, 220

Payne, E. *The Pharaohs of Ancient Egypt*, 122

Payne, P. S. R. *Three Worlds of Albert Schweitzer*, 158

Payne, R. *The Splendor of Persia*, 126

Peacocke, M. D. *H.R.H., The*

AUTHOR INDEX

Duke of Edinburgh, 110
Peare, C. O. *Charles Dickens: His Life,* 104; *Jules Verne: His Life,* 27; *Mahatma Gandhi: The Father of Nonviolence,* 144; *Robert Louis Stevenson, His Life,* 113
Pearlman, M. *The Zealots of Masada: Story of a Dig,* 130
—*See* Comay, J. jt. auth.
Peart, H. *The Loyal Grenvilles,* 88; *Red Falcons of Trémoine,* 83
Peck, A. M. *The Pageant of Canadian History,* 168; *Pageant of Middle American History,* 190; *Pageant of South American History,* 179
Peet, C. *The First Book of Bridges,* 227, 231
Pelagie, D. *St. Francis,* 51
Pendle, G. *The Land and People of Argentina,* 181; *The Land and People of Chile,* 183; *The Land and People of Peru,* 186; *The Lands and Peoples of Paraguay and Uruguay,* 185, 187
Pepper, C. G. *The Pope's Back Yard,* 114
Perkins, C. M. *The Shattered Skull: A Safari to Man's Past,* 223
Perl, L. *Yugoslavia, Romania, Bulgaria: New Era in the Balkans,* 14, 62, 116
Petersham, Maud and Petersham, Miska. *Story of Jesus,* 120
Petersham, Miska. *See* Petersham, Maud, jt. auth.
Peterson, B. N. *See* Peterson, E. C. jt. auth.
Peterson, E. C. and Peterson, B. N. *To Find Jesus,* 120
Peterson, H. L. *A History of Body Armor,* 233; *A History of Firearms,* 233
Pfeiffer, J. E. *The Search for Early Man,* 223
Phelan, J. A. *Heroes and Aeroplanes of the Great War 1914-1918,* 7
Philipson, M. H. *The Count Who Wished He Were a Peasant,* 78
Phillips, Ted. *Getting to Know Saudi Arabia,* 132
Picard, B. L. *Celtic Tales,* 44; *Hero-Tales from the British Isles,* 81; *Lost John,* 86; *Ransom for a Knight,* 83; *Stories of King Arthur and His Knights,* 81; *Tales of the British People,* 81; *The Young Pretenders,* 91
Pickering, J. S. *Famous Astronomers,* 228
Pierson, S. *What Does a U.N. Soldier Do?* 220
Pike, E. R. *Ancient India,* 143; *Ancient Persia,* 126; *Republican Rome,* 49
Pilkington, R. *The Eisenbart Mystery,* 29
Pine, T. S. and Levine, J. *Africans Knew,* 156; *Incas Knew,* 186; *Chinese Knew,* 138; *Egyptians Knew,* 122
Pinney, R. *Quest for the Unknown: Explorers of Today,* 216
Pittenger, N. *See* Pittenger, W. N.
Pittenger, W. N. *Henry VIII of England,* 107; *The Life of Jesus Christ,* 120; *The Life of St. Paul,* 115; *The Life of Saint Peter,* 115; *Martin Luther: The Great Reformer,* 33; *Richard the Lionhearted: The Crusader King,* 111; *Saint Thomas Aquinas, the Angelic Doctor,* 54
Place, M. J. *Gold Down Under:*

The Story of the Australian Gold Rush, 197
Place, M. T. *The Yukon,* 168
Plaidy, J. *The Young Elizabeth,* 105; *Young Mary, Queen of Scots,* 108
Plutarch. *Parallel Lives,* 41, 50
Polatnick, F. T. and Saletan, A. L. *Shapers of Africa,* 157
Polking, K. *Let's Go on the Half Moon With Henry Hudson,* 171
Polland, M. A. *City of the Golden House,* 115; *Deirdre,* 44; *Mission to Cathay,* 141
Pond, S. G. *Ferdinand Magellan: Master Mariner,* 61
Poole, F. K. *First Book of Southeast Asia,* 151; *Indonesia,* 198; *The Philippines,* 200
Popescu, J. and Caldwell, J. C. *Let's Visit Russia,* 73; *Let's Visit Yugoslavia,* 116
—and others. *Rivers of the World, v 1: Danube, Amazon, Niger, Ganges,* 210, 218
Porter, J. *The Scottish Chiefs,* 101
Powell, B. *Modern Japan: A Brief History from 800 A.D. to the Present Day,* 146
Powell, G. E. *Latest Aztec Discoveries; Origin and Untold Riches,* 176
Power-Waters, A. S. *The Crusadder: The Story of Richard the Lionheart,* 111
Powers, A. *Alexander's Horses,* 37; *Hannibal's Elephants,* 46
Powers, R. M. *Cave Dwellers: In the Old Stone Age,* 223
Pownall, E. *Exploring Australia,* 197
Prago, A. *The Revolution in Spanish America: The Independence Movements of 1808-1825,* 179

Pratt, F. *All About Famous Inventors and Their Inventions,* 228
Pratt, S. *The French Revolution,* 21
Preston, E. *Marco Polo: A Story of the Middle Ages,* 141
Price, C. *Cities of Gold and Isles of Spice,* 139; *Made in Ancient Egypt,* 122; *Made in Ancient Greece,* 40
Price, O. *Story of Marco Polo,* 141
Priestley, H. *John Stranger,* 91
Pringle, P. *Highwaymen,* 99; *Napoleon's Hundred Days,* 21; *Young Dickens,* 104; *Young Livingstone,* 157
Proctor, G. L. *Ancient Scandinavia,* 64
Prodanovic, N. C. *Heroes of Serbia,* 116; *Heroes of Siberia,* 74
Pumphrey, G. H. *Conquering the English Channel,* 100
Purdy, C. L. *Gilbert and Sullivan: Masters of Mirth and Melody,* 106; *Song of the North: The Story of Edvard Grieg,* 58; *Stormy Victory: The Story of Tchaikovsky,* 78
Purton, R. W. *Captain Scott,* 204; *Doctor Livingstone,* 157
Pyle, H. *Howard Pyle's Book of Pirates,* 192; *Men of Iron,* 86; *The Merry Adventures of Robin Hood of Great Renown in Nottinghamshire,* 86; *Otto of the Silver Hand,* 28; *Story of King Arthur and His Knights,* 81; *The Story of Sir Launcelot and His Companions,* 81; *The Story of the Champions of the Round Table,* 81; *The Story of the Grail and the Passing of Arthur,* 81

AUTHOR INDEX

Quadflieg, J. *The Book of The Twelve Apostles*, 119; *The Saints and Your Name*, 213

Quennell, C. H. *See* Quennell, M. jt. auth.

Quennell, M. and Quennell, C. H. *Everyday Life in Prehistoric Times*, 223; *Everyday Life in Roman and Anglo-Saxon Times*, 95; *Everyday Things in Ancient Greece*, 40

Quest, O. W. H. *See* Hall-Quest, O. W.

Quigley, L. F. *Ireland*, 45

Quinn, V. *Picture Map Geography of Africa*, 156; *Picture Map Geography of Asia*, 138; *Picture Map Geography of Canada and Alaska*, 168; *Picture Map Geography of Mexico, Central America, and the West Indies*, 190, 192; *Picture Map Geography of South America*, 179; *Picture Map Geography of the Pacific Islands*, 195

Rachleff, O. S. *Young Israel: A History of the Modern Nation*, 129

Rachlis, E. *The Voyages of Henry Hudson*, 171

Rappaport, U. *The Story of the Dead Sea Scrolls*, 129

Rapport, S. B. *See* Wright, H. jt. ed.

Raswan, C. R. *Drinkers of the Wind*, 124

Rau, M. *The Yangtze River*, 138; *The Yellow River*, 138

Ray, M. *Standing Lions*, 39

Raymond, L. *See* Alexander, B. pseud.

Reader, W. J. *Life in Victorian England*, 99

Redford, L. B. *Getting to Know the Central Himalayas: Nepal, Sikkim, Bhutan*, 149; *Getting to Know the Northern Himalayas: Kashmir, Tibet, Assam*, 149

Reeder, R. *The Story of the First World War*, 7; *The Story of the Second World War:* [v 1] *The Axis Strikes (1939-1942)*, 8; *The Story of the Second World War:* [v 2] *The Allies Conquer (1942-1945)*, 9

Reeder, R. P. *See* Reeder, R.

Reese, M. M. *William Shakespeare*, 112

Reeves, J. *The Trojan Horse*, 36

Reilly, R. *Red Hugh, Prince of Donegal*, 44

Reingold, C. B. *Johann Sebastian Bach: Revolutionary of Music*, 30

Reit, S. *See* Bailey, A. jt. auth.

Renault, M. *The Lion in the Gateway*, 40

Reynolds, Q. J. *The Battle of Britain*, 94; *The Life of Saint Patrick*, 45; *Winston Churchill*, 103

Reynolds, R. *The True Story of Gandhi, Man of Peace*, 144

Reynolds, R. L. *Commodore Perry in Japan*, 147

Rhijn, A. van. *The Tide in the Attic*, 54

Ribbons, I. *Monday, 21 October 1805: The Day of Trafalgar*, 99; *Tuesday 4 August 1914: The First Day of World War I*, 7

Rice, T. T. *Byzantium*, 134; *Czars and Czarinas of Russia*, 74; *Everyday Life in Byzantium*, 134; *Finding Out About the Early Russians*, 74

Rich, L. D. *The First Book of the Vikings*, 64

Richards, K. G. *Albert Schweitzer*, 158; *Sir Winston Churchill*, 103

Richards, N. *Pope John XXIII*, 115

Richardson, J. *Young Louis Pasteur*, 26

Richter, W. *Bismarck*, 31

Ridle, J. B. *Mohawk Gamble*, 166

Rieber, A. J. and Nelson, R. C. *A Study of the USSR and Communism: An Historical Approach*, 75

Riedman, S. R. *Antoine Lavoisier — Scientist and Citizen*, 25; *Charles Darwin*, 104; *Men and Women Behind the Atom*, 229

Riesenberg, F. *Balboa: Swordsman and Conquistador*, 190

Rink, P. *Quest for Freedom; Bolivar and the South American Revolution*, 180

Ripley, E. *Goya*, 68; *Leonardo da Vinci*, 52; *Michelangelo*, 53; *Rubens*, 14; *Titian: A Biography*, 54; *Velázquez*, 69; *Vincent Van Gogh*, 56

Ripley, S. N. *Matthew Henson: Arctic Hero*, 206

Ritchie, C. T. *Runner of the Woods: Story of Young Radisson*, 172

Ritchie, E. *Totalitarianism and the Great Depression*, 9; *World War II and the Modern Age*, 9

Ritchie, P. *Australia*, 197

Ritchie, R. *Enemy at the Gate*, 43; *Golden Hawks of Genghis Khan*, 137; *Night Coach to Paris*, 19; *Secret Beyond the Mountains*, 137; *The Year of the Horse*, 137

Rittenhouse, M. *Seven Women Explorers*, 217

Robbin, I. *Giants of Medicine*, 229; *How and Why Wonder Book of Polar Regions*, 202

Robbins, R. *The Emperor and the Drummer Boy*, 19

Roberts, E. M. *Lenin and the Downfall of Tsarist Russia*, 77; *Mao Tse-tung and the Chinese Communist Revolution*, 140; *Stalin: Man of Steel*, 77

Robins, E. *Getting to Know the Congo River*, 156

Robinson, C. A. Jr. *Alexander the Great: Conqueror and Creator of a New World*, 41; *The First Book of Ancient Bible Lands*, 118; *The First Book of Ancient Crete and Mycenae*, 39; *The First Book of Ancient Egypt*, 122; *The First Book of Ancient Greece*, 40; *The First Book of Ancient Mesopotamia and Persia*, 127; *The First Book of Ancient Rome*, 49

Robinson, M. G. *Rival Cities — Venice and Genoa*, 48

Robinson, M. L. *King Arthur and His Knights*, 81

Rockwell, A. F. *Temple on a Hill*, 40

Roesch, R. F. *World's Fairs: Yesterday, Today, Tomorrow*, 210

Rogers, F. and Beard, A. *Heels, Wheels and Wire: The Story of Messages and Signals*, 214

Rogers, W. G. *Mightier Than the Sword; Cartoon, Caricature, Social Comment*, 210

Roland, A. *The Philippines*, 201; *Profiles from the New Asia*, 138

Rollins, F. *Getting to Know Canada*, 168

Rónay, I. C. *See* Csicsery-Rónay, I.

AUTHOR INDEX

Rosen, S. *Galileo and the Magic Numbers,* 51; *The Harmonious World of Johann Kepler,* 33

Rosenbaum, M. *London,* 94

Rosenblum, M. *Heroes of Mexico,* 176

Rosenfeld, S. *The First Song,* 72

Ross, B. *Mexico: Land of Eagle and Serpent,* 174

Ross, F. A. *The Land and People of Canada,* 168

Ross, F. X. *See* Frank, R. Jr. pseud.

Ross, N. W. *Joan of Arc,* 24

Ross, S. *The English Civil War,* 99

Ross, Z. L. *See* McDonald, L. S. jt. auth.

Rossif, F. and Chapsal, M. *Portrait of a Revolution,* 75

Rothkopf, C. *Jean Henri Dunant: Father of the Red Cross,* 71; *Leo Tolstoy,* 78; *The Red Cross,* 220; *Yugoslavia,* 116

Rowe, J. *United Nations Workers: Their Jobs, Their Goals, Their Triumphs,* 220

Rowland, J. *Ernest Rutherford, Master of the Atom,* 111

Roy, A. E. *Great Moments in Astronomy,* 227

Rubin, E. *The Curies and Radium,* 23

Ruffo, V. *Let's Go to the New World With Christopher Columbus,* 68

Rush, P. *The Young Shelley,* 112

Rushmore, R. *Fanny Kemble,* 107

Ruskin, A. *Spy for Liberty: The Adventurous Life of Beaumarchais,* 22

Russ, Lavinia and Russ, Liza, eds. *Forever England: Poetry and Prose About England and the English,* 94

Russ, Liza. *See* Russ, Lavinia, jt. ed.

Russell, J. *Clive of India,* 144

Rutland, J. *Looking at Denmark,* 16

Sadie, S. *Beethoven,* 31; *Handel,* 32

Sale, J. K. *The Land and People of Ghana,* 160

Saletan, A. L. *See* Polatnick, F. T. jt. auth.

Salisbury, H. E. *The Key to Moscow,* 73; *Russia,* 73

Salter, R. J. *Great Moments in Engineering,* 227

Samachson, D. and Samachson, J. *Good Digging: The Story of Archaeology,* 225

Samachson, J. *See* Samachson, D. jt. auth.

Samat, M. T. *See* Toussaint-Samat, M.

Sammis, E. R. *Last Stand at Stalingrad: The Battle That Saved the World,* 76

Samuel, R. *Israel and the Holy Land,* 129

Samuels, G. *B-G. Fighter of Goliaths: The Story of David Ben-Gurion,* 131

Sanderlin, G. W. (ed.) *Across the Ocean Sea: A Journal of Columbus's Voyage,* 66, 68; *Eastward to India: Vasco da Gama's Voyage,* 60; (ed.) *First Around the World: A Journal of Magellan's Voyage,* 60; *The Sea-Dragon: Journals of Francis Drake's Voyage Around the World,* 98

Sanders, R. M. *See* Manning-Sanders, R.

Sankey, J. F. *See* Filmer-Sankey, J.
Sasek, M. *This Is Edinburgh*, 94; *This Is Greece*, 38; *This Is Hong Kong*, 141; *This Is Ireland*, 45; *This Is Israel*, 129; *This Is London*, 94; *This Is Paris*, 20; *This Is Rome*, 48; *This Is Venice*, 48
Saunders, F. W. *Crossroads of Conquerors: The West Indies*, 192
Saunders, L. S. *See* Hartman, G. jt. auth.
Sauter, E. Jr. *See* Hennessey, M. N. jt. auth.
Savage, K. *People and Power: The Story of Three Nations*, 30, 73, 146; *Story of Africa: South of the Sahara*, 156; *The Story of Marxism and Communism*, 211; *Story of the Second World War*, 9; *Story of the United Nations*, 220; *Story of World Religions*, 211
Savory, P. *Congo Fireside Tales*, 159
Scarf, M. *Antarctica: Exploring the Frozen Continent*, 203
Schaaf, W. L. *Carl Friedrich Gauss: Prince of Mathematicians*, 32
Scharff, R. *See* Gelinas, P. J. jt. auth.
Scheele, W. E. *Cave Hunters*, 223; *Mound Builders*, 223; *Prehistoric Man and the Primates*, 223
Scheib, I. *What Happened: The Science Stories Behind the News*, 227
Scherman, K. *Catherine The Great*, 76; *The Slave Who Freed Haiti: The Story of Toussaint L'Ouverture*, 193; *William Tell*, 71
Schickel, R. *World of Goya*, 69

Schlein, M. *Amuny, Boy of Old Egypt*, 121
Schlining, P. *United Nations and What It Does*, 220
Schneider, E. ed. *King Arthur and the Knights of the Round Table*, 82
Schroeder, M. *The Hunted Prince*, 63
Schull, J. *Battle for the Rock: The Story of Wolfe and Montcalm*, 170
Schultz, B. *The Secret of the Pharaohs*, 121
Scoggin, M. ed. *Escapes and Rescues*, 216
Scott, J. *China, The Hungry Dragon*, 138
Scott, Sir W. *Ivanhoe*, 83; *Quentin Durward*, 18
Sears, S. W. *Desert War in North Africa*, 163
Seed, J. *The Voice of the Great Elephant*, 153, 157
Seeger, E. *The Five Sons of King Pandu*, 142; *The Pageant of Chinese History*, 138; *Pageant of Russian History*, 73
Seeger, M. L. *The Day of the Earthquake*, 37
Seegers, K. *Brazil: Awakening Giant*, 182
Seigel, K. *See* Feigenbaum, L. jt. auth.
Selden, G. *Heinrich Schliemann: Discoverer of Buried Treasure*, 42; *Sir Arthur Evans: Discoverer of Knossos*, 106
Sellew, C. F. *Adventures With the Heroes*, 63
Sellman, R. R. *Ancient Egypt*, 123; *The Anglo-Saxons*, 96; *Civil War and the Commonwealth*, 99; *The Crusades*, 3;

AUTHOR INDEX

Elizabethan Seamen, 98; *The First World War*, 7; *Medieval English Warfare*, 97; *Norman England*, 97; *Prehistoric Britain*, 96; *Roman Britain*, 96; *The Second World War*, 9; *The Vikings*, 64

Selsam, M. E. *Around the World With Darwin*, 104; *The Quest of Captain Cook*, 196

Sen, G. *Pageant of India's History*, 143

Serage, N. *The Prince Who Gave Up a Throne: A Story of the Buddha*, 144

Seroff, V. *Wolfgang Amadeus Mozart*, 13

Serraillier, I. *Chaucer and His World*, 102; *The Clashing Rocks: The Story of Jason*, 36; *A Fall from the Sky: The Story of Daedalus*, 36; *The Gorgon's Head: The Story of Perseus*, 37; *Havelok the Dane*, 16; *Robin and His Merry Men*, 86; *The Way of Danger: The Story of Theseus*, 37

Seth, R. *Spies: Their Trade and Tricks*, 233

Severn, B. *Free But Not Equal: How Women Won the Right to Vote*, 211

Sewell, B. and Lynch, P. *The Story of Ancient Egypt*, 123

Seymour, A. H. *Toward Morning: A Story of the Hungarian Freedom Fighters*, 43; *When the Dikes Broke*, 54

Shamir, G. *See* Shamir, M. jt. auth.

Shamir, M. and Shamir G. *The Story of Israel in Stamps*, 129

Shapiro, I. *The Golden Book of the Renaissance*, 5

Shapiro, W. E. ed. *D-Day*, 9; *Lenin and Trotsky*, 77, 78; *Pope Paul VI*, 115; *Trial at Nuremberg*, 30

Shearman, J. *The Land and People of Iran*, 126

Sheldon, W. J. *The Key to Tokyo*, 146; *Tiger in the Rice: A Short History of Vietnam*, 152

Shepherd, D. *We Were There at the Battle of the Bulge*, 30

Sheppard, S. *The First Book of Brazil*, 183

Sherlock, P. *The Land and People of the West Indies*, 192

Shippen, K. B. *Leif Eriksson: First Voyager to America*, 58; *Moses*, 121; *Pool of Knowledge: How the United Nations Share Their Skills*, 220; *Portals to the Past: The Story of Archaeology*, 225

Shirer, W. L. *Rise and Fall of Adolf Hitler*, 33; *The Sinking of the Bismarck*, 100

Shirley, J. *Leonardo da Vinci*, 52; *Shakespeare*, 112

Showers, P. *Columbus Day*, 68

Shuttlesworth, D. *The Tower of London: Grim and Glamorous*, 94

Siedel, F. and Siedel, J. M. *Pioneers in Science*, 229

Siedel, J. M. *See* Siedel, F. jt. auth.

Silver, S. M. *See* Braverman, L. L. jt. auth.

Silverberg, R. *Fifteen Battles That Changed the World*, 233; *The Seven Wonders of the Ancient World*, 211; *Socrates*, 42; *Stormy Voyager: The Story of Charles Wilkes*, 204; *Wonders of Ancient Chinese Science*, 139
—*See also* Chapman, W. pseud.

Silverstein, A. and Silverstein, V. *Carl Linnaeus: The Man Who*

WORLD HISTORY IN JUVENILE BOOKS

Put the World of Life in Order, 70

Silverstein, V. *See* Silverstein, A. jt. auth.

Simon, C. M. *All Men Are Brothers: A Portrait of Albert Schweitzer,* 158; *Dag Hammarskjold,* 70; *The Sun and the Birch: The Story of Crown Prince Akihito and Crown Princess Michiko,* 148

Simon, T. *North Pole: The Story of Robert E. Peary,* 207

Simpson, J. *Everyday Life in the Viking Age,* 64

Simpson, J. H. *See* Hope-Simpson, J.

Sims, B. B. *Confucius,* 140

Sisson, R. *Young Shakespeare,* 112

Skinner, E. *See* Chu, D. jt. auth.

Slinkman, J. *Duel to the Death: Eyewitness Accounts of Great Battles at Sea,* 234

Smaridge, N. *The Light Within: The Story of Maria Montessori,* 53

Smart, J. D. *A Promise to Keep,* 119

Smith, D. C. Jr. *The Land and People of Indonesia,* 198

Smith, E. B. *See* Meredith, R. K. jt. auth.

Smith, F. *Stanley: African Explorer,* 158

Smith, F. C. *The World of the Arctic,* 205

Smith, I. *Paris,* 20

Smith, J. W. D. *Bible Background,* 119

Smith, N. D. *Winston Churchill,* 103

Smith, P. *See* Francis, H. jt. auth.

Smith, R. L. *Getting to Know the World Health Organization,* 220

Smither, E. L. *Early Old Testament Stories,* 119; *Later Old Testament Stories,* 119; *Picture Book of Palestine,* 129

Snedeker, C. D. *The Forgotten Daughter,* 38; *Lysis Goes to the Play,* 37; *Theras and His Town,* 37; *A Triumph for Flavius,* 46; *The White Isle,* 78

Snellgrove, L. E. *Franco and the Spanish Civil War,* 68

Snow, D. J. *Henry Hudson, Explorer of the North,* 172

Snyder, L. L. *Bismarck and German Unification,* 31; *The First Book of the Long Armistice,* 9; *The First Book of the Soviet Union,* 76; *The First Book of World War I,* 7; *The First Book of World War II,* 9; *Hitler and Nazism,* 33

—and Brown, I. M. *Frederick the Great: Prussian Warrior and Statesman,* 32

Sobol, D. J. *The First Book of Medieval Man,* 3

Softly, B. *Place Mill,* 88; *Plain Jane,* 88; *A Stone in a Pool,* 88

Sommerfelt, A. *Miriam,* 57

Soni, W. H. *Getting to Know the River Ganges,* 143

Sootin, H. *Gregor Mendel: Father of the Science of Genetics,* 12

Speiser, J. *UNICEF and the World,* 220

Spencer, C. *Ancient China,* 139; *Chiang Kai-shek: Generalissimo of Nationalist China,* 140; *China's Leaders in Ideas and Action,* 140; *Claim to Freedom: The Rise of the Afro-Asian Peoples,* 156; *Keeping Ahead of Machines: The Human Side of the Automation Revolution,* 227;

AUTHOR INDEX

The Land of the Chinese People, 138; *Made in China,* 138; *Modern China,* 139; *The Song in the Streets,* 21; *Sun Yat-sen: Founder of the Chinese Republic,* 141; *The Yangtze: China's River Highway,* 138

Spencer, W. *The Land and People of Morocco,* 163; *The Land and People of Tunisia,* 163; *The Land and People of Turkey,* 134

Sperry, A. *All About the Arctic and Antarctic,* 202; *The Amazon: River Sea of Brazil,* 183; *Captain Cook Explores the South Seas,* 196; *Pacific Islands Speaking,* 195; *The Voyages of Christopher Columbus,* 68

Spier, P. *Of Dikes and Windmills,* 55

Spink, R. *Young Hans Andersen,* 16

Sprague, R. *Fife and Fandango,* 65

Stafford, A. *Young Bernadette,* 22

Stafford, M. P. *Discoverer of the North Pole, the Story of Robert E. Peary,* 207

Stahl, B. *Blackbeard's Ghost,* 191

Stambler, I. *Wonders of Underwater Exploration,* 216

Stanley-Wrench, M. *The Conscience of a King: The Story of Thomas More,* 109

Stearns, M. *Charlemagne,* 23; *Dante: Poet of Love,* 51; *Elizabeth I of England,* 105; *Goethe: Pattern of Genius,* 32; *Goya and His Times,* 69; *Louis XIV of France: Pattern of Majesty,* 25; *Michelangelo,* 53; *Rembrandt and His World,* 55; *Richard Wagner: Titan of Music,* 34; *Wolfgang Amadeus Mozart: Master of Pure Music,* 13

Steele, W. O. *Story of Leif Ericson,* 58

Stefansson, E. *Here Is the Far North,* 205

Steffan, J. *The Long Fellow,* 45

Steffensen, J. L. *The Renaissance,* 5

—See Johnston, J. jt. auth.

Steinberg, R. *Japan,* 146

Stephens, P. J. *Battle for Destiny,* 86; *Outlaw King: The Story of Robert the Bruce,* 101

Sterling, D. *United Nations, N.Y.,* 221

Sterling, T. L. *Exploration of Africa,* 156

Sterling Publishing Company, Editors of. *Belgium and Luxembourg in Pictures,* 14; *Berlin East and West in Pictures,* 30; *Canada in Pictures,* 168; *Caribbean—The English-Speaking Islands in Pictures,* 192; *Ceylon in Pictures,* 136; *Chile in Pictures,* 183; *Czechoslovakia in Pictures,* 15; *Ecuador in Pictures,* 184; *France in Pictures,* 20; *French Canada in Pictures,* 168; *Holland in Pictures,* 55; *Honduras in Pictures,* 190; *Hong Kong in Pictures,* 141; *Iceland in Pictures,* 44; *Iran in Pictures,* 126; *Ireland in Pictures,* 45; *Israel in Pictures,* 129; *Italy in Pictures,* 48; *Jamaica in Pictures,* 192; *Kenya: In Pictures,* 161; *Lebanon in Pictures,* 132; *Liberia in Pictures,* 161; *Pakistan in Pictures,* 150; *Panama and the Canal Zone in Pictures,* 190; *Poland in Pictures,* 59; *Portugal in Pictures,* 60; *Russia in Pictures,*

73; *Scotland in Pictures*, 94; *South Africa in Pictures*, 165; *Spain in Pictures*, 66; *Sweden in Pictures*, 70; *Switzerland in Pictures*, 71; *Tahiti and the French Islands of the Pacific—in Pictures*, 199; *Thailand in Pictures*, 152; *Venezuela in Pictures*, 188; *Wales in Pictures*, 95; *West Germany in Pictures*, 30; *Yugoslavia in Pictures*, 116

Sterne, E. G. *Benito Juarez: Builder of a Nation*, 178; *The Long Black Schooner*, 153; *Vasco Nuñez de Balboa*, 190

Stevens, W. O. *Famous Scientists*, 229

Stevenson, R. L. *The Black Arrow*, 86; *Kidnapped*, 91; *Treasure Island*, 91

Stewart, D. S. *Turkey*, 134

Stiles, M. B. *Darkness Over the Land*, 29

Stillman, M. See Tannenbaum, B. jt. auth.

Stilwell, H. *Looking at Man's Past*, 224

Stinetorf, L. A. *Children of Africa*, 156

Stockton, F. R. *Buccaneers and Pirates of Our Coasts*, 192

Stoiber, R. M. *Henri Dunant: Man in White*, 71

Stonaker, F. B. *Famous Mathematicians*, 229

Stone, A. H. See Kelman, P. jt. auth.

Stone, E. *Page Boy for King Arthur*, 82; *Robin Hood's Arrow*, 86; *Squire for King Arthur*, 82

Stone, I. *The Great Adventure of Michelangelo*, 53

Storry, R. *Japan*, 147

Stoutenburg, A. and Baker, L. N. *Beloved Botanist*, 70; *Explorer of the Unconscious: Sigmund Freud*, 12

Strauss, R. *Coal, Steel, Atoms, and Trade: Challenge of Uniting Europe*, 9

Streatfeild, N. *The First Book of England*, 95; *Queen Victoria*, 113; *The Thames: London's River*, 95

Street, A. *The Land of the English People*, 95

Strong, C. S. *We Were There With Byrd at the South Pole*, 202

Strousse, F. *Friar and the Knight: Bartolomé de Olmedo and Cortez*, 177; *John Milton: Clarion Voice of Freedom*, 108

Struchen J. *Joan of Arc: Maid of Orleans*, 24; *Pablo Picasso: Master of Modern Art*, 69; *Pope John XXIII: The Gentle Shepherd*, 115

Styles, S. *First Up Everest*, 150; *Mallory of Everest*, 150; *Midshipman Quinn*, 91; *Midshipman Quinn and Denise, the Spy*, 91; *Quinn of the Fury*, 92

Sufrin, M. *Brave Men: Twelve Portraits of Courage*, 213; *To the Top of the World: Sir Edmund Hillary and the Conquest of Everest*, 150

Suggs, R. C. *Alexander the Great, Scientist-King*, 41; *Lords of the Blue Pacific*, 195

Sullivan, G. *Seven Wonders of the Modern World*, 211

Sully, F. *Age of the Guerrilla: A Background Book for Young People on Modern Guerrilla Warfare*, 234

Sutcliff, R. *Dawn Wind*, 82; *Eagle of the Ninth*, 78; *Heroes and*

AUTHOR INDEX

History, 213; *Knight's Fee,* 83; *Lantern Bearers,* 82; *The Mark of the Horse Lord,* 79; *Outcast,* 79; *Shield Ring,* 83; *Silver Branch,* 79; *Warrior Scarlet,* 79

Sutton, A. and Sutton, M. *Among the Maya Ruins: The Adventures of John Lloyd Stephens and Frederick Catherwood,* 178; *Journey Into Ice: John Franklin and the Northwest Passage,* 206

Sutton, F. *The How and Why Wonder Book of World War II,* 9

Sutton, M. See Sutton, A. jt. auth.

Swindler, W. F. *Magna Carta,* 97

Syme, R. *African Traveler: The Story of Mary Kingsley,* 157; *Alexander Mackenzie, Canadian Explorer,* 172; *Amerigo Vespucci, Scientist and Sailor,* 181; *Balboa, Finder of the Pacific,* 190; *Bay of the North: The Story of Pierre Radisson,* 172; *Bolivar: The Liberator,* 180; *Captain Cook, Pacific Explorer,* 196; *Cartier: Finder of the St. Lawrence,* 171; *Champlain of the St. Lawrence,* 171; *Columbus, Finder of the New World,* 68; *Cortes of Mexico,* 177; *De Soto, Finder of the Mississippi,* 68; *Francis Drake, Sailor of the Unknown Seas,* 105; *Francisco Coronado and the Seven Cities of Gold,* 177; *Francisco Pizarro, Finder of Peru,* 187; *Frontenac of New France,* 171; *Garibaldi: The Man Who Made a Nation,* 52; *Henry Hudson,* 172; *La Salle of the Mississippi,* 172; *Magellan, First Around the World,* 61; *Nigerian Pioneer, the Story of Mary Slessor,* 162; *On Foot to the Arctic: The Story of Samuel Hearne,* 206; *Quesada of Colombia,* 184; *Sir Henry Morgan, Buccaneer,* 193; *Vancouver, Explorer of the Pacific Coast,* 173; *Vasco da Gama, Sailor Toward the Sunrise,* 61; *Walter Raleigh,* 111; *Young Nelson,* 109

Tannenbaum, B. and Stillman, M. *Isaac Newton: Pioneer of Space Mathematics,* 109; *Understanding Maps; Charting the Land, Sea and Sky,* 218

Tappan, E. M. *When Knights Were Bold,* 3

Tarshis, J. *Andreas Vesalius: Father of Modern Anatomy,* 14

Taslitt, I. I. *Soldier of Israel: The Story of General Moshe Dayan,* 131; *Young Samson,* 121

Taylor, A. and Cole, L. D. See Dwight, A. pseud.

Taylor, C. *Getting to Know Burma,* 135; *Getting to Know Indonesia,* 198

Taylor, D. *Ancient Greece,* 40; *Ancient Rome,* 50; *Chaucer's England: Living in England,* 97; *The Elizabethan Age: Living in England,* 98; *Fielding's England,* 92

—and Cochrane, L. *The World of Nations,* 211

Taylor, J. W. *Great Moments in Flying,* 231

Taylor, M. M. See Moore, M.

Teall, K. *From Tsars to Commissars: The Story of the Russian Revolution,* 74

Tennyson, A. L. *Charge of the Light Brigade,* 99

Terraine, J. *The Great War, 1914-1918: A Pictorial History,* 7

Terrien, S. *The Golden Bible Atlas,* 119

Tharp, L. H. *Champlain: Northwest Voyager,* 171; *Company of Adventurers; The Story of the Hudson's Bay Company,* 169

Thayer, C. W. *Russia,* 73

Thomas, Henry. *Copernicus,* 51; *Sister Elizabeth Kenny,* 198

Thomas, Hugh, *Spain,* 66

Thomas, J. *Leonardo da Vinci,* 52; *True Story of Lawrence of Arabia,* 133

Thomas, M. Z. *Albert Schweitzer,* 158; *Alexander von Humboldt: Scientist, Explorer, Adventurer,* 181

Thomas, R. W. *See* Cadell, J. pseud.

Thompson, B. J. *Peter and Paul: The Rock and the Sword,* 115

Thompson, E. B. *Africa: Past and Present,* 156

Thompson, J. *Nelson: Hero of Trafalgar,* 109

Thomsen, G. T. *See* Thorne-Thomsen, G.

Thoorens, L. *The Golden Compass,* 13

Thorne, A. *Story of Madame Curie,* 23

Thorne-Thomsen, G. *In Norway,* 57

Tibbets, A. B. comp. *Salute to the Brave: Stories of World War Two,* 234

Tillyard, A. *The Land and People of Yugoslavia,* 116

Toland, J. *Flying Tigers,* 139

Tolboom, W. *People of the Snow: Eskimos of Arctic Canada,* 206

Tooze, R. *Cambodia: Land of Contrasts,* 135

Tor, R. *Getting to Know Greece,* 38; *Getting to Know the Philippines,* 201

Torgersen, D. A. *Gandhi,* 144

Toussaint-Samat, M. *Stories of the Crusades,* 3

Toye, W. *Cartier Discovers the St. Lawrence,* 171; *St. Lawrence,* 168

Tran Cao Linh. *See* Nguyen Cao Dam, jt. auth.

Trapp, M. A. *The Story of the Trapp Family Singers,* 11

Trease, G. *Bows Against the Barons,* 86; *Cue for Treason,* 86; *Escape to King Alfred,* 82; *Seven Sovereign Queens,* 11; *Victory at Valmy,* 19; *Word to Caesar,* 46

Treece, H. *The Burning of Njal,* 43; *The Centurion,* 79; *Horned Helmet,* 43; *Know About the Crusades,* 3; *The Last Viking,* 63; *Man With a Sword,* 83; *Road to Miklagard,* 63; *Splintered Sword,* 63; *Swords from the North,* 63; *Viking's Dawn,* 63; *War Dog,* 79; *The Windswept City,* 37

Treviño, E. B. de. *Casilda of the Rising Moon,* 65; *Here is Mexico,* 174

Tucker, E. E. *Soldiers and Armies,* 234; *The Story of Fighting Ships,* 234; *The Story of Knights and Armor,* 3

Tunis, E. *Oars, Sails, and Steam,* 231; *Weapons: A Pictorial History,* 234; *Wheels: A Pictorial History,* 231

Turlington, B. *Socrates: The Father of Western Philosophy,* 42

AUTHOR INDEX

Turnbull, C. M. *The Peoples of Africa,* 156

Turner, P. *Steam on the Line,* 92

Twain, M. *The Prince and the Pauper,* 86

Uden, G. *A Dictionary of Chivalry,* 3; *Hero Tales from the Age of Chivalry: Retold from the Froissart Chronicles,* 3

Underwood, P. S. *Getting to Know Eastern Europe,* 117

Undset, S. *Sigurd and His Brave Companions: A Tale of Medieval Norway,* 56; *True and Untrue,* 63

Unstead, R. J. *British Castles,* 95; *Looking at Ancient History,* 127; *Looking at History,* 95; *Royal Adventurers,* 11; *Some Kings and Queens,* 11; *The Story of Britain,* 95

Untermeyer, B. and Untermeyer, L. eds. *Adventure Stories,* 1

Untermeyer, L. *See* Untermeyer, B. jt. ed.

Vaeth, J. G. *To the Ends of the Earth: The Explorations of Roald Amundsen,* 204

Vance, E. *Adventures of Robin Hood,* 86

Vance, M. *Ashes of Empire: Carlota and Maximilian of Mexico,* 176, 178; *Dark Eminence: Catherine De Medici and Her Children,* 22; *Elizabeth Tudor, Sovereign Lady,* 105; *The Empress Josephine from Martinique to Malmaison,* 24; *Lady Jane Grey, Reluctant Queen,* 106; *Marie Antoinette: Daughter of an Empress,* 25; *Scotland's Queen; The Story of Mary Stuart,* 108; *Six Queens: The Wives of Henry VIII,* 107; *Song for a Lute,* 111

Van Riper, G. *Richard Byrd: Boy Who Braved the Unknown,* 204

Vaughan, J. B. *The Land and People of Japan,* 147; *The Land and People of the Philippines,* 201

Vaughan-Jackson, G. *Animals and Men in Armor,* 234; *Carramore,* 44

Vergil. *The Aeneid,* 37, 46

Verne, J. *Michael Strogoff,* 72

Villiers, A. J. *The Battle of Trafalgar,* 100

Vining, E. G. *Windows for the Crown Prince,* 148

Vinton, I. *Story of Edith Cavell,* 102

Vittengl, M. J. *All Round Hong Kong,* 142

Vivian, A. C. *See* Mann, A. L. jt. auth.

Vlahos, O. *African Beginnings,* 128; *The Battle-Ax People: Beginnings of Western Culture,* 3; *Human Beginnings,* 224; *New World Beginnings: Indian Cultures in the Americas,* 180

Von Hagen, V. W. *The Incas: People of the Sun,* 187; *Maya: Land of the Turkey and the Deer,* 175; *Roman Roads,* 50; *The Sun Kingdom of the Aztecs,* 176

Von Maltitz, F. W. *The Rhone: River of Contrasts,* 1

Walker, R. L. *First Book of Ancient China,* 139

Wallace, J. A. *Getting to Know Egypt,* 124; *Getting to Know France,* 20; *Getting to Know*

Poland, 59; *Getting to Know the Soviet Union*, 76
Wallace, L. *The Boys' Ben-Hur; a Tale of the Christ*, 47
Wallace, R. *Rise of Russia*, 74; *The World of Van Gogh, 1853-1890*, 56
Wallhauser, H. T. *Pioneers of Flight*, 231
Wallower, L. *The Lost Prince: Louis XVII of France*, 19, 25
Walsh, G. P. *See* Paton Walsh, G.
Walsh, J. P. *See* Paton Walsh, G.
Walsh R. J. *The Adventures and Discoveries of Marco Polo*, 141
Walworth, N. Z. *See* Brooks, P. S. jt. auth.
Ward, L. *See* McNeer, M. jt. auth.
Warner, O. *Captain Cook and the South Pacific*, 196; *Nelson and the Age of Fighting Sail*, 100
Warren, R. *The First Book of Modern Greece*, 41; *The First Book of the Arab World*, 132; *Muhammad: Prophet of Islam*, 133; *The Nile — The Story of Pharaohs, Farmers, and Explorers*, 124
Warwick, A. R. *Let's Look at Castles*, 3
Waters, A. S. P. *See* Power-Waters, A. S.
Watson, James Wreford. *Canada: Giant Nation of the North*, 168; *Egypt: Child of the Nile*, 124; *Ethiopia: Mountain Kingdom*, 160; *Greece: Land of Golden Light*, 38; *India: Old Land, New Nation*, 143; *The Indus: South Asia's Highway of History*, 143; *Iran: Crossroads of Caravans*, 126; *Japan: Islands of the Rising Sun*, 147; *Nigeria: Republic of a Hundred Kings*, 162; *Peru: Land Astride the Andes*, 186; *Thailand: Rice Bowl of Asia*, 152
Watson, Jane Werner. *See* Paloheimo, L. jt. auth.
Watson, S. *To Build a Land*, 129; *Witch of the Glens*, 88
Webb, R. N. *Attila: King of the Huns*, 50; *Genghis Khan: Conqueror of the Medieval World*, 140; *Hannibal, Invader from Carthage*, 52; *The How and Why Wonder Book of Florence Nightingale*, 110; *James Watt: Inventor of a Steam Engine*, 113; *Jean Jacques Rousseau: The Father of Romanticism*, 27; *Leaders of Our Time: v3*, 213; *Leaders of Our Time: v4*, 213; *Marco Polo: The Great Traveler*, 141; *Simón Bolívar: The Liberator*, 180; *We Were There With Caesar's Legions*, 47; *We Were There With Florence Nightingale in the Crimea*, 92; *We Were There With Richard the Lionhearted in the Crusades*, 83; *Winston Churchill: Man of the Century*, 103
Webster, G. *The Man Who Found Out Why: The Story of Gregor Mendel*, 12
Webster, T. B. *Everyday Life in Classical Athens*, 40
Wedgwood, C. V. *Milton and His World*, 108; *The World of Rubens, 1577-1640*, 14
Weingarten, V. *Ganges: Sacred River of India*, 143; *The Jordan: River of the Promised Land*, 131; *The Nile: Lifeline of Egypt*, 124
Weir, R. *High Courage*, 83; *The Lion and the Rose*, 88

AUTHOR INDEX

Weir, R. C. *Leif Ericson, Explorer,* 58

Weisgard, L. *The Athenians in the Classical Period,* 40; *Beginnings of Cities,* 211; *First Farmers: In the Stone Age,* 224

Weiss, D. A. *Great Fire of London,* 99

Welch, R. *Bowman of Crécy,* 83; *Ferdinand Magellan,* 61; *For the King,* 89; *Nicholas Carey,* 92

Weller, G. *Story of Submarines,* 234

Wells, R. F. *On Land and Sea With Caesar; or, Following the Eagles,* 47; *With Caesar's Legions,* 47

Wentworth, E. *Mission to Metlakatla,* 170

Werstein, I. *All the Furious Battles: The Saga of Israel's Army,* 131; *Betrayal: The Munich Pact of 1938,* 9; *The Cruel Years: The Story of the Spanish Civil War,* 66; *The Franco-Prussian War: Germany's Rise as a World Power,* 30; *I Accuse: The Story of the Dreyfus Case,* 21; *The Long Escape,* 13; *The Many Faces of World War I,* 7; *Ten Days in November,* 76; *That Denmark Might Live,* 15; *Trespassers: Korea, June, 1871,* 149

West, A. *The Crusades,* 3; *Getting to Know the Two Vietnams,* 152

Westcott, F. *Bach,* 30

Weston, C. *Afghanistan,* 135; *Ceylon,* 136

Weyr, T. *World War II,* 9

Wheeler, O. *Adventures of Richard Wagner,* 34; *Frederic Chopin, Son of Poland: Early Years,* 59; *Frederic Chopin, Son of Poland: Later Years,* 59; *Handel at the Court of Kings,* 32; *Hans Andersen, Son of Denmark,* 16; *Ludwig Beethoven and the Chiming Tower Bells,* 31; *Moses,* 121; *Peter Tschaikowsky and the Nutcracker Ballet,* 78; *Robert Schumann and Mascot Ziff,* 34; *Story of Peter Tschaikowsky,* 78

—and Deucher, S. *Franz Schubert and His Merry Friends,* 13; *Joseph Haydn: The Merry Little Peasant,* 12; *Mozart, the Wonder Boy,* 13

Whelpton, B. *Paris Triumphant,* 20

Whipple, A. B. *Famous Pirates of the New World,* 193

White, A. T. *All About Archaeology,* 225; *First Men in the World,* 224; *The Golden Treasury of Myths and Legends,* 1; *Knights of the Table Round,* 82; *Lost Worlds: The Romance of Archaeology,* 225; *The St. Lawrence: Seaway of North America,* 169; *Will Shakespeare and the Globe Theatre,* 112

White, D. M. *Caesar to Churchill,* 95

White, H. *Song Without End: The Love Story of Clara and Robert Schumann,* 34

White, J. M. *Everyday Life in Ancient Egypt,* 123

White, R. J. *Life in Regency England,* 106

Whitehead, A. C. *Standard Bearer: A Story of Army Life in the Time of Caesar,* 47

Whitehouse, A. *The Laughing*

Falcon, 19; *Spies With Wings: The Story of the Lafayette Escadrille*, 19
—and Lancelot, M. *Fighting Wings: The Story of Aerial Combat in World War I*, 7
Whitney, D. C. *Latin America*, 180, 190
Whitridge, A. *Simon Bolivar: The Great Liberator*, 180
Whittam, G. and others. *Rivers of the World, v2: Rhine, Murray, Nile, St. Lawrence*, 211, 218
Wibberley, L. *Epics of Everest*, 149; *Kevin O'Connor and the Light Brigade*, 92; *Life of Winston Churchill*, 103
Widder, A. *Action in Submarines*, 234; *Adventures in Black*, 234
Wilber, D. N. *The Land and People of Ceylon*, 136
Wilhelm, M. *For the Glory of France: The Story of the French Resistance*, 22
Wilkens, F. *Ancient Crete*, 39
Wilkes, J. *Roman Army*, 50
Wilkie, K. E. *Charles Dickens, The Inimitable Boz*, 104; *Ferdinand Magellan: Noble Captain*, 61; *Robert Louis Stevenson: Storyteller and Adventurer*, 113
Wilkinson, B. *Cardinal in Armor: The Story of Richelieu and His Times*, 27; *Cry Spy: True Stories of Twentieth Century Spies and Spy Catchers*, 234; *The Helmet of Navarre*, 23; *Young Louis XIV: The Early Years of the Sun King*, 25
Wilkinson, F. *Arms and Armour*, 234
Willard, B. *Flight to the Forest*, 89
Willets, R. F. *Everyday Life in Ancient Crete*, 39
Williams, Barry. *Struggle for North America*, 170
Williams, Beryl. See Epstein, B.; Epstein, S. jt. auth.
Williams, Byron. *Cuba, the Continuing Revolution*, 194
Williams, E. E. *The Tunnel*, 100; *The Wooden Horse*, 100
Williams, E. N. *Life in Georgian England*, 99
Williams, J. *Battle for the Atlantic*, 101; *Joan of Arc*, 24; *Knights of the Crusades*, 4; *Leonardo da Vinci*, 53; *Life in the Middle Ages*, 4; *The Spanish Armada*, 98; *The Sword of King Arthur*, 82; *Tournament of the Lions*, 4; *World of Titian*, 54
Williams, Paul, il. *The Warrior Knights*, 4, 18
Williams, Penry. *Life in Tudor England*, 98
Williamson, H. R. *Guy Fawkes*, 89
Williamson, J. S. *The Eagles Have Flown*, 47; *The Glorious Conspiracy*, 92; *Hittite Warrior*, 133; *The Iron Charm*, 47; *Jacobin's Daughter*, 19; *To Dream Upon a Crown*, 87
Wilson, B. K. *Australia: Wonderland Down Under*, 197
Wilson, C. M. *Wilderness Explorer: The Story of Samuel de Champlain*, 171
Wilson, H. *Little Marquise: Madame de Lafayette*, 24; *The Seine: River of Paris*, 21; *Story of Lafayette*, 24
Wilton, E. *Riverboat Family*, 196
Winder, V. H. *The Land and People of Lebanon*, 132

AUTHOR INDEX

Winer, B. *Life in the Ancient World*, 128

Winston, R. *Charlemagne*, 23

Wintterle, J. and Cramer, R. S. *Portraits of Nobel Laureates in Peace*, 221

Winwar, F. *The Land of the Italian People*, 48; *Napoleon and the Battle of Waterloo*, 21; *Queen Elizabeth and the Spanish Armada*, 105

Wise, William. *From Scrolls to Satellites*, 214; *Secret Mission to the Philippines: The Story of the "Spyron" and the American-Filipino Guerrillas of World War II*, 201; *Two Reigns of Tutankhamen*, 123

Wise, Winifred. *Fanny Kemble: Actress, Author, Abolitionist*, 107

Witker, J. *Getting to Know Scandinavia: Denmark, Norway, & Sweden*, 64

Witting, A. *Treasury of Greek Mythology*, 37

Witton, D. *Our World: Mexico*, 175

Wohlrabe, R. A. and Krusch, W. *The Key to Vienna*, 11; *Land and People of Austria*, 11; *The Land and People of Denmark*, 16; *The Land and People of Germany*, 30; *The Land and People of Portugal*, 60; *The Land and People of Venezuela*, 188; *Picture Map Geography of Western Europe*, 1

Wolcott, C. *See* Wolcott, L. jt. auth.

Wolcott, J. *See* Burch, G. jt. auth.

Wolcott, L. and Wolcott, C. *Religions Around the World*, 211

Wolfe, L. *Ifrikiya: Stories About Africa and Africans*, 153; *Let's Go to the Klondike Gold Rush*, 166

Wolseley, R. E. *Low Countries: Gateways to Europe*, 14, 55

Wood, D. *Enchantment of Canada*, 169

Wood, F. E. *Enchantment of Mexico*, 175

Wood, J. P. *The Lantern Bearer: A Life of Robert Louis Stevenson*, 113; *The Queen's Most Honorable Pirate*, 87

Wood, K. M. *The Holy Apostles Peter and Paul*, 115

Wood, L. N. *Louis Pasteur*, 26

Wood, W. H. *See* Holwood, W. pseud.

Woodford, P. *Mozart*, 13

Worcester, D. E. *Makers of Latin America*, 180; *Three Worlds of Latin America: Mexico, Central America, South America*, 175, 180, 190

Wren, M. C. *Ancient Russia*, 74

Wrench, M. S. *See* Stanley-Wrench, M.

Wright, H. and R. S. B. eds. *Great Adventures in Science*, 227; *Great Undersea Adventures*, 216

Wyatt, I. *The Dream of King Alfdan*, 57

Wyler, R. *See* Ames, G. jt. auth.

Wymer, N. G. *Gilbert and Sullivan*, 106

Wyndham, L. *Florence Nightingale, Nurse to the World*, 110; (ed.) *Folk Tales of China*, 137; (ed.) *Folk Tales of India*, 142; *Tales the People Tell in Russia*, 72

Yadin, Y. *The Story of Masada*, 130

Yates, E. *Children of the Bible*, 119; *Rainbow Round the World: A Story of UNICEF*, 221; *With Pipe, Paddle, and Song: A Story of the French-Canadian Voyageurs, circa 1750*, 169

Yaukey, G. S. *See* Spencer, C. pseud.

Yolen, J. *Pirates in Petticoats*, 193

Yonge, C. M. *Little Duke*, 17

Young, B. and Young, J. *The Last Emperor: The Story of Mexico's Fight for Freedom*, 176; *Liberators of Latin America*, 180; *Simon Bolivar: The George Washington of South America*, 180

Young, J. *See* Young, B. jt. auth.

Young, P. M. *Beethoven*, 31; *Handel*, 32; *Haydn*, 12; *Stravinsky*, 77; *Tchaikovsky*, 78

Zinkin, T. *India and Her Neighbors*, 143; *The Story of Gandhi*, 145

Zottmann, T. M. *See* Thomas, M. Z. pseud.

BIOGRAPHICAL SUBJECT INDEX

Material about individuals listed in this index is to be found on the pages indicated under the appropriate name headings. Authors of the biographies are noted below only for individuals whose names are not used in headings—e.g., Michiko, crown princess of Japan. *In* Simon, 148 (a biography listed under the heading *Akimoto*); Leakey, Louis Seymour Bazett. *In* Mulvey, 225 (material to be found in a biography under general heading).

Açoka. *See* Asoka
Akihito, crown prince of Japan, 148
Alexander the Great, 41; *also in* Appell, 217
Alfred the Great (King of the West Saxons). *In* Churchill, 101
Amenhotep (King of Egypt), 124
Amundsen, Roald, 203-4
Andersen, Hans Christian, 16
Ankhsenamen (Queen of Egypt), 125
Anne (Queen of Britain and Ireland), 101
Anne, consort of Richard III (King of England). *In* Vance, 111
Anne of Brittany (Queen of France), 22
Aquinas, Saint Thomas, 54
Archimedes, 41
Aristotle, 41
Ashmun, Jehudi, 161
Asoka the Great, 143
Ataturk, 134
Attila (King of the Huns), 50
Augustine, Saint, 114

Bach, Johann Sebastian, 30
Baden-Powell, Sir Robert Stephenson Smyth, 1st baron, 101

Balboa, Vasco Nuñez de, 190
Beaumarchais, Pierre Augustin Caron de, 22
Becket, Thomas à, 101
Beethoven, Ludwig van, 31
Ben-Gurion, David, 131
Bernadette of Lourdes, Saint, 22
Bernier, Joseph Elzéar, 206
Bismarck, 31
Bolívar, Simón, 180
Boz. *See* Dickens, C. J. H.
Brahms, Johannes, 31
Brazza, Pierre Paul François Camille Savorgnan de, 159
Brock, Sir Isaac, 170
Broz, Josip. *See* Tito
Bruce (Robert VIII, King of Scotland), 101
Buddha, 143-4
Burton, Sir Richard Francis, 101
Byrd, Richard Evelyn, 204

Cabot, John, 170
Caesar, Gaius Julius, 50-1
Carlota (Empress of Mexico), 176
Cartier, Jacques, 170-1
Catherine de Medicis, 22
Catherine the Great (Empress of Russia), 76
Cavell, Edith Louisa, 102
Cellini, Benvenuto, 51

295

Cervantes, Saavedra, Miguel de, 66
Cézanne, Paul, 22
Chaka (Zulu chief), 157
Champlain, Samuel de, 171
Champollion, Jean François, 125
Charlemagne (King of the Franks, Emperor of the West), 23
Charles II (King of Great Britain and Ireland), 102
Charles V (Holy Roman Emperor), 31
Charles the Great. See Charlemagne
Charles the Wise. See Charles V
Chaucer, Geoffrey, 102
Chiang Kai-shek, 140
Chinese Gordon, 106
Chopin, Frédéric François, 59
Chou En-lai. In Spencer, 140
Christ, Jesus, 120
Churchill, Winston Leonard Spencer, 102-3
Cicero, Marcus Tullius, 51
Cleopatra (Queen of Egypt), 125
Clive, Robert, baron Clive of Plassey, 144
Cockcroft, Sir John, 103
Coeur de Lion, Richard. See Richard I (King of England)
Columbus, Christopher, 67-8
Confucius, 140; also in Spencer, 140
Cook, James (Captain Cook), 195-6
Copernicus, Nicolaus, 51
Coronado, Francisco Vásquez, 176-7
Cortes, Hernando, 177
Cousteau, Jacques Yves. In Dugan, 217
Cromwell, Oliver, 103
Cunard, Sir Samuel, 103
Curie, Irène, 23

Curie, Marie, 23
Curie, Pierre, 23

Da Gama, Vasco, 61
Daniel, 119
Dante, 51
Darwin, Charles Robert, 103-4
David (King of Judah and Israel), 119-20
Davy, Sir Humphry, 104
Dayan, Moshe, 131
De Brazza, Savorgnan, 159
De Gaulle, Charles André Joseph Marie, 23
De Lesseps, 125
Descartes, René, 23
De Soto, Hernando, 68
De Valera, Eamon, 45
Dewey, John. In Friedman, 212
Dickens, Charles John Huffam, 104
Disraeli, Benjamin, 1st earl of Beaconsfield, 104-5
Drake, Sir Francis, 105
Dunant, Jean Henri, 71

Edinburgh, Duke of. See Philip, Prince
Elizabeth I (Queen of England and Ireland), 105
Elizabeth II (Queen of Great Britain and Northern Ireland), 105; also in Boyd, 212
Éminence rouge. See Richelieu
Ericson, Leif, 58
Esther, 120
Euclid, 42; also in Stonaker, 229
Evans, Sir Arthur John, 106

Faraday, Michael, 106
Ferdinand V (King of Castile), 68
Fontaine, Charles. See Louis XVII
Francis of Assisi, Saint, 51

BIOGRAPHICAL SUBJECT INDEX

Franco, Francisco, 68
Frederick II (King of Prussia). *See* Frederick the Great
Frederick the Great (King of Prussia), 32
Freud, Sigmund, 12
Frontenac, Louis de Buade, comte de Palluau et de, 171
Fuchs, Sir Vivian Ernest, 204

Galileo, 51
Gandhi, Indira, 144
Gandhi, Mahatma, 144-5
Garibaldi, Giuseppe, 52
Gaulle, Charles de, 23
Gauss, Karl Friedrich, 32
Gautama Buddha, 143-4
Genghis Khan, 140
Gerbert. *See* Sylvester II, Pope
Gilbert, Sir William Schwenk, 106
Gilbert and Sullivan, 106
Goethe, Johann Wolfgang, 32
Gogh, Vincent van, 56
Goliath. *In* De Regniers, 119; Hazen, 120
Gordon, Charles George, 106
Goya, 68-9
Grey, Lady Jane, 106
Grieg, Edvard, 58
Grieg, Nina, 58
Gustavus Adolphus (Gustavus II, King of Sweden), 70

Haile Selassie I (Emperor of Ethiopia), 160
Hammarskjöld, Dag, 70
Handel, George Frederick, 32
Hannibal, 52
Harvey, William, 106
Hatshepsut (Queen of ancient Egypt). *In* Boyd, 212
Havelok the Dane, 16
Haydn, Joseph, 12
Hearne, Samuel, 206

Henry IV (King of France), 23
Henry VIII (King of England), 107
Henry the Navigator (Prince of Portugal), 61
Henson, Matthew Alexander, 206
Hillary, Sir Edmund Percival, 150
Hindenburg, Paul von, 32
Hippocrates, 42
Hitler, Adolf, 32-3
Hudson, Henry, 171-2
Humboldt, Baron Alexander von, 181
Huxley, Sir Julian Sorell, 107

Ignatius Loyola, Saint, 69
Imhotep, 125
Indira Gandhi, 144
Isabella I (Queen of Castile and Aragon), 69

Jacob. *In* Komroff, 119
Jenner, Edward, 107
Jesus Christ, 120
Jiménez de Quesada, Gonzalo. *See* Quesada, G. J. de
Joan of Arc, Saint, 23-4
John XXIII, Pope, 114-15
Johnson, Samuel, 107
Joliet, Louis, 172
Joliot-Curie, Irène. See Curie, I.
Joseph, 120
Josephine (Empress of France), 24
Juárez, Benito Pablo, 177-8
Justinian I (ruler of Eastern Roman Empire), 134
Justinian the Great, 134

Keats, John, 107
Kemal Ataturk, 134
Kemble, Fanny (Frances Anne), 107

297

Kenny, Elizabeth, 198
Kenyatta, Jomo (Johnstone), 161
Kepler, Johannes, 33
Khrushchev, Nikita Sergeevich, 76
Kingsley, Mary Henrietta, 157
Kipling, Rudyard, 107
Koch, Robert, 33
Kosciuszko, Tadeusz, 59
Kossuth, Lajos, 43
Kublai Khan, 140

Lafayette, Marie Adrienne Françoise (de Noailles), marquise de, 24
Lafayette, Marie Joseph Paul Yves Roch Gilbert du Motier, marquis de, 24
La Salle, Robert Cavalier, sieur de, 172; *also in* Meredith and Smith, 170
Lavoisier, Antoine Laurent, 25
Lawrence of Arabia. *See* Lawrence, T. E.
Lawrence, Thomas Edward, 132-3
Leakey, Louis Seymour Bazett. *In* Mulvey, 225
Leif the Lucky. *See* Ericson, L.
Leigh-Mallory, George Herbert, 150
Lenin, Nikolai, 76-7
Leonardo da Vinci, 52-3
Lesseps, Vicomte Ferdinand Marie de, 125
Linnaeus, Carolus, 70
Lion of Judah. *See* Haile Selassie
Livingstone, David, 157
Louis XIV (King of France), 25
Louis XVII (the lost prince of France), 25
Loyola, Saint Ignatius, 69
Ludendorff, Erich Friedrich Wilhelm, 33
Luther, Martin, 33

Mackenzie, Sir Alexander, 172
Magellan, Ferdinand, 61; *also in* Duvoisin, 217
Magsaysay, Ramón, 201
Mahatma Gandhi, 144-5
Maid of Orleans. *See* Joan of Arc, Saint
Mallory, George Herbert Leigh-, 150
Mao Tse-tung, 140
Marco Polo, 140-1
Marie Antoinette (Queen of France), 25
Marquette, Jacques (Père Marquette), 172
Martin, Thérèse. *See* Teresa of Lisieux, Saint
Marx, Karl, 34
Mary II (Queen of England, Scotland, and Ireland), 108
Mary Stuart (Mary, Queen of Scots), 108
Maximilian (Emperor of Mexico), 178
Maxwell, James Clerk, 108
Medicis, Catherine de, 22
Mendel, Gregor Johann, 12
Merry Monarch. *See* Charles II
Metternich, Prince Klemens Wenzel Nepomuk Lothar von, 12
Michelangelo, 53
Michiko, crown princess of Japan. *In* Simon, 148
Milton, John, 108
Mohammed. *See* Muhammad
Montessori, Maria, 53
Montezuma II (Emperor of Mexico). *In* Appel, 177
Montgomery, Sir Bernard Law, 1st viscount Montgomery of Alamein, 108
More, Sir Thomas (Saint Thomas More), 109
Morgan, Sir Henry, 193

BIOGRAPHICAL SUBJECT INDEX

Moses, 120-1; *also in* Komroff, 119
Mozart, Wolfgang Amadeus, 12-13
Muhammad, 133
Mussolini, Benito, 53
Mustafa Kemal. *See* Ataturk

Nansen, Fridtjof, 206
Napoleon I (Emperor of the French), 25-6
Nehru, Jawaharlal, 145
Nelson, Horatio, Viscount Nelson, 109
Newton, Sir Isaac, 109
Ney, Michel, 26
Nightingale, Florence, 109-10
Noah. *In* Komroff, 119
Nobel, Alfred Bernhard, 70

Olmedo, Bartolomé de. *In* Strousse, 177

Paderewski, Ignace, 59
Pankhurst, Emmeline, 110
Pasteur, Louis, 26
Patrick, Saint, 45
Paul, Saint, 115; *also in* Thompson, 115, *and in* Wood, 115
Paul VI, Pope, 115
Peary, Robert Edwin, 207
Pepys, Samuel, 110
Peter, Saint, 115
Peter the Great, (Czar of Russia), 77
Philip, Prince, duke of Edinburgh, 110
Picasso, Pablo, 69
Pizzaro, Francisco, 187
Polo, Marco, 140-1
Ponce de León, Juan, 193
Priestley, Joseph, 110
Pulaski, Casimir, 59

Quesada, Gonzalo Jimínez de, 184
Quezon, Manuel (Manuel Luis Quezon y Molina), 201

Radisson, Pierre Esprit, 172
Raleigh, Sir Walter, 111
Raphael, 53
Razin, Stepan Timofeevich, 77
The Red Baron. *See* Richthofen, M. A.
Rembrandt, 55
Ricci, Mateo, 141
Richard I (King of England), 111
Richard III (King of England), 111
Richelieu, Armand Jean du Plessis, duc de, 27
Richthofen, Manfred Albrecht, freiherr von, 34
Robert the Bruce. *See* Bruce
Röntgen, Wilhelm Konrad, 34
Ross, Sir Ronald, 145
Rousseau, Jean Jacques, 27
Rubens, Peter Paul, 14
Rutherford, Ernest, 1st baron Rutherford of Nelson, 111

Sakyamuni. *See* Buddha
Samson, 121
Santayana. *In* Loeper, 213
Saul. *See* Paul
Schliemann, Heinrich, 42
Schubert, Franz Peter, 13
Schumann, Clara, 34
Schumann, Robert, 34
Schweitzer, Albert, 157-8
Scott, Robert Falcon, 204
Scott, Sir Walter, 111
Selkirk, Alexander, 111
Shackleton, Sir Ernest Henry, 204
Shakespeare, William, 112
Shelley, Percy Bysshe, 112
Siddartha, Prince. *See* Buddha

Simon Peter. *See* Peter
Slessor, Mary Mitchell, 162
Smith, John, 112
Smuts, Jan Christiaan, 165
Smyth, Sir Robert Stephenson, 1st baron Baden-Powell, 101
Socrates, 42; *also in* Friedman, 212; Loeper, 213
Soto, Hernando de. *See* De Soto, H.
Soubirous, Bernadette. *See* Bernadette of Lourdes
Stalin, Joseph, 77
Stanley, Sir Henry Morton, 158
Stefansson, Vilhjalmur, 207
Stephens, John Lloyd, 178
Stevenson, Robert Louis, 112-13
Stravinsky, Igor Fëdorovich, 77
Sullivan, Sir Arthur Seymour, 106
The Sun King. *See* Louis XIV
Sun Yat-sen, 141
Sylvester II, Pope, 116

Talleyrand-Périgord, Charles Maurice de, prince de Bénévent, 27
Tchaikovsky, Peter Ilyitch, 78
Tennyson, Alfred, 1st baron Tennyson, 113
Teresa of Lisieux, Saint, 27
Thomas Aquinas, Saint, 54
Thomas Becket, Saint, 101
Titian, 54
Tito (Josip Broz), 117
Tolstoy, Leo, count, 78
Toussaint L'Ouverture, Pierre Dominique, 193
Trotsky, Leon, 78

Tutankhamon (King of Egypt), 125

Valera, Eamon de, 45
Vancouver, George, 173
Van Gogh, Vincent, 56
Vasco da Gama, 61
Velázquez, Diego Rodríguez de Silva y, 69
Verdi, Giuseppe, 54
Vermeer, Jan, 56
Verne, Jules, 27
Vesalius, Andreas, 14
Vespucci, Amerigo, 181
Victoria (Queen of the United Kingdom of Great Britain and Ireland, Empress of India), 113; *also in* Churchill, 101
Vinci, Leonardo da, 52-3
Volta, Alessandro, count, 54

Wagner, Richard, 34
Watt, James, 113
Weizmann, Chaim, 131
Wesley, John, 113-14
Wheeler, Sir Robert Eric Mortimer. *In* Clark, 225
Wilkes, Charles, 204
William I (King of England), 114
William the Conqueror. *See* William I (King of England)
William I (Prince of Orange). *See* William the Silent
William the Silent, 56
Wren, Sir Christopher, 114

Yadin, Rav-Aloof Yigael, 131

TITLE INDEX

A Is for Africa, Bond, 154
Aborigines of Australia, Hoyt, 197
About Cave Men of the Old Stone Age, Kramer, 222
Abraham Lincoln's World, Foster, 209
Across the Ocean Sea: A Journal of Columbus's Voyage, Sanderlin, 66, 68
Action in Submarines, Widder, 234
Adam of the Road, Gray, 91
Admiral Byrd of Antarctica, Gladych, 204
Admiral Nelson, Bellis, 109
Adventure North: The Story of Fridtjof Nansen, Denzel, 206
Adventure of Man, Gregor, 222
Adventure Stories, Untermeyer and Untermeyer, 1
The Adventures and Discoveries of Marco Polo, Walsh, 141
Adventures in Archaeology, Fletcher, 224
Adventures in Black, Widder, 234
Adventures of Hercules, Fadiman, 35
The Adventures of Johnny Van Bart, Manson and Manson, 199
Adventures of Richard Wagner, Wheeler, 34
Adventures of Robin Hood, Vance, 86
The Adventures of Tom Leigh, Bentley, 89
Adventures With the Heroes, Sellew, 63

Adventuring in Archaeology, Burland, 224
The Aeneid, Vergil, 37, 46
Afghanistan, Weston, 135
Africa: Adventures in Eyewitness History, Hoff, 155
Africa and Asia, Hillyer and Huey, 155
Africa: Awakening Giant, Lens, 155
Africa: Background for Today, MacGregor-Hastie, 155
Africa in History, Davidson, 154
Africa Is People: Firsthand Accounts from Contemporary Africa, Nolen, 156
Africa: Past and Present, Thompson, 156
African Beginnings, Vlahos, 128
African Firebrand: Kenyatta of Kenya, Archer, 161
African Heroes, Mitchison, 157
African Samson, Harman, 153
African Traveler: The Story of Mary Kingsley, Syme, 157
Africans Knew, Pine and Levine, 156
Against All Odds, Jacobs, 217
Against Odds, Heatter, 215
The Age of Enlightenment, Bowman, 4
Age of Faith, Fremantle, 2
The Age of Great Kings, Firoozi and Klein, 10
Age of Napoleon, Herold, 26
The Age of Revolution, Lindquist, 6
Age of the Guerrilla: A Back-

301

ground Book for Young People on Modern Guerrilla Warfare, Sully, 234
Air War in the Pacific: Air Power Leads the Way, Dupuy, 147
Air War in the Pacific: Victory in the Air, Dupuy, 147
The Air War in the West: June 1941-April 1945, Dupuy, 7
The Air War in the West; September 1939-May 1941, Dupuy, 7
Aircraft of World War I: Fighters, Scouts, Bombers, and Observation Planes, Colby, 5
Airship Over the Pole: The Story of the Italia, Hogg, 205
Aku-Aku: The Secret of Easter Island, Heyerdahl, 199
Albert Schweitzer, Richards, 158
Albert Schweitzer, Thomas, 158
Albert Schweitzer: Genius in the Jungle, Gollomb, 158
Alessandro Volta and the Electric Battery, Dibner, 54
Alexander Mackenzie, Canadian Explorer, Syme, 172
Alexander the Great, Gunther, 41
Alexander the Great, Mercer, 41
Alexander the Great: Conqueror and Creator of a New World, Robinson, 41
Alexander the Great, Scientist-King, Suggs, 41
Alexander von Humboldt: Scientist, Explorer, Adventurer, Thomas, 181
Alexander's Great March, Baumann, 37
Alexander's Horses, Powers, 37
All Aboard for Freedom! McSwigan, 15
All About Archaeology, White, 225
All About Famous Inventors and Their Inventions, Pratt, 228
All About Maps and Mapmaking, Marsh, 218
All About Prehistoric Cave Men, Epstein and Epstein, 222
All About Sailing the Seven Seas, Brindze, 215
All About the Arctic and Antarctic, Sperry, 202
All About Undersea Exploration, Brindze, 215
All About Us, Evans, 209
All Men Are Brothers: A Portrait of Albert Schweitzer, Simon, 158
All Round Hong Kong, Vittengl, 142
All the Furious Battles: The Saga of Israel's Army, Werstein, 131
An Alphabet of Ancient Greece; Book 1: Early Days, Chubb, 39
An Alphabet of Ancient Greece; Book 2: The Golden Years, Chubb, 39
The Amazon — River of Promise, Malkus, 182
The Amazon: River Sea of Brazil, Sperry, 183
Americans Before Columbus, Baity, 179
Americas [Canada, Mexico and South America], Hillyer and Huey, 167, 174, 179
America's First Christmas, Pauli, 65
Amerigo Vespucci, Baker, 181
Amerigo Vespucci, Knoop, 181
Amerigo Vespucci, Scientist and and Sailor, Syme, 181
Among the Maya Ruins: The Adventures of John Lloyd Stephens and Frederick Catherwood, Sutton and Sutton, 178

TITLE INDEX

Amuny, Boy of Old Egypt, Schlein, 121
The Anchor of Mercy, Mac Orlan, 19
Ancient China, Burland, 138
Ancient China, Spencer, 139
Ancient Crete, Wilkens, 39
Ancient Egypt, Burland, 122
Ancient Egypt, Green, 122
Ancient Egypt, Sellman, 123
Ancient Greece, Burland, 39
Ancient Greece, Green, 40
Ancient Greece, Taylor, 40
Ancient India, Pike, 143
Ancient Japan, Kidder, 147
The Ancient Maya, Burland, 175
Ancient Persia, Pike, 126
Ancient Rome, Burland, 48
Ancient Rome, Taylor, 50
Ancient Russia, Wren, 74
Ancient Scandinavia, Proctor, 64
And Tomorrow the Stars: The Story of John Cabot, Hill, 170
Andean Republics, Johnson, 179
Andreas Vesalius: Father of Modern Anatomy, Tarshis, 14
The Anglo-Saxons, Sellman, 96
The Angry Earth, Kidwell, 173
Animals and Men in Armor, Vaughan-Jackson, 234
Animals of Doctor Schweitzer, Fritz, 154
Answer Book of History, Elting and Folsom, 208
Antarctic World, Euller, 203
Antarctica: Exploring the Frozen Continent, Scarf, 203
Antarctica: The Worst Place in the World, Baum, 203
Antoine Lavoisier and the Revolution in Chemistry, Marcus, 25
Antoine Lavoisier – Scientist and Citizen, Riedman, 25
Anvil Chorus: The Story of Giuseppe Verdi, Kaufmann, 54
The Apple and the Arrow, Buff, 71
The Arabs, Ellis, 132
Archaeologists and What They Do, Braidwood, 224
Archimedes and His Wonderful Discoveries, Jonas, 41
Archimedes and the Door of Science, Bendick, 41
Archimedes: Mathematician and Inventor, Gardner, 41
Archimedes Takes a Bath, Lexau, 40
Arctic Rovings, Hall, 205
Arctic Tundra, Goetz, 205
Arctic World, Euller, 205
Argentina, Carpenter, 181
Argentina, Paraguay and Uruguay, Hornos, 181, 185, 187
Aristotle: Dean of Early Science, Downey, 41
The Ark, Benary-Isbert, 28
Armed With Courage, McNeer, 213
Armor, Morrison, 233
Arms and Armour, Wilkinson, 234
Around the World With Darwin, Selsam, 104
Arrow Messenger, Burleigh, 136
The Ashanti of Ghana, Bleeker, 160
Ashes of Empire: Carlota and Maximilian of Mexico, Vance, 176, 178
Asian and Axis Resistance Movements, Dupuy, 8, 147
Asiatic Land Battles: Allied Victories in China and Burma, Dupuy, 147
Asiatic Land Battles: Japanese Ambitions in the Pacific, Dupuy, 147
Asoka the Great: India's Royal Missionary, Lengyel, 143

303

Assassination: A Special Kind of Murder, Heaps, 209
At the Lion Gate, Palmer, 36
At the Seven Stars, Beatty and Beatty, 89
At the Sign of the Globe, Bowers, 112
At the Sign of the Golden Compass, Kelly, 84
The Athenians in the Classical Period, Weisgard, 40
Attila: King of the Huns, Webb, 50
Augustus Caesar's World, Foster, 49, 209
Australia, Ritchie, 197
Australia and New Zealand, MacInnes, 197, 200
Australia and New Zealand: Pacific Community, Harrington, 197, 200
Australia: Wonderland Down Under, Wilson, 197
Austria, Graham, 11
Autobiography, Cellini, 51
Away to Central America, Nevins, 190
Away to East Africa, Nevins, 156
Away to Mexico, Nevins, 174
Away to the Lands of the Andes, Nevins, 179
Away to Venezuela, Nevins, 188
The Aztec, Indians of Mexico, Bleeker, 175
Aztecs, Burland, 175
Aztecs of Mexico, the Lost Civilization, Chambers, 174

B-G. Fighter of Goliaths: The Story of David Ben-Gurion, Samuels, 131
Bach, Holst, 30
Bach, Westcott, 30
Baden-Powell: Chief Scout of the World, Blassingame, 101

Balboa: Discoverer of the Pacific, Mirsky, 190
Balboa, Finder of the Pacific, Syme, 190
Balboa: Swordsman and Conquistador, Riesenberg, 190
Banner Over Me, Greenleaf, 82
The Barbary Pirates, Forester, 163
Barque of the Brothers, Baumann, 60
Battle Against the Sea: How the Dutch Made Holland, Lauber, 55
The Battle-Ax People: Beginnings of Western Culture, Vlahos, 3
Battle for Destiny, Stephens, 86
Battle for Quebec, Mason, 169
Battle for the Atlantic, Williams, 101
Battle for the Rock: The Story of Wolfe and Montcalm, Schull, 170
The Battle of Austerlitz: Napoleon's Greatest Victory, Dupuy, 21
The Battle of Britain, Reynolds, 94
The Battle of El Alamein — Decision in the Desert, Barnett, 100
The Battle of Hastings, Gray, 96
The Battle of Jerusalem: The Six-Day War of June, 1967, Irving, 130
The Battle of Lepanto, 1571, Marx, 5
The Battle of the Spanish Armada, 1588, Marx, 98
The Battle of Trafalgar, Villiers, 100
The Battle of Waterloo, Herold, 99
The Battle of Waterloo: One Hundred Days of Destiny, Komroff, 99
Bay of the North: The Story of Pierre Radisson, Syme, 172

TITLE INDEX

The Bayeux Tapestry; the Story of the Norman Conquest: 1066, Denny and Filmer-Sankey, 96
Bedouins, Hoyt, 132
Beethoven, Mirsky, 31
Beethoven, Sadie, 31
Beethoven, Young, 31
Beethoven: Master Composer, Gimpel, 31
Beethoven: Master Musician, Goss, 31
Beggar's Daughter, Hunt, 88
Beginnings of Cities, Weisgard, 211
Behold Your Queen, Malvern, 120
Belgium, Gerson, 13
Belgium and Luxembourg in Pictures, Sterling Publishing Company, 14
Beloved Botanist, Stoutenburg and Baker, 70
Ben-Gurion and the Birth of Israel, Comay, 131
Ben-Gurion's Israel, Appel, 130
Benito Juarez: Builder of a Nation, Sterne, 178
Benjamin Disraeli: Prime Minister Extraordinary, Grant, 104
Berlin East and West in Pictures, Sterling Publishing Company, 30
Betrayal: The Munich Pact of 1938, Werstein, 9
Bible Background, Smith, 119
The Bible Story for Boys and Girls: New Testament, Bowie, 118
Big John's Secret, Jewett, 83
Birthdays of Freedom, I, Foster, 40
Birthdays of Freedom, II, Foster, 209
Bismarck, Richter, 31
Bismarck and German Unification, Snyder, 31
The Bitter Choice: Eight South Africans' Resistance to Racial Tyranny, Legum and Legum, 165
Black Africa on the Move, Lacy, 155
The Black Arrow, Stevenson, 86
Black Explorer at the North Pole, Henson, 206
Black Flags and Pieces of Eight, Boyd, 192
Black Patriot and Martyr: Toussaint of Haiti, Griffiths, 193
Blackbeard's Ghost, Stahl, 191
The Blind Cross: A Novel of the Children's Crusade, Mott, 1
Blood, Banners and Wild Boars: Tales of Early Spain, Lauritzen, 66
The Boer War, Barbary, 165
Boer War, Martin, 165
Bolivar: The Liberator, Syme, 180
Bolivia, Carpenter and Lyon, 181
Bomber Planes That Made History, Cooke, 232
A Book of Famous Queens, Farmer, 212
Book of the Ancient World, Mills, 127
The Book of The Twelve Apostles, Quadflieg, 119
The Borrowed Crown, Maiden, 85
The Bounty Trilogy, Nordhoff and Hall, 91
Bounty's Boy, Edmonds, 198
Bowman of Crécy, Welch, 83
Bows Against the Barons, Trease, 86
The Boxer Rebellion, Martin, 139
A Boy Hears Stories from the Old Testament, Fraser, 118
The Boy Jesus, Doane, 120
The Boy Knight of Reims, Lownsbery, 18

WORLD HISTORY IN JUVENILE BOOKS

A Boy of Old Prague, Ish-Kishor, 14
A Boy of the Lost Crusade, Hewes, 18
Boy of the Pyramids, Jones, 121
Boyhoods of Great Composers, Book I, Gough, 10
Boyhoods of Great Composers, Book II, Gough, 10
The Boys' Ben-Hur; a Tale of the Christ, Wallace, 47
Boys' Book of the Wonders of Man and His Achievements, Mellersh, 210
Boys in Battle, Laffin, 233
Brahms, Mirsky, 31
Brave Men: Twelve Portraits of Courage, Sufrin, 213
Brazil: Awakening Giant, Seegers, 182
Breakthroughs in Science, Asimov, 226
Britain, Osborne, 94
British Castles, Unstead, 95
The British Empire, an American View of Its History from 1776 to 1945, Johnson, 93
The British Empire and Commonwealth of Nations, Liversidge, 93
British Isles, Clayton, 93
Brother to Galahad, Bowers, 79
Bruno and Karen of Berlin, Holbrook, 28
Buccaneer Harbor, Briggs, 191
Buccaneers and Pirates of Our Coasts, Stockton, 192
Buddha, Cohen, 143
Builders of the Old World, Hartman and Saunders, 2
Building the Suez Canal, Burchell, 123
Buildings of Ancient Egypt, Leacroft and Leacroft, 122

The Buildings of Ancient Greece, Leacroft and Leacroft, 40
Buried Cities, Hall, 225
The Buried Treasure of Archaeology, Brennan, 224
The Burning of Njal, Treece, 43
By Gravel and Gum: Story of a Pioneer Family, Keesing, 196
By Sail and Wind: The Story of the Bahamas, Bothwell, 191
By Star and Compass: The Story of Navigation, Coggins, 215, 226, 229
The Byzantines, Chubb, 134
Byzantium, Rice, 134

Caesar, Isenberg, 51
Caesar to Churchill, 95
Caesar's Gallic War, Coolidge, 49
Cambodia: Land of Contrasts, Tooze, 135
Came Liberty Beyond Our Hope, a Story of Hanukkah, Cohen, 130
Campaigns in Southern Europe, Dupuy and Mayo, 8
Campaigns on the Turkish Fronts, Dupuy and Hayes, 134
Campion Towers, Beatty and Beatty, 87
Canada, Heaton, 167
Canada, Lineaweaver, 168
Canada and Her Story, Bonner, 167
Canada: Giant Nation of the North, Watson, 168
Canada in Pictures, Sterling Publishing Company, 168
Canada: Wonderland of Surprises, Braithwaite, 167
Canada, Young Giant of the North, Leitch, 168

TITLE INDEX

The Canadian Story, McNeer, 168
A Candle at Dusk, Almedingen, 17
The Canterbury Tales, Chaucer, 82
Capital Without a Country, Holbrook, 29
Captain Cook, Bellis, 195
Captain Cook and the South Pacific, Warner, 196
Captain Cook Explores the South Seas, Sperry, 196
Captain Cook, Pacific Explorer, Syme, 196
Captain Cortes Conquers Mexico, Johnson, 177
Captain Deadlock, Hyde, 91
Captain James Cook, Merrett, 196
Captain James Cook: Genius Afloat, Carrison, 195
Captain Scott, Purton, 204
Captured by the Mohawks, North, 166
Cardinal in Armor: The Story of Richelieu and His Times, Wilkinson, 27
Caribbean — The English-Speaking Islands in Pictures, Sterling Publishing Company, 192
Carl Friedrich Gauss: Prince of Mathematicians, Schaaf, 32
Carl Linnaeus: Pioneer of Modern Botany, Dickinson, 70
Carl Linnaeus: The Man Who Put the World of Life in Order, Silverstein and Silverstein, 70
Carramore, Vaughan-Jackson, 44
Cartier Discovers the St. Lawrence, Toye, 171
Cartier: Finder of the St. Lawrence, Syme, 171
Cartier Sails the St. Lawrence, Averill, 170

Casilda of the Rising Moon, Treviño, 65
Castle, Abbey and Town: How People Lived in the Middle Ages, Black, 2
The Castle Book, Duggan, 2
Castles, Boardman, 2
Castors Away, Burton, 90
Catherine the Great, Scherman, 76
A Cavalcade of Kings, Farjeon and Mayne, 212
A Cavalcade of Queens, Farjeon and Mayne, 212
Cave Dwellers: In the Old Stone Age, Powers, 223
Cave Hunters, Scheele, 223
Caveman to Spaceman, Friskey, 230
The Caves of the Great Hunters, Baumann, 222
Celtic Tales, Picard, 44
Central America, Colvin, 189
Central America: Lands Seeking Unity, May, 189
The Centurion, Treece, 79
Ceylon, Weston, 136
Ceylon in Pictures, Sterling Publishing Company, 136
The Chagres: Power of the Panama Canal, Latham, 189
Chaim Weizmann: Builder of a Nation, Baker, 131
Chaka: King of the Zulus, Keating, 157
Challenge for a Throne; The Wars of the Roses, Hamilton, 96
Challenge of the Unknown, Hillary, 215
Champion of World Peace: Dag Hammarskjöld, Levine, 70
Champions of Peace: Winners of

307

the Nobel Peace Prize, Meyer, 221
Champions of the Four Freedoms, Meyer, 213
Champlain; Father of New France, Edwards, 171
Champlain: Northwest Voyager, Tharp, 171
Champlain of the St. Lawrence, Syme, 171
Changing the Face of North America: Challenge of the St. Lawrence Seaway, Lauber, 167
Charge of the Light Brigade, Tennyson, 99
Charlemagne, Komroff, 23
Charlemagne, Stearns, 23
Charlemagne, Winston, 23
Charles Darwin, Greene, 103
Charles Darwin, Gregor, 103
Charles Darwin, Riedman, 104
Charles Darwin and Natural Selection, Dickinson, 103
Charles Dickens, Haines, 104
Charles Dickens: His Life, Peare, 104
Charles Dickens, the Inimitable Boz, Wilkie, 104
Charles V, Holy Roman Emperor, Grant, 31
Charro: Mexican Horseman, Norman, 174
Chaucer and His World, Serraillier, 102
Chaucer in His Time, Brewer, 102
Chaucer's England: Living in England, Taylor, 97
Chiang Kai-shek, Curtis, 140
Chiang Kai-shek: Generalissimo of Nationalist China, Spencer, 140
Chief of the Cossacks, Lamb, 77
Child of the Sun: A Pharaoh of Egypt, Edwards, 124
Children of Africa, Stinetorf, 156
Children of Ancient Rome, Lamprey, 49
Children of Dickens, Crothers, 90
Children of Odin, Colum, 62
Children of the Bible, Yates, 119
The Children of the New Forest, Marryat, 88
Children of the Resistance, Cowan, 7
The Children's Bible, Krause and others, 118
Children's Book of London, Bullock, 93
The Children's Picture Atlas of the World, Bacon, 218
Chile, Carpenter, 183
Chile in Pictures, Sterling Publishing Company, 183
Chile: Progress on Trial, May, 183
China: Adventures in Eyewitness History, Hoff, 137
China, The Hungry Dragon, Scott, 138
China's Leaders in Ideas and Action, Spencer, 140
Chinese Gordon: Hero of Khartoum, Ormont, 106
Chinese Knew, Pine and Levine, 138
Chinese Way of Life, Lin Yu-t'ang, 137
Chivalry and the Mailed Knight, Buehr, 2
Chopin, Chissell, 59
Christopher Columbus, Judson, 67
Christopher Columbus, Kaufman, 67
Christopher Columbus, Olds, 68
Christopher Columbus and His Brothers, Hogelboom, 67

TITLE INDEX

Christopher Columbus, Discoverer, Graham, 67
Christopher Columbus: Navigator to the New World, Carrison, 67
Christopher Columbus: Sailor and Dreamer, Bailey, 67
Chronological Military History of World War II, Dupuy, 8
The Church of Our Fathers, Bainton, 118
Churchill, Dolan, 102
Churchill's England, Nathan, 100
Cities of Gold and Isles of Spice, Price, 139
City of the Golden House, Polland, 115
Civil War and the Commonwealth, Sellman, 99
The Civil War in Spain, Goldston, 66
Claim to Freedom: The Rise of the Afro-Asian Peoples, Spencer, 156
The Clashing Rocks: The Story of Jason, Serraillier, 36
Claymore and Kilt; Tales of Scottish Kings and Castles, Nic Leodhas, 94
Cleopatra, Crayder, 125
Cleopatra of Egypt, Hornblow, 125
Cleopatra: Sister of the Moon, Leighton, 125
Clive of India, Russell, 144
A Cloud Over Hiroshima: The Story of the Atomic Bomb, Hirschfeld, 148
Coal, Steel, Atoms, and Trade: Challenge of Uniting Europe, Strauss, 9
Codes and Ciphers: Secret Writing Through the Ages, Laffin, 233

The Cold War, Heller and Heller, 75
Colombia and Venezuela and the Guianas, MacEoin, 182, 184, 188
Colossus of Europe: Metternich, Archer, 12
Columbus, Aulaire and Aulaire, 67
Columbus and the New World, Derleth, 67
Columbus Day, Showers, 68
Columbus, Finder of the New World, Syme, 68
Columbus Sails, Hodges, 67
The Columbus Story, Dalgliesh, 67
Combat Leaders of World War II, Dupuy, 10
The Commandos: British Raider Heroes of World War II, Mason, 100
The Commandos of World War II, Carter, 100
Commodore Perry in Japan, Reynolds, 147
The Common Market, Ellis, 8
Communication, Adler and Adler, 213
Communication: From Cave Writing to Television, Batchelor, 213
Communication: From Primitive Tom-Toms to Telstar, Foster, 214
Communication: From Stone Age to Space Age, Neal, 214
Communism, an American's View, Johnson, 75
Communism in Our World, Caldwell, 208
Company of Adventurers; The Story of the Hudson's Bay Company, Tharp, 169
Confucius, Sims, 140
Congo Explorer, Carbonnier, 159

Congo Fireside Tales, Savory, 159
The Congo: River Into Central Africa, Lauber, 155
The Congo — River of Mystery, McKown, 155
Conquering the English Channel, Pumphrey, 100
Conquest of the North and South Poles, Owen, 202
The Conquistadors, Kerby, 186
Conquistadors and Pueblos: The Story of the American Southwest, 1540-1848, Hall-Quest, 176
The Conscience of a King: The Story of Thomas More, Stanley-Wrench, 109
Conscripts on the March: The Story of the Soldier from Napoleon to the Nuclear Age, Ellacott, 232
Continent in a Hurry: The Challenge of Africa Today, Griffin, 154
Copernicus, Thomas, 51
Copernicus: Titan of Modern Astronomy, Knight, 51
Coronado and His Captains, Campbell, 176
Cortes and the Aztec Conquest, Blacker, 177
Cortes of Mexico, Syme, 177
The Cossacks, Bartos-Höppner, 72
The Count Who Wished He Were a Peasant, Philipson, 78
Courageous Companions, Finger, 60, 61
Cradle of Civilization, Kramer, 127
Crete: Island of Mystery, Cottrell, 38
The Cross and the Sword of Cortes, Coleman, 177
Crossroads of Conquerors: The West Indies, Saunders, 192
A Crown for Thomas Peters, Hennessey and Sauter, 153
The Cruel Years: The Story of the Spanish Civil War, Werstein, 66
The Crusader: The Story of Richard the Lionheart, Power-Waters, 111
The Crusaders, Bell, 2
The Crusaders, Buehr, 2
The Crusaders, Hamilton, 2
The Crusades, Sellman, 3
The Crusades, West, 3
A Cry of Players, Jowett, 84
Cry Spy:True Stories of Twentieth Century Spies and Spy Catchers, Wilkinson, 234
Cuba, Matthews, 194
Cuba, the Continuing Revolution, Williams, 194
The Cuban Revolution, Goldston, 193
Cue for Treason, Trease, 86
The Curies and Radium, Rubin, 23
Czars and Czarinas of Russia, Rice, 74
Czechoslovakia in Pictures, Sterling Publishing Company, 15

D-Day, Gray, 100
D-Day, Shapiro, 9
D-Day: The Invasion of Europe, Hine, 8
D-Day, the Sixth of June, 1944, Howarth, 8
Dag Hammarskjöld, Simon, 70
Dag Hammarskjöld: A Biography, Kelen, 70
Daily Life at Versailles in the 17th and 18th Centuries, Levron, 21
Daily Life in Early Canada, Douville and Casanova, 169
Daily Life in Peru in the Time of the Spaniards, Descola, 186

TITLE INDEX

Danger Is the Password: Stories of Wartime Spies, Fenner, 232
Danger Point: The Wreck of the Birkenhead, Corbett, 99
Dangerfoot, Brown, 89
Dangerous Journey, Hamori, 42
The Dangerous World of Spies and Spying, Liston, 233
Daniel, Bolliger, 119
Dante: Poet of Love, Stearns, 51
Dark Ages, Asimov, 1
Dark Eminence: Catherine De Medici and Her Children, Vance, 22
The Dark Frigate, Hawes, 87
Dark Venture, Beyer, 153
Darkness Over the Land, Stiles, 29
David and Goliath, De Regniers, 119
David and Goliath, Hazen, 120
David Livingstone: Foe of Darkness, Eaton, 157
Dawn Wind, Sutcliff, 82
The Day of the Bomb, Bruckner, 147
The Day of the Earthquake, Seeger, 37
Deadly Craft: Fire Ships to PT Boats, Hoyt, 232
Dear to Behold: An Intimate Portrait of Indira Gandhi, Hutheesing, 144
Death to the King: The Story of the English Civil War, Alderman, 98
Debbie of the Green Gate, Daringer, 87
Decade of Development: The Challenge of the Underdeveloped Nations, Joyce, 220
Defrosting Antarctic Secrets, Francis and Smith, 203
Defy and Endure: Great Sieges of Modern History, Belfield, 231

De Gaulle: King Without a Crown, Lester, 23
Deirdre, Polland, 44
De Lesseps: Builder of Suez, Long, 125
Denmark: Wonderland of Work and Play, Bailey, 15
Desert Caravans: Challenge of the Changing Sahara, Joy, 163
Desert Fighter: The Story of General Yigael Yadin and the Dead Sea Scrolls, Miller, 131
Desert War in North Africa, Sears, 163
De Soto, Finder of the Mississippi, Syme, 68
Devil in Print, Drewery, 84
Devil in the Fog, Garfield, 90
Dickens and His Works, Burton, 104
Dickens and His World, Brown, 104
Dickens in His Time, Brown, 104
Dictators, Archer, 211
A Dictionary of Chivalry, Uden, 3
Digging Into Yesterday, Friedman, 224
Digging Up Adam: The Story of L.S.B. Leakey, Mulvey, 225
Digs and Diggers, Cottrell, 224
Dirigibles That Made History, Cooke, 230
Discoverer of the North Pole, the Story of Robert E. Peary, Stafford, 207
Discovering the Bible, Lampe and Daniell, 119
Discovering the Royal Tombs at Ur, Glubok, 123
Discovering Tut-Ankh-Amen's Tomb, Glubok, 123
Disraeli, Komroff, 105
Dr. Johnson and His World, Brown, 107

Doctor Livingstone, Purton, 157
Doctor William Harvey and the Discovery of Circulation, Harrison, 106
The Dolphin Crossing, Paton Walsh, 92
Don Quixote of La Mancha, Cervantes Saavedra, 65
Down the Long Stairs, Cawley, 87
Drake: The Man They Called a Pirate, Latham, 105
The Dream of King Alfdan, Wyatt, 57
Drinkers of the Wind, Raswan, 124
Drummer Boy for Montcalm, Hays, 166
Drums in the Forest, Dwight, 166
Duel for the Sky: Fighter Planes and Fighting Pilots of World War II, Mason, 8
Duel in the Shadows, Orbaan, 29
Duel to the Death: Eyewitness Accounts of Great Battles at Sea, Slinkman, 234
Duet: The Story of Clara and Robert Schumann, Kyle, 34
Duke's Command, Berk, 32
Dynamite and Peace: Story of Alfred Nobel, Meyer, 70

Eagle of the Ninth, Sutcliff, 78
Eagle of the Philippines: President Manuel Quezon, Goettel, 201
The Eagles Have Flown, Williamson, 47
The Earliest English, Cramp and Gummer, 95
Early Birds of War; The Daring Pilots and Fighter Airplanes of World War I, Funderburk, 232

Early Days of Man, Burrell, 222
Early Explorers to A.D. 1500, Hobley, 217
Early Japan, Leonard, 147
Early Man, Howell, 222
Early Old Testament Stories, Smither, 119
East Africa: Kenya, Uganda and Tanzania, Kirby, 155, 161, 164
Eastward to India: Vasco da Gama's Voyage, Sanderlin, 60
Ecuador in Pictures, Sterling Publishing Company, 184
Edith Cavell: Heroic Nurse, Elkon, 102
Edith Cavell: Nurse, Spy, Heroine, De Leeuw, 102
Edvard Grieg, Boy of the Northland, Deucher, 58
Edward Jenner and Smallpox Vaccination, Eberle, 107
Egypt: Child of the Nile, Watson, 124
Egypt, Gift of the Nile, Fairservis, 123
Egyptian Adventures, Coolidge, 121
The Egyptian Necklace, Palmer, 121
The Egyptians, Asimov, 122
The Egyptians in the Middle Kingdom, Ochsenschlager and Miller, 122
Egyptians Knew, Pine and Levine, 122
Egypt's Queen: Cleopatra, Noble, 125
The Eisenbart Mystery, Pilkington, 29
Eleven: Time to Think of Marriage, Farhut, Kalish, 150
Elizabeth the First, Cammiade, 105

TITLE INDEX

Elizabeth I of England, Stearns, 105

Elizabeth Tudor, Sovereign Lady, Vance, 105

The Elizabethan Age: Living in England, Taylor, 98

Elizabethan Seamen, Sellman, 98

The Emperor and the Drummer Boy, Robbins, 19

The Emperor's Arrow, Boyce, 17

The Empress Josephine from Martinique to Malmaison, Vance, 24

Empress of All Russia: Catherine the Great, Noble, 76

Enchantment of Canada, Wood, 169

Enchantment of Mexico, Wood, 175

Enchantment of South America: Brazil, Carpenter, 182

Enchantment of South America: Colombia, Carpenter and Lyon, 183

Enchantment of South America: Paraguay, Carpenter and Balow, 184

Enchantment of South America: Peru, Carpenter, 185

Enchantment of South America: Venezuela, Carpenter and Haan, 188

The Endless Steppe: Growing Up in Siberia, Hautzig, 58

Enemy at the Gate, Ritchie, 43

The Engine and the Gun, Barbary, 89

Engineers of the World, Evans, 228

England, Middleton, 94

The English Civil War, Ross, 99

English Explorers of North America, Grant, 170

Epics of Everest, Wibberley, 149

Ernest Rutherford: Architect of the Atom, Kelman and Stone, 111

Ernest Rutherford, Master of the Atom, Rowland, 111

Escape to King Alfred, Trease, 82

Escapes and Rescues, Scoggin, 216

The Eskimo, Arctic Hunters and Trappers, Bleeker, 202

Ethiopia, Nolen, 159

Ethiopia: Mountain Kingdom, Watson, 160

Euclid and Geometry, De Lacy, 42

Europe, Hillyer and Huey, 1

European Folk Festivals, Epstein and Williams, 1

European Land Battles, 1939-1943, Dupuy, 8

European Land Battles, 1944-1945, Dupuy, 8

European Resistance Movements, Dupuy, 8

Everyday Life in Ancient Crete, Willets, 39

Everyday Life in Ancient Egypt, White, 123

Everyday Life in Ancient Rome, Cowell, 49

Everyday Life in Byzantium, Rice, 134

Everyday Life in Classical Athens, Webster, 40

Everyday Life in Early Imperial China During the Han Period 202 B.C.-A.D. 220, Loewe, 138

Everyday Life in Prehistoric Times, Quennell and Quennell, 223

Everyday Life in Roman and Anglo-Saxon Times, Quennell and Quennell, 95

Everyday Life in the Viking Age, Simpson, 64

Everyday Life of the Aztecs, Bray, 175

Everyday Things in Ancient Greece, Quennell and Quennell, 40

Exploits in Africa, Bayliss, 154

Exploration of Africa, Sterling, 156

Explorations of Père Marquette, Kjelgaard, 172

Explorer of the Unconscious: Sigmund Freud, Stoutenburg and Baker, 12

Explorer's Digest, Clark, 217

Explorers of the Arctic and Antarctic, Dolan, 202

Explorers of the Pacific, Day, 195

Explorers of the World, Clark, 217

Exploring Australia, Pownall, 197

Exploring Maps, Moore and Brinton, 218

Exploring the Americas, Hobley, 179

Exploring the Earth, Evans, 215

Exploring the Great River: Early Voyagers on the Mississippi from De Soto to La Salle, Meredith and Smith, 170

Exploring the Himalayas, Douglas, 149

Exploring the Pacific, Hobley, 195

Exploring the World, Moore, 216

Exploring the World of Archaeology, Cleator, 224

The Face of War, Laffin, 233

Fair World for All, Fisher, 219

The Falcon and the Dove: A Life of Thomas Becket of Canterbury, Duggan, 101

Falcons of France, Nordhoff and Hall, 22

A Fall from the Sky: The Story of Daedalus, Serraillier, 36

The Fall of Constantinople, Kielty, 134

The Fall of the Aztecs, Glubok, 175

The Fall of the Incas, Glubok, 186

Famous Astronomers, Pickering, 228

Famous Composers for Young People, Burch and Wolcott, 10

Famous Explorers for Young People, Coffman and Goodman, 217

Famous Fighters of World War I, Army Times, 9

Famous Firsts in Exploration, Mason, 216

Famous Generals and Admirals Young People, Coffman and Goodman, 235

Famous Historians, Hill, 212

Famous Inventors for Young People, Eberle, 228

Famous Kings and Queens for Young People, Coffman and Goodman, 212

Famous Latin-American Liberators, Bailey, 180

Famous Mathematicians, Stonaker, 229

Famous Men of Medicine, Chandler, 228

Famous Men of Science, Bolton, 228

Famous Modern Explorers, Bailey, 217

Famous Myths of the Golden Age, Alexander, 35

Famous Old Masters of Painting, McKinney, 10

Famous Physicists, Mann and Vivian, 228

Famous Pirates of the New World, Whipple, 193

Famous Scientists, Stevens, 229

Famous Twentieth Century Leaders, Donovan, 212

TITLE INDEX

Famous Voyages in Small Boats, Merrett, 216

Fanny Kemble, Rushmore, 107

Fanny Kemble: Actress, Author, Abolitionist, Wise, 107

Far Voyager: The Story of James Cook, Latham, 196

The Faraway Lurs, Behn, 221

Farewell to Troy, Johnson, 36

Fearless Adventurer: Sir Richard Burton, Orrmont, 101

Ferdinand and Isabella, McKendrick, 68, 69

Ferdinand Magellan, Welch, 61

Ferdinand Magellan: Master Mariner, Pond, 61

Ferdinand Magellan: Noble Captain, Wilkie, 61

Fielding's England, Taylor, 92

Fife and Fandango, Sprague, 65

Fifteen Battles That Changed the World, Silverberg, 233

Fifty-Five Days of Terror: The Story of the Boxer Rebellion, Hirschfeld, 139

Fight for Korea: From the War of 1950 to the Pueblo Incident, Fehrenbach, 148

Fight in the Mountains, Bernhardsen, 57

Fighter Against Slavery: Jehudi Ashmun, Orrmont, 161

Fighter for Independence: Jawaharlal Nehru, Apsler, 145

Fighter Parade: Headliners in Fighter Plane History, Colby, 232

Fighter Planes That Made History, Cooke, 232

Fighting Ships and Seamen, MacIntyre, 233

Fighting Wings: The Story of Aerial Combat in World War I, Whitehouse and Lancelot, 7

Finding Out About Ancient Egypt, Mellersh, 122

Finding Out About the Early Russians, Rice, 74

Finding Out About the Past, Freeman, 224

Finland: Champion of Independence, Paloheimo and Watson, 17

Fire in Your Life, Adler, 225

First Around the World: A Journal of Magellan's Voyage, Sanderlin, 60

The First Book of Africa, Hughes, 155

The First Book of Ancient Bible Lands, Robinson, 118

First Book of Ancient China, Walker, 139

The First Book of Ancient Crete and Mycenae, Robinson, 39

The First Book of Ancient Egypt, Robinson, 122

The First Book of Ancient Greece, Robinson, 40

The First Book of Ancient Mesopotamia and Persia, Robinson, 127

The First Book of Ancient Rome, Robinson, 49

The First Book of Archaeology, Kubie, 225

First Book of Arctic Exploration, Liversidge, 205

The First Book of Australia, Kaula, 197

The First Book of Berlin: Tale of a Divided City, Knight, 29

The First Book of Bolivia, Carter, 182

The First Book of Brazil, Sheppard, 183

The First Book of Bridges, Creighton, 227, 231
The First Book of Central America and Panama, Markun, 189
First Book of Colombia, Beck, 183
The First Book of Communist China, Kinmond, 139
First Book of Denmark, Lobsenz, 16
The First Book of East Africa, Lobsenz, 155
The First Book of England, Streatfeild, 95
The First Book of Fiji, Cavanna, 199
The First Book of Hungary, Csicsery-Rónay, 43
The First Book of India, Bothwell, 142
First Book of Israel, Kubie, 129
The First Book of Italy, Epstein and Epstein, 48
First Book of Japan, Miller and Katoh, 146
First Book of Kenya, Foster, 160
The First Book of Maps and Globes, Epstein and Epstein, 218
The First Book of Medieval Man, Sobol, 3
The First Book of Mexico, Epstein and Epstein, 174
The First Book of Modern Greece, Warren, 41
First Book of Morocco, Cavanna, 163
First Book of Niagara Falls, Howard, 167
The First Book of Norway, Merrick, 57
The First Book of Roads, Bothwell, 229
The First Book of Ships, Bendick, 229
First Book of Southeast Asia, Poole, 151
The First Book of Stone Age Man, Dickinson, 222
The First Book of Submarines, Icenhower, 232
The First Book of Switzerland, Epstein and Epstein, 71
The First Book of the Ancient Maya, Beck, 175
The First Book of the Antarctic, Icenhower, 203
The First Book of the Arab World, Warren, 132
The First Book of the Arctic, Liversidge, 205
The First Book of the Aztecs, Beck, 175
First Book of the Bantu Africans, Kaula, 155
The First Book of the Guianas, Hoke, 184
First Book of the Incas, Beck, 186
The First Book of the Long Armistice, Snyder, 9
The First Book of the Mediterranean, Gottlieb, 38, 48, 163
The First Book of the Netherlands, Cohn, 55
First Book of the Panama Canal, Markun, 189
The First Book of the Soviet Union, Snyder, 76
First Book of the Vatican, Deedy, 114
The First Book of the Vikings, Rich, 64
First Book of Turkey, Lengyel, 134
First Book of Venezuela, Beck, 187
The First Book of West Germany, Lobsenz, 30

TITLE INDEX

The First Book of World War I, Snyder, 7

The First Book of World War II, Snyder, 9

The First Bow and Arrow, Osborne, 221

First Farmers: In the Stone Age, Weisgard, 224

The First Lake Dwellers, Osborne, 221

First Men, May, 223

First Men in the World, White, 224

First Men: The Story of Human Beginnings, Goldman and Goldman, 222

First Northwest Passage, O'Meara, 172

First People in the World, Ames and Wyler, 221

The First Song, Rosenfeld, 72

The First 3000 Years: Ancient Civilizations of the Tigris, Euphrates, and Nile River Valleys, and the Mediterranean Sea, Falls, 127

First Under the North Pole: The Voyage of the Nautilus, Anderson, 205

First Up Everest, Styles, 150

The First Wheel, Osborne, 221

The First World War, Sellman, 7

Five Queens of Ancient Egypt, Cottrell, 124

Five Ships West — The Story of Magellan, Israel, 61

The Five Sons of King Pandu, Seeger, 142

Flags of All Nations and the People Who Live Under Them, Elting and Folsom, 209

Flame of Freedom: The Peasants' Revolt of 1381, Alderman, 96

Flight and Adventures of Charles II, Norman, 102

Flight to the Forest, Willard, 89

Flight Toward Home, Ecke, 28

Flights That Made History, Cooke, 230

Florence Nightingale, Hume, 110

Florence Nightingale, Nolan, 110

Florence Nightingale: Founder of Modern Nursing, Harmelink, 110

Florence Nightingale, Nurse to the World, Wyndham, 110

Florence Nightingale: War Nurse, Colver, 109

The Florentine Giraffe: A Tale of the Italian Renaissance, Patton, 47

Flying Aces of World War I, Gurney, 6

Flying Tigers, Toland, 139

Folk Tales of China, Wyndham, 137

Folk Tales of England, Corcoran, 78

Folk Tales of France, Curren, 17

Folk Tales of India, Wyndham, 142

Folk Tales of Japan, Newman, 145

Folk Tales of Latin America, Newman, 179

Folk Tales of North America, Corcoran, 166

Folk Tales of Scandinavia, Curren, 62

Following Columbus: The Voyage of the Nina II, Marx, 191

Footlights to Fame: The Life of Fanny Kemble, Kerr, 107

For Charlemagne, Andrews, 17

For Glory and the King, McDonald and Ross, 176

For the Glory of France: The Story of the French Resistance, Wilhelm, 22

For the King, Welch, 89
For Valour: The Story of the Victoria Cross, Leyland, 93
Forest Doctor: The Story of Albert Schweitzer, Northcott, 158
Forever England: Poetry and Prose About England and the English, Russ and Russ, 94
The Forgotten Daughter, Snedeker, 38
The Four Corners of the World, Duvoisin, 187
Four Ways of Being Human, Lisitzky, 222
France, Barry, 19
France, Brogan, 20
France: A First-Look-At-Geography Book, Longley, 20
France in Pictures, Sterling Publishing Company, 20
Francis Drake, Sailor of the Unknown Seas, Syme, 105
Francisco Coronado and the Seven Cities of Gold, Syme, 177
Francisco Pizarro, Finder of Peru, Syme, 187
Franco and the Spanish Civil War, Snellgrove, 68
The Franco-Prussian War: Germany's Rise as a World Power, Werstein, 30
Franz Schubert and His Merry Friends, Wheeler and Deucher, 13
Frederic Chopin, Son of Poland: Early Years, Wheeler, 59
Frederic Chopin, Son of Poland: Later Years, Wheeler, 59
Frederick the Great: Prussian Warrior and Statesman, Snyder and Brown, 32
Free But Not Equal: How Women Won the Right to Vote, Severn, 211

Freedom Builders: Great Teachers from Socrates to John Dewey, Friedman, 212
Freedom Fighter: Casimir Pulaski, Abodaher, 59
French Canada in Pictures, Sterling Publishing Company, 168
French Explorers in America, Buehr, 170
The French Explorers of North America, Abodaher, 170
The French Foreign Legion, Blassingame, 21
The French Revolution, Dowd, 21
The French Revolution, Pratt, 21
French Roundabout, Bishop, 20
Friar and the Knight: Bartolomé de Olmedo and Cortez, Strousse, 177
Fridtjof Nansen, Berry, 206
Fridtjof Nansen: Arctic Explorer, Noel-Baker, 206
Friend Within the Gates, the Story of Nurse Edith Cavell, Grey, 102
Friendly Frontier, Meyer, 168
Friendship Road: Challenge of the Pan American Highway, Ingraham, 230
The Frightened Hero: A Story of the Siege of Latham House, Latham, 88
From Bush to City: A Look at the New Africa, Bernheim and Bernheim, 154
From Drumbeat to Tickertape, Osmond, 214
From Flying Horse to Man in the Moon: History of Flight from Its Earliest Beginnings to the Conquest of Space, De Leeuw, 230
From Scrolls to Satellites, Wise, 214

TITLE INDEX

From Sea to Sea: The Story of Canada in the Nineteenth and Twentieth Centuries, Field and Dennis, 167, 169

From Tsars to Commissars: The Story of the Russian Revolution, Teall, 74

Frontenac of New France, Syme, 171

Frossia: A Novel of Russia, Almedingen, 72

Galileo and Experimental Science, Marcus, 51

Galileo and the Magic Numbers, Rosen, 51

Galileo: First Observer of Marvelous Things, Levinger, 51

Galleys and Galleons, Buehr, 229

Gandhi, Torgersen, 144

Gandhi: Fighter Without a Sword, Eaton, 144

Gandhi: Peaceful Fighter, Montgomery, 144

Gandhi, Soldier of Nonviolence: His Effect on India and the World Today, Kytle, 144

Gandhi's Story, Masani, 144

Ganges: Sacred River of India, Weingarten, 143

Garibaldi: Father of Modern Italy, Davenport, 52

Garibaldi: The Man Who Made a Nation, Syme, 52

A Garland for Gandhi, Jacob, 144

Gautama Buddha, in Life and Legend, Kelen, 144

General Brock and Niagara Falls, Adams, 170

Genghis Khan and the Mongol Horde, Lamb, 140

Genghis Khan: Conqueror of the Medieval World, Webb, 140

Gentle Falcon, Lewis, 83

George Washington's World, Foster, 209

Germany: East and West, Holbrook, 29

Germany: The Divided Nation, Homze and Homze, 29

Getting to Know Africa's French Community, Olden, 156

Getting to Know Algeria, Deming, 163

Getting to Know Argentina, Olden, 181

Getting to Know Australia, Parke, 197

Getting to Know Brazil, Breetveld, 182

Getting to Know Burma, Taylor, 135

Getting to Know Canada, Rollins, 168

Getting to Know Chile, Breetveld, 183

Getting to Know Colombia, Halsell, 183

Getting to Know Costa Rica, El Salvador, and Nicaragua, Joy, 189

Getting to Know Cuba, Laschever, 194

Getting to Know Eastern Europe, Underwood, 117

Getting to Know Egypt, Wallace, 124

Getting to Know England, Scotland, and Ireland, Joy, 45, 93

Getting to Know France, Wallace, 20

Getting to Know Greece, Tor, 38

Getting to Know Guatemala and the Two Honduras, Halsell, 189

Getting to Know Hong Kong, Joy, 141

Getting to Know India, Laschever, 143

319

WORLD HISTORY IN JUVENILE BOOKS

Getting to Know Indonesia, Taylor, 198
Getting to Know Iran and Iraq, Bahar, 126
Getting to Know Israel, Joy, 129
Getting to Know Italy, Craz, 48
Getting to Know Japan, Jakeman, 146
Getting to Know Kenya, Ingalls, 160
Getting to Know Lebanon, Breetveld, 132
Getting to Know Malaysia and Singapore, King, 149
Getting to Know Mexico, Gómez, 174
Getting to Know Nigeria, Olden, 162
Getting to Know Pakistan, Laschever, 150
Getting to Know Panama, Day, 189
Getting to Know Peru, Halsell, 185
Getting to Know Poland, Wallace, 59
Getting to Know Saudi Arabia, Phillips, 132
Getting to Know Scandinavia: Denmark, Norway, & Sweden, Witker, 64
Getting to Know South Africa, Ingalls, 165
Getting to Know Southern Rhodesia, Zambia, and Malawi, Clements, 154, 164
Getting to Know Spain, Day, 65
Getting to Know Switzerland, Lauber, 71
Getting to Know Tanzania, Joy, 164
Getting to Know Thailand, Ayer, 151
Getting to Know the Arctic, Ogle, 205
Getting to Know the Central Himalayas: Nepal, Sikkim, Bhutan, Redford, 149
Getting to Know the Congo River, Robins, 156
Getting to Know the Northern Himalayas: Kashmir, Tibet, Assam, Redford, 149
Getting to Know the Philippines, Tor, 201
Getting to Know the River Amazon, Joy, 182
Getting to Know the River Ganges, Soni, 143
Getting to Know the Sahara, Joy, 163
Getting to Know the South Pacific, Joy, 199
Getting to Know the Soviet Union, Wallace, 76
Getting to Know the Tigris and Euphrates, Joy, 127
Getting to Know the Two Chinas, Joy, 137
Getting to Know the Two Germanys, Holbrook, 29
Getting to Know the Two Koreas, Johnston, 149
Getting to Know the Two Vietnams, West, 152
Getting to Know the World Health Organization, Smith, 220
Getting to Know Turkey, Davis, 134
Getting to Know UNESCO: How U.N. Crusaders Fight Ignorance, Griffin, 219
Getting to Know United Nations Crusaders: How UNICEF Saves Children, Breetveld, 219
Getting to Know Venezuela, Laschever, 188

TITLE INDEX

Giant of the Atom: Ernest Rutherford, McKown, 111
Giants of Medicine, Robbin, 229
Giants of Science, Cane, 228
Gift of the River, Meadowcroft, 124
Gilbert and Sullivan, Wymer, 106
Gilbert and Sullivan: Masters of Mirth and Melody, Purdy, 106
The Girl in White Armor, Paine, 24
A Glorious Age in Africa: The Story of Three Great African Empires, Chu and Skinner, 154
The Glorious Conspiracy, Williamson, 92
Goethe: Pattern of Genius, Stearns, 32
Gold and Gods of Peru, Baumann, 186
Gold Down Under: The Story of the Australian Gold Rush, Place, 197
The Golden Bible Atlas, Terrien, 119
The Golden Book of the Renaissance, Shapiro, 5
The Golden Compass, Thoorens, 13
The Golden Days of Greece, Coolidge, 39
The Golden Fleece and the Heroes Who Lived Before Achilles, Colum, 35
Golden Hawks of Genghis Khan, Ritchie, 137
The Golden Pharaoh, Bruckner, 125
The Golden Treasury of Myths and Legends, White, 1
Good Digging: The Story of Archaeology, Samachson and Samachson, 225
Good Sense and Good Fortune, and Other Polish Folk Tales, Borski, 58
The Good Ways, Ansley, 1, 208
The Gorgon's Head: The Story of Perseus, Serraillier, 37
Goya, Ripley, 68
Goya and His Times, Stearns, 69
Granada, Surrender! Kidwell, 65
The Grand Canal of China, Harrington, 137
Great Accidents in Science That Changed the World, Meyer, 227
The Great Adventure of Michelangelo, Stone, 53
Great Adventurers, Appell, 217
Great Adventures in Science, Wright and Rapport, 227
Great Air Battles: World Wars I and II, Lawson, 6
Great Ambitions: A Story of the Early Years of Charles Dickens, Kyle, 104
The Great Archaeologists, Daugherty, 225
Great Cities of Canada, May, 168
Great Day in Ghana; Gwasi Goes to Town, Kaye, 160
Great Day in Norway: the 17th of May, Hopp, 57
The Great Fire, Hope-Simpson, 88
Great Fire of London, Weiss, 99
Great Flights and Air Adventures: From Balloons to Spacecraft, Macmillan, 216, 231
Great Ideas in Communications, Brown, 213
Great Ideas of Science, Asimov, 226
The Great Invasion: The Norman Conquest of 1066, Alderman, 96
Great Leaders of Greece and Rome, Cottrell, 50

321

Great Moments at Sea, Campbell, 215
Great Moments in Archaeology, Hume, 225
Great Moments in Astronomy, Roy, 227
Great Moments in Engineering, Salter, 227
Great Moments in Escaping, Clark, 215
Great Moments in Espionage, Clark, 231
Great Moments in Exploration, Hopkins, 215
Great Moments in Flying, Taylor, 231
Great Moments in Medicine, Ludovici, 227
Great Moments in Mountaineering, Clark, 215
Great Moments in Music, Nettel, 10
Great Moments in Rescue Work, Clark, 215
Great Rulers of the African Past, Dobler and Brown, 156
The Great Trade Routes, Duché, 208, 218
Great Undersea Adventures, Wright and Rapport, 216
The Great War, 1914-1918: A Pictorial History, Terraine, 7
Greece, Miller, 38
Greece: A Book to Begin On, Fenton, 38
Greece: Land of Golden Light, Watson, 38
Greece: Wonderland of the Past and Present, Johnson, 38
Greek Gods and Heroes, Graves, 36
Greek Myths, Coolidge, 35
Greek Stories, Dolch and Dolch, 35
Greeks: A Great Adventure, Asimov, 39
Green, Green Sea: A Story of Greece, Cone, 38
Gregor Mendel, Greene, 12
Gregor Mendel: Father of the Science of Genetics, Sootin, 12
Grettir the Strong, Newman, 63
Growing Up in Israel, Holisher, 129
Growing Up in Thirteenth Century England, Duggan, 96
Growing Up With the Norman Conquest, Duggan, 96
Guerrilla Scout, Cassiday, 47
A Guide to African History, Davidson, 154
Guns, Ellacott, 232
Guns at Quebec, Dwight, 166
The Guns of Valmy, Bourliaguet, 18
Guy Fawkes, Williamson, 89

H. R. H., The Duke of Edinburgh, Peacocke, 110
Hakon of Rogen's Saga, Haugaard, 56
Half a Hemisphere: The Story of Latin America, Goetz, 179
Hamid and the Palm Sunday Donkey, Drewery, 128
The Hand of Apollo, Coatsworth, 37
Hand of the King, Morgan, 126
Hand Upon Time: A Life of Charles Dickens, Cooper, 104
Handel, Sadie, 32
Handel, Young, 32
Handel at the Court of Kings, Wheeler, 32
Hannibal, Invader from Carthage, Webb, 52
Hannibal's Elephants, Powers, 46

TITLE INDEX

Hans Andersen, Son of Denmark, Wheeler, 16
Hans Christian Andersen: Immortal Storyteller, Montgomery, 16
The Harmonious World of Johann Kepler, Rosen, 33
The Haunted Journey, Murphy, 74
Havelok the Dane, Crossley-Holland, 16
Havelok the Dane, Serraillier, 16
Haydn, Mirsky, 12
Haydn, Young, 12
He Freed the Minds of Men: René Descartes, Hoyt, 23
He Sailed With Captain Cook, Borden, 195
He Served Two Masters, Haller, 173
He Went With Champlain, Kent, 166
He Went With Christopher Columbus, Kent, 65
He Went With Drake, Kent, 85
He Went With Hannibal, Kent, 46
He Went With Magellan, Kent, 60
He Went With Marco Polo, Kent, 137
He Went With Vasco da Gama, Kent, 60
He Who Saw Everything: The Epic of Gilgamesh, Feagles, 126
He Wouldn't Be King: The Story of Simon Bolivar, Baker, 180
Hebrew People: A History of the Jews, Kamm, 130
Heels, Wheels and Wire: The Story of Messages and Signals, Rogers and Beard, 214
Heinrich Schliemann: Discoverer of Buried Treasure, Selden, 42
Heir to Pendarrow, Fecher, 84
Helicopters That Made History, Cooke, 230
The Helmet of Navarre, Wilkinson, 23
Hengest's Tale, Paton Walsh, 81
Henri Dunant: Man in White, Stoiber, 71
Henry Hudson, Baker, 171
Henry Hudson, Syme, 172
Henry Hudson: Captain of the Icebound Sea, Carmer, 171
Henry Hudson, Explorer of the North, Snow, 172
Henry Morton Stanley, Graves, 158
Henry Stanley, Alter, 158
Henry VIII of England, Pittenger, 107
Henry the Navigator, Prince of Portugal, Anderson, 61
Heraldry: The Story of Armorial Bearings, Buehr, 231
Here Comes Harry, Lewis, 85
Here Is England, Burton, 93
Here Is France, Bishop, 20
Here Is Mexico, Treviño, 174
Here Is the Far North, Stefansson, 205
Hernando Cortes, Graff, 177
Hernando de Soto, Montgomery, 68
Hero Tales from the Age of Chivalry: Retold from the Froissart Chronicles, Uden, 3
Hero-Tales from the British Isles, Picard, 81
Heroes, Kingsley, 36
Heroes and Aeroplanes of the Great War 1914-1918, Phelan, 7
Heroes and History, Sutcliff, 213
Heroes of Asgard: Tales from Scandinavian Mythology, Keary and Keary, 62
Heroes of Civilization, Cottler and Jaffe, 212

WORLD HISTORY IN JUVENILE BOOKS

Heroes of Greece and Troy, Green, 36

Heroes of History, Churchill, 101

Heroes of Mexico, Rosenblum, 176

Heroes of Polar Exploration, Andrist, 202

Heroes of Siberia, Prodanovic, 74, 116

Heroes of the Bible, Komroff, 119

Heroes of the International Red Cross, Deming, 219

Heroes of the Kalevala, Deutsch, 17

The Hidden Treasure of Glaston, Jewett, 83

High Courage, Weir, 83

Highwaymen, Pringle, 99

Highways Across Waterways, Gramet, 230

Hippocrates: Father of Medicine, Goldberg, 42

Hiroshima, Hersey, 148

His Own Good Daughter, Newell, 109

History and Historians, Boardman, 208

History Can Be Fun, Leaf, 210

A History of Body Armor, Peterson, 233

A History of Everyday Things in England, Ellacott, 93

A History of Firearms, Peterson, 233

A History of Invention, Larsen, 227

History of the Western World, Cheney, 208

History of the World for Young Readers, Gelinas and Scharff, 209

History's Hundred Greatest Events, De Witt, 208

Hitler and Nazism, Snyder, 33

Hitler and the Rise of Nazism, Browne, 32

Hitler: From Power to Ruin, Appel, 32

Hittite Warrior, Williamson, 133

Holland in Pictures, Sterling Publishing Company, 55

The Holy Apostles Peter and Paul, Wood, 115

The Holy Land in the Time of Jesus, Kotker, 130

Honduras in Pictures, Sterling Publishing Company, 190

Honey of the Nile, Berry, 121

Hong Kong in Pictures, Sterling Publishing Company, 141

The Honor of Balboa, Noble, 190

The Honorable Sword, Lewis, 145

Hooray for Peace, Hurrah for War; the United States During World War I, Jantzen, 6

Hornblower Goes to Sea, Forester, 90

Hornblower in Captivity, Forester 90

Hornblower Takes Command, Forester, 90

Hornblower's Triumph, Forester, 90

Horned Helmet, Treece, 43

Horsemen of the Steppes, Fairservis, 72

Horses Across the Ages, Mellin, 231

Horses of Anger, Forman, 28

Hostage to Alexander, Andrews, 37

The How and Why Wonder Book of Florence Nightingale, Webb, 110

How and Why Wonder Book of Polar Regions, Robbin, 202

How and Why Wonder Book of Primitive Man, Barr, 222

The How and Why Wonder Book

TITLE INDEX

of World War II, Sutton, 9
How Man Began, Bateman, 222
How the United Nations Works, Galt, 219
How the World's First Cities Began, Gregor, 127
Howard Pyle's Book of Pirates, Pyle, 192
The Hudson's Bay Company, Morenus, 169
Human Beginnings, Vlahos, 224
Humphry Davy and Chemical Discovery, Carrier, 104
Hungarian Heroes and Legends, Domjan, 42
The Hunted Prince, Schroeder, 63
Hunters of Siberia, Bartos-Höppner, 72

I Accuse: The Story of the Dreyfus Case, Werstein, 21
I Discover Columbus, Lawson, 65
I Marched With Hannibal, Baumann, 46
I Will Adventure, Gray, 97
The Ibo of Biafra, Bleeker, 162
Ice Island: The Story of Antarctica, Frank, 203
Ice, Ships, and Men, Euller, 205
Iceland in Pictures, Sterling Publishing Company, 44
Ifrikiya: Stories About Africa and Africans, Wolfe, 153
Ignace Paderewski: Musician and Statesman, Lengyel, 59
Ignatius of Loyola: The Soldier Saint, Liversidge, 69
The Iliad, Homer, 36
Illustrated Book of Knights, Appel, 1
Images of the Universe: Leonardo da Vinci, the Artist as Scientist, McLanathan, 52
Imhotep: Builder in Stone, Cormack, 125
Imperial Rome, Hadas, 49
Imperial Rome, Mellersh, 49
The Impossible Journey of Sir Ernest Shackleton, Bixby, 204
In Bible Days, Hartman, 118
In France, Clement, 20
In Norway, Thorne-Thomsen, 57
In Pursuit of the Spanish Galleon, De Witt, 90
In the Land of Ur: The Discovery of Ancient Mesopotamia, Baumann, 126
In the Morning of the World, Lowrey, 36
The Inca, Indians of the Andes, Bleeker, 186
Inca Peru, Burland, 186
Incas Knew, Pine and Levine, 186
The Incas: People of the Sun, Von Hagen, 187
India, Fairservis, 142
India, Lamb, 143
India and Her Neighbors, Zinkin, 143
India in Pictures, Katz, 143
India: Land of Rivers, Bryce, 142
India: Old Land, New Nation, Watson, 143
Indonesia, Poole, 198
The Indus: South Asia's Highway of History, Watson, 143
Industrial Revolution and Nationalism, Lindquist, 6
Ingri and Edgar Parin d'Aulaire's Book of Greek Myths, Aulaire and Aulaire, 35
The Innocent Wayfaring, Chute, 82
Introducing Beethoven, Harris, 31
The Invaders of Rome, Keating, 49
Inventions of Leonardo da Vinci, Cooper, 52
Inventions That Made History,

Cooke, 226
Inventors of the World, Evans, 228
The Invincible Armada, Gray, 97
Iran: Crossroads of Caravans, Watson, 126
Iran in Pictures, Sterling Publishing Company, 126
Ireland, Quigley, 45
Ireland: Bewitching Wonderland, Erdoes, 45
Ireland in Pictures, Sterling Publishing Company, 45
Iron Chancellor: Otto von Bismarck, Apsler, 31
The Iron Charm, Williamson, 47
Isaac Newton, Moore, 109
Isaac Newton: Mastermind of Science, Knight, 109
Isaac Newton: Pioneer of Space Mathematics, Tannenbaum and Stillman, 109
Isabella, Young Queen of Spain, Criss, 69
Island Hero: The Story of Ramón Magsaysay, Gray, 201
Island in the Desert: Challenge of the Nile, Joy, 123
Israel, Comay and Pearlman, 128
Israel and the Holy Land, Samuel, 129
Israel: Crossroads of Conflict, Feigenbaum and Seigel, 128
Israel in Pictures, Sterling Publishing Company, 129
Israel Reborn, Meeker, 130
Italy in Pictures, Sterling Publishing Company, 48
Italy: Modern Renaissance, Dobrin, 50
Ivanhoe, Scott, 83

Jacobin's Daughter, Williamson, 19

Jamaica in Pictures, Sterling Publishing Company, 192
James Clerk Maxwell and Electromagnetism, May, 108
James Cook, De Leeuw, 196
James Watt: Inventor of a Steam Engine, Webb, 113
Japan, Steinberg, 146
Japan, Storry, 147
Japan: Crossroads of East and West, Kirk, 146
Japan in Story and Pictures, Edelman, 146
Japan: Islands of the Rising Sun, Watson, 147
The Japanese: People of the 3 Treasures, Newman, 146
Jawaharlal Nehru: the Brahman from Kashmir, Lengyel, 145
Jean Henri Dunant: Father of the Red Cross, Rothkopf, 71
Jean Jacques Rousseau: The Father of Romanticism, Webb, 27
Jeanne d'Arc, Fisher, 23
Jesus and the World, Colby, 120
Jesus of Israel, Chute, 120
Jesus of Nazareth, Fosdick, 120
Joan of Arc, Churchill, 23
Joan of Arc, Ross, 24
Joan of Arc, Williams, 24
Joan of Arc: Maid of Orleans, Struchen, 24
Joel of the Hanging Gardens, Edmonds, 128
Johann Sebastian Bach, Mirsky, 30
Johann Sebastian Bach: Revolutionary of Music, Reingold, 30
Johannes Kepler and Planetary Motion, Knight, 33
John Lloyd Stephens: Explorer of Lost Worlds, O'Connor, 178
John Milton, Fuller, 108
John Milton; Clarion Voice of Freedom, Strousse, 108

TITLE INDEX

John Smith: A World Explorer, Graves, 112
John Stranger, Priestley, 91
John Wesley, McNeer and Ward, 114
The Jordan: River of the Promised Land, Weingarten, 131
Joseph, Bolliger, 120
Joseph Haydn: The Merry Little Peasant, Wheeler and Deucher, 12
Joseph Priestley, Pioneer Chemist, Marcus, 110
Joseph Stalin, Liversidge, 77
Journey for a Princess, Leighton, 81
Journey for Tobiyah, Morgan, 133
Journey Into Ice: John Franklin and the Northwest Passage, Sutton and Sutton, 206
Journey to America, Levitin, 28
Juan Ponce de León, Baker, 193
Juarez, Hero of Mexico, Baker, 177
Jules Verne, Becker, 27
Jules Verne: His Life, Peare, 27
Jules Verne: The Man Who Invented the Future, Born, 27
Julia Valeria, Gale, 46
Julius Caesar, David, 50
Julius Caesar, Gunther, 50
Julius Caesar, Komroff, 51
Jungle Doctors, McGrady, 228
Justinian the Great: Roman Emperor of the East, FitzGerald, 134

Karl Marx: The Father of Modern Socialism, Alexander, 34
Karl Marx: The Passionate Logician, Carmichael, 34
Katherine Leslie, Beyer, 89
Keeping Ahead of Machines: The Human Side of the Automation Revolution, Spencer, 227

Kenya: In Pictures, Sterling Publishing Company, 161
Kevin O'Connor and the Light Brigade, Wibberley, 92
The Key to Moscow, Salisbury, 73
The Key to Paris, Douglas, 20
The Key to Tokyo, Sheldon, 146
The Key to Vienna, Wohlrabe and Krusch, 11
The Khmers of Cambodia: The Story of a Mysterious People, Edmonds, 135
Khrushchev, Hirschfeld, 76
Kidnapped, Stevenson, 91
A Kind of Secret Weapon, Arnold, 15
King Arthur and His Knights, Frith, 80
King Arthur and His Knights, Robinson, 81
King Arthur and the Knights of the Round Table, Schneider, 82
King Arthur and the Round Table, Hadfield, 80
King Nobody Wanted, Langford, 120
The King's Contest and Other North African Tales, Holding, 162
The King's Jewel, Berry, 79
The King's Road, Holland, 28
A Knight and His Armor, Oakeshott, 3
A Knight and His Horse, Oakeshott, 3
A Knight and His Weapons, Oakeshott, 3
The Knight of the Cart, Hieatt, 80
Knights and Castles and Feudal Life, Buehr, 2
Knights Besieged, Faulkner, 133
Knight's Castle, Eager, 82
Knight's Fee, Sutcliff, 83

Knights in Armor, Glubok, 2
Knights of the Air: Canadian Aces of World War I, Harris, 170
Knights of the Crusades, Williams, 4
The Knights of the Golden Table, Almedingen, 71
Knights of the Table Round, White, 82
Know About the Armada, Garnett, 97
Know About the Crusades, Treece, 3
Kon-Tiki, Heyerdahl, 199
Korea: Land of the 38th Parallel, Gosfield and Hurwood, 149
Kublai Khan: Lord of Xanadu, Chapman, 140

Lady Jane Grey, Reluctant Queen, Vance, 106
Lady Queen Anne, Hodges, 101
Lafayette: French-American Hero, Bishop, 24
Lafayette: Friend of America, Graham, 24
Lafayette in America, Maurois, 24
Lajos Kossuth: Hungary's Great Patriot, Lengyel, 43
The Lance of Kanana, French, 132
The Land and People of Argentina, Hall, 181
The Land and People of Argentina, Pendle, 181
The Land and People of Australia, Blunden, 196
The Land and People of Australia, Cairns, 196
Land and People of Austria, Wohlrabe and Krusch, 11
Land and People of Belgium, Loder, 13
The Land and People of Brazil, Brown, 182
Land and People of Brazil, MacDonald, 182
The Land and People of Burma, Landry, 135
The Land and People of Burma, Maxwell-Lefroy, 135
The Land and People of Canada, Gordon, 167
The Land and People of Canada, Ross, 168
The Land and People of Central America, Karen, 189
The Land and People of Ceylon, Maxwell-Lefroy, 136
The Land and People of Ceylon, Wilber, 136
The Land and People of Chile, Bowen, 183
The Land and People of Chile, Pendle, 183
The Land and People of China, Bryan, 137
The Land and People of Czechoslovakia, Hall, 15
The Land and People of Denmark, Wohlrabe and Krusch, 16
The Land and People of Egypt, Mahmoud, 123
The Land and People of Ethiopia, Kaula, 159
The Land and People of Finland, Berry, 17
The Land and People of France, Bragdon, 20
The Land and People of Germany, Wohlrabe and Krusch, 30
The Land and People of Ghana, Sale, 160
The Land and People of Greece, Gianakoulis, 38
The Land and People of Holland, Barnouw, 55

TITLE INDEX

The Land and People of Hungary, Lengyel, 43

Land and People of Iceland, Berry, 44

The Land and People of India, Modak, 143

The Land and People of Indonesia, Smith, 198

The Land and People of Iran, Hinckley, 126

The Land and People of Iran, Shearman, 126

The Land and People of Iraq, Lovejoy, 127

The Land and People of Ireland, O'Brien, 45

The Land and People of Israel, Hoffman, 129

The Land and People of Japan, Vaughan, 147

The Land and People of Jordan, Copeland, 131

The Land and People of Kenya, Kaula, 161

The Land and People of Korea, Evans, 148

The Land and People of Lebanon, Winder, 132

The Land and People of Libya, Copeland, 163

The Land and People of Mexico, Larralde, 174

The Land and People of Morocco, Martin, 163

The Land and People of Morocco, Spencer, 163

The Land and People of New Zealand, Kaula, 200

The Land and People of Nigeria, Forman and Forman, 162

The Land and People of Norway, Hall, 57

The Land and People of Pakistan, Feldman, 150

The Land and People of Pakistan, Lang, 150

The Land and People of Peru, Bowen, 185

The Land and People of Peru, Pendle, 186

The Land and People of Poland, Charnock, 59

The Land and People of Poland, Kelly and Kostich, 59

The Land and People of Portugal, Wohlrabe and Krusch, 60

The Land and People of Rhodesia, Kaula, 164

The Land and People of Russia, Nazaroff, 73

The Land and People of Scotland, Buchanan, 93

The Land and People of South Africa, Paton, 165

The Land and People of Spain, Loder, 66

The Land and People of Sweden, Nano, 69

The Land and People of Switzerland, Bragdon, 70

The Land and People of Syria, Copeland, 133

The Land and People of Tanganyika, Kaula, 164

The Land and People of Thailand, Exell, 152

The Land and People of Thailand, Matthew, 152

The Land and People of the Balkans, Kostich, 14, 62, 116

The Land and People of the Guianas, Fletcher, 184

The Land and People of the Philippines, Vaughan, 201

The Land and People of the West Indies, Sherlock, 192

The Land and People of Tunisia, Spencer, 163

The Land and People of Turkey, Spencer, 134

The Land and People of Uruguay, Dobler, 187

The Land and People of Venezuela, Wohlrabe and Krusch, 188

The Land and People of Yugoslavia, Tillyard, 116

Land Battles: North Africa, Sicily, and Italy, Dupuy, 8

Land Between: The Middle East, Copeland, 118

Land in the Sun: The Story of West Africa, Davis and Ashabranner, 154

Land of Promise: The Story of Early Canada, Field and Dennis, 169

Land of the Afghans: A Book for Children, Cruit, 135

The Land of the Chinese People, Spencer, 138

The Land of the English People, Street, 95

The Land of the Italian People, Winwar, 48

Land of the Mayas; Yesterday and Today, Beals, 175

Land of the Pharaohs, Cottrell, 122

Land of the Two Rivers, Cottrell, 127

The Land Seekers, Boucher, 43

The Lands and Peoples of Kenya, Tanzania and Uganda, Grundy, 160

The Lands and Peoples of Paraguay and Uruguay, Pendle, 185, 187

The Language of Cities, Hosken, 214

The Lantern Bearer: A Life of Robert Louis Stevenson, Wood, 113

Lantern Bearers, Sutcliff, 82

La Salle and the Grand Enterprise, Nolan, 172

La Salle of the Mississippi, Syme, 172

La Salle, River Explorer, Graham, 172

The Last Emperor: The Story of Mexico's Fight for Freedom, Young and Young, 176

Last Nine Days of the Bismarck, Forester, 100

Last Stand at Stalingrad: The Battle That Saved the World, Sammis, 76

The Last Viking, Treece, 63

Later Old Testament Stories, Smither, 119

Latest Aztec Discoveries; Origin and Untold Riches, Powell, 176

Latin America, Whitney, 180, 190

The Laughing Falcon, Whitehouse, 19

Lawrence and His Desert Raiders, Barbary, 132

Lawrence of Arabia, MacLean, 133

Leaders of New Nations, Kenworthy and Ferrari, 212

Leaders of Our Time: v3, Webb, 213

Leaders of Our Time: v4, Webb, 213

Leaders of the New Africa, Kaula, 156

Leaders of the People, Kamm, 131

Lebanon in Pictures, Sterling Publishing Company, 132

Legacy of a Pharaoh, Christie, 123

The Legend of the Cid, Goldston, 66

TITLE INDEX

Legends of the Alhambra, Irving, 66
Legends of the North, Coolidge, 62
Leif Ericson, Explorer, Weir, 58
Leif Eriksson: First Voyager to America, Shippen, 58
Leif the Lucky, Aulaire and Aulaire, 58
Leif the Lucky: Discoverer of America, Berry, 58
Lenin, Baker, 76
Lenin and the Downfall of Tsarist Russia, Roberts, 77
Lenin and Trotsky, Shapiro, 77, 78
Lenin: Genius of Revolution, Liversidge, 77
Lenin: The Man Who Made a Revolution, Levine, 76
Leo Tolstoy, Rothkoff, 78
Leonardo da Vinci, Hahn, 52
Leonardo da Vinci, Ripley, 52
Leonardo da Vinci, Shirley, 52
Leonardo da Vinci, Thomas, 52
Leonardo da Vinci, Williams, 53
Leonardo da Vinci: Pathfinder of Science, Gillette, 52
Leonardo da Vinci, Prince of Painters, Newcomb, 52
Let's Go Down the Mississippi with La Salle, Buchheimer, 172
Let's Go Exploring With Magellan, Granberg, 61
Let's Go on the Half Moon With Henry Hudson, Polking, 171
Let's Go to Europe, Mercer, 1
Let's Go to the Klondike Gold Rush, Wolfe, 166
Let's Go to the New World With Christopher Columbus, Ruffo, 68
Let's Go to the United Nations Headquarters, Cochrane, 219

Let's Look at Castles, Warwick, 3
Let's Travel in Australia, Currie, 197
Let's Travel in Canada, Downing and Dyra, 167
Let's Travel in China, Geis, 137
Let's Travel in England, Geis, 93
Let's Travel in France, Geis, 20
Let's Travel in Greece, Geis, 38
Let's Travel in Holland, Irwin, 55
Let's Travel in Hong Kong, Geis, 141
Let's Travel in India, Geis, 142
Let's Travel in Italy, Geis, 48
Let's Travel in Japan, Geis, 146
Let's Travel in Mexico, Geis, 174
Let's Travel in Nigeria and Ghana, Kittler, 162
Let's Travel in Spain, Geis, 65
Let's Travel in Switzerland, Geis, 71
Let's Travel in Thailand, Geis, 152
Let's Travel in the Congo, Kittler, 159
Let's Travel in the Holy Land, Geis, 128
Let's Travel in the Philippines, Geis, 200
Let's Travel in the South Seas, Geis, 199
Let's Travel in the Soviet Union, Geis, 75
Let's Travel in West Germany, Dyra, 29
Let's Visit Afghanistan, Caldwell, 135
Let's Visit Argentina, Caldwell, 181
Let's Visit Australia, Caldwell, 197
Let's Visit Brazil, Caldwell, 182
Let's Visit Canada, Caldwell, 167
Let's Visit Central America, Caldwell, 189

Let's Visit Chile, Caldwell, 183
Let's Visit China, Caldwell, 137
Let's Visit Colombia, Caldwell, 183
Let's Visit Formosa, Caldwell, 151
Let's Visit France, Newman and Caldwell, 20
Let's Visit Germany, Moore and Caldwell, 30
Let's Visit India, Caldwell, 142
Let's Visit Ireland, Caldwell and others, 44
Let's Visit Italy, Bartlett and Caldwell, 47
Let's Visit Japan, Caldwell, 145
Let's Visit Korea, Caldwell, 148
Let's Visit Malaysia, Caldwell, 149
Let's Visit Mexico, Caldwell, 173
Let's Visit Micronesia: Guam (USA), and Trust Territory of the Pacific Islands, Caldwell, 199
Let's Visit Middle Africa, Caldwell, 154
Let's Visit New Zealand, Caldwell, 199
Let's Visit Nigeria, Freville and Caldwell, 162
Let's Visit Pakistan, Caldwell, 150
Let's Visit Peru, Caldwell, 185
Let's Visit Russia, Popescu and Caldwell, 73
Let's Visit Scotland, MacVicar and Caldwell, 94
Let's Visit South Africa, Caldwell and Newman, 165
Let's Visit Southeast Asia, Caldwell, 151
Let's Visit Thailand, Caldwell, 151
Let's Visit the Middle East, Caldwell, 118
Let's Visit the Philippines, Caldwell, 200
Let's Visit the South Pacific, Caldwell, 199
Let's Visit the West Indies, Caldwell, 191
Let's Visit Turkey, Caldwell, 134
Let's Visit Venezuela, Caldwell, 187
Let's Visit Viet Nam, Caldwell, 152
Let's Visit West Africa, Caldwell, 154
Let's Visit Yugoslavia, Popescu and Caldwell, 116
The Level Land, De Jong, 54
Liberators of Latin America, Young and Young, 180
Liberia in Pictures, Sterling Publishing Company, 161
Liberty, Equality, Fraternity: The Story of the French Revolution, Alderman, 21
The Life and Death of Nazi Germany, Goldston, 29
The Life and Death of the Aztec Nation, Keating, 176
Life in Elizabethan England, Dodd, 97
Life in Georgian England, Williams, 99
Life in Italy at the Time of the Medici, Gage, 50
Life in Regency England, White, 100
Life in Roman Britain, Birley, 95
Life in Russia Today, Miller, 75
Life in Russia Under Catherine the Great, Kochan, 74
Life in Stuart England, Ashley, 98
Life in the Age of Charlemagne, Manz, 3
Life in the Ancient World, Winer, 128
Life in the Middle Ages, Williams, 4

TITLE INDEX

Life in the Renaissance, Gail, 4
Life in Tudor England, Williams, 98
Life in Victorian England, Reader, 99
The Life of Jesus Christ, Pittenger, 120
The Life of Saint Augustine, Hansel, 114
The Life of Saint Patrick, Reynolds, 45
Life of St. Paul, Fosdick, 115
The Life of St. Paul, Pittenger, 115
The Life of Saint Peter, Pittenger 115
Life of Winston Churchill, Wibberley, 103
The Light Within: The Story of Maria Montessori, Smaridge, 53
The Lion and the Rose, Weir, 88
Lion Gate and Labyrinth, Baumann, 38
The Lion in the Gateway, Renault, 40
Lion of Judah: The Story of Haile Selassie I, Emperor of Ethiopia, Gorham, 160
The Lion of Poland: The Story of Paderewski, Hume and Hume, 59
Little Duke, Yonge, 17
Little Foreign Devil, Alexander, 136
Little Marquise: Madame de Lafayette, Wilson, 24
Little Martin Luther, Hummel, 33
Lives of Famous Romans, Coolidge, 50
Living in Tokyo, Boardman, 145
The Locked Crowns, Garthwaite, 15
London, Rosenbaum, 94

London's River — The Story of a City, De Maré, 93
Loneliest Continent: The Story of Antarctic Discovery, Chapman, 203
The Long Black Schooner, Sterne, 153
The Long Bows of Agincourt, Norman, 97
The Long Escape, Werstein, 13
The Long Fellow, Steffan, 45
The Long Pilgrimage, Finkel, 17
Looking at Ancient History, Unstead, 127
Looking at Denmark, Rutland, 16
Looking at France, Church, 20
Looking at Greece, Noel-Baker, 38
Looking at History, Unstead, 95
Looking at Holland, Loman, 55
Looking at Italy, Martin, 48
Looking at Man's Past, Stilwell, 224
Looking at Norway, Ashby, 57
Lords of the Blue Pacific, Suggs, 195
The Lost Dragon of Wessex, Bowers, 79
Lost John, Picard, 86
The Lost Prince: Louis XVII of France, Wallower, 19, 25
The Lost Queen of Egypt, Morrison, 125
Lost Worlds: The Romance of Archaeology, White, 225
Louis Pasteur, Wood, 26
Louis Pasteur: Founder of Microbiology, Burton, 26
Louis Pasteur, the Germ Killer, Mann, 26
Louis XIV of France: Pattern of Majesty, Stearns, 25
Low Countries: Gateways to Europe, Wolseley, 14, 55
The Loyal Grenvilles, Peart, 88

Lucius: Adventures of a Roman Boy, Church, 46
The Lucky Ones, Coatsworth, 219
Ludwig Beethoven and the Chiming Tower Bells, Wheeler, 31
Lysis Goes to the Play, Snedeker, 37

Machines and the Men Who Made the World of Industry, Hartman, 214
The MacKenzie: River to the Top of the World, Lambie, 167
Madame Prime Minister: The Story of Indira Gandhi, Garnett, 144
Made in Ancient Egypt, Price, 122
Made in Ancient Greece, Price, 40
Made in China, Spencer, 138
Made in Iceland, Golden, 44
Made in Thailand, Ayer, 151
Magellan, First Around the World, Syme, 61
Magna Carta, Daugherty, 96
Magna Carta, Swindler, 97
Magna Carta: Story of Britain, Hodges, 97
Mahatma Gandhi: The Father of Nonviolence, Peare, 144
Mahatma Gandhi: The Great Soul, Lengyel, 144
Main Streets of Southeast Asia, Buell, 151
Makers of Latin America, Worcester, 180
Makers of the Red Revolution, Coolidge, 74, 76
Makon and the Dauphin, Agle, 18
Malaria Ross: A Story Biography, Kamm, 145
Mallory of Everest, Styles, 150
Man Against the Unknown, Icenhower, 216
Man and His Tools, Burns, 226

Man from St. Malo, Ferguson, 171
Man in the Making, Friedman, 222
A Man Named Columbus, Norman, 68
Man of Steel: Joseph Stalin, Archer, 77
The Man Who Changed China: The Story of Sun Yat-sen, Buck, 141
The Man Who Could Read Stones: Champollion and the Rosetta Stone, Honour, 125
The Man Who Found Out Why: The Story of Gregor Mendel, Webster, 12
The Man Who Transformed the World: James Watt, Crane, 113
The Man Who Was Don Quixote: The Story of Miguel Cervantes, Busoni, 66
Man With a Sword, Treece, 83
Man's First Million Years, Lucas, 223
Man's Way: From Cave to Skyscraper, Linton and Linton, 210
The Many Faces of World War I, Werstein, 7
Mao Tse-tung and the Chinese Communist Revolution, Roberts, 140
The Maoris of New Zealand, McGuire, 200
Maps Mean Adventure, McFall, 216, 218
Marathon Looks on the Sea, Coolidge, 35
Marco Polo, Graves, 140
Marco Polo, Komroff, 140
Marco Polo: A Story of the Middle Ages, Preston, 141
Marco Polo: The Great Traveler, Webb, 141
Marie Antoinette, Kielty, 25

TITLE INDEX

Marie Antoinette, Komroff and Komroff, 25
Marie Antoinette: Daughter of an Empress, Vance, 25
Marie Curie, McKown, 23
The Mark of the Horse Lord, Sutcliff, 79
Marquette and Joliet, Kelly, 172
The Marquis de Lafayette, Carter, 24
The Marsh King, Hodges, 80
Martin Luther, Fosdick, 33
Martin Luther, McNeer and Ward, 33
Martin Luther: The Great Reformer, Pittenger, 33
Mary, Queen of Scots, Hahn, 108
The Masai; Herders of East Africa, Bleeker, 160, 164
Matter of Life and Death: How Wars Get Started — or Are Prevented, Carr, 231
Matthew Henson: Arctic Hero, Ripley, 206
The Maya, Indians of Central America, Bleeker, 175
Maya: Land of the Turkey and the Deer, Von Hagen, 175
The Medieval Castle, Foster, 2
Medieval Days and Ways, Hartman, 2
Medieval English Warfare, Sellman, 97
Mediterranean Africa; Four Muslim Nations, Kittler, 163
Meet Christopher Columbus, De Kay, 67
Meet North Africa, Gunther and others, 163
Meet South Africa, Gunther and others, 165
Meet Soviet Russia, Gunther, 75
Meet the Congo and Its Neighbors, Gunther, 155

Meeting With a Stranger, Bradley, 159
Men Against Distance: The Story of Communications, Floherty, 214
Men Against the Sea, Nordhoff and Hall, 198
Men and Women Behind the Atom, Riedman, 229
Men, Moss, and Reindeer: Challenge of Lapland, Berry, 64
Men of Athens, Coolidge, 39
Men of Ideas, Loeper, 213
Men of Iron, Pyle, 86
Men of Science and Invention, Blow, 227
Men of Sherwood, Cooke, 84
Men Under the Sea, Larsen, 216
Men Who Changed the Map, Berry and Best, 211
Men Who Changed the World, Larsen, 228
Men Who Fought for Freedom, Larsen, 212
Men Who Shaped the Future, Larsen, 228
Merlin's Mistake, Newman, 81
The Merry Adventures of Robin Hood of Great Renown in Nottinghamshire, Pyle, 86
Mesopotamia: The Civilization That Rose Out of the Clay, Fairservis, 127
Messenger from K'itai, Burleigh, 136
Mexican Assignment, McClarren, 174
The Mexican Story, McNeer, 174
Mexicans, Coy, 174
Mexico, Hancock, 174
Mexico: Land of Eagle and Serpent, Ross, 174
Mexico: Land of Hidden Treasure, Credle, 174

Mexico: Land of the Plumed Serpent, Grant, 174
Michael Faraday and the Electric Dynamo, May, 106
Michael Strogoff, Verne, 72
Michelangelo, Ripley, 53
Michelangelo, Stearns, 53
Microbe Man, Doorly, 26
Midshipman Quinn, Styles, 91
Midshipman Quinn and Denise, the Spy, Styles, 91
Mightier Than the Sword; Cartoon, Caricature, Social Comment, Rogers, 210
The Mighty Mekong, Liss, 151
The Mighty Ones: Great Men and Women of Early Bible Days, De Jong, 119
The Military History of the Chinese Civil War, Dupuy, 139
The Military History of the Korean War, Marshall, 149
The Military History of the Spanish-American War: The War to Free Cuba, Marshall, 194
The Military Life of Adolph Hitler, Führer of Germany, Dupuy, 32
The Military Life of Alexander the Great of Macedon, Dupuy, 41
The Military Life of Frederick the Great of Prussia, Dupuy, 32
The Military Life of Gustavus Adolphus, Father of Modern War, Dupuy, 70
The Military Life of Hannibal, Father of Strategy, Dupuy, 52
The Military Life of Julius Caesar, Imperator, Dupuy, 50
The Military Life of Napoleon, Emperor of the French, Dupuy, 26
The Military Life of Winston Churchill of Britain, Dupuy, 102
The Military Lives of Hindenburg and Ludendorff of Imperial Germany, Dupuy, 32, 33
Milton and His World, Wedgwood, 108
The Minoans of Ancient Crete, Field, 39
Miranda the Great, Estes, 46
Miriam, Sommerfelt, 57
Mission to Cathay, Polland, 141
Mission to Metlakatla, Wentworth, 170
Mister Arctic: An Account of Vilhjalmur Stefansson, Berry, 207
Modern China, Spencer, 139
Modern Composers for Young People, Burch, 10
Modern Japan: A Brief History from 800 A.D. to the Present Day, Powell, 146
Mohawk Gamble, Ridle, 166
Molly and the Regicides, Crandell, 87
A Moment of Silence, Janssen, 54
The Monarch of Juan Fernández, Ballard, 111
Monday, 21 October 1805: The Day of Trafalgar, Ribbons, 99
Montgomery of Alamein, Clark, 108
More Heroes of Civilization, Cottler and Jaffe, 212
Le Morte d'Arthur, Malory, 81
Moses, Shippen, 121
Moses, Wheeler, 121
Most Gracious Majesty, Parker, 105
Mound Builders, Scheele, 223
Mountains in the Sea: Challenge of Crowded Japan, Gallant, 146
Mozart, Komroff, 13

TITLE INDEX

Mozart, Mirsky, 13
Mozart, Woodford, 13
Mozart: Child Wonder, Great Composer, Gass, 12
Mozart: Music Magician, Bishop, 12
Mozart, the Wonder Boy, Wheeler and Deucher, 13
Muhammad: Prophet of Islam, Warren, 133
Mussolini and the Rise of Italian Fascism, Absolem, 53
Mutiny on the Bounty, Nordhoff and Hall, 198
My Cousin, the Arab, Nurenberg, 128
My Enemy, My Brother, Forman, 128
My Friend in Africa, Franck, 157
My Japan, 1930-1951, Nakamoto, 148

The Namesake: A Story of King Alfred, Hodges, 80
Napoleon, Cammiade, 25
Napoleon, Komroff, 26
Napoleon and the Battle of Waterloo, Winwar, 21
Napoleon, Man of Destiny, Gimpel, 26
Napoleon's Hundred Days, Pringle, 21
Napoleon's Marshal: The Life of Michel Ney, Foster, 26
Naval and Overseas War, 1914-1915, Dupuy, 5
Naval and Overseas War, 1916-1918, Dupuy and Hayes, 6
Naval War in the Pacific: On to Tokyo, Dupuy, 147
Naval War in the Pacific: Rising Sun of Nippon, Dupuy, 147
The Naval War in the West: The Raiders, Dupuy, 5

The Naval War in the West: The Wolf Packs, Dupuy, 5
Navigation: Land, Sea and Sky, Hellman, 230
The Nehrus of India: Three Generations of Leadership, Lamb, 145
Neighbors to the South, Goetz, 179
Nelson and the Age of Fighting Sail, Warner, 100
Nelson: Hero of Trafalgar, Thompson, 109
The Netherlands, Carew, 55
The New Africa, Gatti and Gatti, 154
The New Popular History of the World; The Story of Mankind from Earliest Times to the Present Day, Caldwell and Merrill, 208
New World Beginnings: Indian Cultures in the Americas, Vlahos, 180
New Worlds Ahead, Hampden, 93
New Zealand, Longley, 200
New Zealand, Marsh, 200
Nicholas Carey, Welch, 92
Nigeria: Republic of a Hundred Kings, Watson, 162
Nigerian Pioneer, the Story of Mary Slessor, Syme, 162
Night Coach to Paris, Ritchie, 19
Night of the Wall, Goldthwait, 28
The Nile: Lifeline of Egypt, Weingarten, 124
The Nile — The Story of Pharaohs, Farmers, and Explorers, Warren, 124
1918: Decision in the West, Dupuy and Crick, 6
1918: Gamble for Victory — The Greatest Attack of World War I, Cowley, 5

1918: The German Offensives, Dupuy and Crick, 6
1914: The Battles in the East, Dupuy, 5
1914: The Battles in the West, Dupuy, 6
No Beat of Drums, Burton, 90
No Time for Glory: Stories of World War II, Fenner, 232
The Norman Conquest: Story of Britain, Hodges, 97
Norman England, Sellman, 97
The Norman Invasion, Ellacott, 96
Norse Gods and Giants, Aulaire, and Aulaire, 62
North Pole: The Story of Robert E. Peary, Simon, 207
North to Freedom, Holm, 15
The Northmen, Chubb, 64
Norwegian Folk Tales, Asbjørnsen, 56
Nubia: A Drowning Land, Drower, 123

O Canada! Barclay, 167
Oars, Sails, and Steam, Tunis, 231
Oath of Silence, Bentley, 89
The Odyssey, Homer, 36
Of Dikes and Windmills, Spier, 55
Of Maps and Men, Neal, 218
Olaf's Sword, Knight, 63
Oliver Cromwell, Levine, 103
Omen for a Princess: The Story of Jahanara, Royal Poet of the Seventeenth Century, Bothwell, 142
Omen of the Birds, Behn, 46
On Course! Navigating in Sea, Air, and Space, Hirsch, 230
On Foot to the Arctic: The Story of Samuel Hearne, Syme, 206
On Land and Sea With Caesar; or Following the Eagles, Wells, 47

Once the Hodja, Kelsey, 134
One Day in Ancient Rome, Kirtland, 49
One Day in Aztec Mexico, Kirtland, 176
One Day in Elizabethan England, Kirtland, 98
Opening Africa, Hobley, 155
Operation Sippacik, Godden, 134
Organization of African Unity, Addona, 153
Organization of American States: The Challenge of the Americas, Haverstock, 220
The Orient — Australia and the South Sea Islands, Hillyer and Huey, 195, 197
Orient Express: The Birth, Life, and Death of a Great Train, Hogg, 230
The Origins of Man, Napier, 223
Other Bible Lands, Lovejoy, 118
Otto of the Silver Hand, Pyle, 28
Our Navy Explores Antarctica, Euller, 203
Our Neighbors in Africa, Caldwell and Caldwell, 154
Our Neighbors in Australia and New Zealand, Caldwell and Caldwell, 197, 200
Our Neighbors in Brazil, Caldwell, and Caldwell, 182
Our Neighbors in Central America, Caldwell and Caldwell, 189
Our Neighbors in India, Caldwell and Caldwell, 142
Our Neighbors in Japan, Caldwell and Caldwell, 146
Our Neighbors in Korea, Caldwell and Caldwell, 148
Our Neighbors in Peru, Caldwell and Caldwell, 185
Our Neighbors in Thailand, Caldwell and Caldwell, 151

TITLE INDEX

Our Neighbors in the Philippines, Caldwell and Caldwell, 200
Our World: Bulgaria, Burt, 14
Our World: Mexico, Witton, 175
Our World: The Taming of Israel's Negev, Golann, 129
Outcast, Sutcliff, 79
Outlaw King: The Story of Robert the Bruce, Stephens, 101
Outpost of Peril, Malkus, 166

Pablo Picasso: Master of Modern Art, Struchen, 69
Pacific Islands Speaking, Sperry, 195
Page Boy for King Arthur, Stone, 82
The Pageant of Canadian History, Peck, 168
The Pageant of Chinese History, Seeger, 138
Pageant of India's History, Sen, 143
Pageant of Japanese History, Dilts, 146
The Pageant of Medieval Art and Life, McLanathan, 3
Pageant of Middle American History, Peck, 190
Pageant of Russian History, Seeger, 73
Pageant of South American History, Peck, 179
Pakistan in Pictures, Sterling Publishing Company, 150
Panama and the Canal Zone in Pictures, Sterling Publishing Company, 190
Parallel Lives, Plutarch, 41, 50
Paris, Smith, 20
Paris Triumphant, Whelpton, 20
Passage to the West: The Great Voyages of Henry Hudson, Gerson, 171
Passover to Freedom, Cohen, 128
Paul and the World's Most Famous Letters, Haughton, 115
Peace Is an Adventure: The Men and Women of the U.N. in Action Around the World, Kelen, 220
Peary to the Pole, Lord, 207
The Peasant Boy Who Became Pope, Lattin, 116
Pebbles from a Broken Jar: Fables and Hero Stories from Old China, Alexander, 136
People and Places, Mead, 223
People and Power: The Story of Three Nations, Savage, 30, 73, 146
People and Things in Early Greece, Jupo, 40
People in Palestine, Coolidge, 130
The People of Ancient Israel, Mills, 130
People of Long Ago, Barker and Hammer, 221
People of the Arctic, Osmond, 205
People of the Snow: Eskimos of Arctic Canada, Tolboom, 206
The Peoples of Africa, Turnbull, 156
Peru, Halsell, 185
Peru, Bolivia, Ecuador: The Indian Andes, May, 182, 184, 185
Peru: Land Astride the Andes, Watson, 186
Peter, Holm, 88
Peter and Paul: The Rock and the Sword, Thompson, 115
Peter the Great, Baker, 77
Peter the Great, Joseph, 77
Peter the Great, Liversidge, 77
Peter Tschaikovsky and the Nutcracker Ballet, Wheeler, 78
The Pharaohs of Ancient Egypt, Payne, 122

WORLD HISTORY IN JUVENILE BOOKS

Pharaohs of Egypt, Hawkes, 124
The Philippines, Poole, 200
The Philippines, Roland, 201
Philippines' Fight for Freedom, Archer, 200
The Philippines: Wonderland of Many Cultures, Brooks, 200
Picture Book of Palestine, Smither, 129
A Picture History of Ancient Rome, Erdoes, 49
A Picture History of Britain, Hutton, 93
A Picture History of India, Hampden, 142
Picture Map Geography of Africa, Quinn, 156
Picture Map Geography of Asia, Quinn, 138
Picture Map Geography of Canada and Alaska, Quinn, 168
Picture Map Geography of Eastern Europe, Hall and Criner, 14, 15, 43, 59, 62, 73, 116
Picture Map Geography of Mexico, Central America, and the West Indies, Quinn, 190, 192
Picture Map Geography of South America, Quinn, 179
Picture Map Geography of the Pacific Islands, Quinn, 195
Picture Map Geography of Western Europe, Wohlrabe and Krusch, 1
The Picture Story of Denmark, O'Neill, 16
The Picture Story of Japan, Carr, 146
Pilgrim Kate, Daringer, 87
Pioneers in Science, Siedel and Siedel, 229
Pioneers of Flight, Wallhauser, 231
Piper to the Clan, Clarke, 87

Pirate Book, Davidson, 192
Pirate Chase, Miers, 191
Pirate Port: The Story of the Sunken City of Port Royal, Marx, 191
Pirate Royal, Beatty and Beatty, 193
Pirates and Highwaymen, Jenkins, 192
Pirates and Privateers, McCall, 192
Pirates in Petticoats, Yolen, 193
Pirates of the Pacific, Day, 195
Pirates of the Spanish Main, Cochran, 192
A Pistol in Greenyards, Hunter, 91
Pizarro and the Conquest of Peru, Howard, 187
Place Mill, Softly, 88
Plague and Fire, Gray, 98
Plain Jane, Softly, 88
The Planes the Allies Flew in World War II, Cooke, 7
The Planes They Flew in World War I, Cooke, 5
Poland in Pictures, Sterling Publishing Company, 59
Polar Aviation, Glines, 202
The Polynesian Triangle, Berry and Best, 198
Ponce de León, Blassingame, 193
Pool of Knowledge: How the United Nations Share Their Skills, Shippen, 220
Pope John XXIII, MacGregor-Hastie, 114
Pope John XXIII, Richards, 115
Pope John XXIII: The Gentle Shepherd, Struchen, 115
Pope Paul VI, MacGregor-Hastie, 115
Pope Paul VI, Pallenberg, 115
Pope Paul VI, Shapiro, 115
The Pope's Back Yard, Pepper, 114

TITLE INDEX

Portals to the Past: The Story of Archaeology, Shippen, 225

Portrait of a Revolution, Rossif and Chapsal, 75

Portrait of Bach, Manton, 30

Portraits of Nobel Laureates in Peace, Wintterle and Cramer, 221

Portugal, Carew, 60

Portugal in Pictures, Sterling Publishing Company, 60

The Portuguese Explorers, Buehr, 60, 61

Powder and Steel: Notable Battles of the 1800s from New Orleans to the Zulu War, Orbaan, 233

Prehistoric Britain, Sellman, 96

Prehistoric Cave Paintings, Marcus, 223

Prehistoric Man and the Primates, Scheele, 223

The Prince and the Pauper, Twain, 86

Prince Henry the Navigator and the Highways of the Sea, Chubb, 61

The Prince of Mexico, Cesco, 173

Prince Valiant and the Golden Princess, Foster, 80

Prince Valiant and the Three Challenges, Foster, 80

Prince Valiant Fights Attila the Hun, Foster, 80

Prince Valiant in the Days of King Arthur, Foster, 80

Prince Valiant in the New World, Foster, 80

Prince Valiant on the Inland Sea, Foster, 80

Prince Valiant's Perilous Voyage, Foster, 80

The Prince Who Gave Up a Throne: A Story of the Buddha, Serage, 144

The Princess and the Lion, Coatsworth, 159

Princess of Orange, Kyle, 108

Prisoner of the Indies, Household, 84

Profile of Kenya, Kenworthy, 161

Profile of Nigeria, Kenworthy, 162

Profiles from the New Asia, Roland, 138

A Promise to Keep, Smart, 119

Prophet of Revolution: Karl Marx, Apsler, 34

Pugnax, the Gladiator, Anderson, 45

Puzzle of the Lost Dauphin, Kimball, 18

The Pygmies; Africans of the Congo Forest, Bleeker, 159

Queen Elizabeth and the Spanish Armada, Winwar, 105

Queen Elizabeth I, Bigland, 105

Queen Most Fair, Oliver, 85, 108

Queen Victoria, Haycraft, 113

Queen Victoria, Streatfeild, 113

The Queen's Most Honorable Pirate, Wood, 87

The Queen's Wizard, Beatty and Beatty, 87

Quentin Durward, Scott, 18

Quesada of Colombia, Syme, 184

Quest for Freedom; Bolivar and the South American Revolution, Rink, 180

Quest for Prehistory, Palmer and Lloyd, 127, 225

Quest for the Dead Sea Scrolls, Palmer, 129

Quest for the Unknown: Explorers of Today, Pinney, 216

The Quest of Captain Cook, Selsam, 196

Quest of Columbus, Meredith and Smith, 67

The Quest of Johannes Kepler, Astronomer, Land, 33,
The Quest of Louis Pasteur, Lauber, 26
The Quest of Michael Faraday, Harvey, 106
The Quetzal Feather, Duncombe, 189
Quinn of the Fury, Styles, 92

Race Between Food and People: The Challenge of a Hungry World, Joy, 209
Racing Cars That Made History, Cooke, 230
Rainbow Round the World: A Story of UNICEF, Yates, 221
Ransom for a Knight, Picard, 83
Raphael: Painter of the Renaissance, Gillette, 53
The Red Bonnet, Garnett, 18
Red Carpet for Lafayette, Foster, 18
The Red Cross, Rothkopf, 220
Red Falcons of Trémoine, Peart, 83
Red Hugh, Prince of Donegal, Reilly, 44
Red Rebel: Tito of Yugoslavia, Archer, 117
Red Revolutionary: A Life of Lenin, Charnock, 76
The Reformation, Cowie, 10
Reformation and Exploration, Johnston and Steffensen, 4
Religions Around the World, Wolcott and Wolcott, 211
The Reluctant Queen, Haycraft, 84
Rembrandt and His World, Stearns, 55
Remember Vera Cruz! Knight, 85
The Renaissance, Bull, 4
The Renaissance, Grant, 4

The Renaissance, Steffensen, 5
Renaissance and Reformation Times, Mills, 5
Republican Rome, Pike, 49
Retreat from Moscow, Almedingen, 74
Return to Hiroshima, Lifton, 148
Revolts and Revolutions, Edmonds, 208
Revolution: France 1789-1794, Eimerl, 21
The Revolution in Spanish America: The Independence Movements of 1808-1825, Prago, 179
The Rhone: River of Contrasts, Von Maltitz, 1
Richard Byrd: Boy Who Braved the Unknown, Van Riper, 204
Richard E. Byrd, Olds, 204
Richard E. Byrd: Adventurer to the Poles, De Leeuw, 204
Richard the Lionhearted: The Crusader King, Pittenger, 111
Richard Wagner: Titan of Music, Stearns, 34
Richthofen, the Red Baron, Fisk, 34
The Riddle of the Incas: The Story of Hiram Bingham and Macchu Picchu, Norman, 186
Ride the Far Wind, Jones, 137
Riding With Coronado, Meredith and Smith, 177
The Rimac: River of Peru, Crosby, 185
The Ring of Danger: A Tale of Elizabethan England, Bill, 84
Ring the Judas Bell, Forman, 35
Rise and Fall of Adolf Hitler, Shirer, 33
The Rise of Red China, Goldston, 139
Rise of Russia, Wallace, 74

TITLE INDEX

Rival Cities — Venice and Genoa, Robinson, 48

Rivals in Parliament: William Pitt and Charles Fox, Noble, 99

Riverboat Family, Wilton, 196

Rivers of the World, v 1: Danube, Amazon, Niger, Ganges, Popescu and others, 210, 218

Rivers of the World, v2: Rhine, Murray, Nile, St. Lawrence, Whittam and others, 211, 218

The Rivers Ran East, Clark, 182

Road to Miklagard, Treece, 63

Roads of Man, Hoag, 230

Roald Amundsen, De Leeuw, 203

Roald Amundsen: A Saga of the Polar Seas, Kugelmass, 203

Robert Bruce: King of Scots, Baker, 101

Robert E. Peary: North Pole Conqueror, Berry, 207

Robert Koch: Father of Bacteriology, Knight, 33

Robert Louis Stevenson: His Life, Peare, 113

Robert Louis Stevenson: Storyteller and Adventurer, Wilkie, 113

Robert Peary: Boy of the North Pole, Clark, 207

Robert Schumann and Mascot Ziff, Wheeler, 34

Robin and His Merry Men, Serraillier, 86

Robin Hood, Creswick, 84

Robin Hood, Oman, 86

Robin Hood and His Merry Outlaws, McSpadden, 85

Robin Hood of Sherwood Forest, McGovern, 85

Robin Hood Stories, Dolch and Dolch, 84

Robin Hood's Arrow, Stone, 86

Rockets' Red Glare: Challenge of Outer Space, Lawrence, 216

Roman Army, Wilkes, 50

Roman Britain, Fox, 95

Roman Britain, Sellman, 96

The Roman Empire, Asimov, 49

Roman People, Coolidge, 48

Roman Republic, Asimov, 48

Roman Roads, Von Hagen, 50

Roman Way, Hamilton, 49

The Romans, Duggan, 49

The Romans in the Days of the Empire, Miller, 49

Royal Adventurers, Unstead, 11

Royal Canadian Mounted Police, Neuberger, 168

The Royal Dirk, Beatty and Beatty, 89

Rubens, Ripley, 14

Rudyard Kipling: Creative Adventurer, Manley, 107

Rulers in Petticoats, Boyd, 212

Runner for the King, Bennett, 185

Runner of the Woods: Story of Young Radisson, Ritchie, 172

Russia, Lawrence, 73

Russia, Salisbury, 73

Russia, Thayer, 73

Russia: Adventures in Eyewitness History, Hoff, 73

Russia and Her Neighbors, Edwards, 74

Russia in Pictures, Sterling Publishing Company, 73

Russia in Revolution, Halliday, 75

Russia Invaded, from Genghis Khan to Hitler, Francini, 73

Russia: The Story of a Nation, Habberton, 73

Russia Under the Czars, Moscow, 74

The Russian Revolution, Goldston, 75

The Russian Revolution, Kochan, 75

The Russian Revolutions, Footman, 75
The Russo-Japanese War, Martin, 148

The Sacred Jewel, Faulkner, 78
St. Francis, Pelagie, 51
Saint Francis of Assisi, Liversidge, 51
St. Lawrence, Toye, 168
Saint Lawrence Seaway, Judson, 167
The St. Lawrence: Seaway of North America, White, 169
Saint Thomas Aquinas, the Angelic Doctor, Pittenger, 54
Saint Thomas More of London Town, Brady, 109
Saints: Adventures in Courage, O'Neill, 11
The Saints and Your Name, Quadflieg, 213
Salute to the Brave: Stories of World War II, Tibbets, 234
Samuel Cunard — Pioneer of the Atlantic Steamship, Grant, 103
The Sapphire Pendant, Beyer, 89
Save the Khan, Bartos-Höppner, 72
Scandinavia, Innes, 64
Scandinavia: The Challenge of Welfare, Edwards, 64
Scarab for Luck: A story of Ancient Egypt, Meadowcroft, 121
The Scarlet Force: Making of the Mounted Police, Longstreeth, 169
The Scarlet Pimpernel, Orczy, 19
Science and Serendipity; Great Discoveries by Accident, Halacy, 226
Science and the Secret of Man's Past, Folsom, 222, 226

Science, Science, Science, Hamilton, 226
Scotland in Pictures, Sterling Publishing Company, 94
Scotland's Queen; The Story of Mary Stuart, Vance, 108
Scotland's Story, Marshall, 94
The Scottish Chiefs, Porter, 101
The Sea-Dragon: Journals of Francis Drake's Voyage Around the World, Sanderlin, 98
Sea Fights, Daniell, 232
Sea Fights Under Sail, Lloyd, 233
Seafarers of the Pacific, Newton, 199
The Seals, Dillon, 44
Seaplanes That Made History, Cooke, 230
Search for a Lost City, Elkin, 42
The Search for Early Man, Pfeiffer, 223
Searchers of the Sea: Pioneers in Oceanography, Daugherty, 215
The Second World War, Sellman, 9
Secret Beyond the Mountains, Ritchie, 137
Secret Mission to the Philippines: The Story of the "Spyron" and the American-Filipino Guerrillas of World War II, Wise, 201
The Secret of the Pharaohs, Schultz, 121
Secrets from Ancient Graves, Cohen, 224
Seeing London, Maxey, 94
Seeking New Lands, Barker and Hammer, 214
The Seine — from Its Source to the the Sea, Davenport, 20
The Seine: River of Paris, Wilson, 21
Sending the Word: The Story of Communications, Buehr, 214

TITLE INDEX

Seven Sovereign Queens, Trease, 11

Seven Women Explorers, Rittenhouse, 217

The Seven Wonders of the Ancient World, Silverberg, 211

Seven Wonders of the Modern World, Sullivan, 211

Shackleton's Epic Voyage, Brown, 204

Shakespeare, Shirley, 112

Shakespeare and His World, Brown, 112

Shakespeare and the Players, Hodges, 97

Shakespeare in His Time, Brown, 112

Shakespeare's England, Horizon Magazine, 98, 112

Shakespeare's Theatre, Hodges, 98

The Shannon: River of Loughs and Legends, Nowlan, 45

Shapers of Africa, Polatnick and Saletan, 157

The Shaping of England, Asimov, 92

The Shattered Skull: A Safari to Man's Past, Perkins, 223

She Lived for Science: Irène Joliot-Curie, McKown, 23

Shepherd of the Sun, Appel, 186

Shepherdess of France: Remembrances of Jeanne d'Arc, Masefield, 23

The Shield of Achilles, Forman, 133

Shield Ring, Sutcliff, 83

Ships of Adventure, Bethers, 229

Short History of Science, Gregor, 226

A Short History of Science, v 1: Ancient Science, Hoyt, 226

A Short History of Science, v 2: Modern Science, Hoyt, 227

The Siege and Fall of Troy, Graves, 36

Siegfried, the Mighty Warrior, De Vivanco, 27

Sigmund Freud, Klagsbrun, 12

Sigurd and His Brave Companions: A Tale of Medieval Norway, Undset, 56

The Silent Cities — Civilizations Lost and Found, Boyd, 127

Silver Branch, Sutcliff, 79

The Silver Dagger, Dwight, 193

Simon Bolivar: The George Washington of South America, Young and Young, 180

Simon Bolivar: The Great Liberator, Whitridge, 180

Simón Bolívar: The Liberator, Webb, 180

The Sinking of the Bismarck, Shirer, 100

Sir Arthur Evans: Discoverer of Knossos, Selden, 106

Sir Christopher Wren: Renaissance Architect, Philosopher, and Scientist, Gould, 114

Sir Francis Drake: A World Explorer, Foster, 105

Sir Gawain and the Green Knight, Hieatt, 80

Sir Henry Morgan, Buccaneer, Syme, 193

Sir Isaac Newton, Houston and De Vault, 109

Sir John Cockcroft, Clark, 103

Sir Julian Huxley, Clark, 107

Sir Mortimer Wheeler, Clark, 225

Sir Tristan of All Time, Holbrook, 28

Sir Vivian Fuchs, Larsen, 204

Sir Walter Raleigh, Baker, 111

Sir Walter Raleigh: A World Explorer, De Leeuw, 111

Sir Winston Churchill, Clark, 102

345

Sir Winston Churchill, Farrell, 103
Sir Winston Churchill, Richards, 103
Sister Elizabeth Kenny, Thomas, 198
The Six-Day Warriors, Braverman and Silver, 130
Six Queens: The Wives of Henry VIII, Vance, 107
The Six Wives of Henry VIII, Malvern, 107
The Skies of Crete, Forman, 36
Slave Doctor, Diekmann, 191
Slave of Catiline, Anderson, 45
The Slave Who Freed Haiti: The Story of Toussaint L'Ouverture, Scherman, 193
Slavery: From the Rise of Western Civilization to the Renaissance, Meltzer, 210
A Slave's Tale, Haugaard, 62
Slavic Peoples, Chubb, 73
The Small War of Sergeant Donkey, Daly, 47
Smith, Garfield, 91
Snow Treasure, McSwigan, 57
So What About History? Morgan, 210
Socrates, Silverberg, 42
Socrates: The Father of Western Philosophy, Turlington, 42
Soldier of Africa, Hennessey and Sauter, 153
Soldier of Israel: The Story of General Moshe Dayan, Taslitt, 131
Soldiers and Armies, Tucker, 234
Some Kings and Queens, Unstead, 11
Song for a Lute, Vance, 111
The Song in the Streets, Spencer, 21
Song of Robin Hood, Malcolmson, 85
The Song of Roland, 17
Song of the North: The Story of Edvard Grieg, Purdy, 58
Song of the Waterfall: The Story of Edvard and Nina Grieg, Kyle, 58
Song Without End: The Love Story of Clara and Robert Schumann, White, 34
Sons of the Desert, Gidal and Gidal, 132
Sons of the Steppe, Baumann, 136
South Africa in Pictures, Sterling Publishing Company, 165
South African Statesman: Jan Christiaan Smuts, Joseph, 165
The Soviet Union: A View from Within, Folsom, 74
The Soviet Union: An Introduction, Lensen, 75
Spain, Brinton, 65
Spain, Goldston, 66
Spain, Thomas, 66
Spain & Portugal: Iberian Portrait, Madden, 60, 66
Spain in Pictures, Sterling Publishing Company, 66
Spain: Wonderland of Contrasts, Daly, 65
Spain's Golden Queen Isabella, Noble, 69
The Spaniards Are Coming, Manning-Sanders, 85
Spanish Armada, Buehr, 97
The Spanish Armada, Hodges, 98
The Spanish Armada, Williams, 98
The Spanish Armada: The Story of a Glorious Defeat, Hirschfeld, 97
The Spanish Letters, Hunter, 91
Spanish Plateau: Challenge of a Dry Land, Buckley, 65
Spearman to Minuteman: The

TITLE INDEX

Story of the Soldier: 2000 B.C. to 1783 A.D., Ellacott, 232

Spice and the Devil's Cave, Hewes, 60

Spice Ho! A Story of Discovery, Hewes, 215

Spies: Their Trade and Tricks, Seth, 233

Spies With Wings: The Story of the Lafayette Escadrille, Whitehouse, 19

The Splendor of Persia, Payne, 126

Splintered Sword, Treece, 63

Spy for Liberty: The Adventurous Life of Beaumarchais, Ruskin, 22

Spy: The Story of Modern Espionage, Irving, 8

Squire for King Arthur, Stone, 82

Stalemate in the Trenches, Dupuy, 6

Stalin: Man of Steel, Roberts, 77

Stallion of the Desert, Frost, 162

Stampede for Gold: The Story of the Klondike, Berton, 169

Stamps Tell the Story of the United Nations, Kelen, 220

Stamps Tell the Story of the Vatican, Kelen, 114

Standard Bearer: A Story of Army Life in the Time of Caesar, Whitehead, 47

Standing Lions, Ray, 39

Stanley: African Explorer, Smith, 158

Star Mountain and Other Legends of Mexico, Campbell, 173

Star of Danger, Levin, 15

A State Is Born: The Story of Israel, Hirschfeld, 129

Steam on the Line, Turner, 92

A Stone in a Pool, Softly, 88

Stonehenge of the Kings: A People Appear, Crampton, 95

Stories from Herodotus, Downey, 40

Stories from Other Lands, Disney (Walt) Productions, 79

Stories of Famous Explorers by Sea, Knight, 217

Stories of Famous Sea Fights, Knight, 232

Stories of Famous Ships, Knight, 231

Stories of King Arthur and His Knights, Picard, 81

Stories of the Crusades, Toussaint-Samat, 3

Stories of the Gods and Heroes, Benson, 211

Stories Told by the Aztecs: Before the Spaniards Came, Beals, 173

Storm Over the Caucasus, Bartos-Höppner, 72

Stormy Victory: The Story of Tchaikovsky, Purdy, 78

Stormy Voyager: The Story of Charles Wilkes, Silverberg, 204

The Story Behind Great Inventions, Montgomery, 227

The Story Behind Great Medical Discoveries, Montgomery, 227

Story of Africa: South of the Sahara, Savage, 156

The Story of Albert Schweitzer, Daniel, 157

The Story of Albert Schweitzer, Manton, 158

The Story of Ancient Athens, Barker, 39

The Story of Ancient Egypt, Sewell and Lynch, 123

The Story of Archaeology in the Americas, Elting and Folsom, 224

The Story of Australia, Day, 197

Story of Beethoven, Kaufmann, 31

The Story of Britain, Unstead, 95

347

Story of Christopher Columbus, Baker, 67
The Story of Christopher Columbus, McGovern, 67
Story of D-Day: June 6, 1944, Bliven, 7
Story of Edith Cavell, Vinton, 102
The Story of Emmeline Pankhurst, Kamm, 110
Story of England, Brown and Arbuthnot, 93
The Story of Fighting Ships, Tucker, 234
The Story of Florence Nightingale, Leighton, 110
The Story of Gandhi, Zinkin, 145
Story of Hans Andersen: Swan of Denmark, Manning-Sanders, 16
The Story of Haydn, Kaufmann, 12
Story of India, Bothwell, 142
The Story of Israel in Stamps, Shamir and Shamir, 129
Story of Jesus, Petersham and Petersham, 120
The Story of Jesus: For Young People, Bowie, 120
Story of Joan of Arc, Nolan, 24
Story of John Keats, Gittings and Manton, 107
Story of King Arthur and His Knights, Pyle, 81
The Story of Knights and Armor, Tucker, 3
Story of Lafayette, Wilson, 24
Story of Leif Ericson, Steele, 58
Story of Louis Pasteur, Malkus, 26
Story of Madame Curie, Thorne, 23
A Story of Man, Jacobson, 222
Story of Marco Polo, Price, 141
The Story of Marxism and Communism, Savage, 211

The Story of Masada, Yadin, 130
The Story of Michelangelo, Allen, 53
The Story of Moses, Klagsbrun, 121
Story of Mozart, Kaufmann, 13
Story of Our Ancestors, Edel, 222
Story of Peter Tschaikowsky, Wheeler, 78
Story of Robert Louis Stevenson, Howard, 113
The Story of Roman Britain, Barker, 95
The Story of Rome, Corney, 48
The Story of Siegfried, Baldwin, 27
The Story of Sir Launcelot and His Companions, Pyle, 81
Story of Submarines, Weller, 234
The Story of the Blue Nile, Moorehead, 124
The Story of the Canterbury Pilgrims, Darton, 96
The Story of the Champions of the Round Table, Pyle, 81
The Story of the Dead Sea Scrolls, Rappaport, 129
The Story of the First World War, Reeder, 7
The Story of the Grail and the Passing of Arthur, Pyle, 81
The Story of the Incas: Mightiest Empire of the Early Americas, McKown, 186
Story of the International Red Cross, Epstein and Epstein, 219
The Story of the Negro, Bontemps, 154
Story of the Second World War, Savage, 9
The Story of the Second World war: [v 1] The Axis Strikes (1939-1942), Reeder, 8
The Story of the Second World

TITLE INDEX

War: [v 2] The Allies Conquer (1942-1945), Reeder, 9

Story of the Steppes: Kazakh Folk Tales, Masey, 72

The Story of the Trapp Family Singers, Trapp, 11

Story of the United Nations, Savage, 220

The Story of the White Nile, Moorehead, 155

The Story of Vietnam: A Background Book for Young People, Dareff, 152

Story of Winston Churchill, Malkus, 103

Story of World Religions, Savage, 211

The Story of World War I, Leckie, 6

Story of World War II, Leckie, 8

Strategic Direction of World War II, Dupuy, 8

Stravinsky, Young, 77

Struggle for North America, Williams, 170

Student Buccaneer, Barbary, 191

A Study of the USSR and Communism: An Historical Approach, Rieber and Nelson, 75

Sumer and Babylon, Mellersh, 127

Summation: Strategic and Combat Leadership, Dupuy, 6

The Sun and the Birch: The Story of Crown Prince Akihito and and Crown Princess Michiko, Simon, 148

The Sun King: Louis XIV of France, Apsler, 25

The Sun Kingdom of the Aztecs, Von Hagen, 176

Sun Yat-sen, Baker, 141

Sun Yat-sen: Founder of the Chinese Republic, Spencer, 141

Swan of the East: The Life and Death of the German Cruiser Emden in World War I, Hoyt, 29

Sweden in Pictures, Sterling Publishing Company, 70

Switzerland, Kubly, 71

Switzerland in Pictures, Sterling Publishing Company, 71

The Sword in the Tree, Bulla, 79

The Sword of King Arthur, Williams, 82

Sword of the Hausas, Hennessey and Sauter, 153

The Sword of the Raven, Boucher, 43

Swords Against Carthage, Donauer, 46

Swords from the North, Treece, 63

Tahiti and the French Islands of the Pacific — in Pictures, Sterling Publishing Company, 199

A Tale of Two Cities, Dickens, 18

Tales from Shakespeare, Lamb and Lamb, 85

Tales of Ancient Egypt, Green, 122

Tales of Maui, Hill, 198

Tales of the British People, Picard, 81

Tales of Troy and Greece, Lang, 36

Tales the People Tell in Russia, Wyndham, 72

Talleyrand, Komroff, 27

Tamar, Malvern, 46

Taming the Columbia River: The Challenge of American-Canadian Cooperation, Holbrook, 167

Tchaikovsky, Young, 78

Teen-Age Treasury of Imagination and Discovery, Manley and Lewis, 216

WORLD HISTORY IN JUVENILE BOOKS

Tell Me About Tokyo, Miller, 146
Temple on a Hill, Rockwell, 40
Ten Days in November, Werstein, 76
Ten Saints, Farjeon, 114
1006, Hamilton, 96
Ten Thousand Heroes, Barbary, 39
Thailand in Pictures, Sterling Publishing Company, 152
Thailand: Rice Bowl of Asia, Watson, 152
The Thames: London's River, Streatfeild, 95
That Denmark Might Live, Werstein, 15
That Men Shall Be Free: The Story of the Magna Carta, Alderman, 96
Theras and His Town, Snedeker, 37
There Was a Time: The Story of Evolution, Morrow, 223
Therese Martin, Haughton, 27
They Called Him Ataturk, Lengyel, 134
They Didn't Come Back, Berna, 215
They Explored, Hoff and De Terra, 217
They Flew to Glory, Bowen, 22
They Gave Their Names to Science, Halacy, 228
They Lived Like This in Ancient Africa, Neurath, 155
They Lived Like This in Ancient Britain, Neurath, 95
They Lived Like This in Ancient China, Neurath, 138
They Lived Like This in Ancient Crete, Neurath, 39
They Lived Like This in Ancient Egypt, Neurath, 122
They Lived Like This in Ancient India, Neurath, 143
They Lived Like This in Ancient Mesopotamia, Neurath, 127
They Lived Like This in Ancient Palestine, Neurath, 130
They Lived Like This in Ancient Persia, Neurath, 126
They Lived Like This in Ancient Peru, Neurath, 186
They Lived Like This in Ancient Rome, Neurath, 49
They Lived Like This in Chaucer's England, Neurath, 97
They Lived Like This in Old Japan, Neurath, 147
They Lived Like This in Shakespeare's England, Neurath, 98
They Lived Like This in the Old Stone Age, Neurath, 223
They Lived Like This: The Ancient Maya, Neurath, 176
They Lived Like This: The Vikings, Neurath, 64
They Peopled the Pacific, Day, 195
They Put Out to Sea, Duvoisin, 217, 218
They Stand Invincible; the Men Who Are Reshaping Our World, Bartlett, 211
They Told Mr. Hakluyt, Knight, 85, 216
This Is Antarctica, Dukert, 203
This Is Canada, Lindsay and McAulay, 168
This Is Edinburgh, Sasek, 94
This Is Greece, Sasek, 38
This Is Hong Kong, Sasek, 141
This Is Ireland, Sasek, 45
This Is Israel, Sasek, 129
This Is London, Sasek, 94
This Is Paris, Sasek, 20
This Is Rome, Sasek, 48

TITLE INDEX

This Is Venice, Sasek, 48
Thread of Victory, Lobdell, 91
Three Conquistadors: Cortes, Coronado, Pizarro, Garst, 177, 187
Three Dictators: Mussolini, Hitler, Stalin, King-Hall, 33, 53, 77
The Three Musketeers, Dumas, 18
Three Promises to You, Leaf, 220
Three Worlds of Albert Schweitzer, Payne, 158
Three Worlds of Latin America: Mexico, Central America, South America, Worcester, 175, 180, 190
The Throne of Peter: A History of the Papacy, MacGregor-Hastie, 114
Through the Frozen Frontier, Dufek, 203
The Tiber: The Roman River, Nowlan, 48
The Tide in the Attic, Rhijn, 54
Tiger in the Rice: A Short History of Vietnam, Sheldon, 152
The Tilted Sombrero, Lampman, 173
Time of Trial, Burton, 90
A Time to Love, Benary-Isbert, 28
Titian: A Biography, Ripley, 54
To Build a Land, Watson, 129
To Dream Upon a Crown, Williamson, 87
To Find Jesus, Peterson and Peterson, 120
To Remember Robert Louis Stevenson, Bailey, 112
To the Ends of the Earth: The Explorations of Roald Amundsen, Vaeth, 204
To the Top of the World: Sir Edmund Hillary and the Conquest of Everest, Sufrin, 150
To the Top of the World: the Story of Peary and Henson, Angell, 207
Too Near the Throne, Haycraft, 84
Tools: Shapers of Civilization, Esterer, 226
Tormented Genius: The Struggles of Vincent Van Gogh, Honour, 56
Totalitarianism and the Great Depression, Ritchie, 9
Tournament of the Lions, Williams, 4
Toward Democracy: Great Documents of History, Montgomery, 210
Toward Morning: A Story of the Hungarian Freedom Fighters, Seymour, 43
Toward Peace: The Nobel Prizes and the Struggle for Peace, Pauli, 220
The Tower of London: Grim and Glamorous, Shuttlesworth, 94
Town Life Through the Ages, Morris, 210
Trade: The World's Lifeblood, Paradis, 210
Traders North, MacArthur, 166
Trail Blazers of Technology, Manchester, 228
The Traitors, Forman, 28
Transport Planes That Made History, Cooke, 232
Transport, Trade, and Travel Through the Ages, Morris, 210, 231
Traveling Into Tomorrow: Transportation for the Future, Aylesworth, 229
Treasure Fleets of the Spanish Main, Marx, 192
Treasure Island, Stevenson, 91

WORLD HISTORY IN JUVENILE BOOKS

The Treasure of Siegfried, Almedingen, 27
Treasures of Yesterday, Garnett, 225
Treasury of Greek Mythology, Witting, 37
Trespassers: Korea, June, 1871, Werstein, 149
Trial at Nuremberg, Shapiro, 30
A Triumph for Flavius, Snedeker, 46
Triumphs and Tragedies in the East, Dupuy, 6
Triumphs of Modern Science, Berger, 226
The Trojan Horse, Barker, 35
The Trojan Horse, Reeves, 36
Trojan War, Coolidge, 35
True Adventures of Spies, Komroff, 233
True and Untrue, Undset, 63
True Book of Communication, Miner, 214
True Book of Knights, Lewellen, 2
True Book of Maps, Carlisle and Carlisle, 218
True North: Story of Captain Joseph Bernier, Fairley and Israel, 206
True Story of Albert Schweitzer, Humanitarian, Merrett, 158
True Story of Captain Scott at the South Pole, Holwood, 204
True Story of David Livingstone, Arnold, 157
The True Story of Gandhi, Man of Peace, Reynolds, 144
True Story of Lawrence of Arabia, Thomas, 133
The True Story of Lord Nelson, Naval Hero, Houghton, 109
True Story of Napoleon, Corley, 26
The True Story of Queen Victoria, Booth, 113
The True Story of Sir Francis Drake, Privateer, Holwood, 105
The True Story of Sir Winston Churchill, Booth, 102
The Trumpeter of Krakow, Kelly, 58
The Tuareg, Nomads and Warriors of the Sahara, Bleeker, 163
Tuesday 4 August 1914: The First Day of World War I, Ribbons, 7
The Tunnel, Williams, 100
Turkey, Stewart, 134
Twelve at War: Great Photographers Under Fire, Hood, 235
Twelve Citizens of the World, Kenworthy, 212
Twentieth Century Caesar: Benito Mussolini, Archer, 53
Twenty and Ten, Bishop, 19
The Twenty Children of Johann Sebastian Bach, Arkin, 30
Twice Queen of France: Anne of Brittany, Butler, 22
The Twig of Cypress, Cooper, 47
Two Reigns of Tutankhamen, Wise, 123
The Two Worlds of Damyan, Bloch, 72

The U.N. in Action, Comay, 219
The U.S.S.R., Clayton, 74
Under Secret Orders, Kullman, 11
Under the Pirate Flag, Hyde, 192
Undersea Explorer: The Story of Captain Cousteau, Dugan, 217
Understanding Maps; Charting the Land, Sea and Sky, Tannenbaum and Stillman, 218
UNICEF and the World, Speiser, 220
United Kingdom: A New Britain, Moore, 94

TITLE INDEX

United Nations and What It Does, Schlining, 220

The United Nations in War and Peace, Fehrenbach, 219

United Nations, N.Y., Sterling, 221

United Nations Workers: Their Jobs, Their Goals, Their Triumphs, Rowe, 220

The Universe of Galileo and Newton, Bixby, 4

Vancouver, Explorer of the Pacific Coast, Syme, 173

Vasco da Gama, Sailor Toward the Sunrise, Syme, 61

Vasco Nuñez de Balboa, Knoop, 190

Vasco Nuñez de Balboa, Sterne, 190

Velázquez, Ripley, 69

The Venetians: Merchant Princes, Chubb, 50

Venezuela in Pictures, Sterling Publishing Company, 188

Venture for a Crown, Fecher, 87

Victoria's Reign, Cammiade, 99

Victory at Valmy, Trease, 19

Viet Nam: Land of Many Dragons, Buell, 152

Vietnam, Our Beloved Land, Nguyen Cao Dam and Tran Cao Linh, 152

Vietnam Today: The Challenge of a Divided Nation, O'Daniel, 152

Viking Explorers, Buehr, 64

The Vikings, Burland, 64

The Vikings, Donovan, 64

The Vikings, Janeway, 64

The Vikings, Sellman, 64

The Vikings at Home and Abroad, Barker, 63

Viking's Dawn, Treece, 63

Vilhjalmur Stefansson: Young Arctic Explorer, Myers and Burnett, 207

Vincent Van Gogh, Ripley, 56

The Vital Link: The Story of the Suez Canal, Hirschfeld, 123

Viva Mexico, Bruckner, 173

The Voice of the Great Elephant, Seed, 153, 157

Voices from the Past: Stories of Great Biblical Discoveries, Eisenberg, 118

Volcanoes and Glaciers: Challenge of Iceland, Cary, 44

The Volga: Lifeline of Russia, Hall, 73

Voyage to Coromandel, Leighton, 63

The Voyages of Christopher Columbus, Sperry, 68

The Voyages of Henry Hudson, Rachlis, 171

The Voyages of Ulysses, Fadiman, 35

Wales in Pictures, Sterling Publishing Company, 95

The Wall of Shame, Heaps, 29

Walls, Gates, and Avenues: The Story of the Town, Jupo, 210

Walls of Windy Troy: A Biography of Heinrich Schliemann, Braymer, 42

Walter Raleigh, Syme, 111

Walter Raleigh: Man of Two Worlds, Buckmaster, 111

War Dog, Treece, 79

The War in Korea: 1950-1953, Leckie, 149

The War in the Air, Dupuy, 6

Ward of the Sun King, Butler, 18

Warlord of the Genji, Carlson, 145

The Warrior Knights, Williams, 4, 18

Warrior on Two Continents:

Thaddeus Kosciuszko, Abodaher, 59

The Warrior Pharaohs, Cottrell, 124

Warrior Scarlet, Sutcliff, 79

Warriors and Worthies; Arms and Armor Through the Ages, Nickel, 10, 233

Warriors With Wings, Jablonski, 22

Watch Fires to the North, Finkel, 80

Watch for the Morning, Oliver, 86

The Way of Danger: The Story of Theseus, Serraillier, 37

We Die Alone, Howarth, 57

We Were There at the Battle of Britain, Knight, 92

We Were There at the Battle of the Bulge, Shepherd, 30

We Were There at the Normandy Invasion, Knight, 92

We Were There in the Klondike Gold Rush, Appel, 166

We Were There With Byrd at the South Pole, Strong, 202

We Were There With Caesar's Legions, Webb, 47

We Were There With Charles Darwin on H.M.S. Beagle, Eisenberg, 90

We Were There With Cortes and Montezuma, Appel, 177

We Were There With Florence Nightingale in the Crimea, Webb, 92

We Were There With Richard the Lionhearted in the Crusades, Webb, 83

We Were There With the Lafayette Escadrille, Knight and Knight, 19

Weapons: A Pictorial History, Tunis, 234

West Germany in Pictures, Sterling Publishing Company, 30

The West in the Middle Ages, Bailey and Reit, 2

West Indies: Islands in the Sun, Cartey, 191

Westward Ho! Kingsley, 85

What Does a U.N. Soldier Do? Pierson, 220

What Happened: The Science Stories Behind the News, Scheib, 227

Wheels: A Pictorial History, Tunis, 231

Wheels: From Ox Carts to Sports Cars, Fleming, 230

Wheels, Wings, and Water: The Story of Cargo Transport, Coombs, 230

When Jays Fly to Bárbmo, Balderson, 57

When Knights Were Bold, Tappan, 3

When the Dikes Broke, Seymour, 54

Whistling Sword, Green, 136

White Boy, Manzi, 164

The White Cockade, Cordell, 44

The White Isle, Snedeker, 78

Who Goes Next: True Stories of Strange Escapes, Alter, 214

Why the Chinese Are the Way They Are, Appel, 137

Why the Russians Are the Way They Are, Appel, 72

Wilderness Explorer: The Story of Samuel de Champlain, Wilson, 171

Wilhelm Conrad Röntgen and the Discovery of X-Rays, Dibner, 34

Will Shakespeare and the Globe Theatre, White, 112

TITLE INDEX

William, Father of the Netherlands, Hall, 56

William Harvey: Trailblazer of Scientific Medicine, Marcus, 106

William Mayne's Book of Heroes; Stories and Poems, Mayne, 213

William Shakespeare, Noble, 112

William Shakespeare, Reese, 112

William Shakespeare and His Plays, Haines, 112

William Tell, Scherman, 71

William Tell and His Son, Hürlimann, 71

William the Conqueror, Costain, 114

William the Conqueror, Lucock, 114

William the Silent, Baker, 56

Windows for the Crown Prince, Vining, 148

The Windswept City, Treece, 37

Winston Churchill, Gilbert, 103

Winston Churchill, Reynolds, 103

Winston Churchill, Smith, 103

Winston Churchill and the Story of Two World Wars, Coolidge, 102

Winston Churchill: Man of the Century, Webb, 103

Witch Dog, Beatty and Beatty, 14

Witch of the Glens, Watson, 88

With Caesar's Legions, Wells, 47

With Pipe, Paddle, and Song: A Story of the French-Canadian Voyageurs, circa 1750, Yates, 169

With Stanley in Africa, Hall-Quest, 158

With the Eagles, Anderson, 46

With Wolfe in Canada, Henty, 169

Wolfgang Amadeus Mozart, Seroff, 13

Wolfgang Amadeus Mozart: Master of Pure Music, Stearns, 13

Wonder World of Snow and Ice, Neurath, 202

Wonders of Ancient Chinese Science, Silverberg, 139

Wonders of Prehistoric Man, Martin, 223

Wonders of the Antarctic, Berrill, 203

Wonders of the Arctic, Berrill, 205

Wonders of Underwater Exploration, Stambler, 216

The Wooden Horse, Williams, 100

Word to Caesar, Trease, 46

Wordhoard, Paton Walsh and Crossley-Holland, 81

Words of Science and the History Behind Them, Asimov, 226

Workshops for the World: The United Nations Family of Agencies, Beckel and Lee, 219

The World Awakes: The Renaissance in Western Europe, Brooks and Walworth, 10

World Book of Great Inventions, Meyer, 227

A World Explorer: Ferdinand Magellan, Groh, 61

A World Explorer; Francisco Coronado, Knoop, 177

World of Captain John Smith, Foster, 10, 209

World of Cézanne, Murphy, 22

The World of Columbus and Sons, Foster, 4

World of Goya, Schickel, 69

The World of Marco Polo, Buehr, 140

World of Michelangelo, Coughlan, 53

The World of Nations, Taylor and Cochrane, 211

The World of Prehistory, Baldwin, 221

WORLD HISTORY IN JUVENILE BOOKS

The World of Red China, Buell, 139
The World of Rice, Boesch, 208
The World of Rubens, 1577-1640, Wedgwood, 14
The World of the Arctic, Smith, 205
The World of the Pharaohs, Baumann, 122
World of Titian, Williams, 54
The World of Tomorrow, Goldstein, 226
The World of Van Gogh, 1853-1890, Wallace, 56
World of Velázquez, 1599-1660, Brown, 69
The World of Vermeer, 1632-1675, Koningsberger, 56
The World of Walls: The Middle Ages in Western Europe, Brooks and Walworth, 10
World War II, Weyr, 9
World War II and the Modern Age, Ritchie, 9
The World We Live In and How It Came to Be, Hartman, 209
World's Fairs: Yesterday, Today, Tomorrow, Roesch, 210
World's Lost and Found: Discoveries in Biblical Archaeology, Eisenberg and Elkins, 118
Worlds Without End, Barclay, 217

The Yangtze: China's River Highway, Spencer, 138
The Yangtze River, Rau, 138
Year of Columbus, 1492, Foster, 4, 209
The Year of the Horse, Ritchie, 137
Year of the Pilgrims, 1620, Foster, 209
The Yellow Hat, Faulkner, 82
The Yellow River, Rau, 138

Yesterday's Daughter, Daringer, 35
You and the United Nations, Fisher, 219
The Young Alexander the Great, Mitchison, 41
Young Bernadette, Stafford, 22
The Young Brahms, Deucher, 31
Young Captain Cook, Knight, 196
Young Catherine the Great, Almedingen, 76
Young Charles Darwin, Hope, 104
Young Cicero, Barbary, 51
Young Columbus, Knight, 67
Young Dickens, Pringle, 104
Young Drake, Knight, 105
The Young Elizabeth, Plaidy, 105
The Young Florence Nightingale, Cooper, 110
The Young Gilbert and Sullivan, Harris, 106
Young Hans Andersen, Spink, 16
Young Hans Christian Andersen, Collin, 16
Young Inca Prince, Malkus, 185
Young Israel: A History of the Modern Nation, Rachleff, 129
The Young John Wesley, Clifford, 113
Young Lawrence of Arabia, Cadell, 133
Young Leonardo da Vinci, Almedingen, 52
Young Livingstone, Pringle, 157
Young Louis Pasteur, Richardson, 26
Young Louis XIV: The Early Years of the Sun King, Wilkinson, 25
The Young Martin Luther, Elder, 33
Young Mary, Queen of Scots, Plaidy, 108

TITLE INDEX

Young Mary Stuart: Queen of Scots, King, 108
The Young Milton, Hobbs, 108
The Young Moses, Haughton, 120
The Young Mozart, Jenkins, 13
Young Napoleon, Cooper, 25
Young Nelson, Syme, 109
The Young Pretenders, Picard, 91
The Young Robert Bruce, Oliver, 101
The Young Robert Louis Stevenson, Finlay, 113
Young Samson, Taslitt, 121
The Young Samuel Pepys, Gunston, 110
Young Shakespeare, Sisson, 112
The Young Shelley, Rush, 112
The Young Tennyson, Hope, 113
The Young Thomas More, Haughton, 109
Young Traveler in Australia, Monypenny, 197
Young Traveler in Austria, Esterházy, 11
The Young Victoria, Cooper, 113
Young Walter Scott, Gray, 111
The Youngest Conquistador, Mantel, 173
The Youngest General: A Story of Lafayette, Gottschalk, 24
Your Book of Maps and Map Reading, Matkin, 218
Yugoslavia, Auty, 116
Yugoslavia, Rothkopf, 116
Yugoslavia in Pictures, Sterling Publishing Company, 116
Yugoslavia, Romania, Bulgaria: New Era in the Balkans, Perl, 14, 62, 116
The Yukon, Place, 168

The Zealots of Masada: Story of a Dig, Pearlman, 130
Zulu Boy, Goldie, 164
The Zulu of South Africa; Cattlemen, Farmers, and Warriors, Bleeker, 165